Melville and Repose

MELVILLE AND REPOSE

The Rhetoric of Humor in the American Renaissance

John Bryant

New York   Oxford
OXFORD UNIVERSITY PRESS
1993

Oxford University Press

Oxford   New York   Toronto
Delhi   Bombay   Calcutta   Madras   Karachi
Kuala Lumpur   Singapore   Hong Kong   Tokyo
Nairobi   Dar es Salaam   Cape Town
Melbourne   Auckland   Madrid

and associated companies in
Berlin   Ibadan

New material copyright © 1993 by Oxford University Press, Inc.

Published by Oxford University Press, Inc.,
200 Madison Avenue, New York, New York 10016

Oxford is a registered trademark of Oxford University Press

Library of Congress Cataloging-in-Publication Data
Bryant, John, 1949–
Melville and repose :
the rhetoric of humor in the American Renaissance /
John Bryant.
p.   cm.   Includes bibliographical references and index.
ISBN 0–19–507782–2
1. Melville, Herman, 1819–1891—Humor.
2. American literature–19th century—History and criticism.
3. Humorous stories, American—History and criticism.
4. Rhetoric—United States—History—19th century.
5. Comic, The, in literature.   6. Narration (Rhetoric)
I. Title.   PS2388.S2B79   1993   813′.3—dc20   92–46150

Selections from Chapter 1 were published under the title ''Melville's Comic Debate'' in *American Literature* 55:2, copyright 1983 Duke University Press, and are reprinted with permission of the publisher. Other portions of that chapter first appeared in ''Melville's Picturesque,'' in *Savage Eye*, ed. Christopher Sten (Kent, Ohio, 1991), and are reprinted with permission of The Kent State University Press. Part of Chapter 6 was previously printed in '' 'Nowhere a Stranger': Melville and Cosmopolitanism,'' *Nineteenth-Century Fiction* 39:3 (December 1984), pp. 275–291, copyright 1984 by the Regents of the University of California. Selections from this chapter were also published under the title ''Citizens of a World to Come: Melville and the Millennial Cosmopolite,'' in *American Literature* 59:1, copyright 1987 Duke University Press; they are reprinted here with permission of the publisher. The discussion of ''Melville's L-Word'' in Chapter 8 was first recorded in *The New England Quarterly* (March 1990), and Chapter 13 originally appeared as ''Allegory and Breakdown in *The Confidence-Man*,'' *Philological Quarterly* 65:1 (Winter 1986). Both are reprinted with permission of the publishers. Selections from the *Typee* manuscript in Chapters 7, 8, and 9 are quoted from the Gansevoort-Lansing Collection, Rare Books and Manuscripts Division, The New York Public Library, Astor, Lenox and Tilden Foundations.

2   4   6   8   9   7   5   3   1

Printed in the United States of America
on acid-free paper

For
Ginny, Emma, and Eliza

Preface

In April 1890, *Harper's Magazine* published an encyclopedic article by Henry Clay Lukens on "America's Literary Comedians," which included one eccentric detail: Tucked into its list of midcentury humorists of "rare talent" was the name Herman Melville.[1] Melville, then a retired customs inspector living comfortably in New York City, had not published a piece of prose fiction in thirty-five years. Eighteen months later he was dead, remembered if at all for *Typee* and other sea romances.

The Lukens piece adds a ripe irony to Melville's final years. Here is America's principal tragic voice ignored, if not forgotten, even misnamed "Henry" in one obituary, identified as a mere "literary comedian." But the double irony is that Lukens's designation is not "mere." Melville was a humorist in the deepest sense of the term, and would not have objected to this seemingly monumental underestimation of his talent. He saw himself as he saw the world: "half melancholy, half farcical" (*Log*, 549). Nor would Melville's early contemporaries have demurred. Although Melville was not a professional humorist like T. B. Thorpe or Oliver Wendell Holmes, he used humor as would any professional writer hoping to make a living. And beyond this, he used humor because it was a metaphysical and aesthetic imperative.

If art must strive to balance head and heart, and if it works to engage readers in what, to paraphrase Melville, may be called the deep thought of laughter, then humor's relevance is undeniable. Of course, we may argue that Melville was constitutionally unprepared to adopt this Romantic code, that he failed in the marketplace because he refused to accept its strictures, and that he failed even more when like Poe he tried to force humor in his work. The French critic Philarète Chasles, an early and close reader of *Mardi*, declared Melville a "Rabelais without gaiety, a Cervantes without grace, and a Voltaire without taste."[2] But Chasles's final message is that Melville is less a failed humorist than one struggling for the proper accommodation of variant humors. Other critics aligned Melville with such comic greats as Burton and Sterne, who perhaps shared Melville's precariously poised sensibility. Melville was not the melancholiac we would like to think him; indeed, humor was fundamental to his rhetoric, intrinsic to his sense of Being and self, crucial to the fabric of the nation. In a very real sense, humor takes us to the heart of Melville's condition as an artist.

Part I of this book supports these unorthodox claims by exploring the comic conventions and rhetorical models available in Melville's culture. Overall, these contextual chapters focus on a long-standing cultural "debate" between integrative and subversive comic modes of amiable humor and what I call the rhetoric of deceit. Each mode presumes its own ontology (benevolence versus misanthropy); its own ethics (faith versus doubt); its own rhetoric (sincerity versus unreliability). The problem for writers of the American Renaissance was how to resolve this comic debate by incorporating humor and satire in ways that would satisfy artistic and social needs. They were in search of a voice that could contain selfhood but also prod an audience immersed in the problems of the emergent democracy. The development of Melville's narrative voice is inextricably bound to his evolving comic sensibility, and that evolution is in turn shaped by certain "facts": that humor (apart from satire) was fundamental to Melville's romantic sense of being; that an "aesthetics of repose" was equally fundamental to this idea of humor; that America required a subordination of satire to humor for its comic and political survival; and that to achieve aesthetic repose Melville experimented with various narrative strategies shifting from *Typee* to *Moby-Dick* to *The Confidence-Man*. Melville concocted his own resolution of the comic debate by drawing upon the amiable and picturesque styles of Irving and Hawthorne, by experimenting with forms of unreliability typical of Poe and Thorpe, and by synthesizing both ironic and reposeful modes through his own notion of cosmopolitanism. Melville's humor also takes us to the heart of the condition of the artist and reader in America.

The problem in studying the comic is the tendency to wear the subject like a chip. Although irony is the preferred mode of expression in "The Modern Age of the Absurd," and though Wylie Sypher argues that comedy "can tell us many things about our situation even tragedy cannot,"[3] the fact remains that the analysis of humor is, at best, a secondary concern. At worst, critics place humor on a patronizing pedestal, too good to be ruined by prolonged study. Nothing spoils a good laugh more than discourse upon it. As James Cox reminds us, "the fate of humor" is that it is taken to be "mere."[4] Humor remains marginalized, even among Americanists, despite the remarkable efforts of Constance Rourke, Walter Blair, and Hamlin Hill. As a consequence, any study of humor—especially one on such a solemn figure as Melville—inevitably includes an apology like the one you are reading now. But just as feminists have awakened us to the power of sentimental fictions, so too might we legitimize "mere" humor and discover new vitalities in old places. Melville included.

My larger purpose in writing *Melville and Repose* is to demonstrate a version of what I call "pluralistic historicism." By pluralism, I do not mean to invoke the current usage equating it to multiculturalism—although that is a valid consideration and one particularly relevant (in the form of cosmopolitanism) to a significant phase of Melville's work—but rather I mean a synthesis of two seemingly divergent approaches to a text, its creation and its reception, which intersect briefly but vitally at those moments when an Author surrenders to a Reader. Often, such surrendering is just as effective for the author as it is for the reader in that a literary expression will serve as both a cogent articulation of one's being as well as a persuasive means of awakening readers to the conditions of their existence. But just as often, it can lead to disastrous compromises. Surrender occurs the moment an author projects a reader and begins to compose. Here, the effusions, restraints, and self-censorings begin. Further expansions or repressions of self and reader occur even as a text, frozen in print, is altered from edition to edition. How writers write reveals the mechanisms and complex vectors of force that shape their surrender. We also see how ideologies emerge and evolve. And given that a writer's writing is never fully done, the writing process and the author's relation to ideology are always inchoate. Writers are always "essaying." At the same time, an author creates structures that ask, demand, tease, or trick us as readers to "play along" with the text. This vital relation to the reader, then, is as exploratory and experimental as the relations to self and ideology. Any critical approach that attempts to freeze either of these sides of the author's creative act (both his or her writing and our reading) necessarily misrepresents the "facts" of the literary process. For Melville, writing and reading were inseparable components of his creative act; hence, any historicist approach must in equivalent fashion be pluralistic; it must enlighten the rhetorical conditions of the author's creativity.

Writers, Texts, and Readers evolve. Critics seek to determine what these mean, even to the extent of trying to retrieve an author's intentions and assessing what successive generations of readers might understand. Given these goals, pluralistic historicism, as it focuses on the interactions between writer and readers, requires a renewed critical imperative: The Author exists. One need not rehearse the past 50 years of criticism to note that successive waves of the New Criticism, structuralism, and deconstruction have so privileged Language itself over Author that biography and historicism have been largely devalued. Most disheartening, I would think, for the neglected traditional historicist is that the advent of the New Historicism, which, in its bid to contextualize literary study should in some sense revalorize the Author, in fact recapitulates poststructuralist assumptions concerning the irrelevance of individual creators. For those such as myself who hope to draw upon the best of the traditional and the new, it is equally disheartening to find that new historicist approaches in their pursuit of a "political unconsciousness" too often rely upon that weakest of historicist methodologies, or what I call "the fallacy of parallel developments" wherein perceived homologies between social and literary structures stand in substitution for harder evidence connecting milieu to text. What is deleted in this form of thinking are studies of authors whose conscious or even accidental acts of creation constitute the "event" that convert a social force into text. In order to avoid the fallacy of parallel structures and focus more upon the transformative "person in between," historicists need to reconsider those arenas of critical inquiry now generally denigrated—causation and intentionality—which while they may lead to speculation nevertheless focus our attention on the very initializing force that makes Language and Text possible—once again, the Author.

My privileging of the Author is likely to draw hurrahs from the "single author societies" and hoots from theorists. But neither response is particularly appropriate. Studying an author simply for the sake of it is as unfulfilling as discovering utterly predictable convergences (or divergences) between a unique text and a general theory of Text (or of Context). Of course, what I offer here is, inevitably, "my" Melville, the product of objective research and unavoidable subjectivities of mind. But it is, I hope, a Melville that can converse with "your" Melville, and one to which we "feel the tie." It is a Melville not so much *framed by* theories of language or culture as it is *revealed through* hypotheses concerning the development of a career, hypotheses that in conjunction with other hypotheses about other creative careers may help us eventually derive a theory of creativity in America.

In writing this book, I have tried to give equal measure to both creation and reception, and where evidence exists, as it does with *Typee*, I have even gone so far as to suggest a redefinition of what a text might be. In the pursuit of something called "repose," I have found myself meddling with metaphysics, aesthetics, ethics, and rhetoric as well as the minutiae of manuscripts and textual variants; I have interconnected letters and reviews as well as literary and family history. I have become more of a cultural philologist exploring a variety of materials to retrieve for us today earlier meanings of such words as geniality, picturesque, and cosmopolitan. I have as well explored the interpenetrations of Melville's psychology, politics, and sexuality. This is a long book—comprehensive more perhaps in its intent than actual execution, of course, but as someone once complained, I have heard the printer's devil knocking at the door and must surrender myself to readers. Such closure brings silence and the worry of necessary incompletion, a feeling much like the tense repose Melville felt and transformed into art. And that complex unitary feeling, more than any effort at critical pluralism, may be the truest link I, or any critic, may have to Melville.

I would like to acknowledge the many friends who have helped me with this project. My training in critical thinking and writing began with my parents, John and Doris Bryant, and continued with Norman Maclean in the College of the University of Chicago; I have tried to follow his injunction to put "pressure on my prose," but I am sure some passages (including this one) would have made him wince. A primordial version of this book began as a dissertation at the same university under Hamlin Hill and James E. Miller, Jr. At that time, Walter Blair was gracious enough to interrupt his active retirement from time to time to counsel me on research technique and, again, prose. His characterization of a scholar as one who will "go to the ends of the earth to find and verify a fact" has made me a better (but exhausted) person. Others have read chapters and provided encouragement: Hennig Cohen, Philip Gura, Stanton Garner, Harrison Hayford, Robert Milder, Merton M. Sealts, Jr., and John Wenke. I would also like to thank former colleagues at the Pennsylvania State University who provided valuable critiques: Eric Birdsall, Robert Burkholder, Mary DeJong, Robert Hudspeth, and Philip Young. Let me also thank my colleagues at Hofstra University: Dana Brand, Stanley Brodwin, Thomas Couser, Allan Davis, Rhoda Nathan, Ruth Prigozy, Robert Sargent, and Lee Zimmerman, whose careful critiques and earnest encouragement have been invaluable. My daughters, Emma and Eliza, have grown up with this book; they have nurtured it and me more deeply than they know. Several sources provided funding: the Institute for Arts and Humanistic Studies, the Faculty Scholarship

Support Fund, and Liberal Arts Research Fund—all three of Penn State—as well as the National Endowment for the Humanities and the Newberry Library. But the one foundation that supported me and this project from beginning to end is my friend and wife Virginia Blanford, whose humor, depth, and creativity circle me round.

Scarsdale, N.Y.   J. B.
January 1993

Contents

Abbreviations for Frequently Cited Sources

CM: Herman Melville. *The Confidence-Man: His Masquerade*. Ed. Harrison Hayford, Hershel Parker, and G. Thomas Tanselle. Evanston and Chicago: Northwestern University and The Newberry Library, 1984.

Companion: John Bryant, ed. *A Companion to Melville Studies*. Westport, CT: Greenwood Press, 1986.

Letters: Merrell R. Davis and William H. Gilman, eds. *The Letters of Herman Melville*. New Haven: Yale University Press, 1960.

Log: Jay Leyda, ed. *The Melville Log: A Documentary Life of Herman Melville, 1819–1891*. Reprint with supplement. New York: Gordian Press, 1969.

M: Herman Melville. *Mardi and a Voyage Thither*. Ed. Harrison Hayford, Hershel Parker, and G. Thomas Tanselle. Evanston and Chicago: Northwestern University and The Newberry Library, 1970.

Marginalia: Wilson Walker Cowen. *Melville's Marginalia*. Ph.D. dissertation. Harvard University, 1965.

MD: Herman Melville. *Moby-Dick, or The Whale*. Ed. Harrison Hayford, Hershel Parker, and G. Thomas Tanselle. Evanston and Chicago: Northwestern University Press and Newberry Library, 1988.

Piazza Tales: Herman Melville. *The Piazza Tales, and Other Prose Pieces, 1839–1860*. Ed. Harrison Hayford, Alma A. MacDougall, and G. Thomas Tanselle. Evanston and Chicago: Northwestern University Press and Newberry Library, 1987.

Poems: Herman Melville. *Collected Poems of Herman Melville*. Ed. Howard P. Vincent. Chicago: Hendricks House, 1946.

Sealts: Merton M. Sealts, Jr. *Melville's Reading*. Rev. ed. Columbia, SC: University of South Carolina Press, 1988.

T: Herman Melville. *Typee: A Peep at Polynesian Life*. Ed. Harrison Hayford, Hershel Parker, and G. Thomas Tanselle. Northwestern University and Newberry Library, 1968.

Melville and Repose

There is laughter in heaven, and laughter in hell.
And a deep thought whose language is laughter.
—*Mardi*

Silence is the only Voice of our
God. . . . how can a man
get a Voice out of Silence?
—*Pierre*

1

A Great Intellect in Repose

"The first duty of a critic . . . is to remember that, behind every book there is a man—or rather, that there is a man in every book." Fitz-James O'Brien, one of Herman Melville's friendlier literary associates, wrote this critical imperative as part of a general assessment of Melville's career occasioned by the publication in 1857 of *The Confidence-Man*. In all, O'Brien was pleased with his friend's progress. He was controlling earlier excesses and had a reasonable claim to becoming America's great "prose-poet." "Behind" or rather "in" Melville's books was a creative "man" whose only errors were on the side of the Imagination. This was surely a "personality," O'Brien concluded, that would "inspire" the age.[1] The poignancy of O'Brien's critique lies in the irony of this misplaced prophecy, for in 1857 Melville was on the verge of professional failure, and if he inspired any age, it was not his but ours. Nor does O'Brien seem cognizant of what critics now perceive to be the failure—whether willful or involuntary—of Melville's form and language.

O'Brien's critical assumptions seem fatally naïve. The New Criticism struggled mightily to purge literary analysis of such biographical orientations, and more recently deconstructionists deny the relevance of any authorial presence in a text. Even New Historicists, who study texts in context, ignore authorial intention for broader notions of a "political unconscious."[2] Few modern critics are concerned with the person behind a text. O'Brien exhibits not even an embryonic hint of modernism; he does not look to literature for unified effects, well-wrought urns, metaphors, metonyms, linguistic crises, social negotiations, or cultural symbols. He focuses solidly on that subjective entity that objectivists cringe to hear invoked—personality. O'Brien assumes that an artist's voice is an actual moral presence, not a fictive construct, that it exists along with social contingency, and that the critic's primary "duty" is to tend to the life within that voice.

Melville felt that way too. After all, the idea that fiction was the emanation of a personality was so heavily ingrained in early-nineteenth-century critical thought that Emerson could decree, without much serious contradiction, that "all form is an effect of character."[3] Poe could argue against such "autorial [sic] vanity,"[4] but his insistence upon a "rational" not charismatic basis for literary form was largely ignored—a fact that further validates the persistence in Melville's day of O'Brien's and Emerson's linkage of character and text. *Moby-Dick* is surely Melville's most powerful attempt to meet O'Brien's expectation of controlled self-exposure. But if O'Brien had any complaint, it was that Melville's next book, *Pierre,* overstepped restraint. He gave his public too much of himself, and readers quickly wondered whether he was a man *worth* knowing at all. Melville had his own doubts as well. In a familiar letter to Hawthorne he stated that his deepest self-explorations were "banned" and that he was simply not able to "write the *other* way," for common consumption (*Letters,* 128). And yet he continued to write with a clear sense of how he might use fiction to contain as well as expose himself. My point here is not to argue for a return to O'Brien's critical stance, but to bear in mind that Melville understood the rhetorical expectations of self-exposure and containment, and that to know Melville's texts we must recognize this tension and come to know the man in this tension.

Scholars generally assume that Melville's inability to achieve a salable projection of himself accounts for his lackluster literary performances in the later fiction. My sense of this period, however, is different. Melville's late narrative experiments seem largely designed to create more artful containments of self than Fitz-James O'Brien could imagine. And while such works as "Benito Cereno" and *The Confidence-Man* achieve a virtual obliteration of self, I argue that Melville's increasing detachment was not a result of failure in the literary marketplace but rather was in keeping with his most fundamental aesthetic views, his aesthetics of repose.

The word "repose" does not appear in the King James Bible, nor in much of Shakespeare. It had its vogue in the Romantic era, losing the richness of its meaning in our rather less-than-reposeful century. Like Hawthorne, Melville strove for literary forms that would project a reposeful moral sensibility—one resonant equally in mirth and insight—a voice that could sustain a tension between self-consciousness and transcendent joy. Humor (both its European and its Native American strains) played a crucial role in the creation of Melville's voice of repose. For Melville and his contemporaries, "repose" implied a range of mental states: a sensual indolence and sleep of reason, but also a wakeful balance of awareness and calm. Eventually, Melville modulated that voice into a whisper, but even in his more embittered creations he did not lose sight of the genial underpinnings of his amiable voice of repose. To paraphrase one claim he made, he stood for the heart, and it is his attempts to control this ethical organ that constitute the "man" in his books.

To understand Melville's aesthetics and rhetoric, we are compelled, like O'Brien, to adopt an essentially biographical approach to Melville. Indeed, Melville's texts, in some way autobiographical in all stages, demand such research. The creative process, his "wrestl[ing] with the angel—Art," is often enough the very subject as well as the cause of his dynamic and varied creations. He was a dislodged gentleman growing up in Jacksonian America, who, being denied a higher education and grand tour, went to sea, returned, wrote, became the darling (briefly) of the New York literary circle, fell apart, lapsed into obscurity, died in 1891, and was resurrected in the 1920s by academics and writers seeking (as had Melville himself) something called American Literature. What attract us to Melville the person are his evident potentials and failures as much as his exciting successes. We are drawn, like Robert Milder, to ask how we might "know" Melville within his volatile culture and, like Merton M. Sealts, Jr., to inquire into the "ways of [Melville's] creativity."[5] In doing so, we may learn more about the adaptive, serpentine, experimental trials and errors of individual creation, and hence more about the problems of art in a democracy and the marketplace.

Melville scholarship has generally emphasized the ontological unfolding of Melville's consciousness throughout the earlier works up to *Pierre,* the failure of later works, and the artist's nihilism and perhaps mental instability.[6] I see the life and canon differently. Melville's "unfolding" continued well past *Pierre.* His later works display a healthy narrative experimentation, and his apparent failures are not due to problems inherent in language or being but are the natural fallout of those experiments. Humor was fundamental to the process. Of all the comic modes—wit, satire, burlesque, romance, and the rest—humor is perhaps the most lyric, and in the nineteenth century it was, because of its capacity for depth and gentility, a privileged mode of address. For Coleridge, humor was a vehicle of deep insight, a mode of transcendence. It is digressive, contradictory, and hence natural and imaginative. It is the evocation of a single lyric mind and heart: Cide Hamete Benengeli reflecting on Don Quixote, or Shandy on Toby, or Ishmael on whales. When, in America, different strains of humor grew out of the frontier's oral tradition, the heroes and voices changed in manner, but the lyrical dimension of their laughter remained the same. As Walter Blair notes, American humor is the sound of "a man's voice, speaking."[7] Although the mendacious humorists of the West (and many were women) are more experiential than transcendental, their complex, comic operations are invariably rooted in a single recognizable and insightful voice. The lyricism is evident in Jim Doggett and his Big Bear, Huck and his river, and even Frank Goodman and the tribe of confidence men around him.

Despite the diversity of voices registered and despite the striking particularity of each self-centered voice, these comic minds share in the lyric impulse to transcend self—to sing beyond the sea—and in so doing to rise above mere comic attack, ridicule, and satire. Their humor meets Meredith's test of "true comedy" in that, despite its immersions in self, it achieves a certain impersonality that "awaken[s] thoughtful laughter."[8] It projects but also aesthetically contains the darkest aspects of our lives, offering what Melville calls the "deep thought" of laughter (*M,* 613). The greatness, then, of any humorist is best measured by her lyricism or more specifically the means by which he unites both integrative and subversive humors within a single voice. What Fitz-James O'Brien was calling for when he invoked the man *in* the book was, in fact, a voice that could, in containing the excesses of mind and language, rise beyond selfhood. (The paradox in this lyrical dimension to humor is that self-abnegation is achieved through a comic absorption into self. Hence, Ishmael and Whitman are lyrical confrères because they sing themselves, but they do so out of time and facticity.) The assumption behind the relevance of the comic-lyric voice is that language "speaks" and "sings"; it is to be heard, and like a musical instrument this human organ can harmonize the dissonances of our lives in both the creator's and the auditor's minds. The comic voice, then, not only enables the mingling of satire and genial modes but also invites writer and audience to combine. Laughter empowers both.

For Melville, humor was inalienable from his aesthetics and rhetoric because it was essential to one's Being. The first step to understanding an aesthetics of repose, then, is to grasp the ontological status of humor.

Humor and Being

If the power, but also the fault, in Wit derives from a reduction of idea to a play of words, then Humor is that playful impulse to plunge beneath language to the fundamentals of life: being, creation, awareness, and death.[9] Humor familiarizes these depths, blending enthusiasm and despair in what Carlyle called an "inverse sublimity." Yet amiable humor's failing is its propensity to domesticate anxiety and sentimentalize the past. The problem is to mix deep humor and true wit while avoiding sentiment and burlesque. George Meredith, speaking for his century, put it well:

> If you laugh all round [the ridiculous person], tumble him, roll him about, deal him a smack, and drop a tear on him, own his likeness to you, and yours to your neighbor, spare him as little as you shun, pity him as much as you expose, it is a spirit of Humor that is moving you.[10]

The "spirit" of humor is its fusion of variant states of consciousness, of sweetness and blight.[11] The assumption of humor's capacity to *fuse* disparate visions is deeply rooted in the metaphysics of Meredith's Romantic precursors. More than a literary mode, humor is an emanation of Being; it is a key to the mingled impulses of Selfhood, both its tears and smacks. It is, finally, a process of self-discovery achieved *through* self-containment. This is, at any rate, the *hope* of Romantic humor. Of course, the darker realities of Romantic ontology insist that humor like language itself can only represent, not create, the self; hence it is fated to fail.

Paul de Man offers a succinct statement of this familiar dilemma. Romantic Imagery, he says, is "grounded in the intrinsic ontological primacy of the natural object. Poetic language seems to originate in the desire to draw closer and closer to the ontological status of the object, and its growth and development are determined by this inclination. . . . [T]his movement is essentially paradoxical and condemned in advance to failure. There can be flowers that 'are' and poetic words that 'originate,' but no poetic words that 'originate' as if they 'were.' ''[12] The imitative syntax, let's say, of Wordsworth's "Rolled round in earth's diurnal course, / With rocks, and stones, and trees" can approximate a fusion of motion and stasis reminiscent of Being itself, but they are not in themselves that state. Words can "originate" (i.e. re-create) but can never *be* the "original" objects they represent. Creativity is a sign of our futile desire for ideality.

As Melville put it even more succinctly, "description [cannot] beget reality" (*M,* 314). Language merely approximates nature; thus, ontologically it must fail. The bugbear of "origination" infects Melville's later works. *The Confidence-Man* acknowledges the futility of ever finding "an original genius." Like Bartleby, a writer only copies reality; and like Billy Budd, that author stammers in frustration, creating nothing but dead words and a narrative "that will always have its ragged edges" (128), which will appear always to destroy itself. Along these lines, Edgar Dryden argues that Melville's metaphysical disposition led him to artistic failure.[13] Melville's self-conscious fictions are a result of man's inability to grasp the "scared white doe" of Truth.[14] Nina Baym proposes that Melville's inability to "commit himself to the exigencies of an extended work of fiction" stems from his denial of the transcendental notion of God as a Namer, which is in turn a fatal denial of the efficacy of language.[15]

But the deconstructionist approach[16] overstates Melville's relation to language and underestimates his ability to write in spite of the philosophical limits of language. Indeed, Dryden's and Baym's explications of Melville's "adventure of [the] failure" of the word ignore the sprightly playfulness of Melville's art, or what Warwick Wadlington identifies as the "godly gamesomeness" of his fiction, the delight in, not resignation to, ragged edges.[17] In this regard, Melville was more in keeping with Anne K. Mellor's notion of the Romantic Ironist who is "filled as much with enthusiasm as with skepticism."[18] In direct opposition to de Man, Mellor argues that writing does not recapitulate the failure of the word; it is a "program" of earnest creation and de-creation, a "never-ending process that becomes an analogue for life itself" (Mellor, 4).[19] Thus, when gentle humor can take into itself the kind of "semi-caress" of the reader that Meredith found in irony, when it can create and uncreate at once, then it corresponds to our deepest desires to approach ideal Being; it is a form of Becoming.

As early as *Mardi,* Melville reveled in the "play-acting" aspects of his art, a kind of "dramatism" involving masks, histrionics, and Shakespearean dramaturgy. Rather than reject fiction because of its inherent artificiality, the author preferred to "play along" with the illusion. Melville was, in this respect, what may be called a "pragmatic Platonist." He acknowledged the proximal nature of art and devised rhetorical ploys that allowed readers to confront the tragic implications of that ontology but at the same time maintain a comic distance, to experience the tragic through comic form.

Melville's sense of the ontological validity of humor derives primarily from Coleridge and Carlyle. Coleridge envisions Nature as a humorist when he argues that this "prime *genial* artist" projects a "being within." As with nature so it is with Nature's "chosen poet," Shakespeare, who is himself "a *genial* understanding directing self-consciously a power and an implicit wisdom deeper than our consciousness."[20] A defining feature of Shakespeare and Nature's shared awareness of a deeper sense of being is the word "genial," a principal item in Melville's comic lexicon. More than superficial gladhanding, geniality is a "true image" of our Being, which by itself operates on one "great law": "all opposites . . . temper each other." This "tempering" is homologous to the Romantic Ironist's melding of creation and destruction. Thus, from a Coleridgean perspective, humor is a function of genial temperance.

Thomas Carlyle adds substance to this insight. In *Sartor Resartus,* it remains cunningly undecided whether Professor Teufelsdrockh's "wild tone" is a manifestation of his "real Humour" or of his "Insanity and Inanity." Although Carlyle ranks humor "among the highest qualities of genius," his pretense of confusing it with madness is destabilizing; it pushes geniality beyond programmatic "tempering" toward a more dynamic dialectic, and even to the edges of creation. Carlyle envisions humor as a pool of water in the crater of a volcano that reflects the distant light of the highest stars and simultaneously transmits from below "glances from the Region of Nether Fire." Humor's watery, volcanic fusion of transcendent idealism and the self-negating sublime corresponds to the Professor's own containment of variant "humours"; he, too, "gleams of an ethereal love" and can "clasp the whole Universe into his bosom, and keep it warm." Here, then, is the hearty genialist. But Teufelsdrockh is "sly and still, so imperturbably saturnine; [he] shows such indifference [and] malign coolness towards all that men strive after."[21] Here, too, is the intellectual wit. Carlyle fuses both comic forms. Or does he merely confuse them? Unlike the volcanic symbol, which projects an external repose, Teufelsdrockh seems all the wilder for his mixture of degenerative satire and regenerative humor. However, Carlyle's principal comic model was not the eiron Teufelsdrockh but the humorist Jean Paul Richter.[22] "Jean Paul" (as he was affectionately known) was as widely read as Goethe.[23] With characteristic energy, Carlyle praises the humorist as "a man of feeling, in the noblest sense of that word; for he loves all living with the heart of a brother."[24] As a man "of sensibility" (for the "essence of humour is sensibility; warm, tender fellow-feeling"), Carlyle's gentle Jean Paul shuns irony. It is a "shallow endowment akin to caricature [and] a poor fraction of humour." Similarly, "True humour," he continues,

> springs not more from the head than from the heart; it is not contempt, its essence is love; it issues not in laughter, but in still smiles, which lie far deeper. It is a sort of *inverse sublimity;* exalting, as it were, into our affections what is below us, while sublimity draws down into our affections what is above us. The former is scarcely less precious or heart-affecting than the latter; perhaps it is still rarer, and, as a test of genius, still more decisive. It is, in fact, the bloom and perfume, the purest effluence of a deep, fine and loving nature; a nature in harmony with itself, reconciled to the world and its stintedness and contradiction, nay, finding in this very contradiction new elements of beauty as well as goodness." [16–17, my emphasis]

The notion of humor as a "reconciliation" of contradictions accounts for all of Teufelsdrockh's irony, laughter, and smiles. Like Coleridge, Carlyle makes humor—its origin in love and containment of intellect—into a nature unto itself. And yet Nature is nothing if it is not, like the genial artist, a tempered volcanic pool of contradictions. Thus, humor is an "inverse sublimity" in that it "exalts . . . what is below" and stimulates our awareness of the volcanic "nether fires." It is a means by which philosophical self-awareness rises to enliven but never disintegrate our affections. More than wit and sarcasm or even the sublime itself, humor by its comic fusion of opposites is the "decisive test of genius," for humor manifests an evercoming consciousness of Being; it is "a nature in harmony with itself." To the degree that it controls ironic eruptions, Teufelsdrockh's laughter signifies his redemption; it embodies the inverse sublime.

For Melville, achieving Carlyle's "inverse sublimity" required years of rhetorical experimentation built upon an aesthetics of repose.

Melville's Aesthetics of Repose

Herman Melville published no treatise on Art; he proposed no rigorous theories.[25] His most explicit discussion of the fine arts, a lecture on Roman statuary, comes to us only as a text reconstructed from secondhand reports and auditors' notes. Like a "scared white doe," Melville's aesthetics must be grasped through certain "cunning glimpses": a few reviews, lectures, poems, and discrete passages from the fiction (primarily *Mardi, Moby-Dick,* and *The Confidence-Man*). With only fragments for primary documents, we can only strike toward a Melville aesthetic, but in this patchwork affair, genial humor plays a vital role as manifested in three artistic elements: repose, fusion, and the picturesque.

Fusion and Repose

"Repose" connotes a kind of peaceful stasis, or pliant recumbency of will, a careless state of mind: mild, silent, calm. It implies both release and dependence: a reasonable sleep of anxiety; a sweet surrender of ourselves into the hands of God, nature, or society. In the religious parlance of the nineteenth century, we repose faith in God. In the secular world, we repose confidence in ourselves and others. Nature is God's elegy to man, a proof against death, arguing that all care and worry shall end reposefully beneath the sod. Imbedded in the "still voice" of William Cullen Bryant's "Thanatopsis" is the comfort that death is a communal "couch" (from "coucher," to sleep) upon which all humanity reclines.[26] It is a "surrendering up / Thine individual being" (11.24–25) to the democracy of death.

Passive versions of repose involve two consecutive operations: an abnegation of self and an escape to a higher, benevolent authority. Melville was not above the allurements of "Lotos-land" thinking. In the refrain to his haunting woodland poem "Pontoosuce," he advises us to "Let go, let go" of selfhood (*Poems,* 398). This withdrawal is also implicit in *Mardi* when Aaron is depicted as "repos[ing] upon his sons" (130), and in "The Counterpane" (*MD,* ch. 4), when Ishmael awakens in the arms of Queequeg. Filial and fraternal love require a sleep of personal identity, and one that Taji also experiences in sensual heterosexual love, but only briefly, when he transforms his encounter with Yillah into a "Fairy bower in the fair lagoon, scene of sylvan ease and heart's repose" (*M,* 193). In the middle of Taji's furious quest for Ideality comes the recollection in tranquility of one moment of release when love and nature put self and time to rest.

Repose is not mental oblivion, but rather an active state of mind tempering anxiety and confidence. From a Platonic perspective, repose is at best only a temporal approximation of perfect being and therefore resembles what Diotima, Socrates' mentor in *Symposium,* calls a "daemonic" state of mind: a halfway sensibility that is conscious of Ideality but nevertheless fatally rooted in Actuality. Repose is not a cessation of awareness but a form of desire. Melville pursued in his art an oxymoronic *tense repose:* tense because of its probing toward Being and yet reposeful because of its containment of our anguish over the futility of that quest.

Bryant touches upon this tense repose in his *Lectures on Poetry* (1825) when he distinguishes between the imagination's most "intense exercise [which] sometimes unsettles the reason" (enthusiasm or madness) and the imagination's "gentle sort of activity" (187) or "repose" which is dream. For him, art is a middle ground between the "exercise" of self-indulgence and unconsciousness. Like dream, which rehearses our desire of pure Being, it mediates consciousness and death. But the "gentle activity" of Bryant's dreaming is finally more genteel than genial, more wit than humor. His "couch" is a brave witticism, but it lacks Carlyle's "inverse sublimity." It is more somnolent than reposeful. The distinction illuminates the analogy between humor and repose. Just as humor may aspire to an inverse sublimity but also degenerate into sentimentality, so too does the mind in repose teeter between a sharp confrontation with the awareness of nihility and the desire to end all consciousness. To achieve aesthetic validity, both humor and repose must occupy a liminal state that conjoins sentiment and the sublime.

Poe had little patience for such balancing acts, but he knew the two realms his contemporaries were trying to address. His "Sonnet—Silence" establishes a series of dualities: matter and light, solidity and shade, body and soul. Accordingly, there are two silences. Nature's Wordsworthian silence is experienced primarily through art ("lore") and memory, and is "terrorless." The other is the silence of Being, a realm for God not man, which is the unmediable horror of the sublime, the Silence of Nothingness.[29] Poe proposes no balance of these two silences, only a warning that if caught by the latter "elf," we can only "commend [ourselves] to God." This is not a plea for religion but a little friendly advice from one who knows the terrorist Silence too well. For Poe, repose, like humor, is a facile accommodation of material fears, and never the spiritual silence of the universe. Melville's repose, however, attempts to mediate Poe's unmediable sublime with the "inverse sublime" of Carlylean humor. As with humor, such aesthetic repose is validated through a consciousness of the tensions required to strike the mediation. True repose is always wakeful.

Longfellow saw this mediation even in his shallow effusion "A Psalm of Life." Despite its adolescent chest-thumping, bivouacking, and footprinting, the poem's restive "up and doing" ends with the apothegm, "Learn to labour and to wait."[30] There is both action and stillness, a calm yet fevered expectancy, in the final "wait": a tense repose. In his "Prelude" to *Voices of the Night,* the insomniac Longfellow uses "Fancy's sleepless eyes" first to envision, as might the humorist, "all forms of sorrow and delight" (4). But deeper still in "Hymn to the Night," the poet cures this sleeplessness by drinking from the "cistern" of the night, the deepest recesses of our conscious being. His "spirit drank repose" and "learns to bear / What man has borne before." Both "sorrow and delight" are contained in this reposeful draught, but the resultant "sleep," while it hushes the "*lips* of Care," does not end caring itself. There is only the cessation of complaint: "And they complain no more" (5). Thus, in his waiting repose (and before he must be "up and doing"), Longfellow transforms life's stream of sorrow and delight into "the trailing garments of the Night," a languorous but wakeful image suggesting both lovemaking and "affright." Longfellow's attempts to lift himself up from Bryant's "couch," to articulate an aesthetics of active repose, gives deeper meaning to the familiar opener "the soul is dead that slumbers" ("Psalm," 3).

Repose is a mediation of being and nothingness, of me and not me. But Emerson would not settle for such "daemonic" accommodations, for the transcendentalist reaches true being through an expansion of insight and an abnegation of self effected in intellect, not art. The transparent eyeball *sees* rather than feels. In a journal entry for September 1842 he wrote, "Intellect always puts an interval between the subject & the object. Affection would blend the two. For weal or for woe I clear myself from the thing I contemplate: I grieve, but am not a grief: I love, but am not a love."[29] Given that his son Waldo was only nine months in the grave, the philosopher's insistence upon Reason over despair contains a special urgency. Others "would blend" father and son, griever and grieved; he shall maintain a vital distance. When philosopher became poet in "Threnody," his Wordsworthian elegy for the lost boy, Emerson dramatized the struggle to transcend the subjectivity of "affection," both in the sense of his affections for Waldo and in the larger sense of the affective faculty of self to rise beyond earthly repose. No matter how intellectually engaged, this state of mind is no better than grieving because of its lingering attachment to self. As a form of "Becoming," repose is only a rhetorical approximation, an artistic displacement of the soul, an emblem of a desire for ideality, not ideality itself. "God offers to every mind its choice between truth and repose," Emerson wrote in "Intellect" (1835)." He in whom the love of repose predominates . . . gets rest, commodity and reputation; but he shuts the door of truth" (21). There is an almost heroic vigor in the authenticity of Emerson's transcendent mind that will give no quarter to repose, not as the sleep of reason Longfellow derides nor even the aesthetic mediation of "daemonism." The universe is awake, and if we are to be unleashed from the cave of actuality, we must "startle the sleeper conscience in the deepest cell of [our] repose" (Emerson, 8).

As in life, so too in poetry. Although Emerson equates "the spirit of the world" with "the great calm presence of the Creator" (234), he advocates a poetry of excess that belies repose. The poet's affinity with God is not in self-possession but in his likeness to a liberator, who "speaks adequately . . . only when he speaks somewhat wildly" (233). This "liberating god" (235) is vatic and emphatic, "inflamed and carried away by his thought, to that degree that he forgets the author and the public and heeds only this one dream which holds him like an insanity" (236). The poet reaches the sublime, and "declare[s] it"; he shall "draw us with love and terror" (238). There is no allowance here or need for an "*inverse* sublimity," no genial tempering of the contradictory "lords of life." There is only the wakeful "Experience" of startled confrontation.

Although Melville was strongly attracted to Emerson—"I love all men who *dive*"—far more so than his less tolerant Knickerbocker associates, he firmly allowed, if only to assure Evert Duyckinck of his Dutch stability, that he did not "oscillate in Emerson's rainbow."[30] The fact is that Shakespeare (another of Melville's divers), not Emerson, was Melville's "liberating god," as "gentle, aye, almost as Jesus" and as high as "Gabriel, Raphael and Michael" (77). Emerson's "misfortune" (Melville would not call it a "fault") was that he was "above munching a plain cake in the company of jolly fellows" (80). He lacked Shakespeare's "genial understanding." He lacked as well what Hazlitt called the "strength in the imagination that reposes entirely on nature, which nothing else can supply" (*Marginalia*, 485).

Hazlitt spoke of an actual not transcendent nature, one of paint and words. Truth lies in the creative *approach* to the ideal, not in ideality itself. Melville, who had marked this line in his copy of *Round Table*, addressed the matter in an unanswered interrogative: "Can art, not life, make the ideal?"[31] To achieve a *sense* of ideality in art would require a quiet dramatization of the engagement of both the *me* and the *not me* rather than a dissolving of one for the attainment of a sublime other. Indeed, Melville might have wanted to "speak somewhat wildly," and he did so at times, allowing himself to be "inflamed and carried away with his own thought" even to the point of "insanity." But he also knew that he could not "forget . . . the public," and that he must tone down the Emersonian sublime. He struggled, then, for his own version of an inverse sublimity.

Melville's chief aesthetic problem in dramatizing the struggle toward ideality was necessarily twofold. First, he needed to find ways to give ascendancy to the "mute calm" and "eternal mildness of joy" buried within him (*MD*, 326). But at the same time he needed to impart to this sense of repose a tension acknowledging the "tornadoed Atlantic" of his being. This notion of reposeful restraint has precedence in neoclassical aesthetics, which Melville accessed through painting and sculpture. Melville's tours of Europe in 1849 and 1856–57 included frequent visits to museums and private collections. Later on, he lectured on Roman statuary, collected well over three hundred prints and engravings, and composed various poems on art and artists, including "Art," "Rammon," "Rip Van Winkle's Lilac," and the Burgundy Club sketches. The latter consist of dialogs on the picturesque, a notion that suffuses Melville's work from the beginning. But one artwork that transfixed Melville was the Laocoön.

This first-century Greek sculpture was a principal icon of classical restraint for the eighteenth century. Melville viewed it at the Vatican Museum in 1857 and made it a central example in his lecture "Statues in Rome." In 1766 Lessing had used the sculpture to study the limits of both painting and poetry. For him, the tormented features of Laocoön entangled amidst god-sent serpents showed how beauty precedes truth.[32] A precise rendering of Laocoön's death throes, Lessing argues, would require repugnant bodily contortions. To avoid alienating viewers, Laocoön's creator found an accommodation of truth to beauty by making his snakes conform to sensuous lines and capturing Laocoön's expression not in mid-scream—eyes bulging, mouth agape—but just before his scream. Not only is this mute expectancy beautiful, but it engages us more deeply in the central figure's predicament. Paradoxically, the subduing of harsh truths within stylized forms heightens the effect of terror, leaving us easefully suspended in anticipation of horror.[33] Melville, too, was impressed by the statue's eternal mildness. Like the Apollo Belvedere, it exhibits the "tranquil, subdued air such as men have when under the influence of no passion" (*Lectures*, 407). Laocoön's anguished face, a "symbol of human misfortune," partakes of this tranquility.

Melville saw even more, for Laocoön epitomized the modern condition of deteriorating faith. Poor Laocoön: he saw through the façade of the Trojan Horse; his spear proved its ominous hollowness; he spoke the truth and was killed. Melville saw himself writhing amid those marble snakes. Laocoön's artist had lived during the fall of Roman imperialism and the rise of Christian hegemony. Similarly, in Melville's day America's imperialism threatened the union; civil war was only four years off; shallow evangelism and millennialism on one side and corrosive doubt on the other mocked traditional belief. Both ancient and modern artists were caught in periods of anxious transition. Thus Melville wrote that the sculpture embodied "the doubt and dark groping of speculation in that age when the old mythology was passing away and men's minds had not reposed in the new faith" (*Lectures,* 404). Melville saw through the anguish of the sculpture to the sculptor and found a restrained projection of his own sense of loss and anticipation. Just as Laocoön's creator buried within stone his agony over the "passing away" of one belief, Melville aspired toward a reposeful voice that could articulate his own problem of passing faith without exposing too sharply his "dark gropings." His goal was restraint: to objectify passions and subdue selfhood within art itself. Hence, one of "the finest . . . statements of truth" for him (he later wrote) was Maurice de Guerin's remark: "There is more power and beauty . . . in the well-kept secret of one's self and one's thoughts than in the display of a whole heaven that one may have inside one" (*Log,* 703–4).

Melville recognized in Laocoön the powerful effect of subduing his "doubt and dark groping." The Hellene's wrestling with those theological and ontological snakes reappears in the more Hebraic imagery of Melville's remarkable truncated sonnet, "Art" in which "unlike things must meet and mate . . . And fuse with Jacob's mystic heart, / To wrestle with the angel—Art" (*Poems,* 231). Melville lodges his repose within the "mystic heart," a crucible that can contain the fiery union of "unlike things," the artist's contrary instincts of "Humility—yet pride." Similarly, form and passion fuse within the heart. The final effect is a tense repose. This crucial element in Melville's aesthetic—the subsuming of head within mystic heart, the fusion of light and dark, the ascendency of art over self—indicates a movement toward restraint rather than Poe's terror-ridden, silent sublime. His aesthetics of repose "softens" the sublime; it limits chaos, confines self-indulgence, and restrains speculation. It is a return to Laocoön.

But the fragile nature of repose requires more than the predictable, static patterns of balance. The intellect in repose is full of expectancy. Like Daggoo shouldering Flask in a rocky whale boat on choppy seas, it must be perpetually in and out of balance. There is, then, no exact rhetorical formula for repose, only the recognition that a picturesque "balance" is intermittent, momentary, and always off center. Both Hawthorne and Melville derived their own balance not through precise philosophical argumentation but through a continual Montaignean "essaying" of an idea in order to find out what that idea really is, a "trying out" of themselves in writing, a fictive playing out of various selves. Two such essayings—a casual letter from Melville to his brother Tom and a more formal publication by Hawthorne— indicate the subtle valancies of repose. Melville's letter speaks warmly of the nobility of oblivion:

> Damn your wide-awake and knowing chaps. As for sleepiness, it is one of the noblest qualities of humanity. There is something sociable about it, too. Think of those sensible & sociable millions of good fellows all taking a good friendly snooze together, under the sod—no quarrels, no imaginary grievances, no envies, heart burnings, & thinking how much better that other chap is off—none of this: but all equally free-&-easy, they sleep away & reel off their nine knots an hour, in perfect amity. [*Letters,* 213]

Melville's humor rides the tension between consciousness and repose. He damns the "wide-awake," but the implied pun (wide wake) grants them ballast, a knowing girth and power, and while he commends unconscious sleep, he nevertheless accentuates the very thoughts he would escape: quarrels, grievances, envy, burnings, and thinking. This comic muting recalls Longfellow's hushing of Complaint while still acknowledging Care. In short, Melville did not have to die to gain repose; he could achieve it by essaying death.

Hawthorne also addressed the problem of mediating sleep and consciousness in "The Old Manse."

> Sleep! The world should recline its vast head on the first convenient pillow, and takes an age-long nap. It has gone distracted, through a morbid activity, and, while preternaturally wide-awake, is nevertheless tormented by visions, that seem real to it now, but would assume their truer aspect and character, were all things once set right by an interval of sound repose. This is the only method of getting rid of old delusions, and avoiding new ones—of regenerating our race, so that it might in due time awake, as an infant out of dewy slumber—of restoring to us the simple perception of what is right, and the singlehearted desire to achieve it; both of which have been lost, in consequence of this weary activity of brain and torpor or passion of the heart, that now afflict the universe.[34]

The similarities of idea (the sociability of sleep) and expression ("wide-awake," "sound repose") suggest that Melville had his copy of *Mosses* before him when he wrote his brother. And yet the differences between the two passages reveal the latitude afforded similar thinkers in their separate formulations of repose. Neither writer insists upon a static balance. For Hawthorne, sleep's regenerative rest saves us from too much wakefulness and restores us to childhood; we are infantilized by "dewy slumber." For Melville, however, sleep is a watery end to aging. Although both passages are genially restrained, the humor borders on sentiment. Each expression teeters between wakeful repose and mindless sleep. Each achieves a ripening if not ripeness of vision, a passion verging on yet not quite committing itself to annihilation. And yet this is enough, for ripeness is in the thinking, not the thought.

Melville provides a fuller sense of this off balance repose through an essaying of his sea-calm imagery. Like the doubloon in *Moby-Dick,* a calm mirrors the characters who perceive it. In *Mardi* the Byronic Taji, who lives in and for motion, is forever vexed by calms: They freeze us in "the outer confines of creation, the region of everlasting lull, introductory to a positive vacuity"; they bring on "thoughts of eternity" and soul anxiety (*M,* 10); they make us "madly skeptical" and "almost . . . an infidel" (9). A sea-calm is a "gray chaos" (48) that activates the "instinct" for loneliness and misanthropy. It is Poe's second Silence. But for Babbalanja, a lull provides a more thoughtful "blending" without the "brooding": "This calm is like unto Oro's everlasting serenity, and like unto man's last despair" (267). Where Taji finds only doubt, Babbalanja experiences a tense suspension of both hope and doubt.

This babbling angel contains many selves: the devilish Azzageddi, Bardiana the wise, and Lombardo the author, who like Melville is attempting to discover "Mardi" by writing it out. And like Teufelsdrockh, Babbalanja embraces divergent sensibilities. With the poet Yoomy he projects the Byronic sublime. Poetic truth, he asserts,

> strikes down into the soul's depths; till, intent upon itself, it pierces in upon its
> own essence, and is resolved into its pervading original; becoming a thing con-
> stituent of the all embracing deific; whereby we mortals become part and parcel
> of the gods; our souls to them as thoughts; and we privy to all things occult,
> ineffable, and sublime. [561]

Without this plunge, all songs are worthless. But having waxed Byronic (even Emersonian), Babbalanja rattles off several impenetrable lines of Carlylese ("Rudimental Quincunxes and the Hecatic Spherula") that give King Media a headache. The call for a poetic plunge ends in mumbo-jumbo, and Babbalanja deconstructs the aesthetic principle of sublimity that he has so earnestly created. Once again, Melville's essaying puts us off balance as if to dramatize the precariousness of repose. Departing from the standard Wordsworthian view, he claims that "The greatest fullnesses overflow not spontaneously; and even when decanted, like rich syrups, slowly ooze" (593). In reviewing Hawthorne's *Mosses* two years after the publication of *Mardi,* Melville returned to this odd image of slow "oozings" to characterize the restraint and control of Hawthorne's mirth. As in *Mardi,* the emphasis is not upon quick "piercing" to the soul but rather on the "decanting" of self, as if one's inner truth is a thick port wine contained within a narrow pitcher. Here, there is no Byronic eruption only a genial resolve. This flowing *out* rather than piercing *in* tips the balance back toward a "dewy slumber."

Babbalanja's attachment to an aesthetics of precarious repose is manifest in his rendering of the poet Lombardo's vision of the creative process:

> When Lombardo set about his work, he knew not what it would become. He did
> not build himself in with plans; he wrote right on; and so doing, got deeper and
> deeper into himself; and like a resolute traveler, plunging through baffling woods,
> at last was rewarded for his toils. "In good time," saith he, in his autobiography,
> "I came out into a serene, sunny, ravishing region; full of sweet scents, singing
> birds, wild plaints, roguish laughs, prophetic voices. Here we are at last, then,"
> he cried; "I have created the creative." [595]

In *Typee,* Melville enacts a similar journey when after a period of bafflement in a canebrake, Tommo and Toby make their way to a precipice overlooking paradise with its serene and distant falls. It is an episode of anxiety and then hope symbolic of Tommo's unstable psychology. For Lombardo in *Mardi,* however, this process of entanglement and then picturesque harmony allegorizes the creative interpenetration of doubt and repose: a plunging into baffling woods and an emergence upon a sunny plain. Lombardo's aesthetic paradise stresses the full dimensions of human expression: "wild plaints, roguish laughs, and prophetic voices." Here, the centrality of laughter leads us out of the wild into the visionary. Both Babbalanja's ironic deconstructions and Lombardo's fusion of plaint, laughter, and prophecy require the comic. For Melville, there is no art without repose, and no repose without laughter. Finally, there is no creating the creative without humor.

On completing *Moby-Dick,* Melville told Hawthorne: "I have written a wicked book, and feel spotless as the lamb. Ineffable socialities are in me. . . . It is a strange feeling—no hopefulness is in it, no despair. Content—that is it; and irresponsibility; but without licentious inclination. I speak now of my profoundest sense of being, not of an incidental feeling'' (*Letters,* 142). The ''ineffable socialities'' of Melville's genial ''all-feeling'' recall the ''tranquil subdued air such as men have when under the influence of no passion'' that Melville discerned in Laocoön. Akin to death and sleep, this aesthetic moment transcends actuality: it captures the repose of true Being, a state of ''no hopefulness . . . no despair.'' But what is clear, as in the letter to Tom, is that the ''ineffable socialities'' of geniality are inalienable from Melville's ''profoundest sense of Being.'' Thus, humor and consciousness are inextricably linked in the struggle for repose. Melville's aesthetics occupies a middle ground between the beautiful and the sublime, comedy and tragedy, inland and sea. And that middle ground is best articulated in terms not of the sublime but of the picturesque.

Melville's Picturesque: Toning Down the Green

The general view is that Melville disdained the picturesque as symptomatic of America's shallow optimism.[35] The reasoning is that landscapes that mask the problems of mind and culture with impossible blendings of otherwise obdurate oppositional forces were to Melville inherently false. Ishmael prefers a ''soggy, boggy, squitchy'' painting to the overly patterned Gilpinesque iconography of light and dark. Moreover, those paintings which ''prettify'' squalor—the ''povertiresque'' as Melville put it in *Pierre*—are at best worthy of satire. But given its controlled management of the rough and unexpected, the unpolished picturesque was consonant with Melville's ''half melancholy, half farcical'' approach (*Log,* 549). Thus, if Melville attacks the picturesque at times, it is only to clarify its ethical and aesthetic potentials.[36] The picturesque's critical vocabulary of being and creation encompasses a *chiaroscuro* that empowered Melville to ''fuse'' both bright and dark into what Hawthorne in ''The Old Apple Dealer'' calls ''the moral picturesque.'' In this problematic sketch of a ''generally negative'' Bartleby-like figure, Hawthorne advises that ''Every touch must be *kept down,* or else you destroy the *subdued tone* which is absolutely essential to the whole effect.''[37] In discussing his own version of this ''moral picturesque,'' Melville similarly argued in ''Rip Van Winkle's Lilac'' that one must ''tone down the green'' in both life and art (*Poems,* 289). What emerges, once again, is an artist of self-containment, whose picturesque sensibility is a precarious yet well-modulated fusion—tense yet calm—of anxiety and mirth.[38]

To adapt his principles of fusion and repose within the construct of a moral picturesque, Melville modified a tradition that was by the 1850s essentially passé; and, in view of the generally accepted placement of the movement in modern art, his version was decidedly retrogressive. Picturesque paintings first appeared in the seventeenth century, but they are as diverse in style as Salvator Rosa's moody ruins and Claude's bright landscapes. No serious attempts to clarify the concept appeared until William Gilpin's analectic musings. And though Edmund Burke's study of the sublime does not deal with the subject, subsequent essayists (in particular Uvedale Price and Richard Payne Knight) attempted to define the term by either modifying or rejecting Burke's alignment of the beautiful and sublime with the corresponding human instincts of love and fright.[39]

In expanding Burke's view to encompass the picturesque, Uvedale Price explored a middle ground. If, as Burke argued, beauty physiologically relaxes the nerve fibers that control emotion and the sublime tightens them, then, Price extrapolated, the picturesque leaves them reposed in natural suspension. The emotion aroused is neither pleasure nor pain but "curiosity," and the artistic elements that naturally arouse this sensation are "roughness and sudden variation joined to irregularity."[40] In opposition, associationists such as Gilpin, Archibald Allison, and Knight argued that the picturesque is simply a visual habit, a painterly way of framing the world and transforming nature into a coherent landscape.[41] As stimulating as it was, the controversy between Price and Knight languished as the vogue for the Picturesque passed. Although Price's criterion of a suspension of roughness and irregularity is congruent with Melville's moral *chiaroscuro,* the concept of the picturesque became in Melville's day a quaint derogation of the associationist view meaning little more than "pretty as a picture."

Christopher Hussey's renewed discussion of the "The Picturesque" in 1927 identified the concept as a transitional mode that allowed artists and viewers (from about 1730 to 1830) to adjust their habits of viewing from an appreciation of the "soft and pleasing repose . . . characteristic of the beautiful" (Hussey, 67) to that of the craggy, awe-engendering sublime. Broadly stated, it was a development away from the rational to the imaginative (or intuitive), from seeing with the mind to seeing with the feelings. Along with Uvedale Price and Hussey, Martin Price has more recently acknowledged the mixed nature of the picturesque, but in delineating what he calls "The Picturesque Moment," he explores a frame of mind that encompasses a variety of cultural phenomena: nostalgia, literature, and humor, as well as the "preserving [of] the significant ruin" (261). The picturesque familiarizes the sublime (265), but, like wit and humor, it involves a playful dissociation of object and meaning (279), leaving us suspended between "the full tragedy of the sublime [and] the serene comedy of the beautiful" (277). Nevertheless, the picturesque promotes an energy of mind, "an intensity of awareness" in its middle ground that is "primarily moral." The tension in Martin Price's picturesque moment, then, is a sense of order, or "the limited idea of unity" (279), giving way to accident, change, and chaos.[42]

Martin Price's picturesque resembles Melville's own intense, transitional sensibility, but Melville's "moment" is essentially counterdirectional: It points back toward classicism rather than forward to the sublime. If art fuses "unlike things" within the "mystic heart," it requires an artistic containment of selfhood. Whereas Hussey's and Martin Price's picturesque moment veers ineluctably toward the decay of the Burkean sublime and its incumbent psychological anxiety, Melville's picturesque is "retrogressive" in its continued insistence upon a voice of "eternal mildness" and repose positioned amid despair, one in which urgent self-exposure begets a voice of restraint that in turn begets renewed "flashings-forth" but also further "calms." In Melville's art, then, the dynamic interpenetration of "Hellenic cheer [and] Hebraic grief" (*Clarel* I: xxviii, 34), because of the equal potency given to these elements, effectively forestalls a full embracing of the sublime. And herein lies the power of *Moby-Dick.*

A particularly apt image that conveys Melville's "retrogressive" picturesque moment also contains a critical understanding of the limits of repose. It is the liminal metaphor of "the marge" or shoreline found in "The Enviable Isles." In this poem, the artful fusion of the sublime and beautiful, symbolized by the shoreline union of sea and land, corresponds to a fusion in life of awareness and joy, but Melville also raises an ethical dilemma implicit in both the aesthetics of repose and the picturesque, i.e., the peril of excessive restraint:

> Through storms you reach them and from storms are free.
>   Afar descried, the foremost drear in hue,
> But, nearer, green; and, on the marge, the sea
>   Makes thunder low and mist of rainbowed dew.
>
> But, inland, where the sleep that folds the hills
> A dreamier sleep, the trance of God, instills—
> On uplands hazed, in wandering airs aswoon,
>   Slow-swaying palms salute love's cypress tree
> Adown in vale where pebbly runlets croon
>   A song to lull all sorrow and all glee.
>
> Sweet-fern and moss in many a glade are here,
>   Where, strown in flocks, what cheek-flushed myriads lie
> Dimpling in dream—unconscious slumberers mere,
>   While billows endless round the beaches die.
>
> —*Poems,* 204

The danger of this Tennysonian lotus-land is that the reposeful "trance of God" will "lull all sorrow and all glee" (l. 12); it is a siren song luring us to mindless sleep and nature reduced to Bryant's "couch." Full repose anesthetizes the intellect, transforming us into "dimpling" "unconscious slumberers mere" (l. 13). But in the opening stanza we thoughtful souls not "dimpling in dream" situate ourselves at that picturesque spot "on the marge" (l. 3), where, turning from the sea, we may be shocked by "thunder low" and yet enlivened by "rainbowed dew."[43]

Melville uses his metaphoric delineations of sea-calm and marge to characterize various artists in his poem "At the Hostelry." This ambitious discourse on the picturesque features a score of painters who assemble, at the request of a Marquis de Grandvin, to haggle over aesthetics. Despite their varying styles, familiar elements of Melville's moral *chiaroscuro* clearly emerge. For Tintoretto, the picturesque requires that "Some decay must lurk / In florid things" (*Poems,* 323). Spagnoletto's definition echoes Melville's famous image of the Encantadan tortoise: "Let sunny frankness charm his air, . . . And, mind ye, don't forget the pall" (328). And under Steen's "vineyard, lo, a cavern!" (330). In each case, fertility intermingles with the grotesque. Moreover, the Ishmaelean geniality of Grandvin and Jack Gentian (their very names project mirth) dominates the poem. The Marquis focuses immediately upon the moral complexity that the picturesque attempts to contain: "In best of worlds if all's not bright, / Allow, the shadow's chased by light, / Though rest for neither yet may be" (313). Surely, the balance of light and shadow is expected, but Melville's image of light chasing shadow suggests an ever moving aesthetic space, a kind of perpetual liminality, which, as we shall see, Melville also found in the "ever-moving dawn" of Hawthorne's mirth. The genial Marquis's *chiaroscuro* insists upon a mutual interpenetration of head and heart.

Works by Spagnoletto and Lippi—one "furious," the other "serene"—represent unmediated oppositional styles (319). In them is no true picturesque. But Steen's and Swanevelt's balance of sublimity and beauty implies a reconciliation: the former champions *"Wine and brine* / The mingled brew" (329); the latter praises Leonardo's Medusa wherein "Grace and the Picturesque may dwell / With Terror" (319). To lend credence to these mingled brews of terror and restraint, Melville punctuates the debate with the eloquent silences of the Great Masters themselves, who listen but never speak: Rembrandt is "reserved in self-control"; Leonardo is entranced by "light / Rayed thro' red wine in glass—a gleam / Pink on the polished table bright" (332), and Michael Angelo is mutely withdrawn, sipping water. The silence of these Masters and their picturesque moments of repose evoke a sense of self-control, clarity, and detachment that cannot be articulated but only painted: the sensual repose of pink on bright polish.

The elements of fusion, repose, and the picturesque in Melville's aesthetics clarify the interaction between the artist's conception of being and his projection of that consciousness into art. But to end simply by saying that Melville's art reflects a mind intent upon restraint does not help us apply these aesthetic principles to a critical reading of Melville's texts. To understand how Melville used literary works to bring his readers closer to his vision of repose, we must turn to the rhetorical problem of voice.

Melville's Rhetoric: Voicing the Voiceless

Had Melville been only a thinker, he would have been a philosopher of silence: "Truth is in things, and not in words," he wrote in *Mardi,* "truth is voiceless" (283). Accordingly, the seeker of truth finds reality in matter not language, substance not rhetoric; and since silence is the only true emblem of that reality, the writer's job is, as we have inferred from de Man, inherently problematic if not futile. But Melville takes a step that oddly enough brings him back to a deeper commitment to the word. Finding the truth "in things," he argues, is no simple matter, for as Babbalanja remarks, "things visible" are as delusory as "things imaginative." "If duped by one we are equally duped by the other" (284). Given the deceptive nature of objective reality, we must continually fall back upon "the old interrogatory"— what is truth? "That question," Babbalanja asserts, "is more final than any answer." It is also more final than reality itself; thus we inevitably return to rhetoric, not, however, the rhetoric of "answers" but rather a rhetoric of perpetual interrogation. Melville intuits ideality (in Self, God, Being), knows he cannot grasp it, and yet must settle for the tragicomic torment of asking about it. For if truth is in things, and yet things deceive, our only human recourse is not in *questing,* as though objective reality can be touched, but in *questioning* it, talking toward it, "essaying" its reality. Herein lies the difference between the futile quester Ahab and the resolvent questioner Ishmael.

Melville was not a philosopher. He was at best a pragmatic Platonist and very much a rhetorician. And he saw his rhetorical dilemma clearly: He wanted to give readers some taste of the ominous silence inherent in reality but had only the noise of language with which to body that feeling forth. In *Pierre* he writes: "that profound Silence, that only Voice of our God . . . from that divine thing without a name, those impostor philosophers pretend somehow to have got an answer; which is as absurd as though they should say they had got water out of a stone; for how can a man get a Voice out of Silence" (208). To understand Melville's true unfolding as an artist, we need to recognize that rhetoric not philosophy was his most immediate and vital concern. The rhetorical problem of how to "get a Voice out of Silence" seems hopelessly absurd, for language can only fail if it must be silent. But disregarding this de Manian perspective, Melville aims through endless experimentation for linguistic and dramatistic approximations of truth, not silence itself, but artful evocations of silence either in symbols of whiteness and circularity, walled-in characters, or, oddly enough, in voluble speakers poised before a non-answering void. Writer and artist Maurice Sendak speaks to the effectiveness of this Melvillean rhetoric when he observes from the reader's point of view: "You have to resign yourself to the non-answer and, in fact, when you do, finally, it is the best of all answers. . . . It is the most honest of all answers, and Melville is a kind of beacon in the sense that you begin to love the non-answers."[44] To be sure, the anxiety of the "non-answer" resides at the center of Melville's sense of repose.

In giving voice to his aesthetics of repose, Melville at first created narrators who would speak *about* the silent universe. They were versions of Ishmael, the comic poser of problems left unanswered. Later, after silencing the Ishmaelean voice in his fiction, Melville devised radically distant narrators who, by the very nature of their distancing, stood *for* (rather than spoke about) an uncommunicative universe, and thereby forced readers to enact for themselves the drama of doubt and belief. In voicing the voicelessness of truth, Melville relied on a comic stance grounded in the notion of geniality.

The Genial Instinct: Victim and Voice

No one who reads Melville can deny that there is something negative in the man. He defied the "yes-gentry," said "NO! in thunder" (*Letters,* 125), and found aesthetic merit in "the power of blackness ten times black." Melville came by this streak honestly. His mother was, by most reports, an aloof Calvinist, and though her son grew away from her doctrines, he was continually intrigued by the "mysteries of iniquity."

But Melville's upbringing was not entirely joyless.[45] Newly recovered letters from Herman's mother record her belief in the efficacy of the heart. On 17 October 1838 she admonishes her seventeen-year-old daughter Augusta to "Cultivate the best feelings of the heart & extract from it with the aid of fervent prayer, all the baser passions which are alas so natural to us, in our present state of depravity. Cultivate the Virtues which are also but in a much fainter degree inherent in our nature, and by *careful culture* they will soon thrive & prosper so as eventually to root out and to totally eradicate, or greatly to impair the natural prevalence of evil."[46] Not much joy here; but in a letter dated 10 (?) September 1841, Maria more directly supports the heart: "I hold that running & jumping, when in the country together with hearty, loud, ringing laughter, are conducive to health." Of course, she adds, polite society considers such activities to be "Vulgar"; hence Melville's mother (true daughter of the Puritans) advises that one's running and jumping and laughing should be performed "away from critical observation with proper discretion." That the somber Maria Gansevoort Melville—widow and recluse—was a closet humorist is about as jarring a notion in the context of our prevailing assumptions about Herman's upbringing as the idea of Queen Victoria dancing the Highland fling on Albert's grave, and yet the mother may have passed to her son a crucial set of comic beliefs: that humor is one of the "best feelings of the heart," that it is in some sense "inherent in our nature," that it can be "cultivated," and that through "careful culture" it may "eradicate" or at least "impair" our equally inherent, more clearly visible evil tendency.[47]

If Melville did not learn these principles in youth, he acquired them soon enough, for they are evident throughout his fiction. For him, "the best feelings of the heart" are not learned; they are innate, "inherent in our nature" (to quote Mother Melville) or more appropriately *instinctive*. What I call the "genial instinct" in Melville's ethical view is equivalent to his more familiar "instinct of the knowledge of demonism" (*MD* 194). Just as the Vermont colt that has never seen a buffalo bolts at the shaking of an unseen buffalo robe, we know instinctively that the world threatens our being. If unchecked, our instinct for self-awareness promotes a socially alien, disintegrative, and misanthropic mentality. Without "careful culture," we become victims of that instinct.

For Melville, this instinctive faculty of awareness is a spontaneous mental reflex countered but not negated by the equally inevitable instinct of geniality. Also an inalienable human reflex, the genial instinct is that creative force revealed to Babbalanja in the sympathetic breezes of May mornings. It is "the flower of life springing from some sense of joy in it" ("John Marr," *Poems,* 161). It is the " 'all' feeling" (*Letters,* 131)—that sudden sense of personal coherence and of oneness with others and nature. Like one's demonic awareness, geniality is a survival instinct but in an amative and creative key. In its lowest social manifestation, it is the herding instinct or awareness of safety in numbers; it binds all people into a "common continent." But above all, it is the innate sense of "good nature" that gives birth to the unavoidable human attributes of benevolence, confidence, faith, friendship, fraternity, philanthropy, and democracy.

The danger with instincts—whether subversive or integrative, intellectual or affective—is that they operate automatically and indifferently. They cannot be predicted or fully controlled. Like humor or repose, too much control or absolute suppression of these twin instincts is, as Freud notes, the same as death. Too little control (i.e., giving free rein to either psychic reflex) leads to a series of unpredictable and unlivable manic–depressive states. Melville's most interesting characters, both tragic and comic, are victims of instinct. Without geniality, Jackson in *Redburn* is vicious and sarcastic, Pierre's mind grows "maggotty," Ahab (petulantly tossing his pipe away) becomes a "self-consuming misanthrope," Bartleby curls up, the surly Pitch dries up like an old shoe, and Billy strikes home. Without the opposing instinctive awareness of nihility, Tommo too eagerly embraces cannibals, pie-eyed Redburn is continually snookered, and Captain Amasa Delano dandifies the "monster" Babo. Thus, we are caught up in our own instincts between the fiery dust of Byronism and the shallow hedonism, facile optimism, and sentiment of geniality. These instinctive "humours"—the will to see and know, the will to laugh and create—are both signs of grace and yet inborn tragic flaws. They preserve and humanize; they also destroy and delude. The catch is that they are unavoidable. The trick is to make them balance.[48]

Melville took this balancing act to be a human imperative. In the capitalized, epigrammatic conclusion to "The Conflict of Convictions," he states: "YEA AND NAY—/ EACH HATH HIS SAY; / BUT GOD HE KEEPS THE MIDDLE WAY" (*Poems*, 7). But the Civil War, which occasioned this "Battle-Piece," was the tragic realization that for North and South, there was no godly "middle way." "Bartleby" dramatizes a failure to balance in more human terms. The scrivener's demonic instinct carries isolation to the point of self-destruction; the lawyer's hith-erto unacknowledged geniality draws him inexplicably toward humanity despite himself. The two cannot find a "good natural arrangement," and the result is an absurd comedy in which characters (to borrow the Bergsonian formula) enact the mechanisms of instincts they only vaguely comprehend. There is no middle way, only an acknowledgment in the tale's final equation of Bartleby and humanity of the need for one.

Melville was himself a victim of instinct. Witness the flip-flops in his letters to Hawthorne. In the jaunty "No! in thunder" letter of 16 April 1851, he expresses the ineluctable atheism of total awareness. His claim to sovereignty over God is that they are equally tripped by the concept of Being: "[T]here lies the knot with which we choke ourselves. As soon as you say *Me*, a *God*, a *Nature*, so soon you jump from your stool and hang from the beam. Yes, that word [Being] is the hangman." Our instinct to know ourselves leads to an elevation of self and a debasement of God, but ultimately the knowledge that Ideal Being is an unachievable state abrogates the sovereignty of the Self. Thus Melville concludes that "those who say yes, *lie*" (*Letters*, 125). But Melville's next letter to Hawthorne presents the case for geniality. He begins with a bold statement of individualism, exalts heart over head, and speculates on the illusory nature of the genial instinct, which finally mitigates his initial self-aggrandizement:

> It is a frightful poetical creed that the cultivation of the brain eats out the heart. . . . I stand for the heart. To the dogs with the head! I had rather be a fool with a heart, than Jupiter Olympus with his head. The reason the mass of men fear God, and at bottom dislike Him, is because they rather distrust His heart, and fancy Him all brain like a watch. [129]

In standing for the heart, Melville places faith in the integrative " 'all' feeling," which elevates man and nature above God and toward pure Being. But like the intense "flashings-forth" of demonism, the genial instinct is only a "temporary feeling" (131). Neither instinct can claim sovereignty for long.

Whether we catch Melville "standing for" head or heart, his arguments coil back to his obsession with selfhood and Being. One instinct invariably intrudes upon the other. This pattern of unpredictable intrusion recurs throughout Melville's books. After Tommo's first evening "of drowsy repose" with the Typees, he awakes at midnight suddenly "apprehensive of some evil" (*T*, 93). Redburn climbs the mast and gets "lost in one delirious throb at the center of the All," but this "wild bubbling and bursting . . . at my heart" suddenly abates when he must "set to work like an ass!" on deck (66). In a similar scene, Ishmael is caught in the rhythms of the sea and "lulled into . . . an opium-like listlessness of vacant, unconscious reverie" in which "at last he loses his identity" (*MD*, 159) and nearly plunges to his death. And in *The Confidence-Man* the oft-diddled Mr. Roberts, instinctively drawn to the camaraderie of a glass of champagne, instinctively realizes through the agency of the same champagne that he is about to be duped. His wine activates first one instinct and then another, first "all feeling" then "all truth." Here, human will is reduced to mere impulse and reflex.

We are fated to ride a nonstop teeter-totter, with head and heart randomly and willfully tossing and dropping each other with little hope of calm. And yet Melville's fictions clearly manifest his attempts to give voice to a middle way. He experimented with comic figures and voices—rhetorical versions of the picturesque—that could subsume the demonic *within* the genial. This fused sensibility—outwardly benign, inwardly knowing—grows out of Babbalanja's "deep thought" of laughter and culminates with the godly gamesome Ishmael. Although he could not in any real sense voice the silence of God, Melville could hush the demonism of self-awareness through the restraining faculty of his genial spirit. But amiable humor in Melville's day had gone the way of sentiment, and for Melville to use geniality effectively he had to revitalize it.[49] Making genial humor strong enough to contain "deep thought" would require "careful culture." Aesthetically and rhetorically, he could not sustain a viable voice of repose unless the instinct of geniality were as strong as the demonic is destructive. To cultivate his genial voice, Melville had to correct America's sense of humor, and one significant step in that direction is his essay on Hawthorne.

Hawthorne's Religion of Mirth

For some, Melville's review of "Hawthorne and His *Mosses*" is a manifesto for an art of concealment. Richard Brodhead states the case succinctly: The "author can use the forms and conventions of popular fiction in such a way as to gain the approval of the popular audience, while at the same time smuggling a darker communication past their eyes."[50] There is substance to this notion, for Melville's most memorable lines in his review assert that "the great Art of Telling the Truth" is achieved by providing readers only "cunning glimpses" of truth ("*Mosses*," 244). Presumably, the superficial reader, unused to a careful treading through a text, hurries past a writer's purposeful subversions. Moreover, by concealing blasphemies beneath innocuous symbols, Hawthorne and Melville could be satisfied that knowing readers would appreciate the depths that common readers merely skim. The writer "deceive[s] . . . the superficial skimmer of pages" (251). It was a means of surviving in the literary marketplace while being true to oneself.[51]

But the idea that Hawthorne and Melville were forced by the exigencies of the marketplace to adopt an aesthetics of concealment is not entirely satisfactory. Melville's warning to superficial skimmers must be taken in context. Melville is merely speaking of how such titles as "Young Goodman Brown" promise nothing more

than a "Goody Two Shoes" tale but in fact deliver something "deep as Dante."
Melville admits he is "dolefully dupe[d]" by "harmless" Hawthorne (242, 252),
whose "sublimity . . . seems lost in his sweetness" (252). But the word "seems"
indicates that this deception is a purposely fabricated effect; it is only temporary,
so that the intended reading experience is one of discovery. In discovering unexpected meaning, readers emerge far more chilled than if they had their "moral"
dished out plain. Clearly, Hawthorne intends his concealments to be uncovered.
Like most literary "hoaxers," he "duped" with the idea of being "caught." His
concealments are designed to expose themselves. Hawthorne's "sweetness," then,
is not pap for common readers; it is the medium by which his "sublimity" is artfully
contained and ready for restrained exposure.

Burke's view, "No art is great but that it deceives," echoes a passage from
Carlyle marked in Melville's copy of FitzGerald's *Polonius:* "No good book . . .
shows its best face at first."[52] The assumption here that readers have a shared
expectancy of concealment belies any special aesthetic relevance given to Hawthorne's or Melville's "art" of concealment. We go to a fiction to discover what
is hidden; we know we must decipher and decode an artist's suggestive indirections.
Indeed, Melville's digressive Chapter 14 in *The Confidence-Man* argues that it is
the highly contrived concealments of popular novelists, not the more challenging
"twistings and turnings" of his own ironic fiction, that cheapen a literary work.
Moreover, Hawthorne's concealments are designed to explore the artful effect of
restraining self-indulgent philosophizing.[53] The point is not so much *that* Hawthorne
conceals but *how* he does it, how he expresses the "power and beauty" of "the
well-kept secret" of himself, how he could modulate selfhood within a genial
voice.

"Hawthorne and His *Mosses*" is as much an essay on the artful function of
geniality as it is of "blackness, ten times black" (243).[54] Hawthorne's geniality is
a means of self-containment, and humor is the principal mechanism of that restraint.
Unlike Shakespeare, who was forced to pander to an audience, Hawthorne (Melville
observes) refrains from "all popularizing noise and show of broad farce, and blood-
smeared tragedy"; he is "content with the still, rich utterances of *a great intellect
in repose,* and which sends few thoughts into circulation, except they be arterialized
at his large warm lungs, and expanded in his honest heart" (245, my emphasis).
The heart's dual function is to *express* an inner being but also to *humanize* that
dark entity, to make expression communicable. Like the heart, Hawthorne's "con-
templative humor" rises above the hail-fellow's "rollicking rudeness." It is "so
high, so deep, and yet so richly relishable. . . . It is the very religion of mirth"
(241). Hawthorne allegorizes his relishable yet spiritual humor through images of
suppressed fire and light found in "Fire Worship." The hearth, a metaphor for
both heart and art, exhibits the tense repose of Laocoön. It contains the fire's
potential for "mischief" and "mad destruction" within a warm "domestic kindness." Just as Shakespeare has his "flashings-forth," the fire, Hawthorne writes,
may betray "his wild nature," but its "red tongue" rarely escapes the stony hearth
whose "warm heart atone[s] for all" (241). In its containment of fiery truths, the
hearth resembles Melville's crucible of "Art" wherein "Humility—yet pride and

scorn'' are fused with ''mystic heart.'' Hearth, heart, and art—the three are virtual homophonic emanations of the same genial spirit.

Hawthorne's ''power and beauty'' reside in his comic containment of ''grotesque forms . . . hushed in the noon-day repose of [his] spell'' (241). It is a mystic union of humor, love, and mind. In words that echo Carlyle on Richter, Melville writes,

> But there is no man, in whom humor and love, like mountain peaks, soar to such a rapt height, as to receive the irradiations of the upper skies; —there is no man in whom humor and love are developed in that high form called genius; no such man can exist without also possessing, as the indispensable complement of these, a great, deep intellect, which drops down into the universe like a plummet. Or [else], love and humor are only the eyes, through which such an intellect views this world. [242][55]

Although the thrust of this passage is to demand a deep intellect from genius, Melville clearly requires an equivalent commitment to humor. The consequence of not striking this complementary relation is artistic debasement. Moreover, the last sentence suggests that love and humor are more than Emersonian optics of the intellect. They do not merely feed the intellect with data of the world; they are the indispensable means by which demonic revelations are ''arterialized,'' that is, sent out into the world. Like Carlyle's volcanic pool, Hawthorne's humor allows for a containment of head within heart. It is a form of ''inverse sublimity'' that places the ''intellect in repose.'' It is a rhetorical approximation of silence.

In fusing humor and intellect, Hawthorne achieves the ripeness of ''Indian Summer sunlight'' that unifies the landscape in ''one softness'' yet ''still reveals the distinctive hue of every towering hill, and each far-winding vale'' (242). His golden mirth gives an artful presence to the picturesque topography of the self; yet it subdues the realities of ''hill and vale'' beneath ''one softness.'' It enlivens because it contains. Hawthorne's well-known ''Puritanic gloom,'' then, is not total. Nor is it meant to be fiction's final effect. Hawthorne's ''black conceit'' is only the ''dark half of the physical sphere'' (243) that contains a brighter hemisphere as well; it is a black ''back-ground'' (244) against which his ''flashings-forth'' are set. Melville's point is that darkness and mirth are mutually dependent rhetorical forms. Each delimits the other; each exists in the traces of the other. Hawthorne's darkness, he writes, ''gives more effect to the ever-moving dawn, that forever advances through it, and circumnavigates [the] world'' (243). In this picturesque metaphor prefiguring Grandvin's image of light chasing shadow, Hawthorne's *chiaroscuro* takes on the special light of dawn. It is not merely a balance of day and night but rather the penetration of geniality into gloom. Indeed, Hawthorne's dawnlike mirth subdues as it ''forever advances through'' that darkness. Unlike Wordsworth's ''deeply interfused'' sense of the sublime in ''Whose dwelling is the light of setting suns,''[56] Melville stresses the light of rising suns. Hawthorne's art is a perpetual liminality. His voice, the ''rich utterances of a great intellect in repose,'' grows out of this crepuscular interfusion of opposing sensibilities, out of the mingling of intellect with ''the all-engendering heart'' (243), out of the mutual intrusions of geniality and despair.[57]

In life, Hawthorne's instinct was to hide himself far more than Melville ever could, and his own fictions were marked by a form of restraint that Melville had to work hard at acquiring. In his *American Notebooks,* Hawthorne had worried about the *chiaroscuro* of his mind: "Lights and shadows are continually flitting across my inward sky, and I know neither whence they come nor whither they go; nor do I inquire too closely into them." He feared the intimations of even the brighter truths. For him "there is something more awful [i.e., full of awe] in happiness than in sorrow, —the latter being earthly and finite, the former composed of the substance and texture of eternity, so that spirits still embodied may well tremble at it."[58] Here is Hawthorne's "inverse sublimity," what he called "the fiercer, deeper, and more tragic power of laughter."[59]

No one denies that Melville's famous review alerts us to the "blackness" in Hawthorne. What must be realized, however, is the comic context of this revelation. In stressing the rhetorical "effect" of Hawthorne's *chiaroscuro,* Melville was seeking to educate readers to the darker veins in Hawthorne's humor. In 1850 it was not at all necessary to proclaim Hawthorne's mirth; everyone had already praised it to the skies—in London, Boston, and New York. Edwin P. Whipple, for instance, ranked Hawthorne over a dozen or so wits including Carlyle, Dickens, Irving, and Goldsmith. For him, the author possessed felicity beyond Addison and insight over Steele; his "beautiful depth of cheerful feeling" made him "the very poet of mirth."[60] So much having been said, it is a wonder that Melville bothered to mention Hawthorne's comic gift at all. In fact, he made the effort in order to deepen our sense of Hawthorne's humor. True, Whipple had recognized the "delicate sharpness of satire" in Hawthorne, but like most critics he was content to stress the "gentle, harmless" Hawthorne. None had gone further to identify the "fierceness" in the man's humor and thereby validate the deeper aesthetic necessity of his geniality. Melville's review, then, is a correction of the contemporary view of Hawthorne's mirth.

Reading the "*Mosses*" review this way helps us better understand the strategies of Melville's own *chiaroscuro*. Notice, for instance, the picturesque duality in this familiar warning: "You may be witched by his sunlight, —transported by the bright gildings in the skies he builds over you; —but there is the blackness of darkness beyond; and even his bright gildings but fringe, and play upon the edges of thunderclouds" (243). At first, mirth seems only an adornment on the fringe of meaning. But we come to realize, too, that we cannot know the shape and nature of the thundercloud without the bright outlining. Humor and Insight (sunshine and thunder) give reality to each other. Those who see only mirth have labored under an "absurd misconception"; but equally mistaken are those who find only "gloom." The *totality* of Hawthorne resides in his tense repose, best apprehended through the reader's exercise of the heart. Melville continues: Hawthorne "is immeasurably deeper than the plummet of the mere critic. For it is not the brain that can test such a man; it is only the heart. You cannot come to know greatness by inspecting it; there is no glimpse to be caught of it, except by intuition; you need not ring it, you but touch it, and you find it is gold" (244).

Melville's ultimate focus is how we must read. Reading is an intuitive process; we read not with "eyes" but with feelings. We "touch" a text to find its gold.

The "all-engendering heart" is, in fact, *more* than an organ of self-exposure through which dark insights are "arterialized," more than the fusing crucible of awareness and mirth, more, too, than the site of a "great intellect in repose." It is as well the faculty by which a reader grasps a fiction. The heart is both creative and receptive. It is the source of Hawthorne's genial voice and the means by which we hear it. By extension, true humor—deep, fierce, tragic—is the central controlling art through which writer and reader achieve repose. Indeed, the creative heart engenders the receptive heart. Or so it seemed for Melville when first he read his Hawthorne and let himself "be witched" and "transported" by his words, let himself "touch" Hawthorne's gold and "play upon the edges of thunderclouds," let himself bask in his "noon-day repose." Melville had discovered in Hawthorne not only a kindred genius, but the touchstone for his own sense of what a reader must do.

In a letter to Evert Duyckinck, Sophia Hawthorne proclaimed that the writer of the *"Mosses"* review had "apprehended" her husband far more than any other reader. What Melville apprehended was of both aesthetic and rhetorical value. He grasped the artistic necessity of humor in Hawthorne's picturesque and tied that to his aesthetics of repose. He also learned just how far a reader might go. The only question for Melville, who at the time was in the midst of *Moby-Dick,* was whether he could make his own reader go farther.

Melville and the Reader: "Lord, When Shall We Be Done Changing?"

Melville never wrote the same book twice. Each fiction has its singularity. The reason for so much experimentation is not that he wavered in his aesthetics of repose. That remained a constant. Rather, he was in continual search for new strategies to teach readers how to read him. Melville's commitment to humor also remained constant, but in creating a voice that could project a "great intellect in repose," he also experimented with conflicting forms of laughter, in particular the integrative mode of geniality and the more subversive rhetoric of deceit found in tall tales and literary confidence games. Melville also devised in his later fiction a synthesis of these two associated with his own version of the culturally ambivalent mode of cosmopolitanism. And more: As he experimented with comic modes he also shifted from a picturesque style of fiction to something far more dramatistic, from first-person narrative to more detached third-person speakers. But he did this, as well, in the context of a democratic society's comic debate over how humor and satire could best serve the republic.

The problem was that while satire was decidedly divisive, it had more native authenticity in its sting than did the bland sentiment of what was essentially a British import, amiable humor. America's comic imperative, then, was to give individual political factions their say while at the same time promote the emergence of a unifying voice of the culture. The trick was to compress satiric thrust within good-natured humor, to control the sting of irony and make it useful. For Melville's contemporaries, a true "national literature" would have to be one that could speak sharply and yet embracingly, and could balance the people's divided interests with the nation's need for unity. The difficulties of achieving such a balance were clear to William Gilmore Simms, and equally clear to him was that the pompous Cornelius Mathews, the favored humorist in Melville's New York circle, could not effect that balance. The problem, for instance, with *Puffer Hopkins,* the Southern critic argued, was that it is too satiric, and the problem with satire is that it incites rather than resolves. When Mathews "says 'laugh' . . . we are more disposed to 'lynch.' " In short, Mathews was no "humorist."[63] Where he failed in moderating political attack with amiability, other comic figures succeeded; hence, the emergence of such complex humorists as the community-building ironists Diedrich Knickerbocker and Ishmael and the moral con artists Jim Doggett and Frank Goodman, who could compress their skepticism of Americans within a general love of humanity.

The growth of America's comic sensibility is grounded in the possibility that wit, irony, and satire can be contained within a benevolent voice of humor. Humor could have its sting, and the resultant "innocent wit," according to the humorist Frederick S. Cozzens, would have "sufficient amiability and good sense to keep it [satire] in subjection."[62] This "subjection" was precisely the art of containment that Melville desired. But Melville's geniality had to face American realities. The 1850s were not amiable times. The economic uncertainties of the Jacksonian era had erased the last vestige of privilege from the burgeoning democracy, making the genial longing for a golden, prerevolutionary past wildly inappropriate. Cooper bemoaned the passing of Patroons in a tone of rancor not found in the voice of a De Coverley or Shandy. Good-natured humor in the hands of the ephemeral N. P. Willis had little effect in articulating the problems of a nation bound for civil war. The recusant Irving had focused his admirable talents on the histories of other lands, not the deep thought of American laughter. Emerson had no truck with "whim." The most vital comic movement was America's rustic humor, which reflected more genuinely the fundamental conflicts of the age—urban versus frontier, north versus south, savage versus civilized—but it, too, tended to regionalize, not unify. The crisis in America's comic debate was how to make use of traditional and native materials, and who would be able to effect a new and unifying sense of humor.

Part I outlines the context of this comic debate. Here, I trace the development of amiable humor from British sources to American counterparts, focusing largely upon Irving and his own struggle to control his satiric impulses. I explore the social and rhetorical uses of comic lying as found in both Europe and America. Here the native roots of unreliable narrative are masterfully nurtured in the hoaxes and tall tales of Poe and T. B. Thorpe. Melville knew Irving, Poe, and Thorpe as well as he did Hawthorne, and he found in them ample inspiration for his own comic strategies of sincerity and deceit. Finally, Part I focuses on the eighteenth-century European ideal of cosmopolitanism, a form of liberalism which on the American frontier created a highly ambivalent cultural figure—the citizen of the world—who in most respects resembled a confidence man. Melville was sensitive to both the promise and the danger of cosmopolitanism. Well before today's multicultural debate, he also saw the paradox of our immigrant democracy located in his own cosmopolitan hero, Frank Goodman, who, as a genial misanthrope, synthesizes integrative and subversive humors and challenges readers to test the fabric of their nation.

Melville's most experimental years were his most exhausting. By the time he had finished *The Confidence-Man,* and just as Fitz-James O'Brien was extolling his potential, Melville was sailing for Europe and the Holy Land. According to Hawthorne, who as Consul to Liverpool met Melville on that voyage east, Melville was "about ready to be annihilated." Some hint of his exhaustion can be detected in an earlier remark to Hawthorne, made as he was turning his attention from *Moby-Dick* to the ill-fated *Pierre.* He was, he said, one person while composing his whale, and another with *Pierre.* For that matter, he is a different person at the close of his letter from the one at the beginning. "Lord," he writes, "when will we be done changing" (*Letters,* 143). For Melville, the changes in humor, form, and voice would not cease. But whether composing in the first-person or third-person voice, whether involved in the picturesque or more dramatic forms, whether as a genialist, confidence man, or cosmopolite, he kept before him the goal of writing "still rich utterances of a great intellect in repose."

I

AMERICA'S COMIC DEBATE

2

America's Repose

It is but nature to be shy of a mortal who boldly declares that a thief in jail is as honorable a personage as Gen. George Washington. This is ludicrous. But Truth is the silliest thing under the sun. Try to get a living by the Truth—and go to the Soup Societies. . . . It can hardly be doubted that all Reformers are bottomed upon the truth, more or less; and to the world at large are not reformers almost universally laughing stocks? Why so? Truth is ridiculous to men. Thus easily in my room here do I, conceited and garrulous, reverse the test of my Lord Shaftesbury.

Letters, 127

These words conclude Melville's opening to a letter to Hawthorne. The letter itself is an expansive ramble that begins with farming, ends with Goethe, and in between touches upon democracy, aristocracy, literary fortune ("Dollars damn me"), head, heart, and intellectual "unfolding." Melville's jaunty but obsessive tone—"I feel cheerfully disposed, and therefore I write a little bluely" (*Letters*, 128)—echoes Ishmael, and understandably so; *Moby-Dick* was near completion. Shandyean in its pronouncements and tentative reversals, the heft of the letter obliged Melville to invert the postal custom of that day and pay the freight himself. At issue in these lines is Melville's reversal of Shaftesbury's familiar comic test for truth. Melville's good-natured humor makes a political point even as it suggests the failure of the amiable mode to survive amid the hurly-burly of democratic politics. The amiable undoing of amiability strikes to the heart of America's comic debate.

In privileging humor over wit, Shaftesbury had envisioned a new era of truth in which falsity would be laughed "out of court." But he had not planned on America, where factionalists and frontiersmen only muddied "truth," and any position could be sanctioned with a laugh. It was a divisive age of satire sorely in need of the integrative calm of humor. Melville's "reversal" of Shaftesbury acknowledged the low state of geniality in the culture. In developing his own humor, he was attempting to give new vitality to an increasingly ineffectual but still valued mode. In this project he backed Hazlitt, who had bemoaned the atrophying of amiability in Britain, and the encouragement of "Young America," the New York literary group headed by Evert Duyckinck, for whom humor was a means of "building up good."

Britain's Amiable Tradition

Shaftesbury's "Sober Kind of Cheerfulness"

Anthony Ashley, "my Lord Shaftesbury" and the third of that name, was not the deepest thinker of his age, but his influence on aesthetics spread well into the nineteenth century. More social commentator than philosopher, he was the first among "benevolists," whose insistence upon man's good nature fostered the climate of amiability in eighteenth-century letters and gave birth to Roger de Coverley, Parson Adams, Tristram Shandy, and the Vicar of Wakefield. Shaftesbury's premises derived from his Christian creed: God exists; He is good; Nature embodies His benevolence; and the proof of this lies in man's innate good nature. Shaftesbury's comic test of truth is that an idea should withstand the onslaught of reasonable ridicule. Truth can laugh at itself and be the stronger for it. In his *Characteristics of Men* (1711) and in *Sensus Communis: An Essay on the Freedom of Wit and Humor,* Shaftesbury's amiable ironies reinvigorated Christian humanism. He was a breath of fresh air after Thomas Hobbes, who in the previous century had argued that since self-interest motivates humanity, and since our natural state is one of war, our laughter, caused by a "sudden glory" or recognition of one's superiority over "some deformed thing in another," is a sign of social victory.[1] Shaftesbury reorients Hobbesian self-interest, placing emphasis on our "sense of fellowship."[2] Self-interest is "group interest," an integrative not divisive herding instinct, and laughter stems not from a brutish instinct to prevail but from a desire to enhance the godly benevolence inherent in all men. Laughter is shared in good humor, not inflicted in "sudden glory."

Like Hobbes, Shaftesbury recognized the power of humor as a form of governance. But whereas Hobbes stressed social control through satiric putdown, Shaftesbury saw laughter as a reasonable way to discriminate truth from falsehood, and heavenly inspiration from mere "enthusiasm." The problem was that while religious and poetic "inspiration is a real feeling of the Divine Presence, and enthusiasm a false one[,] the passion they raise is much alike" (36, 37). Cool laughter is the best "antidote" for heated enthusiasm, and Shaftesbury proposed that to dispense this comic medicine, we must "give liberty to wit" (15). If allowed to prosper in a free marketplace of ideas, "politely managed raillery" (65) would weed out false enthusiasm, puncture pretense, expose knavery, and disclose error. In addition, this comedic *laissez-faire* promotes self-awareness by forcing us to adjust to the commonsense ways of God and reason inherent in ourselves; we become "sedate, cool, and impartial, free of every biassing passion, every giddy vapor, or melancholy fume" (39). Just as Socrates' good-natured self-effacement was so finely tuned that he could laugh heartily at Aristophanes' caricatures of himself (23–24), our genial self-laughter shall induce the "sedate, cool" confidence of self-knowledge and repose. It is, Shaftesbury remarked in language that prefigures Melville's deep thinking laughter, a "sober kind of cheerfulness" (12).

But giving liberty to wit can backfire. Speculating on the power of laughter, Shaftesbury quips that if the Jews had laughed at Jesus instead of taking him so seriously, Christianity would not have grown at the pace it did (22). But this counter-example implies (despite Shaftesbury's own beliefs) that raillery can *retard* or thwart divine benevolence itself. Knaves, too, can have reasonable wit, and given liberty they, too, will prosper. Shaftesbury's patrician assumption is that we all share in "Sensus Communis" an instinct for the good, and that in the long run false enthusiasm will be marginalized. He is not willing to admit Gresham's law into his free economy of laughter, wherein the circulation of false wit (like bad paper money) would drive out true wit (or gold). For this benevolent civil libertarian, the consequences of restraining wit and humor are more threatening than giving freedom to knaves. Government restraints force humorists to disguise their jabs in confusing ironies. The result is that under the threat of censorship honest raillery becomes mere "bantering." "The higher the slavery," Shaftesbury notes, "the more exquisite the buffoonery" (49). Under repression, a society laughs parabolically through obscure ironies, masked satires, nonsense, and indirection; the result is "redoubled" disguises, "mysteriousness," and moral confusion. Humor is no longer an honest projection of self but a vacant social gesture—mere burlesque—designed for the evasions of political survival.[3]

Social constraints prevent rather than perfect humor. Our only "antidote" against "the thoroughly profligate knave" or humbug is our freedom to laugh at him. With right reason and polite management, humor "will refine itself. . . . All politeness is owing to liberty. We polish one another, and rub off rough sides by a sort of *amicable collision*. To restrain this is inevitably to bring a rust upon men's sensibility. 'Tis a destroying of good breeding." (Shaftesbury, 46, my emphasis) Moreover, liberty enhances human perception: "An honest heart is only a more cunning one; and honesty and good-nature, a more deliberate or better regulated self-love" (78). Thus, the man of "good breeding" is neither fool nor enthusiast, and armed with his honest but cunning heart he is prepared to engage in "amicable collision" even with knaves. Shaftesbury's seemingly shallow optimism is not so jejune as to ignore the deceptive nature of enthusiasm, the risks of obscure irony, and threat of knavery. He knew that "good breeding" is not inborn but acquired through "amicable" social conflict. "The only rest or repose" we may have from the "perpetual discord of life [and] alternate disquiet and self-dislike," he concludes, is through "one determined, considerate resolution" to bring "temper" into harmony with "mind" and "judgment" (86).

Eighteenth-century Anglicanism lent support to Shaftesbury's view. Though R. S. Crane shows that Shaftesbury occupies only one branch in the "genealogy" of benevolism,[4] his good-natured prose reinforced a profound shift in the comic sensibility of the age. But in the age of Jackson, not King George, in which "enthusiasm" had taken on political and evangelical dimensions unanticipated by Shaftesbury, and in an age of Byron, not Addison, in which an inspired imagination might dress to Gothic excess, Herman Melville could flippantly reverse Shaftesbury's test, deny the immutability of right reason, disavow the efficacy of good humor, and not cause much alarm. Melville's quip, more than Shaftesbury's own concerning Jesus and the Jews who failed to laugh, clearly assumes the powerlessness of good humor in a free marketplace increasingly populated by democratic knaves. That much is certain, let alone the fact that Melville had Promethean doubts about Shaftesbury's most basic assumption: God is good. But the nature of any flippant remark is that it flips two ways, and if Melville seems to reject Shaftesbury because the mass of men ridicule truth, he does not necessarily deny the power of mirth to enliven the individual or even, if "politely managed," enlighten the public. But to gain a fuller sense of what Melville's flip reversal meant, we need to touch briefly upon the development of amiable humor especially up to the time of Hazlitt.

From Shandy to Hazlitt: The Pastoral and the Picturesque

By the turn of the nineteenth century, the world was growing speculative in business, economy, and politics, as well as philosophy. Nations were galloping, and soon steaming, into industrialization. Country gentlemen had to confront the reality of mercantile life. And if the world's getting and spending were too much with us late and soon, the amiable humorist's solution was not to engage in corrective raillery but to retreat into pastoral whimsy. Paradoxically, amiability had become a liberal-minded gentleman's impulse toward conservative non-action. Shaftesbury's benevolent philosophy fed the fires of progress (urged it and even required it through free wit), but its attempts to polish the political animal through the amicable collision of free and witty intercourse proved inadequate as the modern world launched its new "-isms": nationalism, imperialism, cosmopolitanism, Methodism, Millennialism, and the materialism of upward mobility. The amiable humorist's response to the slaps of modernism was to turn the other cheek toward an imagined past and gaze more steadily inward, to indulge in bachelorism, Quixotic whims, and nostalgic reminiscence. Disenchanted with satire as a means of prescribing values and yet constrained by benevolism from lashing out at the perceived evils of a too swiftly progressive age, they made "old values" seem delectable and yet tantalizingly out of reach. Thus, humor lapsed into a version of the pastoral.

As William Empson and Leo Marx have argued, the pastoral mode is an attempt to reconcile the power of a swiftly advancing civilization with the values of the individual through an artful retreat to a middle landscape (both literal and figurative) situated between city and wilderness.[5] When society cannot have Eden, it will invent Arden. The pastoral landscaping found in gardens, paintings, and writings in both Europe and America manifests this mentality, blending civilized art and raw nature. But this reconciliation was, as Leo Marx argues, more myth than reality, the fantasy fulfillment of social desires. It was an escape from revolution. Similarly, amiable humor is a pastoral retreat from corrosive modernisms: It promotes outmoded knighthood, wistful bachelorhood, and besieged husbandry. This comic pastoralism is the humorist's link to an edenic past in which present-day social commentary is meekly implied in the nostalgic sighs over the past. Deeper psychological repressions, the loss of political power, and the fear of sexual impotence are sublimated in whimsy.

The traditional exemplars of this comic pastoral (Quixote, Falstaff, De Coverley) puzzle over the passage of friendship, love, and time. They are rusty nobles pursuing lost causes, men of high sentiment and true feeling despite their eccentricities, petty obsessions, and "madness." In America where rustics outnumber rusty nobles, versions of the comic pastoral were found in the reduced but recognizable circumstances of such Down East monologists as Seba Smith (Jack Downing), B. P. Shillaber (Mrs. Partington), and Frances Whitcher (Widow Bedott). But the most popular avatars in both England and America were the odd eccentrics of Laurence Sterne's *Tristram Shandy:* the punctilious theoretician Walter Shandy, his dreamy obsessive brother Toby, and their diffident chronicler Tristram, who never gets his narrative engaged in a forward gear.

At the heart of Sterne's digressive novel is Uncle Toby's instability, a clear sign of what war and society can do to strip the individual of his power and dignity. And yet our laughter does not permit a too-tragic reading of Toby's loss because Toby's own obsessive nostalgia neutralizes the sting of his "wound." While Toby's endearing whims direct us to his sexual anxieties, they quickly divert our attention from the war that created the inner wreckage to what allows him psychic survival: his model battlefield and irregular courtship of the Widow Wadman. Here, social and psychological anxieties emerge, but only in sentimental eccentricity. Toby's playground is the symbolic cause of the wound that makes his lovemaking impossible—his "hobby-horse" is the phallic replacement of what got wounded—and yet that mock battlefield is the ironic setting of his half-acknowledged desire for the Widow. Toby's nostalgia is the unconscious working out of psychic wounds even as it eludes the power of warring nations. Despite the pastoral regressions, Sterne's brilliance lies in his compression of satiric attacks upon love and war within the safer form of whim.

The problem of such compression, however, is that the amiable humorist risks denying the existence of social and psychological pain. When geniality degenerates into genteel diffidence, Shaftesbury's good-humored gentleman becomes society's fool, and the delicacies of a Sterne become the rank sentimentality of Henry Mackenzie's *Man of Feeling* (1771) and *Man of the World* (1773). To be sure, the parade of naïve benevolists, black-suited misanthropes, tedious paragons of virtue, and hypocritical men of feeling that marches through late-eighteenth-century fiction indicates the culture's continued search for an aesthetic balance of good humor and critical power.[6] Certain amiable figures—Fielding's Squire Allworthy and Parson Adams or Goldsmith's Dr. Primrose—succeed, at times ironically, in balancing social commitment and psychological insight, but despite their compassionate rectitude, these pastoral recluses are too often victims of their sentiment. Surely Charles Lamb reclaimed some of the power inherent in amiable humor. His Wordsworthian blending of thought and feeling, his probing into anxiety and the deeper reaches of sentiment, brought the pastoral mode closer to urban realities, but finally British readers were drawn more to the debased Byronic posings of such dandies as the young Bulwer (whom Carlyle loved to hate).[7]

If in its pastoral phase amiable humor could not fully respond, as one critic puts it, to "the fate of goodness in society,"[8] William Hazlitt argued for a picturesque revitalization. At heart a painter, Hazlitt preferred the immediacy of paint to writing's self-involvement with words. And though he placed the "ideal" in art above the "picturesque," he invariably used the picturesque terminology of contrast and roughness throughout his twenty volumes of criticism. Don Quixote and Sancho Panza are a "picturesque and striking" contrast to the overly polished dandies of modern times. In calling Addison and other good-natured essayists of the previous century "moral historians," he noted their reluctance "to prove all black or all white" and praised their painterly instinct for "[laying] on the intermediate colours."[9] Similarly, in Lamb "there is a fine tone of *chiaroscuro,* a moral perspective in his writings," one that provides "vivid obscurity . . . arch piquancy . . . such picturesque quaintness, such smiling pathos."[10] What made Hogarth a comic genius was his picturesque balance in seeming to be always on the verge of caricature but never falling into it. For Hazlitt, good-natured humor and the picturesque share the same ethical view of man, an insight implicit in his most famous pronouncement: "Man is the only animal that laughs and weeps; for he is the only animal that is struck with the difference between what things are, and what they ought to be" (*CW,* 5). Humor is not a pastoral *place* for retreat but rather a variable *perspective* that situates us between reality and ideality. Its function is not escape but "to account for the condition of human life."

Hazlitt's fondness for earlier genialists derives from the Carlylean conviction that humor approaches poetic creation. The characters in *Don Quixote,* shaped by their "impulses of caprice and accident," are "so true to nature . . . that we not only recognize the fidelity of the representation, but recognize it with all the advantages of novelty superadded. They are in the best sense *originals,* namely, in the sense in which nature has her originals" (*CW,* 110). Moreover—and Shaftesbury would have been pleased to hear it—humor's creation of the "new" stimulates faith in readers. In placing "the ludicrous" above "the ridiculous," Hazlitt continued the tradition of favoring humor over satire. The ludicrous contrasts "what things are" with what is desirable; the ridiculous is merely that which is contrary to sense and reason. Although ridicule strikes home, it is also shrill, hence rhetorically useless— "the same contempt and disapprobation which sharpens and subtilizes our sense of the impropriety, adds a severity to [the ridiculous] inconsistent with perfect ease and enjoyment" (*CW,* 7–8). In short, satiric ridicule lacks Shaftesbury's "politely managed" repose. Humor is superior because, resembling the ways of Nature, it engages readers more effectively.

But Hazlitt's chief contribution to the comic debate is his articulation of humor's limits. The flaw in Shakespeare is that he is too good-natured, too "magnanimous" (*CW,* 35). Hazlitt preferred that humor be a bit bad. Hence, the Restoration was comedy's golden age, for "the town" was full of fools and "fashionable life" (*CW,* 37) providing perfect fodder for wits. But modern manners have progressed too well; the magnanimity of Shakespeare has, in appearance at any rate, outlasted the roughness of the restoration. Everyone reads the same books, writes the same way, has "the same artificial education and the same common stock of ideas, so that we see all objects from the same point of view. . . . we learn to exist, not in ourselves, but in books;—all men become alike mere readers—spectators, not actors in the scene, and lose their proper personal identity" (*CW,* 152). Without "picturesque and striking" originals to depict, humor naturally dissipates for want of subject matter. True "comic excellence" (found in Addison and Sterne) lies in the picturesque "roughness of texture and the sharp angles *not* being worn out by the artificial refinements of intellect, or the frequent *collision* of social intercourse" (*CW,* 152, my emphasis). In echoing Shaftesbury's "amicable collision," Hazlitt registers a final critique: The seeds of comic dissipation are inherent in progressive benevolism, for if good humor promotes the social polishing of varied individuals, then inevitably the need for "raillery" diminishes and, ideally, disappears. As society homogenizes into a great middle class, humor loses its capacity for the picturesque. Carried to its extreme, Shaftesbury's "politely managed" system of comic polishing leads, paradoxically, to the humorless complacency Hazlitt abhors.

Needless to say, Shaftesbury did not project the effects of humor into a utopian vision, nor did Hazlitt believe that English society had, in fact, achieved homogeneity except in the middle class's mulish indifference to the nation's lack of moral progress.[11] Hazlitt's worry is that Shaftesburyan gentility induces a mediocrity that denies the more picturesque reality of humanity. Humor should articulate human roughness, not eradicate it. British society had allowed itself to believe it had achieved a universal sameness among its cultural membership. But few in the literate culture were testing the validity of this insipid fraternalism against the reality of social diversity: the underclasses, the not-me, the alien, and the other.

In short, Hazlitt's amiable contemporaries were frauds, a point he makes in an engaging *Round Table* rant "On Good-Nature." In exposing the good-natured man's self-serving conservativism, Hazlitt reclaims the liberal principles of geniality. His amiable man brings to mind the employer in "Bartleby the Scrivener" for whom "the easiest way of life is the best" (*Piazza Tales,* 14): He "does not . . . make himself uncomfortable about things he cannot mend . . . [and] resents more violently any interruption of his ease and comforts."[12] And yet there is a more genuine form of amiability—"if the truth were known, the most disagreeable people are the most amiable." They are true lovers of man scratching away the placidity of a society committed in manners only to benevolence. Truly amiable men feel an interest in what does not concern them; they regard others, not just themselves. They are fatally attached to "liberty, truth, justice, humanity, and honour. . . . They have a fellow-feeling with all that has been done, said, or thought in the world." The new good-natured man is a radical in the original sense—one who seeks the root of human potential. Hazlitt's apparent rejection of geniality is really a regenerative "amicable collision" with it.

Melville's playful reversal of Shaftesbury is also only an apparent rejection of amiability; more aptly, it is a tentative test of Shaftesbury's test to examine its usefulness in a democratic world. America's picturesque people were not so polished that they could be spared a bit of laughter. The amiable Mrs. Trollope and Mr. Dickens, blasting away at American manners, could attest to that. The only real problem for Melville was *how* to laugh at America: a society richly deserving of satire but one whose diversity required the tolerance of humor.

Melville's reversal of Shaftesbury's test must be taken in the larger context of his preceding discussion of democracy and aristocracy, initiated in Hawthorne's previous letter (now lost). Apparently, Hawthorne had registered serious reservations about Melville's enthusiasm for democracy, and in his own defense Melville acknowledges how one (such as Hawthorne) might be "shy" of taking egalitarianism to the extreme, of ranking thief and president equally. It would be "ludicrous" to go so far. The word "ludicrous" is a touchstone for the anti-Shaftesburyan conclusion: "Truth is the silliest thing under the sun," and among the masses, who laugh truth out of the pulpit and into "Soup Societies." In America, Shaftesbury's free marketplace of wit is a false economy, for democratic "consumers" will "buy" laughter indiscriminately before they buy the truth; they will settle for appearances despite any derision of them, for, all things being equal, one person's laughter at you is no more valid than your laughter at him. A democrat's laughter hounds and obfuscates truth rather than tests the truth. It will protect the parvenu from shame; it legitimizes the mercantile over the ideal; it sanctions complacency, blindness, and greed. It is the laughter of the mob that Robin joins in when he sees his kinsman ridden on a rail in Hawthorne's "My Kinsman, Major Molineux." It is an inverted Hobbesian process, for democratic laughter claims superiority of the inferior man over tradition. "Thus, I reverse Shaftesbury's test," Melville proclaims as if to argue that geniality will never realize its original intended effect of good governance.

But just as Melville flips this coin once, he flips it again. Even though he despises "mankind in the mass," he will not abandon "the unconditional democracy of all things." A sense of individual benevolence still lingers. Thus, the comic debate between democracy and aristocracy is an "endless sermon."

Melville's reluctance to abandon amiability was as much personal and aesthetic as it was political. Immersed in *Moby-Dick,* he had found in the good-natured repose of his most abiding humorist Ishmael an antidote to his poetic enthusiasms. If Melville was to stay out of the Soup Societies, he would have to use humor to tame his fictions. *Mardi* had marked Melville as a Platonic enthusiast, and reviewers frequently cautioned against linguistic excess. Indeed, Melville's enthused letter to Hawthorne attests to his characteristic excitability: He "stands for the heart"; he exalts the "aristocracy of feeling" up to the level of the aristocracy of the brain; he speaks "boldly" and is "conceited and garrulous" in reversing Shaftesbury. In short, Melville is full of every "giddy vapour, or melancholy fume" that Shaftesbury had hoped good humor would neutralize. Melville's reversal is an enthusiast's petulant rejection of the very aesthetic that would wisely restrain him; it is a thumbing of his nose at critics who had deplored his egalitarian and metaphysical excesses. But though his "vapours and fumes" belie the "sedate, cool" Socratic impartiality that Shaftesbury admired, Melville later in his letter articulates a desire for "the calm, the coolness, the silent grass-growing mood" of literary composition. Melville's doubt that he could fully sustain this mood does not negate his recognition of an aesthetic repose that amiable humor could provide. Dollars may damn him; the marketplace may pervert the truth; democracy may reverse Shaftesbury, and Melville may join in the reversal, but geniality—calm and cool—insinuates its way into human affairs. The heart prevails.

Inevitably, Melville goes beyond amiability without rejecting it. He oversteps Shaftesbury's principal metaphor of humor and understanding: the eye. "We can never do more injury to truth," Shaftesbury noted, "than by discovering too much of it on some occasions." The understanding, like our eyes, can stand only so much light. "Whatever is beyond, brings darkness and confusion." "Real humanity" exists in "hid[ing] strong truths from tender eyes . . . by a pleasant amusement" (Shaftesbury, 45). For Shaftesbury, humor is a metaphysical preservative, shaded glasses protecting us from our fatal vision. But, as we have seen in "*Mosses,*" Melville reached beyond this metaphor of the eye (that sacred organ of rationalists and transcendentalists) to the heart as the true organ of our understanding. "Love and humor," he argues, are not merely "tender eyes"; they are the ventricles and auricles wherein geniality and deep thought are circulated and fused. The heart alone, not the eye, is capable of measured insight. Like Hazlitt, Melville required a richer heart than Shaftesbury had surmised, one that could go beyond the superficialities of the shallow "man of sensibility" and could supply a humor that was both "honest" *and* "cunning."

Amiability on Native Ground

Melville was not alone in his desire to amplify the fading tradition of amiability. Although Emerson had no truck with "whim," Melville's associates in the Young America movement were certain that humor rather than satire was the only cure for the Republic. But even they were not in perfect agreement.

Emerson and Comic Defect

Constitutionally, Ralph Waldo Emerson was not disposed to laughter. One fall evening in 1834, after dining with a New Bedford acquaintance, the transcendentalist observed his host tickling his wife and sisters. Emerson had no recourse but to "grow grave." Later, during his midlife visit to London, he admited that "the one thing odious to me now is joking."[13] Although philosophically he was the optimist of his age, his Transcendentalism was rarely expressed in comic forms other than "dry Yankeeisms."[14] "God grant me," he wrote in his Journal on 13 May 1848, "the noble companions whom I have left at home who value merriment less, and virtues and powers more." His dismissal of the arrogant nationalism of British humor in *English Traits* reflects back negatively on America's own growing cadre of regional braggarts. But in castigating the ethnocentrism and egotism of humor, Emerson denied humor any saving grace.

Emerson was not completely joyless; he simply did not see amiable humor as an effective mode of thought for "man thinking." In urging us to draw inspiration from the "nonchalance of boys" in our journey toward "Self Reliance," the philosopher comes close to legitimizing humor: "I would write on the lintels of the door-post, *Whim*." And that seems as strong an endorsement of amiability as one might hope to find. However, he adds, "I hope it is somewhat better than whim at last, but we cannot spend the day in explanation."[15] Had Emerson taken a day off to explain, he might have shown that while "whim" may free us from the "jail" of self-consciousness, it cannot expand our consciousness beyond self into full Being. That is the function of the poet, who places virtue and creation above "merriment." Whim, then, is no passport to transcendence. Unlike his friend Carlyle, Emerson would not equate humor with either poetic imagination or liberation, and not surprisingly his contribution to America's comic debate, an essay on "The Comic," suggests that he would rather write on his lintels "*Satire*."

Unlike Hazlitt, for whom laughter and tears affirm our humanity, Emerson finds that these responses only accentuate the chasm between man and Reason. "Our species," he begins, "is the only joker in nature."[16] We laugh when we recognize how far removed from the ideal we are. "Reason does not joke, and men of reason do not," but when reasoning men discover a "balking of the intellect" or "the break of continuity of the intellect," they see in an instant their "halfness" and laugh ("Comic," 206, 205). There is "no halfness in nature," only in society. Transcendental man expands that fraction to a whole. Along the way, we laugh when, "in comparing fractions with essential integers or wholes" ("Comic," 204), we gain a sudden Hobbesian "glory" in our intellectual growth. As with Carlyle's notion of irony as only a "fraction" of true humor, a joke is a "well-intended halfness" thrust before us to exercise our insight and promote a fuller sense of being. For Hazlitt laughter is the first step toward a fulfillment of that being, but for Emerson it is a mark of Cain, signifying where we have been and how much further we have to go. The truly transcendental sensibility does not need to laugh.

Emerson views the comic with a satirist's, not a humorist's, eye. For him, laughter is a corrective of human deficiencies,[17] best turned inwardly upon our salvageable selves rather than upon society as a whole. "A rogue alive to the ludicrous," he notes, "is still convertible" ("Comic," 208), because the recognition of risible disparities attests to the rogue's awareness of the ideal Beauty beyond him, and in such awareness there is the potential for change. Whereas the humorist would appreciate the rogue's accommodation of himself to the absurdity of the universe, Emerson argues that being "alive to the ludicrous" only hints at the recognized need for a reconstruction. The humorist encourages continued laughter; Emerson envisions a day when it would be unnecessary.

If Emerson seems a transcendental Hobbes, the startling equation lies in our potential spiritual superiority over our remediable actuality. I laugh because I know I can be better. Thus the most familiar passage from "The Comic" may hint at social reform but actually promotes personal regeneration:

> There is no joke so true and deep in actual life as when some pure idealist goes up and down among the institutions of society, attended by a man who knows the world, and who, sympathizing with the philosopher's scrutiny, sympathizes also with the confusion and indignation of the detected, skulking institutions. His perception of disparity, his eye wandering perpetually from the rule to the crooked, lying, thieving fact, makes the eyes run over with laughter. ["Comic," 206]

But while the function of laughter is in "exposing all actual defect," the satiric exposure also broadens human sympathies. Notice that the man of the world gains sympathy for the problems of psychological growth (confusion and indignation) as well as for idealism. Paradoxically, Emerson's satiric agenda acquires a modest hint of good-natured humor.

Nevertheless, Emerson had no taste for those who "celebrate their perception of halfness and a latent lie" ("Comic," 208). There is more to gain from "the sympathetic contemplation of things by the understanding from the philosopher's point of view" ("Comic," 206) than from John Bull's cakes and ale, or for that matter any of the numerous comic figures growing in America's culture. The frontiersman, Yankee, black minstrel, and confidence man are fractions of a national mind, proud but false regionalists heedless of other counties, other worlds. The laughter of such rogues signifies nothing but their subconscious longing to be rid of roguishness. Our native humorists embody the failure of a culture to achieve an ideal oneness. The Boston critic E. P. Whipple put it succinctly: "Life, in harmony with reason, is the only life safe from laughter."[18] Emerson, too, would have us "safe from laughter." Transcendence obviates it. "Man thinking" does not need to laugh.

No stronger opposition to this New England chill existed than in the Knickerbocker humorists of New York. In the pages of *The Knickerbocker* magazine, one essayist argues that while laughter may be abused by the sycophant, cynic, or dandy, there is always in compensation "the good, honest laugher . . . who has a heart to feel and sympathize" and who is "content to drink the cup of life mingled as it is, to enjoy calmly the sweeter portion, and laugh at the bitter." But Knickerbocker amiability reduces humor to a bittersweet mechanism with no philosophy to match Emerson. We are advised to laugh broadly and to drink a little to help that laughter flow. But though one may learn to "gather wisdom even from laughter," laughter, finally, is "incompatible" with wisdom.[19] Humor, then, is a palliative for existence, not a "deep thought," for "Darkness and sorrow are merely transient, and ever 'is the earth's still moon-like confidence in joy at her full.' "[20]

Melville, who began work on *The Confidence-Man* six months after that glib pronouncement, found neither Emersonian nor Knickerbocker approaches acceptable. On the one hand, Mark Winsome and Egbert epitomize the coolness of transcendentalism; on the other, the merchant Roberts learns the perilous effects of "moon-like confidence." But in shaping his own sense of amiability, Melville shared the views of such Young Americans as Evert Duyckinck and William A. Jones, as well as the Southerner William Gilmore Simms, who found social utility in humor and elevated it to a "familiar philosophy."

Young America Laughing

Yankee Doodle came to town in 1847, not on a pony but as a satirical magazine put out by the flamboyant Cornelius Mathews, a cofounder of "Young America," loquacious champion of National Literature, and (oddly enough) Evert Duyckinck's prime candidate for America's "Great Author." The only thing that kept Mathews from achieving such greatness was his stunning lack of talent, laboriously borne out in several undistinguished romances and tales. He is best remembered as an editor. *Yankee Doodle* folded in the year of its birth. Aside from its attacks on the Mexican War, it is memorable largely because Melville published in it his "Anecdotes of Old Zack." These burlesques of General Zachary Taylor were not enough to keep *Yankee Doodle* in circulation or Taylor out of the presidency. In all, the satiric weekly is of little importance in the development of Melville's humor; however, it has bearing on America's comic debate, because its demise inspired Duyckinck to reflect on the relative merits of humor and satire in American culture. Unlike Emerson, Duyckinck viewed laughter not as a reaction to human defect, but as a fostering of democratic potentials; it is equal in imaginative and social power to poetry.

In comparing *Yankee Doodle* to *Punch,* Duyckinck wrote in his diary on 9 October 1847 that the British journal has institutions and classes to satirize, [but] here there are only individuals and individuals resent what classes must endure. There are subjects enough here for Satire but they are not permanent—before you can catch them they have changed. At best the work of the satirist is not the highest. A spice of it does more good than a cartload. The surest way to put down Evil is to build up good.[21]

Seventeen months later, Melville made a similar observation employing Duyckinck's vocabulary. In his 3 March 1849 letter to Duyckinck, he disparages Emerson's arrogant presumption to know the world, concluding that such Platonists

are all cracked right across the brow. And never will the pullers-down be able to cope with the builders-up. And this pulling down is easy enough—a keg of powder blew up B[r]ock's Monument—but the man who applied the match, could not, alone, build such a pile to save his soul from the sharkmaw of the Devil. [*Letters*, 79]

Clearly, Melville and Duyckinck had discussed the problem of "building up good" throughout their early association, and the "pullers-down / builders-up" dichotomy was, therefore, a familiar code for their shared social progressivism. Let's also recall that Melville's letter, which begins "I do not oscillate in Emerson's rainbow," is a clarification of his praise for Emerson in an earlier letter (now lost) that had apparently bothered Duyckinck. In short, Melville is reasserting his nontranscendental, pro–Young America credentials, and his use of the "pullers-down / builders-up" idiom is designed strengthen his tie to Duyckinck.

Whatever rhetorical ploy Melville was using, his critique of Emerson as a puller-down affirms the liberal principle of "building up good." Pulling down individuals or institutions through satire is too easy; but more, in an American context, it is simply not practical, for individuals (not bound to class) have no allegiance to established creeds, not even to cherished social defects. They change rapidly in response to the volatile economy, not to elude a satirist's barbs. To be effective, a satirist must have a sense of social stability, a norm against which to find readers wanting. But, Duyckinck complains, there are no social norms in America. Similarly, there are no spiritual or transcendent norms, and to complain as Emerson does of the defect in our social and spiritual lives is to beat a horse that has already fled the barn. Duyckinck and Melville propose to go beyond Emerson's satiric notion of the comic. The best way to build up good is through the laughter of humor.

Duyckinck had argued as much seven years earlier in a review of Mathews. Here, he draws the familiar distinction between humor and wit traceable from Hobbes and Shaftesbury to Coleridge, Carlyle, and Hazlitt. "Humor is a genial, kindly-affected, natural quality, 'that plays around the heart.' Its essence is good nature. Wit, on the contrary, is prone to sneer, and be sarcastic. Wit separates—humor combines. Humor is social . . . wit stands alone."[22] But the hurly-burly of democracy imposes complications. Whereas the lofty wit sends down largely ineffectual satiric bolts upon a largely implacable crowd, the humorist will mingle, to "kindle hope" and "invite encouragement." He or she is ameliorative, not divisive. Like Don Quixote, he can find "traits of divinity" and "see not discord but variations" (ED, 431). Like Hawthorne, she possesses, then, a picturesque sensibility, a *chiaroscuro* vision of humanity, which "rejoices in the summer field, full of warmth and tender shades'' (ED, 433). But Don Quixote was ''mad,'' and Hawthorne resisted the crowd; hence, the democratic humorist, no matter how benevolent and sincere, is necessarily ''at variance with the rest of the world [which] is to him insincere.'' He is eccentric, not out of whim but because he ''stands as nature made him, original, self-preserved, acting out his own peculiarity, and talking of the world as it is pictured in his peculiar optics'' (ED, 432). The Humorist's ''peculiar'' eye is not Emerson's transparent organ but rather an optic focused on the margins of quotidian life gaining in its detachment a glimpse at the invisible social truths beneath the surface of the mob.[23] The humorist is not higher but deeper than the crowd and closer to man's original state. He therefore stands aloof (not aloft), and yet his benevolence and insight are attractive perhaps precisely because of the odd, genial blending of the two. The humorist, then, is a ''familiar domestic poet'' whose ''unexpected contrasts . . . suggest laughter to the illiterate [and] contain already elements of the serious to the reflective.''[24]

As poet, Duyckinck's humorist performs feats of the imagination tantamount to the explorations of mind projected by Shelley's visionary poet or Emerson's ''liberating god.'' But in a social frame, his humor is a process of self-discovery that illuminates our national character. In it,

> much that now lies hid would be discovered, to do honor to the national character— much to rescue elements essentially good, from the chaos of frivolity and uproar in which they are now lost—many genial qualities brought to light, now not often recognized but inseparable from the heart of man; something thereby to gain the love of other people abroad, to endear us to one another as warm-hearted, kindly-affectioned brethren at home. [ED, 430–31]

Duyckinck does not propose—aside from one of Mathews's forgettable and forgotten characters, Mr. Crumb, a ''sound old man of right feeling'' (ED, 435)— any figure who might capture the affections of readers; rather, he is content (perhaps in deference to Mathews's unoriginal crumbs of humor) to dwell more abstractly on the imaginative and social function of the humorist in a democracy: his ability to inform, not hector, to reveal native strengths and sympathies, to promote self-awareness and national consciousness, to give voice to a National Literature, and to show ''how another human being plays his part in life'' (ED, 431). For Duyckinck, the Republic was a comedy still in rehearsal, and the actors had not yet fully mastered their roles.

Four years after Duyckinck's essay, William Gilmore Simms, the editor, novelist, and southern ally of Duyckinck, wrote his own review of Mathews, focusing as well upon the nature and present state of humor in America. Perry Miller's account of the controversy that ensued stresses the split in the ranks that inevitably led to the dissolution of Young America. As Miller saw it, Simms simply could not contain, in deference to Duyckinck, his distaste for Mathews any longer.[25] We have already sampled some of what spewed forth when Simms let the floodgates open, for it was on this occasion that he claimed that the too-satiric Mathews would rather have us ''lynch'' than ''laugh.'' But there was more to anger Duyckinck: chiefly, Simms's repeated claim that Americans are too ''earnest and irascible'' to be humorous.[26] This provoked Duyckinck's sidekick, William A. Jones, to call down one year later the "shades" of Franklin, Irving, Paulding, Hawthorne, "Harry Franco" (Charles F. Briggs), and "Felix Merry" (Duyckinck) to defend American humor. And when Jones asserted that the French have "keen satire, but no flowing humor,"[27] he in turn drew fire from Poe, who in his *Broadway Journal* missed Jones's point by invoking the "shades" of French satirists Rabelais and Voltaire as examples of humor. Given Poe's own feeble attempts at humor, this failure to grasp Jones's distinction is not surprising. In all, Poe found Jones's attack on fellow Southerner Simms to be the "contemptible . . . composition of an imitator and a quack," whose chief fault was in presuming to write on humor without having read Augustus B. Longstreet (another Southern lion whom Poe, and even much of England for that matter, had praised).[28]

These are the forays that made up the Grand American Humor Skirmish of 1844–45. What is unfortunate is that *if* and when literary historians allude to this mighty war,[29] they emphasize the infighting and personal attacks. Lost are Simms's and Jones's truly insightful utterances on the social and aesthetic functions of humor. In fact, Simms's essay argues for humor's capacity to rise above personality and political faction and to effect a picturesque coalescence of the many into one. It offers, as did Hazlitt and Melville, a radical redefinition of amiability, one that in looking South and West for comic sources proposed a declaration of independence from Europe far more authentic than any Young American up north had been willing to make.

In complaining about Mathews's satiric tendencies, Simms gets to the aesthetic heart of the matter. Satire in its most authentic phase is rooted in personal attack. It is inherently divisive, but more, it suggests a failure of mind and self. As Simms puts it, the satirist lacks the humorist's "mental flexibility" and "pliancy of mood"; and, given this personally entrenched vision of rectitude, the satirist continually insists upon an impossible ideal self, an egocentric version of himself. The satirist has no "jest" but is all "earnest"; he is "one-sided" and incapable of a "many-sided" vision. He is an Ahab. The humorist—and here Simms favors the "democratic" Dickens over the "despotic" Mathews—is able "to go out of himself, to forget himself, to forget his favorite thoughts and fancies, and to throw all the strength of his intellect into the *dramatis personae* under his hands" (Simms, 327). Shakespeare, Homer, and Scott could do this, but not Milton, Byron, or Bulwer. What humor allows is an aesthetic act of self-abnegation that promotes, on the one hand, a psychological repose and, on the other, a cosmopolitan vision of cultural unity. It is a way of building up the nation.

Mathews, however, is a "judge" not a "friend" (Simms, 327). His failing lies precisely in his satiric self-absorption. He writes "as one brought up in a particular school or party. He has imbibed the bias of a sect—and that not a successful one,—and their prejudices constitute the staple of his satire. Satire it is—not description. His materials are due to partisan politics, rather than to his walks among the people" (Simms, 331). In a way—and this shall become more relevant when we discuss Jones—Matthews's brand of "Egotism," jury-rigged upon the bias and prejudice of party politics, disqualifies the writer as democrat and humorist. If one is to impose a "self," it must be a self derived from "the people."

Simms's opposition of Satire and "description" is curious, for we expect "Hu-

mor'' not ''description'' as the second term, but given Hazlitt's equation of humor
and the picturesque, the distinction is finally not surprising. ''Description'' suggests
a certain objectivity that comes with the humorist's open heart. The satirist draws
caricature; the humorist describes character. On the one hand, we find portraits of
defect in both party and self; on the other, we find something large, varied, inclusive,
indeed picturesque. For Simms, the connection between humor and moral picturesque is realized in America's uncertain, picturesque West:

> There grows a hardy and generous nature, untaught, unsophisticated, warm, ardent
> and impetuous, which is yet destined to unfold great destinies in art and literature.
> . . . It is an original and vigourous nature, *rough but rich,* illiterate but fresh, —
> full of virgin flow and enthusiasm. . . . And in the buoyant force and animation of
> its speech, —in its copious fund of expression, —in the audacity of its illustration,
> —its very hyperbole, —the singular force of its analogies, —the pregnant, though
> ludicrous vitality of its pictures, —its queer allusions, *sudden repartee,* and lively
> adaptation of the *foreign and unexpected, to the familiar,* —we recognize the
> presence of genius as likely to embody the humorous as eloquent, —the mirthful
> and the picturesque as the sublime and the imposing.   [Simms, 337–38]

The West replaces Carlyle's volcano. It is ''rough but rich,'' an explosion of vitality
and creation yet one that is ripe and contained; it is ''pregnant.'' As with the
picturesque, we find in it the ''sudden'' and ''unexpected'' and yet the ''familiar.''
It is an ''inverse sublimity'' both ''mirthful'' and ''imposing.''

Literary historians confirm Simms's prophetic view of the West, for America's
humor did indeed find its uniqueness in the tall talk and tall tales of the frontier,
but what is more important here is the picturesque idiom that conveys his prophecy
and bespeaks Melville's tense repose of humor. Like Melville, Simms stresses the
crucial marginality of the picturesque point of view. ''The ludicrous,'' he writes,
''is an Al Sirat—as narrow as that boundary which is supposed to separate the
genius from the madman; and to make his way along this attenuated passage, is at
once the greatest danger and the greatest triumph of the writer, whether his aim be
the humorous or the sublime'' (Simms, 331). In holding to his Al Sirat, the fine,
sharp line between heaven and hell upon which unbelievers trip and believers stand
firm, the humorist like the sublime poet can control, by force of his marginal
sensibility, the excesses of imagination and irrationality.

But despite America's Western potential, our culture remains humorless, for
like Mathews we are an earnest, blowhard nation. Our arrogance, a form of
national egotism that precludes true inclusive humor, is a symptom of our parvenu
culture. We lack confidence; therefore, we boast in compensation. Paradoxically,
American arrogance signifies salvation as well as defect, for our boasting concerns
what might be as well as what is. It is an emblem of our expectation of ''social
progress.'' ''The secret,'' Simms writes, ''of all our amiability [is] a desire for
improvement and for fame'' (Simms, 340). In time, America will match its
earnest desires with confident jests and become a nation of amiable humorists.
Simms was one critic bent on revitalizing geniality. William A. Jones was another.

Although Jones found Simms's denigration of Mathews to be ''singular and
mistaken'' (AH, 212), he tacitly accepted in his essay on ''American Humor''
Simms's larger aesthetic and social views. Reemphasizing Duyckinck's earlier

position that humor is poetic and capable of "serious or even deep gloom" (AH, 213), Jones locates the problem of America's humor in its lack of national scope and cohesion. Like the country itself, our humor—with its scheming Yankees, wild Kentuckians, and genial Virginians—is utterly regional. But the hope for a cosmopolitan coalescence lies not in Simms's West (just another region, no matter how expansive and picturesque) but in the theater where the full panoply of American types (French, German, Dutch; Yankee and black) can be contained upon a single stage. Whereas Simms looked westward for a self-indulgent, redemptive voice, Jones took the retrospective route, finding inspiration in a European forebear: Shaftesbury.

For Jones, Shaftesbury confirms two paired formulations: Tyranny induces satire; freedom, humor. When people are enslaved and forced into compliance or silence, they respond with ironies, burlesques, and other forms of veiled comic attack. The test case for Jones is Italy, where, under the thumb of various sequential despots, the buffoonery of Commedia dell'Arte still thrives at the expense of good-natured humor: "Buffoonery only can exist in an enslaved country. Shaftesbury proves conclusively that court fools can only be found in the palaces of tyrants, and buffoons among a nation of slaves. Humor is a manly quality, and requires the pure air of freedom to expand in."[30] Quite possibly, Jones's remarks about Italian slavery were designed to remind Simms that if the Southerner truly desired a free voice of humor in the West, it would require free-soil states and abolition, not (as Simms and his compatriots would have it) its contaminating extension of slavery into the territories.

Whatever the infra-digs, Jones would have us apply Shaftesbury to the American condition with a positivistic inversion of cause and effect. If freedom induces humor and tyranny, satire, then conversely the practice of good humor and the avoidance of satiric thrust facilitate America's cultural unification. Jones stuck by the liberal optimism of Shaftesbury's free economy of wit and humor; he was not inclined to propose any Melvillean reversal or admit to democractic tyrannies—the marketplace, the critical establishment, the mob—that might diminish his correlation of freedom and humor. He did not see, as did Poe in his last story "Hop-Frog," how critics might reduce artists to buffoonery. Nor did he see, as did Melville in "Benito Cereno" and *The Confidence-Man,* the need to retreat within unstable narrative ironies because his nation could not bear plain speaking. In a civilization where freedom was in fact disproving Shaftesbury, Jones's hope for good humor was visionary. But if Jones's essay on "American Humor" overstates as it reiterates Duyckinck, his other writings elucidate the problem of America's amiability and egotism as well as his own version of amiability, or what he called "The Familiar Philosophy."

Jones found models for America's comic recovery in the balanced repose of such ancient and modern practitioners of amiability as Montaigne, Addison, Steele, Lamb, Hunt, and Hazlitt. Although self-indulgent and erratic, these writers control their otherwise offensive "literary egotism" and factionalism through a redemptive coalescence of feeling and intellect essential to an aesthetics of repose. In his essay "Literary Egotism," Jones writes that "every action and thought [of the egotists] refers to some peculiar circumstances fixed in their memory by the iron chain of association. They are creatures of sentiment as well as intellect. Every idea in their minds is influenced by every pulsation of their hearts."[31] The socializing effect of this form of classically restrained Romantic introspection is to induce readers, through the author's open-hearted familiarity and "self-anatomy," to explore themselves, to discover, as Duyckinck put it, what "lies hid." The discovery of an inner linkage to what might otherwise be considered an alien eccentricity creates a rhetorical bonding that is inherently democratic. We are placed, Jones notes, "upon the footing of a friend" with the literary egotist; we are "charmed" (LE, 222).

Simms would have concurred, for he had rejected Mathews as more "judge" than "friend." But in looking west, he was (in Jones's view) confusing exuberance for the deeper, socially functional "egotism" of traditional amiability. Worse, Simms was championing his region over all others, and this would only trigger the nightmare of one enthused faction tyrannizing the rest. In "Literary Egotism," Jones hoped that the polite management of humor would unite various enthusiasms within a single comic voice. It would not attempt a scrappy congress of different voices but rather search for the common strand of intellect and feeling linking all factions. In turn, this brand of Shaftesburyan thinking would allow for "a union of shrewdness and pathetic power."[32]

Like Duyckinck, Jones's principal concern was that this "Familiar Philosophy" would promote social growth by creating "creatures of sentiment as well as intellect" in the democracy. Not surprisingly (given Young America's link to Hazlitt), Jones's restrained amiability is essentially picturesque. In "mingling the gay colors with the melancholy aspects of Fortune," the familiar philosophy "reveals the natural corruption, as well as the innate goodness (not quite extinct) of the human heart, improves every opportunity of bringing the latter into the service of the public and private good, and palliates the former by considerations of human frailty" (FP, 246, 248). On the surface of it, Jones's utilitarian formulation of the picturesque aesthetics of repose seems at best contradictory in applying an inherently conservative form of humor to a progressive political agenda, and at worst premature in assuming that humor can *shape* rather than simply *reflect* the national character. Young America's faith in amiability rested upon the idea that humor's "self-anatomy" encourages self-awareness, which leads to a discovery of innate benevolence that will in turn root out political faction. But while a recognition of our "frailty" (i.e. benevolence) may "palliate" man's innate "corruption," it cannot guard against depravity. (Here, in fact, is the problematic core of geniality in *The Confidence-Man.*) Yet, Jones's point is that our frail quest for faith is instinctive, hence unavoidable. It can be left uncultivated, but like our instinctive depravity, it cannot be suppressed. Nor should it be if humanity is to preserve its potential for love, peace, divinity. The only way to build up good is to exercise our faculty of sentiment in tandem with our intellect. Thus, "frailty" must be fused with "shrewdness," just as egotism or enthusiasm must be restrained by form and humor. A proper fusion, however, cannot be achieved without knowing the limits of sentiment.

In "Satire and Sentiment" Jones provides the ethical "fine tuning" of his familiar philosophy that sharpens the critical dimensions of America's comic debate. Like

Duyckinck, Jones had little regard for the "rational spirit," which professes "virtue of censure" but too often degenerates into "bigotry" and the "vice of lampoon."[33] Its "unbelief in goodness" leads to "the hard heart and skeptical head" (SS, 90). But our "instinctive appetite" for sentiment is equally prone to corruption (SS, 88). Its "delicate generosity" can become an "ephemeral sensibility" (SS, 88). Worse, "excessive indulgence or feeling paralyzes the active powers"; in a word, it becomes impractical (SS, 89). Sentiment degrades to sentimentality; too much feeling creates too much talk and no action. The language of love replaces loving; charity is never performed. The result is like satire run wild: a hardening of the heart. The sentimentalist attempts "to make a heart in the head; to change the sensitive into the intellectual . . . to make reflective ideas stand for genuine emotions." The effect is to "petrify the affections." Moreover, "this whining sort of philosophy in time grows into a levity of character and utter indifference" (SS, 91). The "whining philosophy" of sentimentality is the debased ruin of the "familiar philosophy" in which true sentiment is found not in a substitution of heart for head but in the fused "offspring of natural feeling and intelligent judgment" (SS, 92).

Jones identifies three kinds of sentiment. The lowest is the "manly" sentiment found, for example, in Izaak Walton's "outbursting of an uncorrupted heart." Mackenzie and Sterne follow with a sensibility "cultivated by education, elevated by Society, purified by Religion." But finally, there is in Wordsworth, Burke, and Shakespeare the "magnificent and swelling character" of poet, patriot, and philanthropist (SS, 93). For Jones the "test of fine sentiment" is not enthusiastic "outbursting" but "magnificence," an enlargement of the heart that by embracing all creates social utility; it is what he calls "practical benevolence." "All else," he concludes, "is little better than an intellectual grace, and the cunning refinement of the elegant courtier." (SS, 91).

Young America's goal in transplanting amiability in native soil was to locate its social function in "philanthropy," to translate *caritas* into charity, and to make benevolence work. Jones derived his familiar philosophy carefully; he knew the power of sentiment. The weakness in his approach is that he does not apply the same critical rigor to his exalted model, the Philanthropist, who in the form of Melville's confidence man conceals an "intellectual grace" and a "cunning refinement" that prick the bubble of amiability. Still, Jones's promotion of Shaftesburyan benevolence, even in the face of Melville's later, more insightful reversal, should not be reduced to a shallow Rotarianism. The alternative to his form of amiable humor was divisive satire, a comic mode not simply distasteful but counterproductive for the democracy.

William A. Jones's fate was to be the forgotten secretary of a movement that failed to endorse a writer who could embody its vision. Melville left Young America, and it abandoned him. But neither could fully dispense with their most amiable of mentors, Washington Irving. Although his humor was conservative, nostalgic, pastoral, and escapist and his use of the picturesque more iconic than dynamic, his contribution to America's comic debate is substantial, if only for his ability to bring a standard of geniality before the democracy. But more than this, his personal achievement was to rise above the satire of *Salmagundi* and land upon the character of Rip Van Winkle, one of the nation's most enduring symbols of amiability. Irving's own comic debate, then, serves us as an example of one writer's search for aesthetic containment and for the rhetorical strategies that would promote that sense of repose.

3

The Example of Irving

On 31 July 1847, Herman Melville, author of *Typee* and *Omoo,* dined at Astor House with Evert Duyckinck, former editor for Putnam's and co-founder of *The Literary World*. At the time, Melville's career was bounding. He was soon to marry Elizabeth Shaw, and by September he would move with her, his mother, sisters, brother, and sister-in-law into a town house near Astor Place. Those Manhattan years were tumultuous: The author would plunge avidly into Duyckinck's library; immerse himself in metaphysics, literature, and politics; and write three books (*Mardi, Redburn, White-Jacket*). He would witness (it is likely) the Astor Place Riot of May 1849 almost on his doorstep, and would travel to England—this time as an accomplished literary figure, not a seaman. It was the beginning of a tremendous "unfolding." Duyckinck had published the American edition of *Typee,* had helped Melville secure a contract for *Omoo,* and had assigned Melville to review a book on whaling for his new magazine. He had sent *Typee* to Hawthorne, and in 1850 he would facilitate the famous meeting between Hawthorne and Melville. More than anyone else, he was Melville's mentor and promoter.[1] Duyckinck was a literary radical despite his conservative demeanor. He founded the Tetractys Club and "Young America" to promote the development of a National Literature. To be anti-establishment in New York was to be anti-Knickerbocker, or at least disparaging of those Jonathan Oldstyle elitists who in the pages of *The Knickerbocker* (headed by Lewis Gaylord Clark) worried over Jacksonianism, attacked such upstarts as Poe, and paid homage to the recusant Washington Irving.[2]

Although by 1847 most of Irving's career was behind him, he was the principal American writer of the day, but for Duyckinck, who admired Irving's genius and "genial humor,"[3] the nation required a more original voice than one canonized as "The American Goldsmith." Melville shared this ambivalence, but for different reasons. Herman's brother Gansevoort had gotten Irving to read *Typee* in proofs, and the author of *The Sketch Book* had pronounced it promising (*Log,* 204; Howard, 96). This private praise must have had the same exhilarating effect on Melville as Emerson's more public "salute" to *Leaves of Grass* had on Whitman. But Melville would later admit to Duyckinck that, compared to Hawthorne, Irving was a "grasshopper" (*Letters,* 121). Nevertheless, his deep affection for Irving endured even to one of his last creative acts, "Rip Van Winkle's Lilac."

Given these affinities and divergences, Duyckinck's diary entry on the Astor House dinner affords an insight into Melville's self-image. Melville "is cheerful company without being very [?] or original and models his writing evidently a great deal on Washington Irving" (*Log*, 253). One almost hears a muted "oh dear" behind that word "evidently." Melville is congenial, but he lacks originality, a fact epitomized in his wish to emulate the imitative Irving. Exactly what Melville saw as a model in Irving—his picturesque style or his preference for semifictional travel literature—is not stated. In any event, Duyckinck soon got more originality out of Melville than he desired, and at some later date he (or someone else) attempted to erase the disparaging remarks concerning Melville, Irving, and originality. All that the mentor left was that Melville had been "cheerful company." Still, Melville's attraction to "the example of Irving" underscores an important factor in his career. For the one thing worth emulating in Irving was his aesthetically pleasing and highly marketable voice. Irving also struggled for this genial voice, and that struggle—a personal debate between satiric impulse and amiable restraint—is analogous to Melville's own search for narrative repose.

Irving's Comic Debate

Washington Irving was born with an Addisonian pen in hand. *Salmagundi* (1807–8) imitated the *Tatler* and *Spectator* even down to its amiable eccentrics. The more original *History of New York* (1809) is reminiscent of Goldsmith, about whom he wrote a credible biography (1840); and his *Sketch Book* (1819) borrowed from Lamb, whose reputation he surpassed, even in England. Irving was not the sole importer of amiability to America, but he standardized for Americans the near-ritualized relationship between amiable humorist and reader; in turning away from satire he reinforced the need for the politically regenerative voice of the humorist: the tone of good-natured and nostalgic insight, the whims and Romantic flights of fancy, the sincere yet playful irony, the political and moral conservativism, the love of humanity. A model for schoolchildren and professionals, Irving's graceful prose appeared in primers beside Addison. A stage production of "Rip Van Winkle" endured throughout the century, and such writers as Paulding, Bryant, and Willis, as well as Hawthorne and Melville, freely dipped into the rich pool of Irving's work.[4] Ishmael could not have been born without Diedrich Knickerbocker and Geoffrey Crayon.

But Irving had detractors. Hazlitt complained with an acrimony bordering on national resentment that he was an imitator of "the wits of Queen Anne" and "mere trifler—a *filigree* man—an English litterateur at second-hand."[5] The manner of Irving's imitation also disturbed Hazlitt:

> Instead of tracing the changes that have taken place in society since Addison or Fielding wrote, [Irving] transcribes their account in a different handwriting, and thus keeps us stationary, at least in our most attractive and praiseworthy qualities of simplicity, honesty, hospitality, modesty, and good-nature. This is a very flattering mode of turning fiction into history or history into fiction.[6]

Hazlitt accepts the sincere flattery of Irving's imitation but wants Irving to serve England better. Unfortunately, Irving was writing for America.

Not having read *Salmagundi* or *The History of New York*, nor having been much impressed by *The Sketch Book* (the only work by Irving he had read), Hazlitt may not have known that his derisive phrase "turning of fiction into history" was precisely the kind of mythy playfulness along the margins of fact and fancy that America (not England) required in its attempt to fashion a lasting culture *ab nihilo*. Hazlitt and Irving were essentially good-natured gentlemen looking to modulate amiable humor, but in opposite directions. While Hazlitt desired more venom to jolt "stationary" British audiences into social reform, Irving instinctively saw the need to tone down the sting of satire, to create through nostalgia opportunities for the conciliation of factions. With amiable humor he could invent a fictive past that would artistically obviate national conflict.

The secret of Irving's surpassing popularity in England lay in his ability to write in various modes—his *Sketch Book* is a medley of styles, including the sentimental, amiable, burlesque, and Gothic.[7] But also important was his talent for confronting the anxious Napoleonic age with a tone that approaches outrage without degenerative misanthropy.[8] Whether this tone suggested the social myopia Hazlitt feared or merely a personal inclination to rise beyond pettifoggery, politics, and economy,[9] its effect was strong. He could politely preach to middle-class readers against the materialism of Gotham and yet reassure them that they were better than it all. Moreover, the very shape of Irving's career had special meaning for America. Irving, the satirist of *Salmagundi,* had evolved into the genial humorist of "Rip Van Winkle" during the nation's most factional age. He symbolized the Tory turned democrat, and valorized both.

Irving's rhetorical development highlights the problems Melville faced. For Irving, humor saved him from political enthusiasms that might otherwise have jeopardized his career. His acute sensitivity to his early satiric inclinations is evident in his final years when, in putting together his collected works, he seriously considered excluding *Salmagundi* altogether and made significant cuts in *The History of New York* to reduce the more caustic politicizing.[10] Such cover-ups were probably unnecessary since his style was so familiar by mid-century that even as careful a reader as Richard Henry Dana found in *Salmagundi* only the amiable Irving he wanted to find.[11] But Irving felt that he could not depend upon future readers to be so friendly as to imagine his satiric "juvenilia" to be so amiable. In retrospect, he wanted to have begun where he had ended; he wanted to lose that part of his past he had successfully expunged. Melville, too, used humor as a means of losing himself. It was a mode of self-abnegation which led to even more objective forms: history for Irving, poetry for Melville. In both cases, each writer took himself out of Time and into Mind. But whereas Melville always takes a plunge, Irving continually refrained. For him writing was a comfort, not a penetration.

The disappointment of Irving is his refusal to expand his humor past nostalgia and myth into psychological realism. Given his personal and sexual anxieties and the instability of his social world, he had no want of material with which to work. But unlike Melville, he chose to mute his talents too severely. His career shows a steady movement deeper into a past of his own making, where he could escape himself through the guise of an inventive historian. He was drawn to the legendary (Columbus) and near-legendary (Goldsmith) for their alleged benevolence. Battered by Time, circumstance, and an unappreciative society, these Irvingesque heroes verge on the tragic, never fully revealing a deeper mental life. Irving found more life in style itself—*lo bello stilo,* the flow of language and image typical of his *Alhambra*—than in the unpredictable flow of thought that may end in fragmentation or nihility. Ultimately, Irving's picturesque style is more a rich slumber than a tense repose. But even though Irving silenced those irritants that could have enlivened his repose, the battle he fought with humor and satire is instructive.

Salmagundi and Some Versions of the Bachelor

Irving came by his imitation of the British amiability honestly or, rather, authentic psychological drives compelled him to it, for as a committed bachelor, he patterned his life on de Coverley as much as he shaped his style on Addison and Steele. Like the fictive knight, Irving was a political conservative and antiquarian who had lost out in love, remained a bachelor, and ended his years in country seclusion. He did not will some of these parallels; unlike the case of the jilted de Coverley, his only love, Matilda Hoffmann, died early in their relationship. But in his salad days he (along with his brother William, James Kirke Paulding, and Henry Brevoort) based his perpetual bachelorhood on the eccentricities of Addison's *Tatler* sketches. Irving and friends gave each other nicknames (the Doctor, the Patroon, Nuncle); they met in Nassau Street taverns and romped at Gouverneur Kemble's country estate; they were bacchanalian; they formed clubs: "The Nine Worthies" and "The Ancient Club of New York."[12] It was as though these postadolescents, having nothing better to do for the year or the rest of their lives, decided on a "whim-wham" to put on a show. It was better than whaling. And the "show" was *Salmagundi,* a journal of criticism, sentiment, politics, and satire. Instead of de Coverley, they had Christopher Cockloft of Cockloft Hall, whose odd relatives were pure Shandy. Their Bickerstaff was Launcelot Langstaff; their Honeycomb, Anthony Evergreen.[13] When the occasion called for cosmopolitan travel sketches, the model was Goldsmith's *Citizen of the World,* even down to "a little man in black." Their pronouncements on fashion, theater, Jefferson, and the French were delivered *ex cathedra,* but genially, their *cathedra* being an amiable "Elbow Chair."

As shameless as its borrowings may be, *Salmagundi* is too much fun to be merely derivative and, indeed, too polemical to be included in Hazlitt's blanket dismissal of Irving's putative "stationary" stance.[14] *Salmagundi* is a "hash," not a rehash: a jaunty mixture of satire, humor, and burlesque; a blending of benevolence and misanthropy. Pulling these disparate modes together is a pervasive bachelor whimsy. In the eighteenth century, the bachelor was generally derided as cynical, self-indulgent, and socially irresponsible. Even for Addison, de Coverley's bachelorhood was a foil to the character's better traits. But Irving's bachelor is different; according to Hedges, "*Salmagundi* made periodical bachelorhood unashamedly Quixotic."[15]

The *Salmagundi* bachelors place the genial fulfillment of life over social and democratic pretensions. This new prioritizing diminishes the corrosive effects of faction by reducing it to whim. Thus, the bachelor aesthetic, which once connoted misanthropy, implies a comic indifference that is paradoxically communal. Ironically, the values of social integration (love and idealism) are invested in the least attached and least committed of individuals, but the fertility of these quixotic bachelors compensates for their detachment. They epitomize the nation's desire for a fusion of total freedom and total commitment to cultural unity.

Irving provides three versions of the bachelor: the utterly whimsical Cocklofts (who provide the largest portion of the journal's burlesque), the caustic Langstaff (our principal satirist), and the amiable Evergreen (our regenerative humorist). Each poses special rhetorical problems.

The Cocklofts and the Problem of Whim

The appeal of whimsy is that it opens the mind to a range of utterly unpredicted associations. The problem is that the connections are as likely to be a meaningless wordplay as a sage insight. Meaning is entirely accidental. The sources of whimsy are equally problematic. A whim may be the symptom of psychological obsessions, which, in the case of an Uncle Toby, may have social relevance, but which (as in Poe) may be the leaden mechanism of an abusive mind. From Shaftesbury's political perspective, whimsical burlesque is the product not of freedom but of tyranny.[16] But the most immediate rhetorical problem is that whim, because of its unpredictably shallow or deep soundings, invariably compromises the author's reliability. We trust a burlesquer only to the degree that at some point the whimsy will turn relevant. The most effective strategy is to *structure* whimsy so that readers can be assured of a connection to their lives but not that they can predict when or where the meaning shall emerge. Whimsy is a purposefully precarious interaction of sense and nonsense. No doubt this radical instability led Emerson to wish for better. But Irving had more patience. His Cockloftian characters reveal the rhetorical limits of whimsy from the delightfully inane to the politically sagacious.

While not a bachelor, Grandfather Cockloft maintains a bachelor's seclusion and exhibits various Shandyan obsessions. "For some incomprehensible purpose, which remains a secret to this day," he is continually blowing up his grounds the better to organize the landscape around his fish pond; he dies on the eve of a new project to blow up the fish pond.[17] Irving does not explore the futility of creativity (or even of gardening) that is submerged in Grandfather's anarchical end. Unlike Uncle Toby's "problem," which yields a rich conclusion to *Tristram Shandy,* Grandfather's nihilism remains "incomprehensible." Langstaff defends his grandfather's gunpowder "whim-whams" on Quixotian principles: If "life is but a dream, happy is he who can make the most of the illusion" (*Sal,* 239). But there follows no reflection on Grandfather's implied self-destruction nor any discussion of the fact that Langstaff himself lacks whimsy, can make nothing of illusion, and must dream vicariously through the antics of his relatives. The moral utility of illusion is a notion to which the world-weary Langstaff can only give lip-service. Grandfather's bachelorisms highlight Langstaff's problematic humorlessness.

The whim-whams of Jeremy Cockloft provide more opportunities for satire. On the surface, Jeremy's indifference is a bit frightening (or satisfying, depending upon your commitment to pets and logic). He once "worried [a cat] to death in an air-pump" to prove the benefits of oxygen (*Sal.,* 102). As an etymologist he derived the word "Mango" from "Jeremiah King" thusly: "Jeremiah King, Jerry King!

Jerking, Girkin! Cucumber, Mango!'' (*Sal* 102). The comical association lies in the sudden shift from a fairly plausible set of derivations based on sound (Jerry King = Jerking) to the unexpected leap from vegetables to fruit at the end. Jeremy is amusing but, sadly, an idiot. Or so it seems. Veiled beneath the inanity is a Marxian (I mean Groucho, not Karl) disrespect for certain cherished assumptions: that the scientific method is humane and that language has logic. Jeremy's other jests, such as his etymology of ''Bridgetown,'' adventitiously turn into satiric commentary. Laboring a syllable at a time, he dispatches ''Bridge'' with pedantic precision. However, his unexpected definition of ''Town'' as ''the accidental assemblage of a church, a tavern, and a blacksmith's shop'' (*Sal.*, 104) delivers a withering indictment of America. It is not enough that American needs are so elemental that they require only three institutions or that a tavern is as valuable as the church. Rather, the satire lies in the fact that the conjoining of these three is purely accidental. Civilization is a coincidental afterthought, and America only a whim. In the spirit of burlesque, Jeremy's logic obliterates knowledge and culture.

In adapting bachelorism to America, Irving pulled social insight out of whimsy without letting satire bruise the Cocklofts' amiability. But no one embroiled in the Federal period could seriously look to either Jeremy or his Grandfather as a political champion: Their obsessions are too strong, their logic too loose, their seclusion (happily enough) too complete. In the final analysis, the stunning alternations of impulse and indifference in Cockloftian whimsy fail to sustain the reader's trust. Since there is no assurance of deep thought in the laughter of whimsy (for to insist upon such assurances would rob whimsy of its essential unpredictability), whimsy can only be political or metaphysical when it self-consciously turns in upon its hidden psychological sources. The same rhetorical problem of achieving reliability in the midst of whimsy existed for Melville, and both writers attempted later in their careers to solve the problem by projecting their voices through various alienated yet genial characters (Knickerbocker and Crayon or Ishmael). Irving was not willing to develop the Cocklofts in this direction. He focused instead upon the psychology of two other bachelors, Launcelot Langstaff and Anthony Evergreen.

Langstaff and the Problem of Satire

Next to a fine lady, ''an old bachelor [is] the most charming being upon earth, in as much as by living in 'single blessedness,' he of course does just as he pleases; and if he has any genius, must acquire a plentiful stock of whims, and oddities, and whalebone habits, without which I esteem a man to be mere beef without mustard, good for nothing at all'' (*Sal.*, 135). This is not Ishmael, although the style and substance would make a credible pastiche. It is Launcelot Langstaff, who, according to the more gracious Anthony Evergreen, is himself ''fertile in whim-whams and bachelorisms'' (*Sal.*, 153). But, in fact, Langstaff is virtually humorless: He ''invests himself with the spleen, and gives audience to the Blue devils from his elbow chair''; he is too often the crabby Diogenes taken in ''a mortal fit of the ''*hyp.*'' He is ''a genuine humorist,'' in the Jonsonian sense that he is a victim of his humours. In practice, Langstaff cannot live up to the good-natured bachelor of his own definition. He is far from ''the most charming being on earth.''

Langstaff does "do what he pleases," but that whimsical liberty invariably leads him to vicious satire. Like his fellow Salmagundians, Langstaff subscribes to a literary manifesto that encourages an open acceptance of the world. "We *care* not what the public think of us," the Salmagundians proclaim. "We write for no other earthly purpose but to please ourselves. . . . We are laughing philosophers," and "true wisdom is a plump, jolly dame, who sits in her armchair, laughs right merrily at the farce of life—and takes the world as it goes" (*Sal.,* 70). While this suits Jeremy Cockloft, it is only a partial portrait of Langstaff, who in satirizing democracy does "*care*" what the public thinks and will not take the world "as it goes."

True, Langstaff has his amiable front, as is evident in his unexpected latitude toward the French. Unlike his Francophobic cousin Pindar, Launcelot loves that "nation of right merry fellows," for their "secret of being happy . . . is nothing more than thinking of nothing, talking about anything, and laughing at every thing" (*Sal.,* 90). He admires the whimsical indifference of the French, but rarely is he "thinking of nothing." Possessing, like his cousin Christopher, "a little vivid spark of toryism . . . in a secret corner of his heart" (*Sal.,* 134), he reviles the consequences of 1789 (foul byproducts of excessive whim) and derides the Francophiliac Jefferson. Like the obsessive personality he is, Langstaff loves what he fears most: freedom, thought, and the French. His ironic praise of French whimsy bespeaks a mental quandary: He cannot be free and easy like the French, although he would like to be, although to be so leads to anarchy and death.

Langstaff's ambivalence only heightens the tension between his proposed amiability and his covert satiric agenda. Take the infamous case of Jefferson's red breeches (*Sal.,* 75). When, in the premiere number of *Salmagundi,* the always decorous Evergreen makes a passing reference to this garment by substituting five asterisks for the word breeches, certain dull readers register confusion over the typographical result: "Jefferson's *****." Or so the sharper-tongued Langstaff reports in the subsequent number. According to him, a Mr. Ichabod Fungus "did not at all like those stars after Mr. Jefferson's name, they had an air of concealment." This thinly veiled derision of readers is ameliorated only slightly by the slightly more enlightened Dick Paddle, who assures Fungus that the elision was not meant to satirize the President; rather, it shows respect in that Evergreen refrained from placing the indelicate word for pants too close to Jefferson's name. (Of course, the deletion more effectively highlights "red" thus exposing Jefferson's radicalism, but Langstaff won't give Fungus or Paddle insight into this irony.) Jefferson is all the more lampooned for Langstaff's presumably indifferent reporting of his readers' responses. But still suspicious of sarcasm, Fungus remains unconvinced; he senses a malicious intent behind the starry concealment of the President's breeches, but without real evidence he can only conclude (with an unconscious wordplay): "thereby *hangs* a tale" (*Sal.,* 81).

We might split hairs to determine which intellect is more refined, Fungus or Paddle; but the final measurement would not put either much higher than ripe fruit. Such teasing of Fungipaddlian readers is as venerable as Cervantes and as fresh as Sterne, but the ungracious suggestion that Jeffersonians are mushrooms adds an uneasy edge to the otherwise benevolent Shandyan device. Dear Reader becomes

Dumb Reader. Langstaff's belittling of readers is a far cry from Evergreen's desire to transform us into laughing philosophers. At this early stage of *Salmagundi*, Langstaff's satiric strategy is to humiliate the very readers he hopes to win.

Langstaff's neurosis is amusing. Everyone can appreciate his melancholic self-indulgence and articulate outrage; his comic type had an established precedent in the "amiable misanthrope" of eighteenth-century England. But Langstaff's impulse to satirize is instinctive; he cannot enter the "farce of life," nor does his laughter cure his rage. He is a satirist despite himself and lacks the socially useful geniality of Anthony Evergreen, his constant apologist.

Evergreen and Langstaff: Seeking the Repose of Humor

Salmagundi's paragon of sensibility is Anthony Evergreen, whose name bespeaks indefatigable optimism and Shaftesburyan benevolence. A sign of Langstaff's potential for comic rehabilitation lies in his championing of Evergreen who, according to the ill-humored conservative, "tempers, so happily, the grave and ceremonious gallantry of the old school with the 'hail fellow' familiarity of the new" (*Sal.*, 71). Such insight may save Langstaff, but his salvation mostly depends on Evergreen's persistent defenses whenever he attacks. Langstaff is remediable only because Evergreen would have us think so. And while this ennobles Evergreen, it also reminds us that humor is primarily a cover-up for Langstaff's impulsive satire. This does not imply deception. Langstaff desires benevolence, and at times he achieves a curative repose, but the instinctual melancholiac always keeps a few barbs in reserve; thus, he remains radically unstable.

Langstaff's potential for comic salvation emerges in the ripe humor of his first Elbow Chair piece in Volume Two, entitled "A Retrospect; or, 'What You Will.' " Langstaff has waited for this August issue to analyze *Salmagundi*'s first year. Late summer induces reflections upon the past, not fruitless speculation on futurity. It is a time "to resort to the pleasures of memory, [rather] than . . . imagination" (*Sal.*, 223). This season of "genial feeling" and "repose" takes Langstaff out of politics and beyond time. But this "sorry amusement" (*Sal.*, 225) only reminds him that his expectations of "raising the world to our own level" have not been met. Surely, certain minor advances in Gotham can be seen in the salubrious lessening of pretense, hypocrisy, and punning (which he disavows, with a pun). But political "slang-whangers" persist, and the Jeffersonian flood will not be damned or dammed. Although Langstaff maintains his opposition, he comes to a double realization: Satire is ineffectual, yet he cannot curb his satiric impulses. Asserting that "a little well applied ridicule" will theoretically rout falsehood (*Sal.*, 227–28), he professes to be a Shaftesburyan humorist, but in reality personality does not conform to theory. Unruly rants stain his benevolism. Recognizing this fated incompatibility, he performs the pastoral humorist's characteristic ritual: He retreats. He will remain a "true and independent bachelor" (*Sal.*, 229) watching "over the welfare of society" from above the fray in Cockloft Hall situated "not so near town . . . nor so distant" (*Sal.*, 238).

There he will write in "retrospect" claiming victory over "mental gloom." The "cheerful exercise of [the] pen" is a "triumph over the spleen" that "retard[s] the furrowing hand of time" (*Sal.*, 229). Writing may not rid America of its "slang-whangers," but the act of "essaying," of containing the anxieties of politics and mortality within the language of memory (not imaginative whim), serves the "mingled motives of selfishness and philanthropy" (*Sal.*, 229). It settles Langstaff's spleen and serves readers as well. By allowing us to observe a satirist's growth toward good humor, Irving shows Langstaff's sincere acceptance of Evergreen's larger project: to make "the whole town . . . a community of laughing philosophers" (*Sal.*, 96). Thus, Irving promotes a kind of "amicable collision" between his abusive satirist and abused reader. Writing shall no longer be a punishment of readers but a communal acceptance of faults shared by writer and reader alike. But while Langstaff's new geniality seems to obviate satire, it does not recast him entirely in the Evergreen mold. As a satirist groping toward humor, he often relapses into satire and must depend greatly upon the kindness of Evergreen to rationalize his attack.

Langstaff's most memorable satire, "On Greatness," is a rant against America's "new man," who "plunges into that mass of obscenity, the *mob;* labours in dirt and oblivion, and makes unto himself the rudiments of a popular name from the admiration and praises of rogues, ignoramuses and blackguards" (*Sal.*, 252). In contrast to this Federalist's nightmare, Langstaff offers up Timothy Dabble, a democratic hero, who nevertheless suffers a degeneration in character. At first, his virtue is rewarded by an election failure because he does not see that "the great object of our political disputes, is not who shall have the *honour* of emancipating the community from the leading-strings of delusion, but who shall have the *profit* of holding the strings and leading the community by the nose" (*Sal.*, 253). But eventually Dabble learns to "succeed"; he becomes another "slang-whanger" destined for the puny pretense of "greatness" in democracy.

Langstaff's attack on Dabble's "slimy progress" follows a proleptic apology by Evergreen. His friend's "paroxysm of his splenetick complaint" is actually therapeutic: "A mental discharge of the kind has a remarkable tendency toward sweetening the temper" (*Sal.*, 250). Langstaff's rant is an unpredictable "flashing-forth," a whim that releases intellectual steam and returns Langstaff to sweet repose. The satire on Dabble revitalizes Langstaff's dormant good humor. Evergreen's defense first legitimizes satire as a purgative that leads to benevolence. Second, it humanizes his friend, thus enhancing his credibility with an already wary audience. But in the end, these two functions work at cross-purposes.

On the surface Evergreen's physiology is convincing. Satire is not an end in itself but a means of flushing out ill humors so that good humor may grow. The attack upon "slang-whangers" effects the union of "selfishness and philanthropy" to which Langstaff aspires. By showing satire's benevolent utility, Evergreen "humorizes" satire, making it more like humor and hence more humane. At the same time, the psychological dimension in Langstaff's satire creates secondary rhetorical benefits. Rather than presume readers will accede to Langstaff's antidemocratic views through the imperious method of *castigat ridendo mores*, Evergreen adopts the humorist's *ad hominem* approach. He drops the presumption that traditional values win instant credibility and attempts to earn credibility for Langstaff by solidifying our faith in him as a person. Paradoxically, Langstaff's instability enhances his reliability; we believe in him because he is so erratic. The logic is that since belief grows out of sympathy, readers will believe in Langstaff to the degree that they recognize in themselves aspects of his personality. As soon as he exposes his desire to fuse "selfishness and philanthropy," he becomes more like us. Langstaff attempts to contain his tendentious impulses within benevolence, fails, vents his spleen, regrets the eruption (but never recants the message), and yet in the process seems more credible than before.

Or so Evergreen would have us think. The problem with purgative satire, in both its psychological and its rhetorical dimensions, is that Langstaff's outbursts, like whim, are uncontrollable. By presenting Langstaff's bitterness within the frame of Evergreen's sweeter temper, Irving attempts to subsume misanthropy within benevolence. But the attempt is as contrived as Evergreen's excuses for Langstaff are thin. Langstaff's anger may eventually cleanse him, but that physiological event is merely the consequence of an organism preserving itself; it is not willed. Langstaff is doomed to endless ventings and purgings, which ease the symptoms of his political anxiety but never cure his inner disorder. There is no true containment of self, only explosion and regret.

Still, Langstaff's deepest insights are bodied forth not in anger but in silence. The moment occurs in a November essay, "Autumnal Reflections," in which Langstaff has lost the genial repose of his summer retrospection but also the bitterness of "On Greatness." He finds himself caught up in a dispiriting cycle of life and death, wherein every season whispers his mortality. His Cousin Pindar, the poet, is different. Although cognizant of the landscape's "dappled livery of decay," he remains "an evergreen of the forest." Langstaff supplies that epithet, but so classifying his cousin does not make Langstaff "evergreen" himself. Pindar consoles him with the idea that the "prevailing color [of the woods] is still green" (*Sal.*, 269) and concludes with a metaphor of mediation—"while, like the lofty mountains of our Southern America, our heads are covered with snow, still, like them, we feel the genial warmth of spring and summer playing upon our bosoms" (*Sal.*, 269). Langstaff's reflection ends here with Pindar's monologue, but without any response of his own. There is only silence.

Irving's choice of a "Southern American" mountain is curious considering that Langstaff and Pindar stand before their own Catskills with plenty of native peaks to inspire them. If the Catskills were simply too tame to give his consolation an epic dimension, the logical alternative would have been the Alps.[18] Although Irving had not at this point witnessed the Alps any more than he had the Andes, they had long been a symbol of the sublime, representing the underlying chaos of Nature. All things being equal, the Alps with their richer poetic associations would have been the expected choice. But Pindar is giving us a New World variant of the European sublime adding a picturesque dimension. Situated on the equator, the Andean range's "bosom" is a middle landscape uniting frozen waste and tropics. This early version of Carlyle's inverse sublimity projects a moral picturesque meant to tame Langstaff's fear of death.

But Langstaff will have none of this. He gives no response to Pindar's picturesque, neither a record of doubt nor one of assent. His silence is a mute deferral of judgment.

A similar standoff occurs in Melville's own South American tale "Benito Cereno," in which the American Captain Delano's insistence upon ever blue skies is met with the Spaniard's darker awareness of human depravity and decay. Their unresolved debate is symbolized by the silence of Babo's severed head. Langstaff's silence is not as profound, but the non-response creates a tense repose between acceptance and rejection, a quietism outstripping noisy satire and brooding misanthropy; it implies both a deeper consciousness and a will to endure. Unlike Cereno's resignation, Langstaff's silence is a voicing of the voiceless, a mooring in Melville's "pondering repose of If." The problem is that Langstaff's mooring is only temporary.

In this silence, Langstaff's former knee-jerk politicizing takes on a new humanism that validates his conservativism. Instead of burlesquing readers, he takes a mountain retreat away from politics and covertly proposes to win us over to his personality by transforming a loathing of political change (i.e. republicanism) into his unvoiced fears of more primal changes: growing old, losing the past, being alone. His autumnal silence goes deeper than "doing what one pleases," and we recognize that Langstaff does not hate democrats so much as he fears change. Democracy, Change, Death: the linkage not only explains the psychological roots of Langstaff's conservativism but also broadens its appeal by removing his conservativism from politics into metaphysics. But though "Autumnal Reflections" articulates Langstaff's commitment to the human condition, he is finally more "selfish" than "philanthropical." With regard to his audience, he remains radically unstable.

Unlike Will Wizard, who concludes *Salmagundi* explicitly "eschewing all spirit of faction, discontent, irreligion, and criticism" (*Sal.*, 316), Langstaff is factional and critical to the end. He berates rather than builds up the good. To be sure, he promises to "part on good terms" with his unreconstructed compatriots: the Funguses, Dabbles, and Paddles. He feels a "glow of parting philanthropy . . . a sentiment of cordial good will toward the numerous host of readers." But it is all another cover-up; he cannot resist a parting shot with his "parting philanthropy." He has criticized America only in "that spirit of hearty affection, with which a schoolmaster drubs an unlucky urchin, or a humane muleteer his recreant animal" (*Sal.*, 306). Suddenly, the glow of geniality dims; our warm smiles grow limp as "we recreant animals" feel Langstaff's pat upon our forelocks. Dear Reader, once Dumb Reader, is now a Mule. Langstaff's condescension underscores the satirist's fate in never combining embrace and derision.

Since scholars attribute much of Langstaff to Irving, and much of Evergreen to Paulding, it might be argued that the two collaborators used each other as foils, balancing Irving's youthful venom with Paulding's geniality. But the two edited each other; thus, their collaboration may have been a true coallition of psyches. Clearly, the collaborators felt as much obliged to moderate one another as to elevate an audience; thus, by placing Langstaff and Evergreen in a dynamic interdependence, Irving and Paulding were tacitly structuring their "hash" of a magazine along the lines of the culture's comic debate. But in "Rip Van Winkle" Irving achieves his fullest fusion of benevolence and satire.

A Rip in the Canvas: Irving's Picturesque

If the conflicts in *Salmagundi* define the limits of satire and humor for Irving—the failure to reconcile Toryism and democracy, to integrate self and other, and to fuse the rhetorics of whimsy, satire, and amiability—then the picturesque vision of "Rip Van Winkle" offers an aesthetically balanced resolution. While the tale is finally more escapist than confrontational in its reposeful conclusion, its fusion of humor and satire is more coherent, even in its silences, and more dynamic than Langstaff's neurotic pastoralism.

To begin with, Rip is himself a coalescence of the Salmagundians. A naïf like the Cocklofts, he enjoys freedom from society and logic; he personifies the whims of youth. Like Langstaff, he is perpetually out of place, indeed out of time, and like Evergreen, he comes to mediate old values and the new. Rip cannot find a proper niche, or rather his wife will not allow him any comfort in the niche he has with the "junto" of indolent "sages" who labor mightily to situate their chairs sagaciously in the shade. Even in the ghostly community of bowlers, he is bewildered, and his improbable resurrection leads him to the brink of madness: "I'm not myself.—I'm somebody else . . . every-thing's changed—and I'm changed—and I can't tell what's my name, or who I am!"[19] But whereas Langstaff neurotically insists upon a humor that he never understands, Rip converts identity crisis into a good-natured humor that mends disputatious America. Rip finally finds his place at home.

In disguising salvos beneath the benevolent mantle of good-natured humor, Irving's Salmagundians take on the inverted position of sophisticates stationed outside the gates of Gotham clamoring to transform the barbarians within. Their bachelorism is mirthful enough, until we sense it is an overprotestation. They call life a farce only because they take it too seriously. Their heroine is a "plump, jolly dame," but they moralize more like Rip's termagant dame. In "Rip Van Winkle," Irving removes these obfuscations. Langstaff's problems—time, mortality, society—are Rip's salvation. Rip's twenty-year furlough valorizes his indolence; he is old enough to be "idle with impunity." Time frees him. He cheats death, avoids revolution, and achieves what Langstaff relishes most: psychological and social permanence. In coalescing earlier types, Rip reconciles humor and satire, benevolence and utility, politics and whim.

Satire in "Rip Van Winkle" is artfully muted. The teasing Dutch portraits, the Yankee Peddler who infuriates Dame Van Winkle to death, the red cap atop a flagpole that replaces the old oak, the ramshackle hotel in place of the comfortable inn, the invidious depiction of the riotous electioneers—all of these jabs are inescapable. Yet this is only wisecracking minus all venom; it promotes no specific political agenda, only a general uneasiness with republican crowds; it does not flap any red breeches. And without any Langstaffian eviscerations, Irving spices his nostalgic humor with sufficient barbs to forestall sentimentality. (He consigns one of the old junto to the anonymity of military death, another to the hell of Congress. Dame Van Winkle's demise signals time's victory over mindless Franklinian industry.) Ironically, Rip's amiable "bachelorism" (perhaps the wrong term for a married man, but then Rip was never really married in spirit) acquires social utility. In former days, Rip did as he pleased. His whim-wham was to "attend to anybody's business but his own" (Rip, 6). Children loved him, dogs never bit. For the Dame this philanthropy was no virtue. But reborn to a new age, Rip is freed from sin; better yet, he has a social function that was denied him in the past: He becomes a favorite among "the rising generation." Those recreant parvenus whom Langstaff would deride, Rip befriends. In turn, they lionize him. Time is not the threat it is in *Salmagundi,* but a process of social integration. It allows Irving a comic detachment that mutes satire without trivializing factional disputes.

What makes these reconciliations work in "Rip" is fantasy. For all its burlesque and whimsy, *Salmagundi* lacks fantasy, the kind of escapist wish-fulfillment that takes an audience beyond satiric defect to delicious unattainable realms of peace, unity, love. To be sure, the pastoral Cockloft Hall provides Langstaff with a fantasy rejuvenation. But such pastoralism has none of Rip's abandonment of social and temporal restraints, nor can it produce Rip's regeneration. Cockloft Hall is a day in the country, not the "wild mountain" sublime where "there was something strange and incomprehensible about the unknown, that inspired awe and checked familiarity" (Rip, 34). But while Rip finds something more than the pastoral, he also experiences something other than the sublime, something picturesque.

After his escape, Rip pauses on a Catskill ledge. It is a silent moment framed by serenity and chaos. Sitting on "the brow of a precipice," Rip "muses" on the vista before him. One side "overlook[s] all of the lower country . . . the lordly Hudson, far, far below him, moving on its silent but majestic course, with the reflection of a purple cloud, or the sail of a lagging bark here and there sleeping on its glassy bosom" (Rip, 33). This world of repose, the sunset of Monarchy, contrasts sharply with Rip's other view, "a deep mountain glen, wild, lonely and shagged, the bottom filled with fragments from the impending cliffs and scarcely lighted by the reflected rays of the setting sun." We might put a carved frame around these words and let them pass for an Asher Durand.

Rip's picturesque vantage provides an iconic *chiaroscuro* of order and decay representing America's political past and future. Submerged in the painterly vision are the materials of satire, boldly abstracted and yet quietly, genially restrained. The mountain picturesque adds to Pindar Cockloft's Andean image. Pindar's mountain rests intellect upon feeling; Langstaff's silence challenges the metaphor. It is sound philosophy but ineffectual therapy, for finally Pindar's metaphor is just another person's words that Langstaff will never fully assimilate because they are not his. But Rip's mountain is experienced directly; he is *in* the picture, and the picture exists because of his recombinative perspective. He mediates landscapes through his physical centrality within the frame. By letting Rip live the metaphor instead of having it forced upon him, Irving depicts a dynamic confrontation of his battered hero and the choices of history. It is a fusion of politics and mind.

Our focus is not on the divided canvas, that is, the two landscapes on either side of Rip, but on Rip, the perceiver perched *between* and *above* the two. What he sees are potentials, not realities—the values of a mythic past, the possibility of democratic misrule. Rip encompasses both in silence. But unlike Langstaff's mute deferral of judgment, Rip's unvoiced "musing" is Irving's refusal to promote a political agenda. It not only restrains satiric impulse but keeps the reader guessing as to the practical outcome of Rip's eventual resurrection. While Rip's identity crisis dramatizes the chaotic half of Rip's picturesque moment, his subsequent social integration regains the mediating perspective of his silent "precipice," where majestic repose and unknown freedom are subsumed in one benevolent heart.

But just as "Rip Van Winkle" marks a substantial advance over *Salmagundi,* Rip's return is too easy. Of course, the bewilderment of a contrived ending is the price we pay for comic fantasy. And yet, in Rip's case, the allegory of his reintegration induces a second allegory of reading that undercuts our sense of a wish fulfilled.

Rip's problematic return has occasioned an endless critical debate of affirmation and doubt. Philip Young's Rip is a pathetic figure with whom the modern world happily connects, for he symbolizes our dissociation from myth and fertility that typifies the postrevolutionary age. Donald Pease tacitly confirms that view in a different key. His Rip represents the kind of "negative freedom" or abandonment of the past that necessitates a radical loss in the American character. Jeffrey Rubin-Dorsky's Rip is a storyteller working out Irving's anxiety over acceptance as a professional writer; he is his claim to legitimacy.[20] But these cogent readings do not address the peculiarity of the "rising generation's" *easy* acceptance of Rip. Although we are not told how Rip embellishes his tale for "the rising generation," we know that he cannot entirely *explain* his inexplicable experience. Irving offers the simple fiction that Rip's details come to us *via* Diedrich Knickerbocker, who omits any discussion of how the townspeople come to accept this tall tale. Why does Irving make "the rising generation" so gullible?

"Rip Van Winkle" offers two allegories: the familiar allegory of political mediation and the covert allegory of the people's will to fall for the first. The fairy tale's primary allegorical apparatus articulates the anxiety of revolution. Rip does not see this allegory; all he knows is that he did the impossible: He slept for twenty years. His act of retelling the story does not fulfill any conscious political function; it simply keeps him sane. Moreover, as the tale becomes a ritual for the town, Rip avoids any re-searchings into any psychological implications of his "sleep." Rip will not "dive" for deeper meanings, but, indolent and amiable to the end, he will tell a tall tale. And who would blame him for this escape? Indeed, we count him lucky to have the creativity to fashion such an artful accommodation of the inexplicable. Why he is believed, however, is Irving's stretcher.

Rip might as well have been kidnapped by aliens. Today, his bearded face would appear on tabloid covers, wide eyes peering out to catch the desperate and bored. Instead, he is loved by those who by any stretch of the imagination would scoff. But the people love Rip's tale not because it explains the past but because it provides an easy fantasy substitute for an uninterpretable history. They might enjoy Rip's eccentricity for its own sake and submit to a vicarious purgation of anxiety through Rip's lucky avoidance of the war they had to fight, but touched for a moment, they will soon go about their business. For them, the tale is only a puzzle, and like Langstaff pondering Pindar's mountain metaphor, they will not be able to experience that puzzle in its original moment. Their present life will go on despite the neatly packaged intrusion from the past that Rip ritualistically provides. They will not do as Rip once did and situate themselves in a silent picturesque of interfused consciousnesses, both past and future. Rather, they will listen to him in order to forget. Through Rip they can compartmentalize the past, reducing the Revolution to one man's symbolic avoidance of it. Rip is not a link to former times and traditions; he is the embodiment of America's desire to marginalize and eventually forget them. The secondary allegory in "Rip Van Winkle," then, tells how Americans fail to "read," how we use fiction to obviate history.

Because of its picturesque vision and its careful striding along the margins of history and mind, "Rip Van Winkle" is far more thoughtful, despite its fantasy, and far more creative, despite its escapism, than any reflections by the Cocklofts, Langstaff, or Evergreen. Thus, for Irving, the tale represents a substantial victory of amiable humor over satire in his work. And, to this degree, it is a monumental achievement in the course of America's comic debate. Still, the ironies implicit in Irving's secondary allegory remain cautiously covert. The issue of whether Americans are gifted or simply foolish in their forgetting of the past is too deftly muted to achieve the interpenetrations of Hawthorne's and Melville's picturesque. Some hint of Irving's awareness of this limitation can be found in his biography of Oliver Goldsmith.

Irving's Goldsmith and the Rhetoric of Geniality

Return now to Astor House, New York City, 31 July 1847. What was there in Irving for Melville to emulate? His silences and picturesque? These he could master by placing himself beside Irving in the grand tradition of "*lo bello stilo.*" What Dante cherished in Virgil, and Irving in Goldsmith, Melville cherished, too: the benevolence, insight, color, and "charm" of "the beautiful style."

Irving's biography of Oliver Goldsmith (1840) is as much an encomium of that style as it is a measured apologia for the whimsical British bachelor and eighteenth-century man of letters who practiced it. Although the volume lacks the thrill of discovery and declaration of independence from European standards that Melville voiced in his homologous encomium of Hawthorne, the biography may be read as Irving's "*Mosses,*" the study of a much-admired predecessor and, indirectly, a manifesto of literary aesthetics. The biography also helps us understand Melville's attachment to Irving.

Two achievements in Irving have precedence in Goldsmith. First, in transplanting Shandyan whimsy to the American democracy, Irving was able to explore the potentials for psychological and social insight within bachelorism. Along these lines he subsumed rancor and anxiety within geniality and thereby demonstrated, as did Goldsmith, the problems of uniting benevolence and understanding. Second, Irving familiarized Americans with an amiable rhetoric in which whimsical speakers gain credibility by dint of their psychological instability. Thus misanthropy, even self-loathing, balances benevolence.

Irving legitimizes these potentials despite Goldsmith's detractors. Against Samuel Johnson's withering claim that Goldsmith mingled with the poor merely because he was once poor himself, Irving insists upon a deeper impulse: Goldsmith went slumming to seek out "what was *comic and characteristic*. It was the feeling of the artist; the feeling which furnished out some of his best scenes in familiar life; the feeling with which [Ben Jonson] sought these very haunts and circles in days of yore, to study 'Every Man in His Humour.' "[21] For Goldsmith (like Coleridge and Hazlitt), painting and writing, like life, are inherently picturesque. The unique, original, and eccentric (not the typical) define our being; hence, the artist's first duty is to investigate the "comic and characteristic." Melville isolates the same "feeling of the artist" in Hawthorne, whose "noon-day repose" transforms the "ruddy" fruits of "twisted, and contorted old trees" (called "humorists and odd-fellows" by Hawthorne) into "ruddy thoughts" that fall "ripe" into our "souls" ("*Mosses,*" 241). Thus, what Samuel Johnson wrongly identifies as Goldsmith's parvenu nostalgia is an instinctive aesthetic attraction to what is deep, ripe, and true in life. Goldsmith was sincere.

But this "feeling of the artist" (a form of benevolence) is problematic. As Irving confirms in various anecdotes, the author's too-artless heart made him "the continual dupe of his benevolence and his trustfulness in human nature" (*OG*, 421). For Johnson, such naïveté was a failing, but, the Doctor concluded, "Let not his frailties be remembered; he was a very great man." Johnson's vague overprotestation, consigning Goldsmith among the near-great, pushes Irving to a defense of Goldsmith's frailties: " 'Let them be remembered' since their tendency is to endear" (*OG*, 426). Goldsmith's defects ensure his reliability; he is great because he is good-natured, comic, and artless, because he is "frail."

But Irving's Goldsmith is no fool; he recognizes the limits of benevolence, which he knows he cannot resist. Goldsmith's critique of Thomas Nash in his *Life of Nash* (as quoted by Irving) clearly applies to Goldsmith himself: "His simplicity in trusting persons whom he had no previous reasons to place confidence in, seems to be one of those lights of his character which, while they impeach his understanding, do honor to his benevolence" (*OG*, 421). The careful juxtaposition here of "understanding" and "benevolence" reveals Goldsmith's tacit awareness of the potential incompatibility of head and heart. Just as Nash's simplicity enlightens Goldsmith's problematic benevolence, so too does Goldsmith's acknowledgment of this dilemma deepen Irving's admiration. Man's fate, these amiable humorists say, lies in our instinct to believe, which proves our divinity while at the same time it threatens our existence.

Goldsmith's style is an extension of his life. His writings ("transcripts of his own heart") are "artless, good-humored, excursive, sensible, whimsical, intelligent" (*OG*, 14). Moreover, his blend of whim and intelligence exacts the endearing reader-responses that epitomize a rhetoric of geniality in which dark truths reside in a sincere and "artless" personality. Notice the strategy as Irving unfolds it: "We read his character in every page, and into familiar intimacy with him as we read. The artless benevolence that beams throughout his work; the whimsical yet amiable views of human life and human nature; the unforced humor, blending so happily with good feeling and good sense, and singularly dashed at times with pleasing melancholy" (*OG*, 13). What gives credence to Goldsmith's intimacy is the open yet restrained self-exposure. Goldsmith's controlled humor is "unforced," but we would have no awareness of this repose unless we were made aware of a "dash" of melancholy that requires restraint. Readers cannot fully recognize stylistic *control* unless they realize that the artist has contrived something that needs to be contained. Thus, Goldsmith's "artless benevolence" is not so artless. It cannot "beam" until countervailing tensions are brought into play. Its appeal lies in the intimate disclosure that it has been battered a bit. The humorist's sincerity is a necessary contrivance in which benevolence and melancholy contain one another. The engaging paradox that informs this rhetoric of geniality is that the reposeful flow of language that suggests an open heart is a conscious fabrication.

But while Irving acknowledges the problematic interdependence of sincerity and craft, he ignores Goldsmith's own admission of artifice, as if to insist upon a natural wellspring of benevolence untainted by rhetorical contrivances of any kind. Irving was content to praise the superficial colorations of Goldsmith's style despite the writer's artifice. By the time he was putting his *Goldsmith* in press, Irving was revising his complete works for an authorized edition, removing (as noted) certain satiric jabs from his earliest works. This self-laundering is part and parcel of his sanitizing of Goldsmith. Just as the American writer created a new edition of himself, he created a version of Goldsmith in line with his own self-portrait, an artist in uncomplicated repose. Needless to say, this is where Melville in his portrait of Hawthorne surpassed Irving, for his insight into Hawthorne's repose exposes rather than conceals the artful tensions that sustain that precarious, *chiaroscuro* interdependency. Some sense of Irving's reticence in admitting to a fabricated sincerity and amiability can be found in his notion of "style."

Irving views Goldsmith's style as "color" (*OG*, 161) and, significantly, as a "magic charm" (*OG*, 418), but he does not explore the full rhetorical consequences of these painterly and necromantic metaphors. There is a potency in these terms beyond Irving's ken; they suggest that style is a transformative and conjurative process. If style is charm or magic, then a stylist is a magician, and *lo bello stilo* a hoax. Magicians (like storytellers) capture us in a spell, and when the trick is done (when we are thoroughly engaged in the fiction) they lead us to guess how it all was done. They perform sleights of hand and word. And as linguistic transformers, they deceive. But in acknowledging Goldsmith's "charm," Irving does not characterize Goldsmith as an ironic rhetorician or self-conscious deceiver. That would impugn the author's natural sincerity. "Goldsmith had no secrets," Irving insists; "his follies, his weaknesses, his errors were all thrown to the surface; his heart was really too guileless and innocent to seek mystery and concealment." Irving's insistence upon a pure Goldsmith despite the implications of the charmer's style seems a willful avoidance of the most harmless of rhetorical truths: that writers manipulate. What gives the lie to this putative guilelessness is Goldsmith's own remark in *The Bee* that "the true end of speech is not so much to express our wants as to conceal them" (*OG*, 230). Irving quotes the aphorism, even notes that it has been falsely attributed to Talleyrand, puzzles a bit over its uncharacteristic insincerity, but never resolves its implied contradiction of Goldsmith's "artless benevolence." In a way, we discover a more crafty Goldsmith than Irving will permit. Goldsmith's gift lies in his "happy knack of extracting sweets from that worldly experience which to others yields nothing but bitterness" (*OG*, 52), and while

Irving can allude to this "knack," he is finally more pleased with the sweets than he is with the containment of bitterness required in the process of extraction. For Melville the fabrication of sincerity is the problematic "given" that enlivens his most self-conscious voices: the anxious Tommo, the resolvent Ishmael, and the necromantic Frank Goodman.

In the three years following his buoyant aspiration to "[model] his writing . . . on Washington Irving," Melville read Shakespeare and Hawthorne deeply. By the summer of 1850, he disavowed one model for another. "Hawthorne and His *Mosses*" is a spirited call for a national literature free from "foreign models." Hawthorne could answer the demand; Irving could not. But the vigor of Melville's manifesto is compromised somewhat by certain ambivalences which both deny a full declaration of independence from Europe and register a lingering affection for Irving. Even as Melville implores America to "prize and cherish her writers," his principal means of legitimizing Hawthorne is to compare him to Shakespeare. And even as he disparages imitators—"there is no hope for us in these smooth pleasing writers that know their powers"—and shouts that "we want no American Gold-smiths," he delivers this critique of Irving's "smooth, pleasing" self-control "without malice, but to speak the plain fact" (*"Mosses,"* 248). The thirty-one-year-old writer had already endured the hostile reception of *Mardi* and the favorable reviews of potboilers for which he had little regard. As he wrote the *"Mosses"* review, he was well-launched into *Moby-Dick,* to be dedicated to Hawthorne, not Irving, and his call for a national literature is as much a plea for a readership responsive to his own original charm as it is a recruitment for new American writers. No doubt, he sensed failure coming; thus, *"Mosses"* is a proleptic defense of his *Whale:* It is "better to fail in originality," he argues, "than to succeed in imitation. . . . Failure is the true test of greatness" (*"Mosses"* 247–48). Melville would win his badge of "greatness" soon enough in various negative reviews, and it is perhaps with a growing anticipation of that fate that Melville softens his attack on Irving's imitative and naïve geniality. He does not reject Irving so much as grow beyond him. The earnest disciple in Duyckinck's diary had graduated. This is the "plain fact" of personal and national growth delivered "without malice" to a former tutor who was happily withdrawn to Sunnyside.

Without a doubt, Melville places Hawthorne over Irving, but what Melville most admired in Hawthorne—his "great intellect in repose," his insight and golden mirth—are elements contained within Irving's amiable pose. We cannot fully un-derstand Melville's own attempts to project an intellect in repose, nor his bookish and genial bachelors, his doubts about democracy, his use of the picturesque, his problematic sincerity and rhetorical gambits, his fading intimacy with readers, without recognizing his attachment to the amiable humor and the rhetoric of geniality that Irving practiced. Melville's geniality touched strains far deeper than Irving's "pleasing melancholy." But to add the requisite satiric "spice" to good-natured humor, to instill in amiable humor a contrasting awareness of its own artificiality, and to engage readers more fully in an understanding of the tensions between benevolence and misanthropy, he experimented with an opposing comic sensibility, not a rhetoric of geniality but one of comic deceit found in the subversive humor of the American tall tale.

4

Playing Along: America and the Rhetoric of Deceit

As a fusion of import and invention, America draws its identity from both foreign traditions and native forms. But more than just the site of cultural fusion, America is the *pressure* to include and expand. In adapting the tenets of amiability to the experiences of the New World, Americans tinkered with old forms to resolve their comic debate. But with the tall tale and its rhetoric of deceit, they created new forms altogether. The "pressure" was in containing divisive satire within a genial frame of humor so as to foster a national comic voice. On the surface of it, the national inclination seemed contrary to Melville's individual aesthetic. Whereas the culture promoted the loud voices of local stereotypes—Yankee, frontiersman, and minstrel—Melville sought a voice of silence. But beyond regional characters was a more compatible humor that thrived on deceptive silences; it was the humor of the American tall tale itself, a narrative structure that trains democratic readers in the dangers of belief. No tradition of humor is richer in America than our affection for liars, for no other form of native humor so richly blends our conflicting desires for social subversion and communal integration. Lying was not exclusive to America, but because the frontier required its denizens to know deception, comic lying became a social and literary art for the nation. Similarly, art forms based on a rhetoric of deceit grew. Writers like Poe and T. B. Thorpe understood the moral effect that tall talk, tall tales, and narrative unreliability had in the democracy, and Melville also adopted the strategies of comic lying to add sting to his genial art. He saw, too, that it was a metaphysical imperative.

The Deep Thought of Laughter

Melville discovered the vitality of the rhetoric of deceit as early as *Mardi,* when in offering a sarcastic comparison of the bachelor to a sterile monk, Babbalanja dramatizes the limits of geniality:

> "Ay, let us laugh: let us roar: let us yell! What, if I was sad but just now? Life is an April day, that both laughs and weeps in a breath. But whoso is wise, laughs when he can. Men fly from a groan, but run to a laugh. . . . And now let us drown away grief . . . it is good to laugh, though the laugh be hollow; and wise to make merry, now and for aye." [*M*, 612–13]

70

Babbalanja pitches his rant just below shrieking. Invoking the mercurial April day metaphor (a standard trope in amiable humor), he exposes the desperation of our whimsy. Laughter is an uncontrollable mechanism, and mirth just hollow roaring. But Babbalanja soon relents, modulating his rant to a resolvent key:

> "There is laughter in heaven, and laughter in hell. And a deep thought whose language is laughter. Though wisdom be wedded to woe, though the way thereto is by tears, yet all ends in a shout. But wisdom wears no weeds; woe is more merry than mirth; . . . Humor, thy laugh is divine; whence, mirth-making idiots have been revered; and therefore may I." [*M*, 613]

The prose rhythm prefigures the lyricism of similar lines in *Moby-Dick*—"There is a wisdom that is woe and a woe that is madness" (*MD*, 425)—and in *The Confidence-Man*—"There is sorrow in the world, but goodness too; and goodness that is not greenness, either, nor more than sorrow is" (*CM*, 24). In each case, Melville defines wisdom through balanced oppositions: heaven and hell, woe and madness, the good and the green, the green and sorrowful. But it is the "voiceless" rocking cadence rather than these voiced terms that finally conveys Melville's deepest pronouncement. Like a harpooner perched on a rocking boat, we must continually adjust to our vaulting and plummeting humors. For Babbalanja, laughter is the solid unstable boat that tips us from heaven to hell and in tipping links the two. It is Simms's Al Sirat. Laughter is an ontological *lingua franca,* the "language" that unites the bright heights and "deep thought" of Being. Through laughter, "mirth and sorrow are kin" (*M*, 613). But this only sets the scene for deeper thought.

Babbalanja's final modulation achieves the serene diction of an aesthetics of repose:

> "I have found that the heart is not whole, but divided; that it seeks a soft cushion whereon to repose; that it vitalizes the blood; which else were weaker than water: I have found that we cannot live without hearts; though the heartless live longest. Yet hug your hearts, ye handful that have them; 'tis a blessed inheritance!" [*M*, 613–14]

The deep thought of laughter is located in the paradox that "we cannot live without hearts" and yet "the heart is not whole." For Ishmael, this is Being's vast practical joke. For Babbalanja, the heart is divided because, as an embodiment of Being, it can only savor, not realize, ideality. Given this perpetual state of becoming, we are as easily "duped" by "things visible" as we are by "things imaginative." Laughter is the truest means of confronting this paradox. Because it is hollow yet deep, and because it fuses lightness and dark, humor brings "imaginative" fictions closer to "visible" reality. It cannot erase the fundamental duplicity in our existence; it can only recapitulate it. Thus, true Laughter balances the hard reality of our divided heart with the desire for soft repose.

The problem for the amiable humorist was that the most effective means of creating a deeply felt experience of duplicity *within* readers was to undermine amiablity itself. The trick of such a rhetoric of deceit, however, was to do this without destroying confidence, even though a betrayal of authorial reliability and the duping of the reader are comic necessities. If laughter were to become the language of deep thought, a new version of amiability would have to be fashioned to invade and capture the very processes of doubt itself. By combining amiability and comic deceit, Melville could genially dupe us into deep thought.

Melville understood the rhetorical complexities of this project. Giving readers a fictive recapitulation of their problematic relation to Being required treating them insincerely, exposing them to equally valid doses of geniality and despair. But humor and authorial betrayal cannot coexist indefinitely; eventually, the tension degenerates into confusion. Thus the repose of humor becomes far more problematic, even as the necessity for it increases. And there was no profit, in mind or marketplace, if, in making readers experience a world of lies, the author lost his readership. Melville's problem was clear; the solution not so simple. His approach was to experiment with the confidence man and the literary confidence game. In forging his rhetoric of deceit, he drew upon European and American traditions. A veracious history of comic lying encompassing humanistic, utilitarian, and amiable perspectives supplies that context.

A Veracious History of Lying

Humanists: Simulation and Dissimulation

Ever since Moses in one of his pricklier moments proclaimed, "Thou shalt not bear false witness," lying has suffered a low reputation. Even the less proscriptive skeptics of the Renaissance share in the disdain for what Montaigne called "an accursed vice."[1] In his essay "On Liars," Montaigne distinguishes two kinds of lies: those that alter facts and those invented out of whole cloth. Later on, Bacon gave terms to these two: dissimulation and simulation. Both thinkers, despite their condemnation, helped to establish lying as an ontologically and psychologically relevant phenomenon.

Montaigne understood that both simulation and dissimulation were doomed to fail because of the structure of mind, in particular that simple human frailty, our memory. The point is not that the truth is easy to acquire, but that lies are hard to remember. In attempting to "alter" the truth, liars will find that "real facts having been the first to lodge in the memory" will inadvertently "dislodge the false version" that they are trying to perpetrate. The same holds for "complete inventions": No memory "could be strong enough to retain all the different shapes" of a pure fantasy or fabrication.[2] To succeed, a liar must not only *create* a new reality, but forever keep it in mind, where it must compete with more veracious facts. Eventually, all lies fail because they do not by nature obtain in mind; they slip away. Asserting the contrapositive of Quintillian's view that a good liar must have a good memory,[3] Montaigne risibly proclaims himself a bad liar because he has such a bad memory.

Eventually, Montaigne came to doubt the notion of a preexistent Truth. There is not "so much misery in us," he said hauntingly, "as emptiness,"[4] and yet he never lost his savor for truth. In his library, he determined that truth was revealed through the self-conscious workings of his mind. However, what Montaigne discovers in "On Liars" is that the least operative brain is the truest. By the same token, Montaigne's poor memory is a source of pleasure, for his inability to retain information makes rereading both necessary and a happy experience of continual rediscovery. The mind is a process, not a storage bin. It flows in unpredictable streams, and in a world defined by intellection the flow of consciousness is more vital than that exercise of memory which freezes thinking into thought. The problem with mendacity is that it dams mental flow by obliging it to adhere to false memories. Lying is wrong not because it varies from truth but because it impedes the natural course of consciousness.

Montaigne does not entertain any Romantic notion that lying may be an act of original creation serving a positive moral function; but his retreat from civil life and his use of the writing experience to "essay" both himself and apparent truths—in short, his reclusive, whimsical, antiquarian, self-conscious, always restrained rhetorical stance—identify him as a grandfather of the amiable humorists. Like them, he favored Democritus, the laughing philosopher, over the weeping Heraclitus, and the wise-guy Diogenes over the misanthropic Timon. Similarly, his assessment of lying as an experiential fact is rooted in a fundamental ontological crisis, the disjuncture between self and truth. An image borrowed from Montaigne in Bacon's discussion "Of Truth" reveals the problem:

> [N]o pleasure is comparable to the standing upon the vantage ground of truth (a hill not to be commanded, and where the air is always clear and serene), and to see the errors, and wanderings, and mists, and tempests in the vale below.[5]

Bacon confidently distinguishes high truth from low error, but despite the authoritarian, indeed military, pose, an ambivalence lurks in his parenthesis.

As a "hill not to be commanded," truth cannot be overthrown, but neither is it a position that is ever fully willed or won; we battle on the slopes of truth only aspiring for, never gaining, the clarity and serenity of such a coign of "vantage." Man's fate is to dwell "in the vale below," to struggle in this world of lies toward truth. Since the Platonic truth cannot be "commanded," it is no longer enough to "know thyself," for this assumes our ability to connect with unattainable reality. Instead, one can only know the *relation* between self and ideal. Survival demands our coming to terms with the illusory multiplicity of experience found in human depths, not on airy mountain heights; it requires an awareness of how lies work.

The key to metaphysical authenticity lies in the association of self with a "questioning" for truth that is flexible, not rigid, one that does not insist upon preexistent certitude on high but rather requires a continual inspection of the picturesque "vale" of "mists and tempests" below. Of course, the immediate ethical problems that arise out of the perpetual questioning are how to coordinate the flow of one's consciousness with the ineffable tides of the world of illusion, how to prevent one's vital skepticism from degenerating into mordant cynicism, and how to reestablish stability and repose without engaging in or falling prey to lies.

Montaigne proposes an aesthetic solution to this ethical dilemma that prefigures Melville's search for repose: His solution is to write. He "essays" an idea on paper, and in doing so "tries out" himself. According to Jean Starobinski, Montaigne's doctrine of *"Que sçais-je?"* led to a redefinition not merely of self but of the very process of self-identification. No longer able to achieve the psychic "repose so sincerely desired" that derives from a philosophical apprehension of an underlying personal reality, Montaigne turned to the author's option of "registering" on paper "the monsters" within him. No longer is truth an objective "vantage ground" high above the vale of error; no longer may the observer separate himself from that which is observed. In Montaigne's essays, Observer and Observed become one; the individual is both the staged "spectacle" of the unfolding consciousness and the audience; he is "a theater in his own right."[6]

Despite the fact that this solipsistic conception of identity necessarily precludes achieving the repose of "an objective moral stability," Starobinski argues that in articulating the "quest for the causes of [that] failure, for the reasons that make repose impossible," the artist in fact achieves a different order of repose. The theater of the self (the observation of our creative thought processes) can be recorded in writing, and "paradoxically, order, stability, and integrity can be the products of self-directed activity."[7] As with the Romantic Ironist, Montaigne's notion of self is defined not in absolute terms but in *relation* to a mutable, illusory world. "The Book," i.e., our writing out or essaying of that relation, is not merely an expression of self but a version of the processes of selfhood itself. Similarly, the reader's experience, the rich unfolding of mind as it engages the world of lies, affords the author's seemingly idle solipsism a significant moral dimension. Montaigne's essays become unified encapsulizations of an unstable reality, and by dint of that containment they approach a tenser sense of intellectual repose. Montaigne wrote not to crystallize truth into precepts but to ramble in "the vale of mists, and tempests" of thinking. Thus he performed the troublesome task in a voice as stable, gentle, and "moral" as a genialist. Although Montaigne's self-exposure inspired later amiable humorists, they rarely matched his metaphysical insight. But Melville, who had read Montaigne repeatedly, who even composed a ditty on the essayist, and whose Ishmael is a Montaignean "essayer," was able to reestablish an accommodation between the amiable voice and Montaigne's sharper vision. After *Moby-Dick,* his literary confidence games expanded the "theater of the self" to engage readers more immediately in the midst of doubt.

Generally more accepting of mendacity than Montaigne, Francis Bacon extended Renaissance notions of lying toward modern utilitarianism. He allowed that the "mixture of a lie" into social intercourse "doth ever add pleasure," and that an occasional lie, rather than impeding consciousness, smooths its flow. He writes:

> Doth any man doubt that, if there were taken out of men's minds vain opinions, flattering hopes, false valuations, imaginations as one would, and the like, but it would leave the minds of a number of men poor shrunken things, full of melancholy and indisposition and unpleasing to themselves.[8]

We are shrunken things without our "imaginations," but in confusing "false valuations" with true, we run the risk of self-delusion,[9] for "It is not the lie that passeth through the mind, but the lie that sinketh and settleth in it, that doth the hurt." Rather than happily fall out of memory, Bacon's lie, through an unavoidable pleasure principle, displaces reality and deludes us. The focus of his metaphor of consciousness is not so much a flowing river as the riverbed that contains the flow.

What impedes the honest currents of thought is the silt of falsehoods that "sink and settle" beneath awareness.

Bacon's assessment of the psychological need to lie is at the root of his broader social utilitarianism. By distinguishing "simulation" (saying what is not) from "dissimulation" (concealing what is), he separates pernicious self-delusions from "every day" lies that facilitate life. Like Montaigne's notion of complete invention, the former lie blasphemously attempts to create knowledge out of nothing. Dissimulation, however, actually implies a sharper awareness of reality than that of the truth-teller. To misdirect others, the dissimulator must have a certain relation to truth. We can mask a truth only if we possess it; thus, a dissimulation is an act of conscious misdirection that necessarily affirms the existence of truth. In a sense, the dissimulator's cunning implies as much self-awareness as malice. He knows the truth he wishes to avoid, whereas the liar who simulates may not know truth at all.

Despite a growing leniency toward mendacity in England, the refusal to give any quarter even to comic lying persisted.[10] In America, however, a good liar could achieve legendary status, and the confidence man could become the nation's "covert hero."[11] But whether in England or America, the dissembling author had to face rhetorical problems far more intriguing than any ethical qualms, for when a lie, even a benevolent one, is exposed as mere lie, the authorial reliability it attempts to secure is destroyed. As Bacon finally notes, a lie is like an alloy in gold, it "may make the metal work the better, but it embaseth it."[12] In the long run, it will not work.

The Utility of Mendacity: Lord Chesterfield and Mr. Barnum

It is the mighty doctrine of "the long run" and an insipid faith in the universal currency of honor that earmark the utilitarian dismissal of lying in eighteenth-century thought and in particular the popular writings of Lord Chesterfield. Taking his cue from Bacon, Chesterfield advised his son that if a social dilemma forces one to some deceptive reaction, the lesser evil is to dissimulate rather than simulate— "concealing the truth, upon proper occasions, is as prudent and innocent as telling a lie, upon any occasion, is infamous and foolish."[13] The sin of lying is in the affront not to God but to one's reputation. "If, in negotiations, you are looked upon as a liar, and a trickster, no confidence will be placed in you." As another high-minded utilitarian put it, truth is "not only our duty, but our interest."[14] It is the fuel of social intercourse. Lying, while it may achieve short-run success, invariably subverts confidence and therefore accrues no long-range benefit.

Chesterfield fully disdained the simulator:

> These people deal in the marvelous; they have seen some things that never existed; they have seen other things which they never really saw, though they did exist, only because they were thought worth seeing. . . . They have done feats themselves, unattempted, or at least unperformed by others. They are always the heroes of their own fables; and think that they gain consideration, or at least present attention, by it. Whereas, in truth, all they get is ridicule and contempt, not without a good

degree of distrust; for one must naturally conclude, that he who will tell any lie from idle vanity, will not scruple telling a greater for interest.[15]

These marvelous liars, "heroes of their own fables," prefigure the boastful tall-talking frontier liar we shall soon meet in a more favorable light. But for Chesterfield there is no humor here; not only do they believe their own lies but they falsely assume their imaginative flights will delight or convince others. Chesterfield's distaste is so strong that he advises his son to avoid the very chance of even appearing to be one, even if that means having to lie. Better to dissimulate than to be taken for a simulator: "Had I really seen anything so very extraordinary as to be almost incredible, I would keep it to myself, rather than, by telling it, give anyone . . . room to doubt for one minute of my veracity." Reputation must be (to recall Shaftesbury) "politely managed," and like any fiction it depends upon considerations of probability and necessity. Society must be convinced of one's sincerity, and the telling of marvels, no matter how true, will damage one's reliability. The courtier manages what is believable; he makes the truth appear truthful. Thus dissimulation in the furtherance of truth is not only justifiable but required.

This is true on the frontier as well as at court. But the American experience also demanded a respect for simulation, pure and simple. The flaw in Chesterfield's utilitarian dismissal of simulation is that it places too much faith in the idea that "the long run" is accessible, that we all have time for truth to rise above falsehood. But with the economic flush times and busts in Jacksonian America, there is no long run; there is only the short dash, usually away from suspicious-sounding owl hoots or specious bank notes. Or more practically speaking, there is only the short dance "for the time being" with potential liars. In the Wilderness, where survival means anticipating the impossible, reputations were built upon the display of one's imaginative ability to play with truth and "play along" with other people's lies. Comic lying was an education. One learns to identify, even perform, lies, not to discern good from evil but to exercise the mind for physical, economic, and psychological survival. Early Americans delighted in teasing each other with tales of superdemons, superbears, and supermen. They even sent the likes of Davy Crocket (hero of his own fables) to Congress. Chesterfield could offer no real utilitarian restraints on this brand of deception. Nor could his paternal advice prepare one for the Big Lies of charismatic Ahabs. "Playing along" with a lie was America's version of Montaigne's essaying of self.

Of course, America outwardly condemned the tall talk that began to seep into literature and the stage. And as native humorists took more to the longbow, the nation's religionists and utilitarians attempted to bring the American experience in line with Chesterfield by amending his text to meet the needs of the democratic gentleman. American editions of Chesterfield enjoyed wide circulation throughout the early days of the republic. Thomas Dobson's Philadelphia edition (1789) supplied Americans with extracts from the 1774 original, and the Reverend John Trusler's 1809 version, aimed at Rip's "rising generation," is a virtual reprint of Dobson.[16] But soon enough Americans were beginning to adapt Chesterfieldian manners to particular national needs. John Grigg's *The American Chesterfield* (1827) provides significant "alterations and additions" to Dobson's initial American edition, especially "suited to the Youth of the United States."[17]

Grigg worries about a new form of mendacity peculiar to the democracy: "Party-lying" is most insidious because distorting truth for the sake of one's political faction converts otherwise honorable gentlemen into mere politicos; it can "seduce even the lover of truth."[18] But his most telling "alteration" is his recasting of Chesterfield's "marvelous lie," renamed the "Narrative or historical lie." Grigg's rustic revision suggests that his admonitions were directed against the now highly visible comic liar, the gamecock woodsman.

> He is always the hero of his own *romances;* he has been in *dangers,* from which *nobody but himself ever escaped;* he has seen with his own eyes whatever other people have heard or read of; he has had *more bonnes fortunes than ever he knew women;* and has *ridden more miles post,* in one day, than ever courier went in two. He is soon discovered and is soon the object of universal contempt and ridicule." [13; my italics]

Grigg substitutes "romance" for Chesterfield's "fable" and the more melodramatic "escaped dangers" for "feats unattempted by others." Unlike Chesterfield's marvelous liar, this American is an adventurer, horseman, and womanizer. He sounds more like lusty Mike Fink than Chesterfield's buffoon, but Grigg insists, despite the popularity of the these "liars" in books, on stage, and even in Washington, that the consequence of their exaggerations is "contempt and ridicule." He was bending Chesterfield to straighten frontier America. He was also whistling against the wind, for the American love of tall talk and hoax was becoming pandemic.

By 1837 the Yankee showman Phineas T. Barnum could exhibit the decrepit ex-slave Joice Heth as the 167-year-old nursemaid of George Washington, and by dint of such audacity gain the attention, dollars, and even respect of the populace. What Grigg condemned as "Narrative or historical" lying could have utility; it could entertain and teach. By 1841 Barnum's American Museum was a center for learning, if you will, based not on the venerable artifacts of history, art, and science, but on marvels, lies, and performances. The attraction was in knowing that one would be humbugged; the learning came out of the challenge to discern true marvels from buncombe. As Neil Harris notes, when receipts from his Heth exhibit began to fall off, Barnum wrote (anonymously) to the papers that the slave was a fake. Crowds returned to see how they had been snookered.[19] Harris links the American love of humbug to the frontier experience: The hoax or practical joke is "a way of reducing a hostile and threatening environment to human scale by manipulating its elements and so demonstrating control over them" (Harris, 71–72). The successful comic lie delights because it provides the otherwise disadvantaged liar a certain psychological dominance. Such lying even delights the victims of a hoax, for the "opportunity to debate the *issue* of falsity, to discover how deception had been practiced, was even more exciting than the discovery of fraud itself" (77). The underlying aesthetic principle is that in an emergent culture, where the individual's fate is wedged between the often inexplicable vagaries of frontier, economy, and faction, certain performed lies sharpen our awareness of the way lies work without physically jeopardizing either liar or victim.

What distinguishes the American love of humbug from earlier attitudes toward lying is that simulation claimed moral validity beyond that of dissimulation. Whereas Montaigne, Bacon, and Chesterfield denigrated the former and tentatively allowed the latter; nineteenth-century Americans willingly embraced the pleasures of both. Even British culture, dubious at first (although Victoria was a fan from the start), drew closer to Barnum. The writer for *Hogg's Instructor* and *Titan* who fancied himself an *"habitué"* of Bacon's "serene summit" of truth calls the "religio-mania" of modern spiritualism (e.g. Mormonism) a humbug and takes special umbrage at Barnum's effrontery in suggesting that a "true history of Humbug" in every "calling and profession" would "startle as well as enlighten the community."[20] The writer is appalled that this man of "overreaching avarice and mammonism" would presume to instruct any community but allows that, given the times, Barnum is ("God forbid!") a suitable "coming man" for the coming age.[21] A *Fraser's* "Essay on Humbug. By a Manchester Man" is even more tolerant: "Humbug is the offspring of civilization and refinement"; it is a "species of deceit, giving pleasure"[22] (or, to quote Hudibras, "the pleasure is as great / Of being cheated as to cheat"), but it condemns Barnum's "exulting confessions" and glorification of mendacity, for they only encourage "a system of delusion" that exhausts faith for profit. And yet the writer concludes that the "judicious appliance of a little humbug" benefits all sectors of life: politics, religion, medicine, and commerce.

British critics did not revile Barnum's lies (the hoaxes, wooly horses, midgets, and various *lusus naturae*) so much as his crowing about them. Indeed, their leniency mirrors the beliefs of Britain's Romantics, who in contrast to Chesterfield found in lying a confirmation of our humanity. As Hazlitt noted, lying "shews spirit and invention; and the more incredible the effrontery, the greater the joke."[23]

The Utility of Mendacity: The Amiable View

A case in point is Samuel Laman Blanchard (1804–45). An actor, poet, and essayist, this genial man of letters modeled his style on Elia and enjoyed the praise and friendship of Dickens, Hunt, and Browning. He begins his good-natured essay on "Every-Day Lying" with the assumption that if "every deviation from truth's straight line constitutes a falsehood, then the human tongue teems with lies. . . . Lying is our language. . . . We write lies, speak lies, think lies, and dream lies."[24] White lies are told out of "pure courtesy," a kind of social reflex which far from being a "hollow" gesture reveals in its spontaneous gratuity "a deeper philanthropic, a sympathetic principle" (Blanchard, 265). Lying based upon this "habit of civility" (266) confirms the unself-conscious benevolence of our geniality. We lie "in good fellowship, in gaiety of heart, and a desire to keep the world alive and merry." After all, Blanchard observes a bit too glibly, the word "lie" constitutes three-fourths of the word "live."

But this discussion of everyday lying is a prelude to the tall tale of Dick Whisk, a merry-making liar who like the American yarn spinner Ovid Bolus seems constitutionally incapable of telling the truth. He lies spontaneously, inveterately, and in spite of himself. He is a lovable, amiable simulator, a character out of Sterne or Dickens, and a precursor of Huck Finn. "Dick's lies were the perfection of lies"—not "tremendous" but "good *level lying*" in the "Every-Day style." However, he is known to tell a *tall* tale or two, and Blanchard gives us one such "Holiday lie." While swimming, Dick is startled by a noise from behind and without looking back sets out to sea. He becomes increasingly alarmed by "the splashing Mystery" upon "the great deep." Is it a shark, a steamer, a seventy-four, Old Neptune, a young Whale? Dick exhausts himself and, finally resigned to his end, turns to meet the "horrible destiny" hotly pursuing him. It is Lord Byron.

Blanchard's stretcher shares a good deal with the American tall tale: the satanic pursuit, mysticism, anticlimax, and even a whale, and yet it is too neatly contained within the framing discussion of rational, everyday lying. We are always reminded that Dick is harmless, and we know that the splashing mystery of the deep will be a humbug. Blanchard teaches us *degrees* of lying and never surrenders his moral authority to the liar. Nor does he encourage the audience to play along with Dick's lie. In fact, his entire purpose seems to be a genial jab at high-flown Romanticism and Blanchard's deceased friend Byron; the lie merely reaffirms rational and moral boundaries.

A more subversive British stretcher can be found in a facetious "Prospectus" for a course of lectures on "The Philosophy of Humbug" appearing in *Bentley's*. The amusing rant by the late Professor Wolfgang von Bibundtucker outlines the universality of humbug in love, politics, flattery, and poetry. We learn that "Deceit is the strong but subtle chain which runs through all the members of a society and links them together; trick or be tricked is the alternative."[25] With a manic mixture of contempt and admiration, the Professor rings changes on a central thesis: "Humbug is knowledge, and knowledge is Humbug." Included here are "the deep feeling, the exquisite pathos, the sublimity, and fanciful touches of poetry. All Humbug, I assure you" (602). Bibundtucker's worry is that lying has fallen into disrepute because it is practiced so poorly; we need better liars, hence better instruction, hence his course of lectures. And his lecture ends with a Carlylean punch: "What a profound Humbug is a patriot, and a physician, and a lawyer, and *a lecturer!*" Bibundtucker, too, is humbug. Thus, his argument is simultaneously affirmed and negated. We are cheated but finally reminded that the professor has only done what he said we all must do, "trick or be tricked."

As comic liars, Whisk and Bibundtucker define the limits of amiable lying. Blanchard's safer lie is tedious for its conservative whimsy. Read allegorically, Dick Whisk is steady John Bull escaping the hocus-pocus of German mysticism; the great depths are just a joke; the sea is water plus salt. But Bibundtucker is German mysticism set free; he is the Romantic *eiron* who invites us into his lair of illusion, even as he warns us of his deceptions. Bibundtucker dismantles the traditional structures of academe and belief that frame his message and knavishly refuses to supply a reliable alternative. What sets him apart from America's frontier liars is the fact that his rant is more of a pastiche of Carlyle than an exercise in imaginative doubt; it is finally an attack on poetic belief, not a playing within it.

George Henry Lewes, companion of George Eliot and the writer for *Colburn's New Monthly Magazine* who signed himself with the Greek letter Mu, provides the most rigorous argument for the Romantic acceptance of lying than either Blanchard or Bibundtucker. In his essay "On the Physiology of Lying," he revises Montaigne and accords equal status to both imagination and memory. We are just as disposed to create facts, he notes, as we are to remember them. On the one hand, memory "revives our sensations in the natural order of their natural occurrence"; whereas imagination "revives our sensations in an order of its own."[26] Thus one faculty brings us in contact with nature; the other, art. We are liars because we imagine, not because we sin.

Experience proves the universal utility of mendacity: Animals deceive by their colorings and evasive behaviors; children lie without hesitation (it is "a spontaneous result of the play of organization"); men and women are endowed with tongues and faces whose sole functions are to fabricate "signs" meant to "impel" others "to trust" ("Physiology," 56–58). Thus, what we perceive to be hypocrisy is, in fact, man's instinctive "play-acting." Poetry, the ultimate system of signs and play-acting, is "expressly devoted to the service of falsehood," not in its mere exaggerations but "by the habitual subordination of reason to imagination" (61). Because "poets are the great professional supporters of every profitable humbug which it is the interest of the masses to maintain," they are to be trusted, cautiously, as one would any liar. However, "their mendacity" has "utility," Lewes wrote, in that poetry's pleasurable falsehoods circumvent what would be for mankind a sterile fixation on death.

Lewes saw that those who assume our only obligation is to truth are not educated to the workings of mind and society; they are too easily impressed by the shams of Chesterfieldian "respectability." Laboring under the false belief in "the truth, whole truth, and nothing but," they are too quickly embittered when Death, "the one great truth of existence," dissolves their "one-sided view" ("Physiology," 61–62). We lie instinctively to damper the reality of death; without the "multitude of false views that we steadfastly take of human nature," suicide would be "epidemic." Our best recourse is to acknowledge our need to lie, and to blend "Truth and falsehood" in our lives consciously, benignly, and without delusion. The two must "continue to jog on together like light and shade; and each will be so tempered by the other, to the end of time, as to let man live through his generation quietly enough, and find his account in the natural balance of the two" (62). Lewes finds in our lies a picturesque sensibility, a Carlylean tempering of fact and imagination, a reposeful union of "light and shade." Lewes's "physiological" position articulates the full potential of amiable humor to embrace a rhetoric of deceit, but it was America's frontier experience that gave form to that view.

The End of Lying: Amiable Confidence Men

As one American, D. McCauley, put it in an essay entitled "Humbugiana," "*incredulity* is the foundation of all wisdom."[27] To survive, Americans must learn to doubt; they must develop what he called "rational belief" through periodic investigations into the faulty mechanisms of human gullibility. Here, "duplicity, deception, fanaticism, and bigotry" would be exposed.

> We would find error borrowing something of truth, in order to make her pass off
> more readily; we would discover the subtlety of grand deceivers, and impostors,

grafting their greatest errors on some well known palpable truth, and we might learn from the investigation, that all men entertain and are influenced by opinions to a much greater extent than persons unacquainted with self-examination are aware, and we might perceive the necessity of rigidly examining every opinion or sentiment before it is adopted as a principle from which any conclusion is to be drawn.   [444]

McCauley's notion of ''rational belief'' is the kind of critical thinking one hopes to instill in all learners: a suspicion of fanaticism, an ability to distinguish intermingled fact and error, and an insistence upon ''self-examination.'' The implication here is that we can never debug the world's humbugs, but we can learn how they work by playing rationally with lies. In effect, we become confidence men.

''The confidence man'' is an American locution for an ancient profession. The term was first used in 1849 to describe a William Thompson (a.k.a. Samuel Willis), who would ask strangers if they had ''confidence in me to trust me with your watch until to-morrow.''[28] Assuming the genteel Thompson to be an unrecollected business acquaintance, the compliant victim surrendered his watch. Mr. Thompson's ''rig'' was cut short when the Manhattan judiciary insisted upon his early retirement upstate. Before there was Thompson, there was ''Jeremy Diddler,'' a swindler in the early American stage production ''Raising the Wind'' (1803), and infinitely before him there were innumerable variations of the ''trickster,'' a comic type indigenous to nearly all cultures, especially primitive, emergent, or repressive societies.[29] American Indians have the larcenous Coyote; Eastern Indians have the monkey; black slaves invented Br'er Rabbit. The Italians gave us Arlecchino; the British, Punch; the French, Tartuffe. America's traditional trio—frontiersman, Yankee Peddler, and black minstrel—share one common feature: They, too, are tricksters.

But for a trickster to be a confidence man, his game must build in some way upon the victim's willingness to believe and be duped. In a confidence game, the con man merely provides the opportunity and mechanisms for larceny; the victim, for whatever benevolent or self-serving reason, sets it in motion. Not only is there a sucker born every minute, but the sucker is his own midwife. He is forever convinced that the scam before him is a swindle of someone else. If trickster legends validate the cleverness amid adversity of the heroic knave, the literary confidence game focuses more upon the interaction of victim and knave, and necessarily upon the fatal human instinct for belief. Indeed, the most satisfying version of any confidence game is the conning of the con man or duping of the knave, for to beat the liar at his own game is to claim a moral victory of imagination over doubt and self-delusion. But it also entails the incorporation of the knave's identity into our own, presumably amiable, nature. In conning the con man, we become a con man ourselves; hence, it is a version of playing along.

The emergence of the confidence man captivated Melville's New York. The original New York *Herald* article reporting Thompson's apprehension was widely reprinted, and a comic interlude called ''The Confidence Man'' (probably by John Brougham) was staged. The new name for an old figure allowed Americans a means to articulate a fuller range of problems related to democracy, self, and belief. Two divergent commentaries—one satiric, the other more amiable—attest to the facility with which social critics adopted the confidence man as a timely metaphor.

"The Confidence Man on a Large Scale" argues bitterly against the fact that a petty thief like Thompson is jailed while the nation's real confidence men, our respected capitalists, are not only free but honored. The rogue Thompson "is collared by the police. [But financiers] are cherished by society. . . . He is a mean, beggarly, timid, narrow-minded wretch. . . . They are respectable, princely, bold, high-soaring 'operators,' who are to be satisfied only with the plunder of the whole community."[30] This "masterly, trenchant satire" drew the praise of Lewis Gaylord Clark in his *Knickerbocker* magazine, but not before his rival, Evert Duyckinck, reprinted in *Literary World* a far more amiable perspective, which had first appeared anonymously in the *Merchants' Ledger*. Here, Thompson's ability to swindle anyone in this age of skeptics actually "speaks well for human nature." Or so the writer for the *Ledger*, echoing Blanchard and Lewes, argued:

> The man who is *always* on his guard, *always* proof against appeal, who cannot be beguiled into the weakness of pity by *any* story—is far gone, in our opinion, toward being himself a hardened villain. He may steer clear of petty larceny and open swindling—but mark that man well in his intercourse with his fellows—they have no confidence in him, as he has none in them. He lives coldly among his people— he walks an iceberg in the marts of trade and social life—and when he dies, may Heaven have that confidence in him which he had not in his fellow mortals.[31]

Pairing the *Knickerbocker* and Young America responses to the confidence man reveals the dilemma of credulity. On the one hand, our democracy encourages the plunder of its own community, and until such hypocrisy is eradicated, the people are best advised to be less gullible. But on the other hand, our ability to believe (even in scoundrels) makes the democracy work. The special kind of comic liar known as "the confidence man" sharpened the nation's sense of culture and self; his entry into the framed tall tale (and Melville's art) was inevitable.

The Lie of Our Land: Forms of Comic Lying

The genres of comic deceit reflect increasingly self-conscious phases of American culture. *Tall talk* is a spontaneous and ritualistic verbal contest between individual combatants on the frontier. The *tall tale* may be an anecdotal rendering of tall talk exaggeration or the literary framing of "barbaric" tall talk by a gentleman narrator; in either case, it is essentially a means of showcasing, criticizing, or controlling America's emergent frontier identity.[32] The third phase, *unreliable narrative,* is by no means an exclusively American invention, but when a tall tale becomes a literary confidence game or hoax designed to victimize the reader, that betrayal, typical of all unreliable fictions, takes on a particularly American flavor.

Tall Talk and Tall Tale: Learning to Play Along

Tall talk is that form of frontier boasting that operates on its own peculiar aesthetics of fat horses and ugly dogs; its own Hobbesian ethics of force, fire, and aqua-fortis; its own psychology of linguistic dominance and poetics of neologism (*vide* "teetotacious exfluncation''); and even its own mathematics, with fractions larger than wholes. Tall talk is invariably associated with America's gamecock woodsman, whose dress is as outrageous as his or her (let's not forget Sal Fink) language. The folklorist Richard Dorson has traced the character type back to such Indian gadabouts as Sam Hyde (the ''Münchhausen of the red man''), who claimed to have killed a whale by plugging its spout hole,[33] and we can add examples of boastful sagamores as early as 1634 in William Wood's pamphlet *New England's Prospect,* in which one brave claims he can ''blow down castles with his breath and conquer kingdoms with his conceit.''[34] But Baron von Münchhausen would remind us that Americans were not the only braggarts, and Walter Blair argues that the character is rooted in the *Miles Gloriosus* of Plautus, a playwright who was not an American but who had a good sense of humor anyway.[35]

When tall talk is showcased in type and exhibited as malarkey, it becomes a tall tale, and the question of the framer's intentionality comes immediately to the fore. Complex versions of the tall tale stretch back to early colonial anecdotes intended for Puritan and European ears. Thomas Morton may have been the first British visitor to New England shores to use excessive language as a ploy to entice his Puritan adversaries toward more flexible modes of thought. A university scalawag, he tacked an obscure, densely allusive and pagan poem on his maypole at Merry-Mount to baffle William Bradford and his pious crowd. It may have been America's first hoax. In interpreting his own poem, Morton later argued in *New English Canaan* that to understand poetry, one must be a Proteus, a godlike shape-shifter, which his former Puritan neighbors surely were not. But the deeper effect of his literary game is that such verbal shape-shifting is also fitting mental preparation for surviving the protean wiles of the Wilderness. Morton's cryptic poem was a hoax, a tall tale intended to tease and to educate no-nonsense Pilgrims. Bradford's response was a musket and an invitation to leave. Other colonial simulators were more successful.

An Englishman and an Indian went afowling one fair morning in the New England woods, but they were overtaken by an ice-storm at noon, and before dusk they froze to death. Their rigid corpses were found the next day. ''The Indian, having gained three flight-shots more of his journey homeward [than the Englishman], was found reared up against a tree with his aquavitae bottle at his head.''[36]

This stretcher recorded by William Wood exhibits a classic rhetorical strategy. The anecdote (exquisitely economical in its lie work) begins with highly probable details (two hunters hunting, a storm, death; morning, noon, dusk), which lead us to the whopping lie of the Indian freeze-dried in his last act of taking a drink. The punch in the punch line is carefully reserved to the last three words—''at his head''— to make sure that the visual impact of the impossible event—a man freezing in the act of drinking—is delivered at the last possible syntactic opportunity. Upon reflection, the reader takes a more complicated attitude toward this simulation. At first the message seems to be that some adversities can be laughed at, but when the last words sink in, we realize that Wood is caricaturing the Indian. Further reflection leads to a retrospective deconstruction of all previous details. Discovering one impossible ''fact,'' we quickly assume that *all* the facts are lies: The Indian corpse was not found in that position, nor in advance of his mate; there may not have been any corpse at all; no storm, no hunters, no hunt. The reader, left to ponder the tale's veracity, is consequently launched into an experience of doubt, forced to mull over the hundred possible ways in which the anecdote may be false. With no hope of determining what really happened, we invariably turn to the issue of intention. Why is the author lying?

The insidious thing is that the tall tale deflects the very concern for intentionality that its impossibilities raise. Wood's wooden Indian argues that Indian stamina is great, that Indian drinking is inveterate, and that American winters are strong enough to freeze alcohol. And these stereotypes percolate in our consciousness even as Wood's lie work strongly suggests they are hogwash. Thus, just as we begin to doubt Wood's motives, we assure ourselves that there may be something true about this Indian and this climate after all. Why would Wood lie about something so trivial, especially if he is trying to entice new settlers? And yet we know he is lying and that he wants us to catch him in his lie. Rather than pit one verbal combatant against another, as in tall talk, the little tall tale mitigates fears by exaggerating them. Wood's primary intention is to minimize the threat of New England adversity. At the same time the lie initiates the victim into a unique culture of knowledge and belief. Lord Chesterfield's strategy would have been to omit any reference to the frozen sagamore for fear the marvel would engender disbelief; he would have dissimulated a more plausible tale. But Wood inflates improbable fact into impossible lie; he simulates reality through a marvelous invention. The winter wind has made drinking companions out of our stiff heroes. Once we laugh at being taken in, we find ourselves assuming that, despite death, the reality of America cannot be as foreboding as Wood's simulation would have it. Of course, Wood cannot be believed, but our perception of his *intention to make us believe* creates in the Old World reader a curious response: I see that you are exaggerating; I know that the Indian was not found this way. But your lie demonstrates significant values (companionship, courage, humor). Moreover, your easily detected lie suggests a desire to tease me out of anxiety. I am therefore lured by the sincerity of your comic spirit if not your veracity. The practical consequences of this lie are that the Old World "victim" may cross the Atlantic to meet that Indian himself. By mitigating New World perils through a playful exaggeration rather than a sober Chesterfieldian explanation (or, worse, silence), Wood's lie work generates in the reader a tentative search for a personally recoverable truth.

And here the playing along begins: Knowing Wood's lie to be a lie, we begin to speculate upon what the truth might in fact be. In this situation, the old saw that truth has one face but falsehood many is effectively inverted: What we know to be certain is the singular falseness of the lie; the truth, however, consists of a "boundless field" of possibilities.[37] For the skeptic denying preexistent Truth, the discovery of a lie is a vital moment of certainty: We may not know what is true, but we surely know what is not. If we are suitably enticed to play along in the game of discerning falsehoods, the tall tale will then initiate in us the impulse to explore, to enter into a culture where the only "true facts" are the imaginative approximations of reality we call lies. New England weather cannot freeze dry a pickled Indian, but it may get colder than we have ever known. It is a fact we can know only through personal experience, so we book passage.

What has only *resembled* knowledge (the lie itself) now becomes the locus of an inquiry that *engenders* a self-conscious process of knowing. That the lie falls into absurdity does not negate this learning process; in fact, it enhances the victim's ratiocination. For if we begin to envision a liar behind the lie, then the inquiry shifts from the simulation or knowledge created to the liar's creativity. The lie invites us to know the liar as well as ourselves, just as a poem invites us to know both poet and Self. Here is one who by nature of his figurative communication argues that we cannot know the world by Fahrenheit or Celsius but by imaginative comparison only; and to know this liar, we must do as he does: We too must lie; we must speculate, and in so doing we create knowledge and belief. By playing along with the liar, we enter a select culture in which the principal Truth is our mutual awareness that we all are *creating* impressions and reactions, the "facts" of our own sensibility. What we know is that we are lying, and in sharing that knowledge, we are united.

A culture may be divided into classes; the culture of the liar determines its classes in terms of knowledge, not possession. I might swallow Wood's lie. Or scoff at its false logic. But to respond in these ways is to be branded a boob or a cynic. I might, however, respond in kind and remark that an Indian so stiff might make a good crowbar. In which case, I enter a third class; I learn to play along by trying to best my opponent, perpetuating the game. I know he is lying; he knows I am lying; we share a certain truth: We are lying. Dupes, Cynics, and Players. In the culture of the liar, the cynic who exposes the lie as a lie is no better than the fool who believes. Both presume that Truth exists, somewhere if not here. On top of the heap, however, is the Player, whose principal truth is the recognition that our shared imaginative interplay is all of reality we can know, and that a culture fabricated out of our shared imaginations is more certain even than "things visible." This class we reserve for Melville.

With comic lying, epistemology begets sociology. One person lying creates knowledge; two people playing along constitute a culture. One's initiation into this ludic culture requires the ability to perceive a lie and the willingness to fabricate a response. It soon establishes a world divided between intellectual haves and have nots, in which the special knowledge that we know we are lying determines those who are "in" as opposed to the boobies and sourpusses who are "out." The individual who ventures out to find Wood's Indian will not find Truth, but he will learn the process that created the Indian. And she may "write home" with new lies that encourage still more to venture out and play along.[38] The ludic culture of comic lying is based on doubt, pure invention, figurative logic, and fantasy; while it subverts convention, it promotes a regenerative, imaginative, and (to use the Romantic term) "original" process of self-awareness and creativity.

As with epistemology and sociology, so too with rhetoric, for "playing along" with a lie is no different from the aesthetic experience we have in reading poetic creations. A poem is a challenge to perception, knowledge, and belief. If your love is like a red, red rose, we have no way of knowing the reality of that love; is it thorny? delicate? enfolded? ephemeral? With nothing more than the poem and our shared language, we attempt to grasp the poet's specific meaning but find that we can only determine the unsatisfying truth of "what it means to me," which is finally no determination at all. The poet has not been fully reached. We read more, playing along in our minds with possible interpretations, until such time as we begin to respond with poet'c inventions of our own, restatements of the poem in our own terms—*my* red depends upon a wagon; my rose is a rose is a rose. We give poem for poem, and we speak in lies such as these because reality cannot be defined (not love, not red, not rose); it can only be circumlocuted. But the circumlocution is an ethical event. We learn that to *read* poetry, one must become something of a poet. And, to return from a poetic to a ludic mode, one must be a liar to know lies.

Comic lying is an aesthetic experience that serves moral and social ends. If the frontier—with its undiscovered regions, unpredictable nature, treacherous Indians, bandits, demons, and politicians—is the fullest manifestation of the world of lies, then the inhabitant of this new world is best prepared by being exposed to vicarious forms of deception. He must not only learn to discern true and false signals; she must learn to create deceptions. But underlying the social ramifications is the liar's "*joie de vivre* [and] exhilarating sense of power" in the invention, perpetration, and development of his lies.[39] For Joseph Baldwin, lying was to be enjoyed in and of itself. His Ovid Bolus is a "natural liar" who "lie[s] with a relish . . . from the delight of invention and the charm of fictitious narrative." For him, lying is "a poetic property" requiring "workmanship" and "polish"; it is one of the "*Belles lettres*"; it is (and forgive Baldwin this pun) "lyric."[40] As Mody Boatright notes, "The frontiersman lied in order to satirize his betters; he lied to cure others of the swell head; he lied in order to initiate recruits to his way of life. He lied to amuse himself and his fellows. He was an artist and like all artists his chief reward was in the exercise of his art."[41]

Framing the Tall Tale: From Ideology to Unreliability

When the anecdotal tall tale becomes a literary genre, more specialized political and aesthetic concerns enter the picture. On the whole, the literary tall tale borrows its form from the convention of the framed narrative in which the author, usually an educated genialist, introduces us to the antics of the liar. The distance between narrator and clown accentuates the distinctions of class, morality, and language between aristocrat and democrat. But the whiggish narrator's willingness to co-opt the Jacksonian clown as an agent of his own satiric attacks on low life and, moreover, his admiration of the liar's expertise in putting down upstarts reveal an inherent ambivalence in the tall tale. Kenneth Lynn interprets this tension as evidence of a decay of whiggish confidence in the face of rising Jacksonianism. The lies of Johnson Hooper's Simon Suggs (who is always "shifty in a new country") work because society, as currently constituted in the great republic, is filled with fools who believe them.[42] Neil Schmitz examines the tension from the "fool's" perspective, arguing that the attraction to the liar reveals Jacksonian man's fear and anxiety in his attempted conquest of nature.[43] Most recently, William Lenz details the complexities of the Jacksonian reader's love–hate relationship with the comic liar as a response to the vicissitudes of "flush times." The reader is given a chance through the tall tale's con man hero to taste the forbidden fruit of immoral behavior while maintaining a modicum of moral elevation. That is, the reader may enjoy the lies, condone the perpetration of con games, and vent frustrations over a Hobbesian world of war, but will not degenerate into an actual confidence man. It is purgative playing along.[44]

Placed in its historical context, the framed tall tale voiced a wide range of political anxieties linked to the uncertain democracy. Early on, Augustus Longstreet showcased his comic liars with the repeated understanding that his "Georgia scenes" reflected the old days before civilization finally reached the South. Longstreet continually asserts the Southern gentleman's distance from such Jacksonian horrors as Ransey Sniffle to affirm his own Southern gentility. It was a message both Poe and Britain heard far more clearly than the Northern establishment that it was intended to convince. Thirty years later, during the Civil War, George Washington Harris reduced the role of his genial narrator in *Sut Lovingood's Yarns* to such a degree that an unmediated Sut became a vicious engine of anti-Lincoln propaganda. Because of its dual structure based on the genial gentleman framing the satiric trickster, the tall tale could, depending upon the humorist and the times, be used in America's comic debate to argue for either assimilation or division.

But the best of literary tall tales finally transcended politics, focusing more upon the interplay of the democracy's citizenry in general than upon the hollow battles of specific factions. In *Huckleberry Finn,* the transformation went deeper into the mind, so that Huck's gift for lying as much reveals his longing for family and human relation as they expose the viciousness of a society that allows his lies to work. America, not nature, is the world of lies, and America is a place one can flee. Huck's escape to the territories is a flight away from the exhaustion of the moral lying required for his social survival and personal integrity. But before *Huck Finn,* there were T. B. Thorpe and Edgar Allan Poe. Both practitioners of the tall tale and literary confidence game used their rhetorical forms to test their readers' social and metaphysical beliefs, and in particular the utility and reality of transcendentalism. Poe excelled in the transcendental hoax, a literary gambit that burlesques the reader's fatal tendency to believe in the attainment of ideality. In his hands, however, the hoax was designed not to transform readers but to humiliate them, to make them play the fool. Thorpe is more amiable in his rhetoric of deceit, placing readers in a moment of silence and expectancy poised between two irresolvable suspicions: Nature is a poetic mystery; Nature is a sham. Melville borrowed from both models of narrative unreliability in pursuing his deep thought of laughter.

5

E. A. Poe and T. B. Thorpe:
Two Models of Deceit

Poe's hoaxes avoid the traditional framed structure of the tall tale, and yet they develop the technique of the unreliable con man narrator to its fullest. As sharp, even bitter attacks upon the reader, they test our wits against the writer's, but somehow the cards are always unfairly stacked against us. Poe's famous tale of ratiocination, "The Murders in the Rue Morgue," does not induce a "perpetual interrogative" of self, nature, illusion, and truth, but suppresses the doubt it raises about irrationality and sex. And in "Ligeia" imagination and transcendence are the bait in an elaborate confidence game against readers. Finally, there is little playing along in Poe; his put-ons are putdowns. Thomas Bangs Thorpe's "Big Bear of Arkansas," however, employs silences (rather than stings) to lure us more effectively into a community of liars and players. This more genial hoax was the better model for containing factionalism and regionalism within a larger metaphysical vision. More than Poe, Thorpe effected a convincing reconciliation of humor and satire within America's comic debate. In Thorpe, we find America and repose; in Poe, the anxieties of self and ideality. Melville combined the best of both.

Poe's Humor

In discussing the curiously strained or "campy" humor of *The Confidence-Man*, Paul Brodtkorb has remarked that it is "the strain, not the humor . . . that amuses."[1] The same might be said of Poe. The writer is so obsessively rationalistic that one of his recurrent jokes is to have a character laugh thusly: Ha ha, He he, Hi hi, Ho ho, Hu hu.[2] Somehow, the sequencing of vowels tickled Poe. Few are amused by either the humor or the strain in this too-earnest jest. That Poe repeated it is an embarrassment critics simply ignore. For whatever reasons, Poe never felt obliged to develop a more amiable pose. He was a satirist specializing in burlesque, parody, and hoax. Humor was not his style, nor benevolence his manner; eccentric Shandyans and Knickerbockers do not populate his fiction. For him, obsession was not whim, and geniality had little to do with beauty. Consequently, Poe's barbed humor is driven by caricature rather than character, and committed to mechanistic wordplay (as with the laughing vowels) rather than heartfelt sentiment.

Certain tales seem to be nothing more than exercises in language, exploding common clichés by extending them to their absurd limits.[3] In this vein "A Loss of Breath" seems hardly worth the effort; its title does most the work. "Hans Pfaall," a space-travel hoax, is based on the premise that, if slowly exposed to ever thinning atmospheres, one can, like a live frog slowly adjusting to a heated skillet, adapt to the vacuum of space; the scientific mumbo-jumbo of this mechanical tall tale leaves us more exhausted—breathless again—than amused. The comic premise of "How to Write a Blackwood Article" is the absurdity of a narrator meticulously relating her own decapitation by the inexorable movement of a clock. This send-up of magazine literature is an early instance of the first-person corpse technique; few narrators have ever been so "detached" as the headless Psyche Zenobia.[4] In "The Devil in the Belfry," time tyrannizes a Dutch community until a devilish fiddler makes the belltower strike thirteen, and the town disintegrates. Music, spontaneity, and originality rout rationality.

Poe's wit is tailored to Bergson's theory that laughter derives from an "encrustation of the mechanical upon the living." But unlike the less pretentious Marx Brothers or more thoughtful Charlie Chaplin, for whom good-natured anarchy is a healthy balance to social anxiety, Poe does not furnish to readers any alternatives to the breathless, headless, heartless world he lampoons. He assaults the reader, rubbing our noses against the flimsy veneer of reason that barely conceals the more tempting irrationality of human obsessions: sex, death, and transcendence. Rather than offer any fusion of sensibilities, he taunts us by playing upon our limited vision. His laughter is an unrestrained release of pent-up emotional tension over an intractably hostile and psychically indeterminate universe; it has no hope of repose.

Although Poe began his career in a comic vein,[5] he had little success raising his humor above the contrivance of burlesque to Hawthorne's "religion of mirth." Curiously, though, his most intriguing use of comic strategies is actually found in his more serious Grotesques and Arabesques, such as "Ligeia." Indeed, G. R. Thompson demonstrates that we cannot separate Poe's Gothicism from his wit, that his grotesques *are* burlesques, and that if he was not an amiable humorist in the tradition of Sterne, Goldsmith, and Irving, he was nevertheless America's chief Romantic ironist. He found in the German school of Schlegel, Tieck, and Hoffmann "a literary technique of indirection involving a deceptive and even 'secret' irony clear only to the reader of superior perceptions. . . . He found a belief in the explorations of novelty through contrasts of incident, through fanciful and even fantastic metaphor, symbol, punning, and general wordplay. And he found, finally, a concept of a superior mind transcending the gloomy chaos of the world through artistic ironic detachment." Poe's laughter, then, is not so hysterical, but rather a means of expressing a "controlled, and therefore skeptical, philosophical despair."[6] Thompson is correct to the extent that comedy may have soothed Poe's inner conflicts, but the comic tales do not extend such reposeful reconciliations to readers; they often preclude our balance of transcendence and doubt.[7] Indeed, they are designed, like any hoax or tall tale, to induce as much anxiety as they may pretend to dispel. Poe may have borrowed his love of a hoax along with his sense of Romantic irony from Germany, but he probably honed his strategies of unreliability on America's tall tale. His highly favorable review of Longstreet's *Georgia Scenes* records his awareness of the tradition.[8] And in that tradition, he was, as Robert Regan puts it, "a literary con-artist."[9]

Poe's con artistry appears more clearly in what may be called his transcendental hoaxes, best exemplified by "The Murders in the Rue Morgue" and "Ligeia." Both tales are contrived, despite quite different narrative stances, to cheat the reader or, better, let readers fall prey to their own transcendental urges and cheat themselves.

The Ape of Unreason: "The Murders in the Rue Morgue"

Poe's best-known tale of ratiocination operates like a tall tale. At first glance tall tale and detective fiction are generic opposites, sharing little more than a fondness for first-person narration. The tall tale is comic; the detective story, serious. One dupes the reader; the other seeks truth. One creates chaos; the other finds order. One thrives on doubt; the other attempts to explain. Nevertheless, the two have a similar effect, for both require us to wander in a world of lies and to experience the unknown. In that process, both wean us from naïve expectations of conventional characterization, plot, or logic, and both thereby sharpen our wits. In tall tale and detective tale, the author challenges the reader to figure out what lies beneath the lies before the detective or liar unravels it for us. As Poe's narrator in "Rue Morgue" puts it, such analysis is "that moral activity which *disentangles*."[10] Readers of detective fiction must, like those of a tall tale, become disentanglers if they are to gain the full measure of the reading experience.

Who is our liar in "Rue Morgue," and how is his lie perpetrated? Dupin is unquestionably the agent of Poe's duplicity. His one-step-behind "Watson" of a narrator, by dint of his slow-wittedness, facilitates their scheme. We are the dupes. The lie is that Dupin's intuitive-analytical method does not work at all to solve the case, for Dupin conceals from us hard evidence, which if revealed to the reader *at the time that Dupin learns of it* would unmask the murderer without any imaginative deduction whatsoever. Moreover, the deep thought within Poe's lie work is Dupin's submerged identification with his Ape nemesis, a symbolic affinity for the irrational that further belies Dupin's controlled rationality. But what is Poe's intention in such a hoax? We begin to find an answer in Poe's other hoaxes.

In "The Philosophy of Composition" Poe's familiar argument is that a writer consciously designs a poem to create a particular effect. It is not spun out "by a species of fine frenzy—an ecstatic intuition," as transcendental poets would have us believe;[11] there is no mystery in its genesis. Its mechanisms are contrived; the causes of its effect are rational, hence knowable. The problem, however, is that Poe's venerable essay is itself a hoax. For while its thesis is plausible, its "proof" cannot hold. Poe's biggest stretcher is that his refrain "Nevermore" did not just spring to mind; he derived it *a priori* from a calculated assessment of the alleged universal sonority of certain consonant and vowel sounds. It grew logically out of an aesthetic requisition. In overstating the mechanistic composition of his poem, Poe almost forces us to become even more wedded to the belief he proposes to dispel, that poems are created through ecstatic inspiration rather than cool premeditation. But Poe's failure to convince seems willful, leaving readers enmeshed in a fruitlessly unstable relation to the act of creation. In overreaching for an absolute rationality that will belie Romantic intuition, he leaves us suspended between two mutually exclusive formulations with no mediation in sight. We may accept Poe's rejection of frenzied creation, but we cannot fully accept his mechanistic alternative. We finish "The Philosophy of Composition" with a pulling sensation in our leg. Ironically, the insincere and contrived essay is the best argument for its own thesis that art is a carefully concealed contrivance. What holds for the essay holds, too, for Poe's tales of ratiocination.

"Thou Art the Man," the last of Poe's tales of ratiocination, makes a point of its contrivances. So implausible are the detective's ploys in snaring a murderer—with a macabre sense of humor, several bits of elastic whalebone, some handy ventriloquism, and a great deal of luck, our hero makes a corpse sit up, talk, and terrify the murderer into a confession—that even halfwitted readers sense Poe's self-parody. Mysteries are contrivances. Poe was bemused by gullible readers who marvel at Dupin's intelligence. In a letter to Philip Cooke, he points out that that intelligence is utterly contrived:

> You are right about the hair-splitting of my French friend:—that is all done for effect. . . . people think [these tales] more ingenious than they are—on account of their method and *air* of method. In the 'Murders in the Rue Morgue,' for instance, where is the ingenuity of unravelling a web which you yourself (the author) have woven for the express purpose of unravelling. The reader is made to confound the ingenuity of the supposititious Dupin with that of the writer of the story. [Poe's *Letters,* 328]

Poe's letter makes explicit what the hoaxy "Philosophy of Composition" and "Thou Art the Man" imply. The detective's intelligence is a device that appears to unravel what the author has purposely raveled up. Dupin's "hair-splitting," his process of "disentangling," may be moral, but it is nevertheless a literary confidence game.

The "confounding" of the reader to accept "the *air* of method" in Dupin's unravelings as a *true* method is echoed in the tale itself when the nameless speaker observes that the analyst's "results brought about by the very soul and essence of method, have in truth, the whole *air of tuition*" (RM, p. 528, my italics). Notice that the turn of phrase takes on a certain duplicity when read in the context of Poe's letter. Dupin's power of analysis only *appears* to be an imaginative process; it possesses only the "air" of genius, just as his intelligence, Poe told Cooke, was only "supposititious." Poe's narrator understands Dupin better than we think, for there is less to Dupin than meets the eye. As we shall see, even his "airs" boil down to nothing more than "hairs."

Yes, Dupin is brilliant. One evening he quite casually reads the narrator's mind. This is not telepathy but the more impressive workings of an imaginative-analytic brain that performs acute observation, deduction, and association. Poe's narrator stands in awe, and, on cue, most readers accept the narrator's high regard of Dupin's ability. But Dupin's acumen is aided by much luck in the fifteen minutes in which he deduces the course of his friend's meditations, and his improbable "deductions" from paving stones to Epicurus to Orion to some Latin phrasing and finally to his friend's most recent thought are based on the feelings and experiences he has shared with his close associate of the night. In fact, there is nothing "intuitive" here. Dupin simply knows his friend well enough to assume his line of thinking. And, of course, just as imagination and rationality are themselves only "airs," this is only the *air* of tuition cooked up by Poe; the true efficacy of Dupin's intelligence remains to be seen at work not on a friend but on the Rue Morgue murderer: the ape. This, too, is carefully contrived, but Poe's hoax does more than expose the contrivance of a mystery. In a tactic now quite familiar to mystery readers, Poe plants a series of "sub-mysteries" that challenge readers to solve the crime by distinguishing real clues from red herrings. The reader expects that the author will deflect and misdirect our attention; it is part of the game. But in "Rue Morgue" Poe does more than misdirect; he actually has Dupin conceal the most damning clue. Readers do not stand a chance in solving the crime for themselves. Manipulated by our own reverence for Dupin's contrived intelligence, we fail to recognize the absurdity of the so-called rational world. We are duped.

Here are the details: Madame L'Espanaye and her daughter have been murdered. One has been decapitated and thrown out the window; the other strangled and stuffed feet first up the chimney. Their room shows signs of fierce struggle, and its doors and windows have been locked from the inside. Neighbors of various nationalities testify to hearing a foreign voice amid the women's shrieks. Slowly but surely Dupin unravels each puzzle. The "sub-mystery" of the neighbors' conflicting testimony is explained: What each assumed was a *foreign* language would have been recognized by one of the other foreign tenants; therefore, the unintelligible "voice" is not human. But Dupin keeps this deduction, and another crucial clue, to himself while he attends to the less important puzzle of the locked windows. Open at the time of the murderer's entrance, the window had fallen shut upon his exit and, Dupin shows us, locked itself by means of the fortuitous activation of a hidden spring in the window. But neither of these sub-mysteries is finally of any relevance, for while Poe has dragged us through the neighbors' tedious depositions and Dupin's slowly unfolding explanations, the detective has held in his hand all along crucial physical evidence of an ape attack, that is, a tuft of tawny Orang-Outang hair that, as Dupin tells us, but only at the end of the tale, he has (and note the word) "*disentangled* . . . from the rigidly clutched fingers of Madame L'Espanaye" (RM, 558).

From the beginning Dupin knows that the ape hair in the victim's clutch can only mean that the murderer is an ape. But Poe and Dupin conceal it, leading us to believe that by unraveling the sub-mysteries—what Poe in his letter to Cooke slyly calls "hair-splitting"—he had intuited a conclusion that any schoolboy could have derived from the *corpus delicti*. Does Dupin use imagination and analysis to find this evidence? No, he simply stumbles on it. Are readers allowed to stumble on this hair, too? Not by a long shot. Here is all that the narrator reports at the moment of Dupin's discovery: "I saw nothing beyond what had been stated in the [newspaper]. Dupin scrutinized everything—not excepting the bodies of the victims. We then went into the other rooms, and into the yard . . . " (RM, 546). Now, a mystery writer with perhaps only a vague sense of obligation for fair play would have at the very least shown Dupin inspecting the victim's *hands* or "extract from them a substance—I know not what—and put it in his waistcoat.'' But not Poe. His only hint that Dupin has stumbled on the hair and knows the plain truth is that he ''scrutinized everything—not excepting the bodies of the victims.'' The litotic ''not excepting'' draws attention, somewhat, to the moment of discovery, but evidently this was the only nudge Poe was willing to give the reader. He was not taking any chances that the reader might suspect Dupin of withholding evidence or Poe of perpetrating a hoax.[12]

There are, of course, games within this con game. The ''moral activity of *disentangling*'' discussed in Poe's letter to Cooke, for instance, is robbed of its authenticity when Dupin repeats the term to describe his surreptitious ''disentangling'' of the ape hair from the corpse's fingers. The physical act, as it calls attention to Dupin's deception, cheapens the purported moral activity. It is, as he admits to Cooke, just ''hair-splitting.'' And more: Dupin's duplicity becomes hypocritical when he begins to disparage the police. Not only does he puff his own ineffectual method of investigation (the intuitive), but he denigrates what is, in fact, the more legitimate one (the inductive). Poe associates this inductive approach with the ''cunning'' inspector Vidocq, who is simply too intense in his investigations. ''He impaired his vision by holding the object too close. He might see, perhaps, one or two points with unusual clearness, but in so doing he, necessarily, lost sight of the matter as a whole. Thus there is such a thing as being too profound'' (RM, 545). But the outrageous truth is that Dupin himself has solved the crime by this very same dull and workmanlike method; he has simply scrutinized Mme. L'Esplanaye's hands. Moreover, by removing the ape hair evidence from the scene of the crime himself, he denies Vidocq any chance of solving the crime. Vidocq's problem is not that he holds things too closely but that Dupin is hiding the facts from him. No doubt if Dupin had left the evidence in Madame L'Espanaye's clutches, the ''too profound'' Vidocq would have solved the case before Dupin could begin to concoct his climactic and flamboyant resolution scene. Given Dupin's subterfuge, we have little choice but to play the fool in Poe's confidence game.

Perhaps Poe does not intend a hoax; perhaps he has simply failed to conceal his contrivances adequately in the little matter of the ape hair. After all, the mere fact that a tale is contrived—and all of them are, Poe rightly claims—does not mean that the contriver intends to mislead the reader or make an issue out of the reader's too-easy acceptance of the tale's simulations. All tales of ratiocination must have some element of misdirection; they are tactical necessities for the creation of suspense. Perhaps Poe is not trying to dupe us.

But, in fact, the business of the ape hair is itself gratuitous; it is planted there, almost perversely, as the whopper in Poe's tall tale hoax that tests our acuity. If the point is to demonstrate what an analytic and imaginative mind can do, we would expect Dupin to be able to deduce his solution, just as he supposedly intuits his friend's train of thought, without such mundane evidence as a tuft of hair. In fact, by the time he discloses the hair, he has already revealed all the circumstantial evidence needed to conclude that the murderer was not human, that it is probably an athletic animal with hands, not paws, that it sounds *almost* human, that it is probably an ape. Dupin could have solved the case, and (all the more astonishingly) without the *prima facie* evidence of the hair. That he includes this unnecessary detail at all and conceals it from the reader argues all the more for a hoax. For while the ape hair superadds a confirmation of Dupin's deduction, it also clues us in to Dupin's cover-up, reminding us that astonishing "deductions" are easy when the detective knows the conclusion in advance. This is precisely what Poe's letter to Cooke is saying: Dupin's intelligence is "supposititious."

But why would Poe inflict this literary con game on his readers? For David Ketterer, deception is a necessity in Poe's aesthetic. Since space, time, and selfhood warp perception, Poe's strategy is to subject readers to "various technical and thematic deceptions of his own" to expose the falsity of "false reality." This is more effective than trying to reveal "the true."[13] In Ketterer's terms, the ape hair is one such "false reality." In the context of its tall tale strategy, the hair is one of many details that keep us from seeing the master contriver behind them all. The more jury-rigged Dupin's powers become, the less convinced we are of Poe's insistence upon the rationality of the imagination. As with "The Philosophy of Composition," we suspect Poe of concealing beneath his pretext of imaginative rationality a controverting truth, that the mind is finally irrational and destructive— like an ape. Let's penetrate Poe's lie work, then, to its symbolic core.

Beneath Poe's careful lines of reasoning, the reader must perform a deeper process of "disentangling." Dupin, we know, has a split personality, or, to use the narrator's term, there is "a double Dupin—the creative and resolvent" (RM, 533). Poe would have us see this doubleness as a positive combination of the imaginative and the analytic, and critics tend to agree that Dupin is "the prime example of [a] balance" of intuition and reason.[14] But in fact he is both unbalanced and unbalancing. To begin with, Dupin's "air" of method and tuition is a cover-up for his obsessive attraction to the irrational. The narrator allows that, living in darkness and wandering at night, both he and Dupin "should have been regarded as madmen" (RM, 532); moreover, Dupin possesses "an excited, or perhaps diseased intelligence" (RM, 533). A seemingly innocuous observation about an exceptionally gifted checker player tells even more. As an analyst, the player "throws himself into the spirit of his opponent, identifies himself therewith, and not infrequently sees thus, at a glance, the sole methods (sometimes indeed absurdly simple ones) by which he may seduce into error or hurry into miscalculation" (RM, 529). Just as player identifies with opponent, the detective Dupin must identify with the criminal he pursues. But the mind he must enter is that of an ape. Dupin would have us believe he performs this feat with detachment, but his "method" is all sham. For pages of unnecessary unfoldings, Dupin seduces us into error by concealing from us the talismanic ape hair, symbolic of the violent beast he must know in order to solve the case. He does not reveal the evidence when he discovers it but harbors it within, throwing himself into the spirit of the beast, and allowing us to think we are observing an imaginative genius when in fact that "diseased intelligence" roots itself more deeply in a fearsome identification with the irrational.

Our unassuming narrator plays a part in this literary confidence game, too. In a tall tale, as in any framed fiction, the reader is naturally dependent upon the narrator to report all we need to know in order to keep pace with the central trickster figure. Poe's particular tactic is to limit his speaker's intelligence, and in "Rue Morgue" our "pacer" narrator is a solid step behind Dupin. Or, at least, this is what we are meant to believe. When the two investigate the scene of the crime, Dupin finds the ape hair, but the narrator sees "nothing beyond what had been stated" in the daily news. Our impression is that the speaker believes only what he reads in the papers. But he is not so impercipient; in fact, his own "erroneous" deductions strike closer to home than Dupin's miraculously accurate resolution, and this is all the more remarkable considering that the narrator, too, has been denied access to the ape hair clue.

The narrator's conclusion is that the murderer is "a madman . . . some raving maniac escaped from a neighboring *Maison de Santé*" (RM, 558). Now, if the murderer is a madman and Dupin identifies with the murderer, then the logical extension of the narrator's conclusion is that Dupin, too, is mad, a "diseased intelligence," just as the narrator had surmised earlier on. Significantly, Dupin has just laid out the evidence (minus the hair) for us and the narrator in such a way as to make this false conclusion of an escaped madman inescapable. But once the notion of madness is breached, Dupin swiftly and ceremoniously whips out his ape hair. What should have been mentioned first (*prima facie*) is saved for last. It is as though Dupin were leading us to the issue of madness and even daring us to call him mad. But just before we do, he reveals the "truth": It is only an ape. This revelation is both anticlimactic and diversionary. The rational explanation, which is meant to astound us (and it does), is dramatically arranged to subvert our growing suspicion that Dupin has more in common with the irrational than with the imaginative.

Dupin's "air of method" is to salt the mines of his fiction with an easy explanation of horror. Such hoaxing permits a glance at madness but finally says less about what we want to know more of: C. Auguste Dupin. Those content to accept Poe's hoax will lionize Dupin; those who are "on to" Poe will doubt his sleuth. Eventually our doubt leads us to conclude that our narrator has stumbled upon Dupin's madness, that Dupin conceals the talismanic hair because of his identification with the ape of unreason, and that, as soon as we begin to ferret out that damning association, the detective releases the evidence that diverts us away from the fact of his "diseased intelligence." Little else explains Dupin's pathological concealment of the evidence.

"Ligeia": Poe's Transcendental Hoax

If read as a hoax, "Rue Morgue" divides its readers into those who take Dupin's "method" at face value and those who see through it. In either case, however, there remains a certain degree of tension in the reader's experience. On the one hand, Dupin's ape deduction if taken as truly intuitive strikes us as far less brilliant than his earlier "mind reading" display. On the other hand, the cover-up reveals a hidden Poe whose self-loathing is as unsettling as the audience-loathing implied in the very act of his hoax. We are not meant to crack this case but to feel, vaguely, that we are somehow deficient. Something of the same effect grows out of "Ligeia," only here the deficiency in us is our natural desire to beat death and to transcend. We are berated for wanting what Poe himself so desperately craved.

Asked by James Russell Lowell in 1844 to write a brief "spiritual autobiography" for *Graham's,* Poe jotted down several pages of credos, or non-credos. "I have no belief in spirituality. I think the word a mere word,'' he wrote, adding: ''My life has been whim—impulse—passion—a longing for the future.''[15] But soon enough he defines music as ''the perfection of the soul, or idea, of Poetry.'' Poe would deny ''spirituality'' but would insist upon impulse, futurity, soul, and Platonic Idea. Perhaps the contradictions can be resolved when seen in the context of Poe's antidemocratic remarks to the more egalitarian Lowell, in which he distinguishes ''man the individual'' from ''man the mass.'' While Poe as an individual soul might ''live continually in a reverie of the future,'' he saw no hope of transcendence for the masses and flatly declared ''no faith in human perfectibility.'' An individual talent may *approach* a state of Platonic perfection, but the mass of man remains hopelessly chained in the cave. Limited by this asymptotic (approachable but un-attainable) futurity, art can only provide ''the *vagueness* of exaltation,'' not real transcendence itself. And, he writes, if the arousals of ''a sweet air'' can be generated through ''affectation''—Poe defends his tinkling rhymes and ara-besques—then such affectation in writing is ''no blemish.''[16] Transcendence is ''a mere word.''

Of course, many cannot forgive Poe his ''affectations.'' But the fact that the writer recognized the contrivances of his ''airs'' in creating the simulation of transcendence suggests a rhetorical purposiveness to his affect. To Lowell: ''I now and then feel stirred up to excel a fool, merely because I hate to let a fool imagine that he may excel me'' (Poe's *Letters,* 20). Here we find the seed of a transcendental hoaxer's strategy. Transmitting the ''vagueness'' or ''suggestiveness'' of ideality to readers requires an initial destabilization of the reader's conventional expecta-tions. And for Poe that also meant a direct challenge to the reader's intellect. He dares us to excel him, to catch him in his contrivances, to expose the hoax and thereby discover in our wonderment at the authorial betrayal a new and vague relation between author and reader that excites our taste of something beyond authority, something transcendent. Thus satiric thrust may induce an awareness of the ideal; at least this is the implied hope. The reality of the reading experience is that readers do not always survive the transcendental operation; they are merely fools for excelling.

In ''Ligeia,'' Poe's strategy is to induce readers to become so engaged in the narrator's bogus transcendentalisms that they fail to see that he has murdered his wife Rowena and placed the blame on a nonexistent phantom he calls Ligeia. It is an alibi only a transcendentalist would buy. As with ''Rue Morgue,'' the rhetoric of this Gothic tall tale is to have us adopt a form of rationality that inevitably destroys itself. In this case, our delusive transcendental logic encourages us to confuse mysticism with murder so that we more readily believe Ligeia to be the agent of Rowena's death than the more obvious culprit, our narrator. Five decades of criticism have laid strong foundations for this argument, establishing Rowena's death as a murder and Ligeia as the narrator's fantasy.[17] But still unexplored are the rationale for the narrator's performance of madness and the ironic effect of this ''affectation'' upon readers.

The first step is to determine the narrator's reliability. At first glance, this is no step at all; he is clearly either a madman or an opium addict, and in either case he cannot be trusted. But in fact he is not so crazy, for he makes a tremendous effort to balance incredulity with sympathy. Unlike other obsessive speakers, our narrator projects himself as an earnest "soul" trying to come to grips with the inexplicable and with himself. Like Ahab, he recognizes "a mad disorder in my thoughts," and he freely admits to his opium use.[18] These frank admissions come as a kind of Montaignean "essaying," an attempt to find himself through his trying-out of the events. If he is mad, he knows it and wants to control it, and in thus establishing his sincerity, we entertain his credibility. This is, of course, only an *air* of credibility, but Poe creates the "affectation" with deadly intent. The issue of Ligeia's last name shows his skill.

The most damning evidence against the narrator's mental disorder is his admission that he "cannot, for my soul, remember" Ligeia's "patronymic" (L, 310). Invoking Montaigne once again, we are inclined to think that this remarkable admission supports the narrator's credibility if only for the fact that no one with such a poor memory could possibly be a liar. This is no hoaxer, and the sincere, parenthetical "for my soul" substantiates the belief. His subsequent explanation is a retrieval of past possibilities, a series of speculations and a discovery of the self that with seeming inadvertency leads to his accepting the possibility of the transcendent soul. First we follow the narrator as he analyzes the cause of his memory lapse: Perhaps long suffering has enfeebled his memory, or perhaps Ligeia's learning, beauty, and eloquence "made their way into my heart by paces so steadily and stealthily progressive that they have been unnoticed and unknown" (L, 310). But then he recalls that he *never* knew Ligeia's name. It is not a matter of forgetting but of not knowing. The attempt to wrestle with the deeper impossibility of his ignorance of Ligeia's name continues: Perhaps it was her "playful charge" to keep it a secret; or perhaps it was her "test of [his] affection"; or perhaps, finally and most nobly, it was his Romantic "caprice" not to inquire, for to do otherwise would be to sully a spiritual love with mundane details. The cagey self-portrait that evolves is of a personality discovering himself, and happily his discoveries prove both his rationality and his intense devotion to "spirituality." The narrator is not mad; he is just a transcendentalist.

Ultimately, the narrator's "fierce moodiness" (L, 323) enhances his reliability. His development through fragile stages of awareness, his self-doubt, his admitted obsessions and "passion to discover" (L, 313) are in fact evidence of an admirably analytic mind. Moreover, we are urged to discount his chemical dependency when we find that he is more fully dependent upon Ligeia as a guide "through the chaotic world of metaphysical investigation" (L, 316) than he is upon drugs. Without this transcendent woman, he is "but a child groping benighted," and like a child he is open to those Wordsworthian wellsprings of creativity. Our deepest point of sympathy occurs when the narrator demonstrates his poetic powers in deriving the meaning of Ligeia's eyes. His process of thought is thoroughly transcendental. He cannot define but can only "suggest" meaning through "a circle of analogies." The eyes share a spiritual connection to "the commonest objects": vine, moth, stream, ocean, meteor, star, music, and word (L, 314). The progression of images recalls Emerson on the Poet. By tale's end, the narrator/child/poet is a fully transformed true believer in Ligeia's transcendental revivification: "Can I never—can I never be mistaken" (L, 330). The reader has little choice but to accept his sincere

self-realization, and this is the heart of Poe's strategy. We are so transfixed with
these mental processes that we miss a simple fact: Ligeia does not exist.

Here the conflict between realism and Poe's "suggestiveness" comes into play.
On the one hand, if Ligeia represents transcendental ideality, she will be, by Poe's
reasoning, "vague" in characterization. On the other, such an immaterial figure
lacks verisimilitude, and hence credibility. Poe's few well-chosen details describing
Ligeia carefully walk the line between both effects. We recognize the material
specificity of her aquiline nose and tightly curled "hyacinthine" hair (L, 312). She
possesses "the softness and majesty, the fullness and spirituality, of the Greek."
Of course, the eyes, despite the myriad descriptive analogies, remain ineffable, and
as Poe piles on the Greek allusions, we begin to wonder if this is a living woman
or an artful representation of one.

Her eyes are the embodiment of beauty and passion; her brow expresses "repose"
(L, 312); she is "outwardly calm, ever-placid" (L, 315). In short, Ligeia is a set
of abstractions culled from a History of Ancient Art. Laden with the symbols of
Western value and the aesthetics of repose, she personifies ideality and control. In
reality, Ligeia is more statue than person; even her flesh is like marble. And the
only real revivification that occurs in the tale stems from the life that the narrator
gives this statue through the sheer force of his language. The vagueness associated
with Ligeia, then, is not Poe's effort to approach ideality but rather the narrator's
finally inept attempt to give reality to a figure he never met, a dream figure that
will serve as the culprit in his murder of his real wife, Rowena.

Only when we meet Rowena—a woman in the flesh—do we begin to arouse
ourselves from the narrator's transcendental hoax. What first awakens us is the odd
particularity of the second wife's name. In contrast to Ligeia, the Lady Rowena
Trevanion of Tremaine has a last name: lots of them. And she has family. We learn
that our wealthy narrator keeps house in an old abbey with a bridal room decorated
in an unsettlingly arabesque manner. So garish is this chamber that the narrator
wonders how Rowena's parents ever allowed their marriage: "Where were the souls
of the haughty family of the bride, when, through thirst of gold, they permitted to
pass the threshold of an apartment so bedecked, a maiden and a daughter so
beloved?" (L, 321). The implication is that, despite the threatening chamber designed to persuade a father of the bride to cancel the nuptials, Mr. Trevanion of
Tremaine has willingly sold his daughter for the honor and wealth of the narrator's
name. The room is a metaphysical torture chamber whose monstrously animated
drapery mirrors unanticipated patterns of mind. In it, we see ourselves "surrounded
by an endless succession of the ghostly forms which belong to the superstitions of
the Norman, or arise in the guilty slumbers of the monk" (L, 322). The narrator
has built this bridal bower of animated fear, guilt, and repressed sexuality all for
Miss Tremaine of good Norman stock, a child bride whose parents have no qualms
about prostituting to a monkish fiend. Like his room, the narrator has also contrived
Ligeia—a fictitious ghost of ideality comparable in linguistic abstraction to his
stylized bridal chamber—to haunt Rowena, innocent pawn and emblem of her
parents' unholy greed.

The final clue that uncovers the hoax is the "three or four large drops of a brilliant
and ruby-colored fluid" (L, 325) that plop out of nowhere into Rowena's wine. A

"literal" reading of this would argue that a real Ligeia poisons Rowena so that she may "revivify" herself within the body of her successor. But murder seems oddly out of character for the "ever-placid" Ligeia, whose eyes are so forcefully connected with growth, fertility, life, and no hint of death. Murder, however, seems precisely in character for the narrator, whose only simple declarative sentence in the tale is "I loathed her with a hatred belonging more to demon than to man" (L, 323). The point, however, is not the *fact* of the narrator's murdering Rowena but rather his *manner* in persuading us that Ligeia did it.

The narrator's apparent madness projects a rationality that makes transcendental logic valid and desirable. We *want* Ligeia to exist because we want her theory of the will to transcend death to work. Transfixed upon the supernatural, we submit to the pleasures of a mimetic transcendence and fail to see the eyes of an ugly truth staring at us between the lines. Poe's rhetoric of deceit is more devastating than the "insinuated mockery of transcendentalism" that Thompson finds.[19] By making the narrator's enthusiasm credible and Ligeia's eyes repositories of value, Poe lures us into thinking like a transcendentalist despite ourselves. We become victims of our assumptions, dupes of our desire for spirituality. More than mocking us, Poe has us transform ourselves into transcendentalists and then watches as that transformation collapses under its own weight.

Poe's problematic relationship with Transcendentalism is well known. He called New England a Frog Pond and castigated its leading Frogpondian, Emerson, as one of several "mystics for mysticism's sake" whose "Orphicism" represented "confusion worse confounded."[20] Poe's attack may have been provoked, for he could easily have seen himself described in Emerson's example of what a poet should *not* be: "a music-box of delicate tunes and rhythms."[21] And he took exception to Emerson's continual assumption that "the soul of the poet [can] come to ripeness of thought" or that "the melodies of the poet ascend and leap and pierce into the deeps of infinite time" (Poet, 232). Poe insisted that poetry is not a "species of fine frenzy" or "ecstatic intuition" (PC, 454), nor is the poet "a liberating god" who "speaks somewhat wildly" (Poet, 235, 233); he is instead a rhetorician shaping words to achieve effects upon readers. He also argued that Emersonians confuse a contrived poetic effect with the ideal state it attempts to mimic. Poetry can only be richly suggestive of meaning, not an embodiment of or "piercing" into ideality. Thus, he complains that "we are too fond of confounding [that '*richness*'] with *the ideal*," and he goes on to shake his finger more fiercely: "It is the *excess* of the suggested meaning . . . which turns into prose . . . the so-called poetry of the so-called transcendentalists" (PC, 463). The problem with the Frogpondians is not only their presumption of "human perfectibility" but their tendency to mistake their own "excess" for truth and their failure to appreciate the necessity of "affectation."[22]

Poe's hoax works only to the degree that transcendental readers make similar metaphysical mistakes. We confuse the narrator's excessive enthusiasms for sincere reportage and self-growth. We confuse the sham of Ligeia's Hellenic ghost with true ideality. We take a murder to be "revivification." And yet, in reflecting back upon just how it was we were "taken in," we recognize that our sympathy for the mad narrator and the ineluctable appeal of Ligeia's eyes engage our need to believe.

The enduring ability of "Ligeia" to dupe us is based upon our willingness to adopt a flimsy transcendental logic that, in purporting to reveal, through Romantic analogies, an immortal truth, in fact covers up a sordid little domestic poisoning. And what is most damning is that the hoax works with the active complicity of the transcendental reader. We dupe ourselves into sham ideality.

Just as a lie is not a lie unless it is believed, a hoax is no hoax unless it is exposed. Readers must have a reasonable chance of "disentangling," otherwise the rhetorical benefits of their hard-won discovery, initial shame, subsequent anger, knowing smile, and then sly perpetuation of the hoax will all be lost; there is no playing along. The problem with Poe's best hoaxes is that they are often too tough to crack. Poe relished "excelling a fool" even to the point of allowing his readers to continue in their delusion. Rather than share the humor of discovery, Poe was content to glory in private satiric victories. T. B. Thorpe's more humorous hoax invites full disclosure and a far more generous spirit of communality.

Thorpe's Big Bear

Like most tall tales, "The Big Bear of Arkansas" is a framed story in which a cultured gentleman introduces the antics of a boastful frontier clown. The contrast between the narrator's refinement and the clown's vulgarity represents the nation's attempt to accommodate both high and low factions. But as the nation became more secure in its love of rusticity, the genteel frame in tall tales tended to attenuate. Thorpe's nameless narrator is suitably detached but not so far removed as to keep him from participating in the hoaxing of the reader; he is Jim Doggett's accomplice. Jim amuses us primarily through a series of lies that build only to collapse anticlimactically under the weight of their absurdity. His victory (and the narrator's) is that he finally puts across a lie so poetic as to seem real. His lies range from epic to mythic and finally transcendent proportions. Jim has seen forty-pound turkeys and has fought mosquitoes big enough to "superate" mere Yankees. Each bear he describes grows toward sublimity and yet is grounded in a real experience of the unconquerable West. Jim's final big bear can "eye" you "as quiet as a pond in low water"; it can descend a tree "as gently as a lady would from a carriage"; it can "[loom] up like a *black mist*" and groan "like a thousand sinners."[23] This animal possesses the fierce beauty of doubt and sin, whose threatening grandeur finally outstrips the paltry lies of frontiersmen like Jim, mere "children of the woods." Myth becomes poetry, or so it seems.

Doggett's tall tale has a two-pronged irony. First, a close reading of Jim's climactic killing of the big bear reveals that it is clearly a hoax. Jim tells us that he sights the bear while crouching "just *from habit*" beside a tree and that in standing and running toward the bear, he trips over his "inexpressibles." Most readers are so wrapped up in the final confrontation between Jim and bear that they fail to translate these details properly. Like another proverbial bear, Jim has been "shitting in the woods" when he sights his bear and is so startled that he fails to button up and thus trips over his pants. In telling his bear tale, Jim exposes his bare tail, but we are so captivated by the liar's rhetoric that we cannot see his tail for the tale. In short, we have been hoaxed. Jim's big bear is no more real than the turkeys and mosquitoes he has lied about before.

But a second irony is that Jim does not seem fully aware of this hoax. As Walter Blair puts it, he draws out a "beautiful lie—such a superbly imagined and performed work of art that he convinces not only his audience but also himself."[24] Thus Thorpe gives us Chesterfield's ultimate Romancer, simulator, and "hero of his own fables," one who lies for the sake of lying and is deluded by his own invention. With this reading, Jim's New World innocence and shallow exuberance are cleverly exposed. And yet one nagging doubt occurs. Is it likely that Jim could perpetrate his defecation hoax in one paragraph and forget the perpetration in the next? Just how self-deluded can a liar be?

Blair interprets Jim's concluding silence as evidence of Jim's confusion of "the real and imagined."[25] But Jim also *breaks* that silence with a call to liquor up: He leads his rapt auditors out of his illusion as purposefully as he has put them there. In addition, our poker-faced narrator makes no reference to the tale's central hoax. Has he too been duped? Although he calls Jim a superstitious child of the woods, he is nevertheless drawn to the "mystery" of the man. But does this mystery refer to Jim's poetry or to his hoax? Given such doubts, we must turn to Jim's intentions. Why should anyone hoodwink these steamboaters with an elaborate "romancing" lie? From Blair's perspective the answer is that this is what "*lyric*" artists do. Like Ovid Bolus, he lies for the pleasure of invention. But Jim has a deeper pleasure in mind; he is out for revenge.

Jim tells us early on who has wronged him, where, and how. Returning home from his first (perhaps last) visit to New Orleans, he confesses to having been made a laughing stock. The gentlemen there had baited him with words he did not understand and played him for the fool. They asked him to discuss the principal "game" in Arkansas. When Jim declared it to be "poker," they laughed, and laughed harder when he offered "rolette" as a reasonable alternative. Jim now knows—for he openly admits it to the passengers of the *Invincible*—that "game" refers not to cards but "how we get our meat." But he has learned this vocabulary lesson bitterly. City folk have called him "green." Humiliated and "thrown away," he calls himself "useless." His boisterous crowing is precisely the kind of tall-talk reaffirmation of identity we might expect from a snubbed outsider returning home. But more: Steaming into the wilder reaches of the Mississippi, Jim will execute more complex verbal actions than were used against him. He will use "game" in its deepest sense by playing a confidence game that will demonstrate his superior verbal expertise. Words, the very ammunition that backfired on him in the city, will now become his "principal game." In his linguistic war of revenge, he will perpetrate a hoax on the same class of individual that humiliated him back in New Orleans. Now the city dwellers are the outsiders.

The rhetoric of Jim's lie work progresses through six phases, each associated with a remarkable personality change. Taken sequentially, they increase Jim's credibility within a heterogeneous, naturally skeptical group of travel-weary auditors. Jim plays the part of a Boaster, Learner, Possessed Man, Social Outcast, Poet, and finally Humbled Believer.

As a tall talker, Jim is believed by no one. At this early stage Jim is not effectively a person at all, but a stereotypical gamecock. We hear him crowing before we see him; and when we see him, he calls himself "Big Bar." His first "whopper" (Jim's term), concerning a turkey so fat that "gobs of tallow" roll out of it when it "busts" open, draws unified exclamations of disbelief from twenty auditors, in particular a persistent "cynical looking Hoosier" who doubts the existence of the bird and derides Arkansas for its mosquitoes. Now, the first step in seizing the imagination of an audience is to eliminate skeptics who spoil the fun by making other fools think too much. Jim has tested the waters of this group with a whopping lie to see who will bite and who will not. No one seriously believes in Jim's turkey, but most will play along with him. The Hoosier, however, is our Malvolio and must therefore be disposed of. Jim's tactic is to "see" the cynic's mosquitoes and "raise" him one hundredfold. Arkansas's mosquitoes are big, but for natives they are no more of a nuisance than an alligator. Besides, they root *under* the skin, so they cannot really hurt much. The only case of injury recorded, however, "was to a Yankee [read Hoosier]" who "swelled up and busted; then he su-per-a-ted." Jim concludes with a bit of verbal grandstanding: The Yankee "took the ager . . . ; then he took a steamboat" home, all because "he took mosquitoes to heart" (Big Bear, 339). Playing on three uses of "took" more than makes up for Jim's linguistic failure back in The Big Easy. Like Jim in New Orleans, the Hoosier is "used up," that is useless, and leaves.

When an Englishman inquires about bears, Jim tests his audience again, gulling them this time a bit further before the inevitable flop. His thesis is that because Arkansas is so rich, bear season is year round; consequently, bears are always fat and huntable. Since "Fat [is] an enemy to speed," the Arkansas bear is easy to snare. But to make one edible, you must "run" it to get the fat mixed with the meat, and when the running is done, you must take great care, for steam will shoot "out of the bullet-hole ten foot in a straight line" like an exploding boiler (Big Bear, 341). Up until this last point, Jim's sober explanation of running the bear and mixing its inner substances sounds informed, hence veracious. That steam, though, sounds a bit tall.

Jim's strategy is *not* to convince us of this lie but, in fact, to expose his mendacity, for by allowing his lie to fall apart he reinforces the gamecock stereotype. With this role established, his subsequent and more believable tales will actually shine as evidence of personal growth. Readers will witness his emergence from a stereotype into true "personhood." The illusion that we are probing past the stereotypical liar to a deeper personality is the organizing principle behind Jim's five remaining performances.

The gentleman narrator initiates this unfolding by asking Jim to relate "some particular bear hunt" (Big Bear, 343). This, Jim promptly does not do. Instead, he establishes a new identity by exposing his past. He shows himself to be a Learner, devoted to the mastery of the hunt. Like the narrator, he "ain't ashamed to gain information." Here is a newfound humility in Jim: He admits to a time when he knew nothing of bears, back when he first learned to measure a bear's size by its scratch marks on a tree and exclaimed with Franklinian glee, "I've learned something new a'ready, and I'll put it to practice" (Big Bear, 343). His "larning" is a mark of maturity and utility. It precludes the kind of imaginative nonsense we have heard already. Jim is no longer a liar but a pragmatist. He is useful, not "used up."

As his mastery grows, Jim grows. He learns all there is to know about bears. But the fate of certitude is monotony. Jim now knows bears too well; hunting them is "as much the same to me as drinking" (Big Bear, 344). He has reached the point of intellectual satiety; he knows "the signs so well" and becomes alienated from his native soil. Thus his discovery of bear marks eight inches higher than normal rushes him into a new phase of learning. His first reaction is that the "sign" is a "hoax." Coming from Jim or any liar, this is a dangerous gambit. Imagine the risk. In the midst of his own hoax, he has mentioned the very word that might alarm his more perspicacious auditors. But their assumption is that if Jim is so cavalier, he must not be a hoaxer. (Barnum knew better.) Jim's utter disbelief turns to the "conviction" that the marks are real—"it came home to my soul like an earthquake" (Big Bear, 344). Suddenly, jaded Jim has a vibrant *soul,* a faculty we did not know he possessed. He continues to read signs. Buzzards lead him to the corpse of a pig and more bear marks—"that sign is certain." The evidence proves a reality; both mind and soul are geared to the certainty of this improbable beast. Jim is alive once more. By following Jim's intellectual growth, we grow more certain that this blowhard is sincere, that his thoughts and beliefs evolve rationally, and that he reads signs well. But confusion returns when Jim cannot catch the bear; it is "puzzling" and "past [his] understanding" (Big Bear, 345). In all, this Learner has moved through certitude, skepticism, conviction, and confusion. The complexity of these sequential phases suggests that Jim is telling the truth.

Confusion becomes paranoia as Jim becomes a Possessed Man. The bear is his obsession: "I would see that bar in everything I did; *he hunted me,* and that, too, like a divil, which I began to think he was" (Big Bear, 345). Roles are reversed: The bear is the hunter, Jim, the prey. Jim's language becomes more direct, less exaggerated. Formerly, he has depended upon fallacious similes: potato hills like Indian mounds. Now the tall-talking simile "like a divil" grows toward full metaphoric identity—"he *was*" a devil. The linguistic transformation seems a clumsy afterthought hurrying to assure us that this devil is no lie. Paradoxically, the clumsiness of the sudden revelation enhances Jim's sincerity; *this* is the "real" Jim. The rhetorical effect is that Jim's subsequent tall-talk similes become more convincing as they become more poetic. He loves the animal "like a brother." It sits like "a pond in low water" and descends from a tree "as gently as a lady."

When Jim finally corners this "brother," he misfires, and his "green-horn" hunting companion fires an ineffectual glancing shot off the bear's forehead. The bear convulses "in a *wrath all over,*" and as if in sympathy, Jim, too, gets his "wrath . . . up" over his friend's bad shot. The confluence of Jim's paranoia and sympathetic identification with the bear suggests Jim's suspicion that the Protean bear (devil, brother, lady, pond) symbolizes the inherent illusoriness of nature. Nature is no longer "spontenacious" or Edenic; it is demonic and deceptive. And worse, it mirrors Jim himself.

When Jim finally bags his bear by drowning it in a lake, he discovers that his "brother" is not the right bear at all but a "she bar." Jim's subdued similes make sense now. Earlier, he had seen the bear in feminine terms as a "pond" and a "lady," and in fact those unconscious projections of the hunter's submerged feminine self not only prophesy the death of a lady bear in a pond but also indicate the full depth of Jim's mentality. His brother is in fact a sister, and for a brief moment the problematic mirroring penetrates to his own sexual identity. Jim's brief self-exposure is as well a foreshadowing of his more ribald exposure of his backside to his audience, which occurs only a few lines later.

Taken together, these moments might lend themselves to a bisexual or homosexual reading of Jim's character, but no such luck. While Jim learns more about himself than he bargained for, what he reveals speaks more to the pansexual (or androgynous) aesthetic of poetic insight than to his sexual orientation. The gentle lady bear dead in the narcissistic pond is the faintly realized symbol of Jim's imagination, a fusion of masculine utilitarianism and feminine creativity. And since this revelation occurs during what Jim takes to be a delusion, an added argument is that Jim's imaginative language is the product of his desire and nature's illusions. That is, poetry reveals only by an apparent warping of nature and mind. It is, then, at this point that we glimpse the poetic foundations of Jim's "*Lyric*" art.

However, we must place these sexual, metaphysical, and aesthetic ruminations in their rhetorical context. Has Jim fabricated the details of his hunting the "she bar" merely to intensify his control over his increasingly open-jawed auditors? Or has he gotten caught up in his own tale to such a degree that (à la Blair) he fails to recognize that his androgynous slip is showing? Or is his "slip" (Freudian or otherwise) well planned to engage the deepest of readers with psychological icings untasted by the *hoi polloi?* Whatever intentions we might impute to this Possessed Man, his ultimate goal of duping the passengers is undiminished.

Jim shifts personalities again, this time to the Social Outcast, the very role he was forced to play in New Orleans. But this time he acts out his shame with relish. Given his reputation as a master hunter, Jim must now endure the sarcasm of fellow huntsmen. This is Jim's lowest point: He has mistaken a regular-size female bear for the mythic male and has even forgotten to load his gun. These tenderfoot errors deserve scorn, but Jim lashes back, making a veiled reference to the tall tale he is telling: "Perhaps you want to call somebody a liar" (Big Bear, 347). His friends, he tells us, laugh harder. Allowing himself to relive his New Orleans humiliation, Jim vents his anxiety while at the same time shoring up more sympathy among his steamboat auditors, even as he challenges them (indirectly) to call him a liar. Bewildered and now alienated, Jim seems as vulnerable as the timid settler a few pages back. Big Jim is little jim, the moral opposite of the frontier stereotype, and this frank self-exposure only contributes to his credibility. Jim's audience is now fully prepared to be hoaxed.

Jim's last two personalities come in swift succession. As Poet, Jim manages to combine ribald indirections and poetic myth within a voice of wonder and control.

> Well, stranger, on the morning previous to the great day of my hunting expedition, I went into the woods near my house, taking my gun and Bowie-knife [his dog] along, just *from habit*, and there sitting down also from habit, what should I see, getting over my fence, but *the bar!* Yes, the old varmint was within a hundred yards of me, and the way he walked *over that fence*—stranger, he loomed up like a *black mist*, he seemed so large, and he walked right towards me. I raised myself,

took deliberate aim, and fired. Instantly the varmint wheeled, gave a yell, and *walked through the fence* like a falling tree would through a cobweb. I started after, but was tripped up by my inexpressibles, which either from habit, or the excitement of the moment, were about my heels, and before I had really gathered myself up, I heard the old varmint groaning in a thicket near by, like a thousand sinners, and by the time I reached him he was a corpse. [Big Bear, 347]

Here, the sublime enormity and fearful mystery of the bear, delivered in effortless cadences, more free verse than prose, are not so much undercut by the bare-bottomed hunter at the center who gives the lie to the picture, as they are made to coexist with that lie. The undeniable hoax is a slap to those cheeky enough to ridicule a master liar and gullible enough to fall for Jim's Romantic questing beast. But the juxtaposition of Jim's less than Edenic defecation and the chilling groan of a thousand sinners is equally irresistible to meaning-makers. Here is the Outcast Adam laboring over his excretions, squatting in his ordure, listening to a chorus of sinners crying to be let back into paradise. Jim's debouchment is somehow a sign of man's fall. Like Ishmael, who saw the universe as one big practical joke, Jim suggests that salvation is one big hoax.

Nevertheless, Jim ends as a Humbled Believer. He did not kill the bear; the bear had simply given up. Strong enough to defeat Sampson in "the twinkling of a dice-box," it has surrendered to a life force higher than itself and Jim. Jim has been merely the unconscious agent of this power. His steamboat auditors have also "bought into" the idea of the mythic sympathy of nature, an idea reinforced by Jim's rhetorical manipulations. Jim appeals to a higher authority, fully validating himself and his word. And Jim's auditors, caught up in their own assumptions of omnipotent nature, have no recourse but to believe.

Beginning as an obvious liar, Jim has led us through a series of precise and quite believable psychological states—skepticism, conviction, sexual confusion, alienation, determination, and belief. He has transformed himself from a lowlife stereotype into a poet and philosopher. Now a humble pilgrim, he has penetrated into the darkest secrets of himself and the woods; he has removed his gamecock mask and shown us his bare truth. But in reality Jim's "character development" is the setup for a hoax; all that he really bears is his bare bottom. His revenge on the gentlemen of the world is that he uses his verbal skills to make them believe his illusion. Nature's sublimity is just a wordy fabrication. Jim's victory lies not in his new-found humility in the face of nature or in his ability to believe in a force greater than his mouth; rather it is his ability to create belief through lies so palpable as to make heaven seem real. But significantly, Jim's lie work allows us to hold both Jims—the Liar and the Believer—together as one. He is the coalescence of the poet and humorist.

To argue, then, that Jim manages naïvely to delude himself with his own lies is to miss a vital, metaphysical tension in the tall tale. Thorpe's message is that belief is a purely willed creation. Jim knows that he has built a structure of belief for his audience, and even though he has hinted that the structure is a hoax, the sense of mystery he has implanted is no less a fantasy than any other human response to the woods. What is important, however, is how his auditors respond. Are they simpletons who believe unreservedly despite their earlier resistance to Jim's exaggerations? Are they cynics who reject it all as humbug? Are they Jim's satiric caricature of those who fall into the trap of personifying nature? Or, do they "play along," finding aesthetic pleasure in his game, benevolently acknowledging the necessity of imagination in the fabrication of belief? Thorpe's conclusion thwarts clear answers. It all ends with "a grave silence," which may be the prelude to derisive laughter or breathless wonder. Thorpe's authorial silence keeps the perpetual interrogatives going—a fact that requires some concluding remarks on the gentleman narrator's complicity in this literary confidence game.

Thorpe's Narrator: Knave or Fool

Poe's literary confidence games reveal at least four narrative options available to the tall tale hoaxer. The framing speaker may be a *disinterested observer,* reliably reporting but not participating in the hoax (as in "Hop-Frog"), or any one of three *participant* narrators: the *unconscious dupe* ("Tarr and Fether"), the *dupe growing in consciousness* ("Rue Morgue"), or a *confidence man* ("Ligeia"). A fifth possibility is the *confederate,* a narrator who actively assists the central liar in his hoax through either significant silences or broad misdirections. Thorpe's genial narrator straddles two options. He seems detached, interested only in the flavor of Jim's address. Like the lawyer in "Bartleby," who announces his fascination with eccentric scriveners, Thorpe's narrator observes the Gamecock Woodsman with anthropological objectivity. But his detachment is almost too distant. He draws no conclusions about Jim, no empathic equations ("Ah Doggett! Ah humanity!"), and no interpretations of the passengers' silence. In fact, his restraint facilitates Jim's hoax, and we suspect he may be *Jim's confederate.*

For the most part, the narrator maintains an amiable and cosmopolitan stance. But he also notes that the vibrant diversity of the steamboat's passengers is a curious encumbrance to brotherhood. The ship's "heterogeneous" crowd has "disposed themselves in little groups" (Big Bear, 338); there is no mingling, no society, no One out of Many. The narrator himself makes "no endeavors to become acquainted with my fellow passengers" (Big Bear, 337). Thorpe's America is a lonely crowd. Significantly, Jim's sudden appearance instantly unites all factions into a genial community. His eyes, according to the narrator, are "good-natured to simplicity"; his boasting is "irresistibly droll"; and his good humor leaves "every face . . . wreathed in a smile." Jim is the tonic that dissuades anomie and encourages democratic growth. The drama of comic performance instantly homogenizes a splintered world. The narrator is a willing advocate of Jim's socializing mirth. He knows Jim is a word twister, and when he applies the epithet of "logician" to Jim after the liar has "argued" the Hoosier into submission on the topic of mosquitoes, we know his sarcasm implies a consciousness of Jim's rhetorical intent. Like a Greek chorus, the narrator speaks for an audience consolidated under Jim's spell, but if he senses duplicity, why does he not expose the hoax? Does he find a communal function in it?

Evidence of the narrator's complicity is small but substantive. First, his coming and going seem oddly timed. He is a day-tripper and boards *The Invincible* at the last possible minute, exiting promptly at Jim's conclusion. That is, he arrives just in time to hear (or aid) Jim and leaves when no longer needed. Second, the narrator is instrumental in urging Jim on to the tale's central hoax. Once Jim has had done with his petty lies (the forty-pound turkey, impaled sow, and steam-boiler bear), he "ramble[s] on to one thing and another." But the narrator gives him direction, "ask[ing him] if he would not give me a description of some particular bear hunt" (Big Bear, 342–43). Whether the narrator is cuing his clown (as if to say "Now's the time") or merely instigating some fun on his own (inflicting Jim on the crowd), the fact remains that his stage direction moves Jim from mere boasting toward his more poetic lies.

Third, the narrator warns the reader of an impending hoax: A "man of observation," he remarks, "need not lack for amusement or instruction in such a crowd," and he "more critically than usual examine[s the] contents" of his paper (Big Bear, 337). The narrator's critical reading inspires our own analysis of Jim's intent. Finally, the narrator nudges us with italics. From the beginning he has silently used the all-too-familiar convention in Southwestern humor of giving typographical emphasis to slang expressions and comic neologisms. But just before Jim's major lie, he draws special attention to the convention telling us that he will italicize Jim's "happy manner . . . of emphasizing the prominent parts of his conversation" (Big Bear, 343). Thus, at a crucial moment he seems to say that if we observe his italics "more critically than usual," we may find a "prominent part" hidden away. Actually, Thorpe italicizes sparingly, giving emphasis to a select few phrases, not the least of which is "just *from habit*," the code phrase that does indeed reveal to acute observers Jim's most "prominent part."

If Thorpe's speaker is both disinterested observer of and genial accomplice in Jim's comic lie, we may find two hoaxes in "The Big Bear of Arkansas." Jim's hoax is a woodsman's personal vendetta against the kind of sophisticates that humiliated him in New Orleans. His weapon (language) had backfired on him in the city, but on the frontier it scores a direct hit. Jim's victory lies in his inducing citified skeptics to believe in a fantasy. The narrator's second, more complex legpull attends to the metaphysical and communal ramifications of hoaxing. With fair enough warning that a lie is in the works, we discover that as Jim's rhetoric escalates, we fail to distinguish fact from illusion. But more, in sharing the passengers' "grave silence," we contemplate the role of lies in creating belief and the flimsy foundations of democratic communities.

However many hoaxes we may discern in "Big Bear," the fact remains that the tale's lie work is firmly encased within an amiable frame. The reader may be misdirected at times but never fully misled or cheated, for the hints of a hoax are evident, the reader has a fair chance to put the hoax together, and he or she will be "amused and instructed." Even though Jim is out to get us literate city folk, and jolly well succeeds, we know there is no folly in falling for this confidence game. Our falling confirms a Romantic and democratic ideology that to remain a skeptic or cynic is a failure of the imagination and of the communal spirit. Jim gets us because we want to be got, and that secret desire to be duped into poetic and social belief is, perhaps, no different from Poe's presumption about his transcendental readers of "Ligeia." But Thorpe allows us to recognize the illusoriness of the comic lie we want so much to accept. It is as though our wish for social unity is both fulfilled and denied. Thus, in the end Thorpe's communalizing rhetoric of deceit is critical, yet amiable and regenerative. Poe's more satiric strategy is to lure us into faulty frames of mind, which by falling apart leave us dispossessed. There is no synthesis of faith and doubt, no alternative balance, no community of fools and friends, no real hope for the efficacy of rationality. There is only the fall.

The tall tale provided American writers with the means by which they could effect a synthesis of humor and satire. Its frame structure allowed for a submergence of subversive ideas (metaphysical, psychological, or political) within an amiable mode. And it gave writers a plethora of narrative stances with which to lead readers in and out of belief and doubt. Melville drew upon these models, making his own confidence man both a character type and a narrative voice. But his personal synthesis was also aided by a third comic concept, one that began with the Enlightenment, expanded in America's democracy, and articulated for the author a rhetorical figure capable of combining amiability and deceit. It is the cosmopolitan ideal.

6

The Genial Misanthrope:
Melville and the Cosmopolitan Ideal

The recent development of multiethnic approaches to literary analysis has excited new interest in an old question: What is an American? As for any immigrant nation, the answer necessarily evolves with every new repositioning of power among its peoples; accordingly, to be American is to be culturally unstable. America itself is not "One culture *out* of Many" but rather "One culture *and* Many." Thus Americans, no matter how far removed in the generations from their initial immigrations, discover an identity in the fusion of their allegiance to an ethnic past with a desire for a transcultural attachment. The repose of self-worth in multiethnic life teeters on the fulcrum of a hyphen, whether to lose that hyphen or to wave it like a flag. In Melville's day the problems of ethnicity were expressed primarily in the idiom of the cosmopolitan ideal, wherein all cultures, races, and creeds would be afforded equal footing. Established in late-eighteenth-century Europe, the ideal nevertheless had its best hope for fulfillment in early-nineteenth-century America, where achieving political and cultural coherence depended upon the harmonizing of factions. America was in potential if not full reality the ultimate cosmopolitical state.

The cosmopolitan ideal was not so clearly delineated as to be the basis for governmental policy, but its language suffuses the culture, emerging in the discourse of evangelists, abolitionists, merchants, woodsmen, artists, and critics. Crèvecoeur speaks a cosmopolitan line when he defines an American:

> I could point out to you a family whose grandfather was an Englishman whose wife was Dutch, whose son married a French woman, and whose present four sons have now four wives of different nations. *He* is an American, who, leaving behind him all his ancient prejudices and manners, receives new ones from the new mode of life he holds.[1]

Farther on in his *Letters from an American Farmer,* Crèvecoeur extends his secular cosmopolitanism into a religious arena; "all sects," he wrote, "are mixed as well as all nations," to create a "religious indifference" that dispels bigotry (*LAF*, 552). And still further, the French immigrant draws upon a specialized cosmopolitan vocabulary to distinguish American and European cultures: "A traveler in Europe becomes a stranger as soon as he quits his own kingdom; but it is otherwise here. We know . . . no strangers; this is every person's country" (555). Crèvecoeur never uses the word cosmopolitan, but his liberal optimism—his assurance that multiethnic life vanquishes "ancient prejudices" and engenders secular and religious "indifference," that it banishes the very notion of "stranger" by giving everyone a home—is unmistakably cosmopolitan. It is also unmistakably naïve.

Eventually, the Civil War and America's imperial policies lead to a culture that associated the cosmopolite with American expatriates, not immigrants—with "ambassadors" seeking identity elsewhere. But in the early republic the citizen of the world was an import to our shores, a denizen of the frontier, a cultural relativist who endorsed the broadest acceptance of all factions, races, and beliefs. As such the American cosmopolite sacrificed the fixed identity of a nationalist, and in declaring himself a "stranger who is at home everywhere," he assured as much distrust of himself as respect. Voicing the ultimate extensions of Democratic faith, the cosmopolitan was simultaneously challenged to a unitary American social identity. The problems of cosmopolitan identity—of being true to all cultures *and* to the culture of one's birth—speak to the dilemma of modern multiethnicity: If I am all nations, creeds, and colors, how do I dig back and down to that seed of being that is uniquely me? Early on, the cosmopolite represented the radically unstable identity of the immigrant American Self. Far more than Crèvecoeur realized, the cosmopolitan ideal was as much a problem for self-awareness as it was the political hope of the world.

Numerous men and women called themselves cosmopolites or citizens of the world in order to command a certain universal audience, and their personalities contribute to our sense of what the American cosmopolitan meant to those around him. Melville was not the first to call someone a "cosmopolitan," but he was the first (in *The Confidence-Man*) to attach the term to a major fictional character. Even earlier in his career, in *Typee* and *Moby-Dick,* he played with the psychological and ethical ramifications of the concept, testing the con man temperament of this ambivalent figure far more deeply than any American before Henry James. Sensing its potential for both amiable humor and comic deceit, he found cosmopolitanism to be an avenue for aesthetic synthesis and a tentative resolution for America's comic debate. He called his cosmopolitan figure "the genial misanthrope."

Melville's Cosmopolite

"A Genial misanthrope! I thought I had stretched the rope pretty hard in talking of genial hangmen. A genial misanthrope is no more conceivable than a surly philanthropist" (*CM,* 176). The incredulous speaker is Charlie Noble, the Mississippi operator soon to be duped by Frank Goodman, the cosmopolitan "hero" of *The Confidence-Man.* The two have met just after Goodman has failed to befriend Pitch, a twice-diddled frontiersman, too wary now to allow himself the luxury of any man's company. Pitch has stormed off, and in his wake Noble arrives declaring Pitch a misanthropist comparable to the Indian-hater Colonel John Moredock. Although upset by Pitch, Goodman will not despise him as Noble wants. For him, Pitch is a "surly philanthropist" whose gruff exterior hides a tender heart. Intending to "fuddle" Goodman, Noble eventually becomes Goodman's dupe. The tables are turned: Goodman cons the con man Noble. Only moments before this climax, Goodman offers up his notion of the genial misanthrope as a "converse" or moral opposite of Pitch's "surly philanthropist." This "new kind of monster," outwardly benevolent but inwardly conscious of human iniquity, is no Timon of Athens, but rather "will take steps, fiddle in hand, and set the tickled world a'dancing. In a word, as the progress of Christianization mellows those in manner whom it cannot mend in mind, much the same will it prove with the progress of genialization. And so, thanks to geniality, the misanthrope, reclaimed from his boorish address, will take on refinement and softness" (*CM*, 177). Noble's response to this prophetic "monster" is the truculent incredulity registered above: To him, a genial misanthrope is no more possible than a surly philanthropist.

At this point Melville's riverboat novel founders in the shifty sands of a moral dilemma. Readers must accept Goodman's genial misanthrope, a complex projection of himself, on the basis of a debate between two speakers of equally problematic reliability. Whom do we trust: the blustering Noble or the suspiciously naïve Goodman? We shall explore the dynamics of this debate more fully in a later chapter. For now, we need to retrieve the reactions Melville's first readers had to Melville's new comic type and its constituent sources in the traditions of eighteenth-century amiable humor: the benevolent misanthrope and the citizen of the world.

Not all misanthropes are alike, but the most salvageable and endearing is the "benevolent misanthrope," epitomized by Smollett's Matthew Bramble.[2] As his name implies, he is a thorny, rambling cynic capable of satiric thrust but given, finally, to genial sentiments. Overall, the benevolent misanthrope not only gave the amiable humorist a device for safely containing satire, he also provided an aesthetic means of portraying the ethics of the "man of feeling" as a moral survivor in a wolfish world. Inwardly, the British benevolent misanthrope cherishes individual human genius; outwardly, he scorns man in the mass. Potentially tragic yet ultimately comic, the character finds redemption in his love of individual souls despite a recognition of human depravity. Melville experiments with both the tragic and the comic potentials when he has Ishmael apply the tenets of benevolent misanthropy to the ship's carpenter—"man alone [is] a wonder, a grandeur, and a woe" but "mankind in mass [is only] a mob of unnecessary duplicates" (*MD* 466). The stolid carpenter is a "wonder" of psychological endurance; Ahab, a woe. And, like both, Pitch in *The Confidence-Man,* a comic Ahab, harbors human affections he would like to deny. But the problem with the benevolent misanthrope as a comic device was that he quickly devolved in the nineteenth century into the lachrymose cynic of sentimental drama. Melville's *genial* misanthrope inverts the traditional *benevolent* misanthrope, so that he is outwardly amiable and yet inwardly wary and thus a direct moral contrast to the ineffectual Pitch, a surly and fatally philanthropic American cousin of Matthew Bramble.

Melville also associates this new amiability with cosmopolitanism. Before Bramble there was Diogenes, who combined both the reliable benevolent misanthrope and more subversive cosmopolitan. Unlike Timon, whose hatred is as virulent as his charity was indiscriminate and who attacks from his isolated cave, Diogenes made himself a market-place cynic for all to experience and try to comprehend. The first self-styled "citizen of the world," he held no particular bias for any localized political unit and pledged allegiance to universal truths that transcend faction and creed. Diogenes does not rail at man; he merely mocks him; he is, to borrow from Melville, "less a man-hater than a man-hooter" (*CM,* 138). Goodman protests too much when he denies any comparison of himself to Diogenes; he is indeed like the Greek (and in clear contrast to Timon) an accessible and amiable cynic.

By making his genial misanthrope the *beau idéal* of his con man cosmopolite, Melville fuses the mutually exclusive sensibilities of idealism and skepticism, and in subjecting readers to this fusion, he promotes a resolvent synthesis. Making this comic experience work required a valorization of the cosmopolitan, and this meant making a radically unstable cultural figure seem reliable. Melville's rhetorical challenge and its meaning for multiethnic readers today cannot be fully appreciated unless we understand the roots of this figure in Europe and America.

Europe's Cosmopolite: "At Home in Every Place"

Ishmael's distinction between "man alone" and "mankind in the mass" is most immediately connected to those Enlightenment thinkers—Locke, Newton, Leibnitz, Hume, Franklin, and Kant—who, according to Thomas Schlereth, were the principal proponents of eighteenth-century cosmopolitanism. They hoped to resolve the conflict between their "belief in the individualism of the elite and an abstract faith in the humanity of the mass" by uncovering the universal principles of taste and human behavior inherent in all men.[3] Tolerant and eclectic, they advocated open markets and a free economy, arguing that the mingling of all nations in world trade would guarantee the amity of all cultures (Schlereth, 50). In short, the cosmopolitan goals of the Age of Reason espoused a healthy cultural relativism and a world government freed from regionalism and prejudice.

For certain *Philosophes,* cosmopolitanism was an inevitability. Kant presupposed a human propensity to resolve our conflicting needs to "*associate*" with others and to "*isolate*" from mankind. The projected synthesis is an "asocial sociability," comparable to the amiable humorist's assimilation of benevolence and misanthropy, which in a political context builds through dialectical conflicts between one triumphant nation-state after another.[4] Nations dissolve and combine through warfare; however, they are the necessary stepping stones toward a civil commonwealth of all nations, a cosmopolitical state. Unfortunately, Kant did not foresee Napoleon and two centuries of imperialism.

Along with its cultural relativism, the cosmopolitan ideal also encouraged a pluralistic engagement of the arts and sciences, in particular the more peaceful evolution of national letters into a world literature. "The idea," wrote Goethe, "is not that the nations shall think alike, but that they shall learn to understand [and] tolerate one another." The route toward this peaceable kingdom was not so much through an appreciation of national "peculiarities" as through the universal ascension of a poetic sensibility, which allows us to apprehend the "unconscious" workings of the "inner traits" of a "whole nation, as well as the individual."[5] Thus, Goethe told Eckermann that he was "more and more convinced that poetry is the universal possession of mankind" and that it precipitates that "degree [of culture] where [national hatred] vanishes altogether, and where one stands . . . *above* nations, and feels the weal and woe of a neighboring people, as if it had happened to one's own." True self-awareness comes only after we assimilate the foreigner, the alien other, and stranger into our being, and that process begins with an uprooting of the Self from the comfortable peculiarities of our nativity. Inevitably, poetry hurries along the cosmopolitan state, for since "the good, noble, and beautiful [are] confined to no particular province or country," the poet of one nation ultimately speaks the language of all nations.[6]

Goethe projected this poetic fusion of All into One within an amiable frame. Laurence Sterne, for instance, was for him the initiator of an "epoch of clearer human knowledge, nobler toleration, gentler humanity,"[7] and his association of cosmopolitanism with the Shandyan pastoral, although seemingly paradoxical, was typical for the age. On the surface, cosmopolitan sensibility hardly seems domestic. If self-possession and aesthetic repose are achieved by an immersion in the multiplicity of life, then travel has priority over home, and travel literature over pastoral. Indeed, the Enlightenment initiated the vogue of touring capitals, Alps, Orient, and New World as well as the genre of the satiric tour conducted by faux-Orientals writing letters home, gently mocking Western ways. Travel defined the citizen of the world, but a sense of *home* (the *heimlich* or the familiar and stable) was also the repository of values that a traveler travels to find. It was as much a factor in the cosmopolitan sensibility as motion and instability. One must finally stop, find repose, and send down roots to cultivate one's garden.

Britain's cosmopolitans addressed the conflicting necessities of travel and home. In *Rasselas* (1759), Johnson's benevolent misanthrope Imlac sees motion as a psychological imperative: "Our minds, like our bodies, are in continual flux. . . . Do not suffer life to stagnate; it will grow muddy for want of motion: commit yourself again to the current of the world."[8] For this cosmopolite, motion defines being. But at the same time, Goldsmith warns against travel as an end in itself: "A man who leaves home to mend himself and others, is a philosopher; but he who goes from country to country, guided by the blind impulse of curiosity, is only a vagabond."[9] To "commit" ourselves, in Goldsmith's view, to Johnson's riverworld is to acknowledge a human lacking that must be filled. Rather than acquiesce to Goethe's awakening of poetic powers buried within, Goldsmith advances cosmopolitanism as a means of resolving personal deficiencies. We lack repose; we hurt, so we travel. And the hurt gives a moral direction to travel that goes beyond escapism. What distinguishes the true cosmopolite from the mere vagabond is the will "to mend."

But healthy travel had its peculiar cosmopolitan pain. The "Swiss disease" (*heimwei* or homesickness), often associated with moments of sublimity experienced in the Alps, was dramatized in shelves of sentimental fictions reminiscent of *The Sorrows of Young Werther* and the *Prelude*. The syndrome pits the impulse to move against the desire for "local attachment."[10] The cosmopolite becomes a stranger, despite all self-searching, to himself. Psychologically, the cosmopolitan posed a paradox: He leaves home to find home and discovers his identity in other nations. Reflecting this paradox Samuel Johnson defined "Cosmopolite" as if to impose a domestic coloration upon his world of flux. His "Cosmopolite" is "one who is *at home* in every place." Johnson's Dictionary places a homey restraint on the psychic need for constant motion. But "home" cannot be "every place": It is not London *and* Paris *and* the Alps *and* (Johnson surely knew) the Hebrides. It is a guarded land, private and particular, inhabited by select individuals, engendering a peculiar idiom, and rooted in time and place. Johnson has little sense of the cosmopolitan's status as a stranger or of how others in their homes would perceive such a figure knocking at the door.

Whether viewed politically, aesthetically, or psychologically, the cosmopolitan sensibility was inherently contradictory. While its goal was one stable, nationless culture of Reason, that goal could be reached, as Kant argued, only through the destabilization of individual political states or, as Goethe felt, through a transcendence of single voices by an exposure to all or, as Johnson urged, through a commitment to flux yet home. Because of the cosmopolite's attempt to reconcile one and many, motion and stasis, self and stranger, this eclectic cultural figure naturally coincided with its equally conflicted counterpart in amiable humor, the benevolent misanthrope. And in literary representations, the traditional cosmopolitan encompassed both humor and satire. No better expression of both the comic and the sentimental sides of the cosmopolitan character can be found than in two "men in black" who bridge the eighteenth and nineteenth centuries: Goldsmith's Drybone in *The Citizen of the World* and Count Charles in Kotzebue's *The Stranger*.

Gentlemen and Strangers

Modeled on Montesquieu's *Lettres persanes* (and itself a model for Irving's *Salmagundi*), Goldsmith's *The Citizen of the World* (a Chinese emissary's epistolary descriptions of London) pairs the baffled Lien Chi Altangi with a troubled "humourist in a nation of humourists," one Drybone, or "the man in black."[11] Lien establishes his cosmopolitanism when he writes, "had I been never from home it is possible I might find an infinite fund of ridicule in [foreigners]." But "long travelling" has made him a tolerant humorist; he will "laugh at folly alone, and ... find nothing truly ridiculous but villainy and vice" (*CW*, 87). While certain individuals may merit ridicule, Lien never vituperates. He comes to see that his own "standard of perfection was founded in prejudice or partiality." Travel cures the Chinese of his regionalism and triggers amiability. In abandoning prejudice, the cosmopolitan commits himself not simply to "the current of the world" but to a code of laughter that prevents satire. As with Johnson, Lien's good nature tames flux.

Drybone is Goldsmith's satirist. As a benevolent misanthrope, this man in black endures a condition of "continual restraint" more pathological than wise. His Shaftesburyan father, who believed that "universal benevolence was the first law of nature," raised his children to be "machines of pity" (*CW*, 128). Good-natured and hence helpless, Drybone is abused by patrons, lovers, and friends. But in debtors' prison, he "reforms" by repressing his benevolence within a crusty misanthropic shell. Outwardly he hates; inwardly his heart "dilated with the most unbounded love to his fellow creatures" (126). Fundamentally a humorist, he poses as a satirist, and is therefore a hypocrite: "If ever I am ask'd a question, whether I know it or not, instead of answering," he boasts, "I only smile and look wise"

(128). But Drybone is a victim of a survival reflex. Born a "machine of pity," he is now a machine of repressed scorn, but the tradeoff has left him no wiser and no less mechanistic.

Goldsmith keeps Drybone from plunging too deeply into sentimentality. But the more lugubrious and popular benevolent misanthrope of the age was Kotzebue's Count Charles, the sentimental protagonist of *The Stranger*. First published in 1787 as *Misanthropy and Repentance,* the play was translated by Richard Sheridan under its more familiar title in 1798. William Dunlop produced the work that season in New York City, and it was "still highly favored" well into the midcentury.[12] According to Epes Sargent, Melville's contemporary at the New York *Mirror* and editor of the play in 1846, *The Stranger* was "much abused by critics" for its melodrama, sentiment, and "exaggerated passions."[13] It was also a scandal. The play's central characters are an estranged couple: the tearful "Mrs. Haller," governess of a remote Manor, and the Stranger (always dressed in black) who camps out beside the manor and grouses about humanity. The unwed Baron of the Manor falls for Mrs. Haller and asks the Stranger (who has saved the Baron's nephew from drowning) to help him pursue her hand. But this plan dissolves when the Stranger recognizes that Mrs. Haller is his wife. Act IV reveals all: The Stranger (Count Charles by name) was cuckolded by a friend, who deceived his wife (our Mrs. Haller) into thinking Charles's inattention was caused by his love for another woman. She left Charles, and he has been a misanthropic wanderer ever since. But this was not the scandal.

Act V was the scandal. Here the husband and wife repent of their faithless indiscretions, revive their marriage, and return home (which now includes Mrs. Haller's illegitimate offspring, whom the Stranger happily accepts). Sheridan removed this last act, leaving the two sinners properly separated and the audience basking in the moral uplift of their misery.

For nineteenth-century Americans, *The Stranger* bolstered the traditional association of cosmopolitanism and benevolent misanthropy. When, in Act One, the servant Francis fails to dissuade Charles from his doubts about humanity, Francis defends his master: "He rails against the whole world, and yet no beggar leaves his door unsatisfied. . . . A hater of society, no doubt; but not by Providence intended to be so. Misanthropy in his head, not in his heart" (Stranger, 9). Like Melville's Francis Goodman, Kotzebue's Francis ranks a "feeling" fool over a "cold skeptic" and sees through Count Charles's Pitch-like insistence upon misanthropy. Charles cannot hide his benevolence. He loves what he scorns, and travels to find himself; he is a stranger searching for a home. But early theatergoers were not ready for so much benevolence. Kotzebue's original intent was to elevate a cosmopolitan sensibility to its highest Christian consequence: After misanthropy and repentance comes forgiveness. The public could not see (because Sheridan would not let them) domesticity depicted as a reward for promiscuity. The cosmopolitanism of *The Stranger* was more libertine than liberal.[14]

While characters like Drybone and the Stranger allowed amiable humorists to place a benevolent frame upon their satiric commentary, their potential for rank sentimentality lessened their potential for conveying deep psychological truths. For Melville, these early versions of Pitch finally served as foils for a higher cosmopolitan sensibility (a "genial misanthropy") that could, like Lien Chi's, maintain an "indifference" toward both benevolence and misanthropy. Warning his son against slipping into misanthropy, Goldsmith's Citizen of the World discards the common belief that a misanthrope is "either a brute or angel." In fact, neither case obtains, for "the censure is too severe, and the praise unmerited" (*CW,* Letter 67). The cosmopolitan views the man-hater neither as the possessor of Truth nor as one possessed: His insight is warped, his madness contrived. Misanthropy results not from the inefficacy of benevolence but from the inability to withstand the disappointment when our instinctual benevolence fails, as it so often does. It is the "unexperienced man" who will substitute ill-advised scorn for overconfident love and thus become a misanthrope. Experience, not Drybone's mechanisms nor the Stranger's providential redemption, is the cosmopolitan's guide. One must love and hate, believe and doubt. Thus Goldsmith concludes with a Confucian analect reminiscent of Johnson's fluxional view: "They must often change . . . who would be constant in happiness or wisdom" (*CW,* 232). Lien commits himself to the current of the world and finds repose amid change. Melville saw this potential in the cosmopolitan, even as he recognized its sentimental weakness. But if the cosmopolitan must be a stranger, might that stranger also be a confidence man? Melville did not have to argue this point; his American readers shared the doubt. It came part and parcel when the cosmopolitan came to the New World.

America's Con Man Cosmopolite: "Nowhere a Stranger"

Cosmopolitanism shaped American thought well into the nineteenth century. In praising the cosmopolitan flavor of Jean Paul's amiable humor for its "lov[ing of] all living with the heart of a brother,"[15] Carlyle gave a democratic face to an aristocratic style. And in America the seemingly localized call for a National literature was actually based on the cosmopolitan hope for a World literature. Like Carlyle, Young America also praised Jean Paul, as if the German were one of their own, a universal democrat. Reviewing Richter's *Walt und Vult,* Duyckinck's *Literary World* argued that since American freedom inspires catholicity "in taste and spirit," we gather "treasures of wisdom and philosophy, of science and letters, from every people and every language."[16] We are the cosmopolitan hope of the world, a vacuum sucking into it all nations. In finding a voice for this vacuum, America had to reject imitation and regionalism and, as Melville argued in "*Mosses,*" aim for those elements of expression that, as Goethe saw it, transcend locality and strike to the human heart. The political constraints that thwarted Shakespeare could not inhibit New World writers from "flashing forth": Hawthorne and Melville were making their bid as delegates to the General Assembly of a universal poetic culture.

The cosmopolitan ethos filtered into the sensibilities of America's more popular writers. Sketcher Bayard Taylor (a possible source for Frank Goodman) recorded his many travels for an international readership, as did the more prosaic N. P. Willis, whose *Inklings of Adventure* begins with "I am a kind of—what-d'ye-call-'em—a sort of here-and-thereian. I am a stranger nowhere."[17] James Lawson, whose ability to gain the combined respect of such infighters as Simms, Clark, Duyckinck, and Poe is itself a cosmopolitan feat, adopted the pseudonym "a Cosmopolite" for his *Tales and Sketches*,[18] and Duyckinck adopted a cosmopolitan rhetoric when he wrote that the poet is "the true mediator among nations."[19] But two anonymous "Monologues Among the Mountains" published in *Graham's* "By a Cosmopolite" more fully indicate the vital presence of cosmopolitanism during the American Romantic period.

The Monologist promotes the Goethean vision of world literature, for it is only through an "understanding of the true nature of Art" that modern man may realize his highest state of mind. "I love my fellows, and I love my country," he claims, but quickly adds, "though, I associate not with the one, and extol not the other." But this brooding isolation from his species only ignites a cosmopolitan rhetoric that urges his "country men [to] come forward into the line of the true greatness of the race."[20] That greatness lies in the mingling of sublimity and repose, which a nation can grasp only when it rises above regional self-definitions and identifies with the whole of humanity. In language that prefigures Melville's review of Hawthorne, the monologist calls for a return to "the life of the Mind!—to the spring and flash of Thought and the boundless sweep of Feelings." He also vitalizes the notion of tense repose:

[The only life worth living is] Hot intense and fiery life, in which the poorness of our mortality is merged and drowned in the flood of the soul's eternal forces,— that fierce existence, in which the buried luster of our creation-flame is *flashed out* from the depths of our nature, to gild and glorify our career.—that thronged, still crescive vehemence of feeling which presses the heart into *calmness through rapture*.[21]

Our anonymous "Cosmopolite" concludes that he "never knew repose but in the tension of faculties." To be sure, his Romantic flame belies Lien Chi's cooler repose, but the choice of metaphor in a *fusion* of faculties rather than Goldsmith's and Johnson's *current* of life involves the same transcendence of self beyond national identity toward a wakeful, universal repose. The Cosmopolite's Carlylean "calmness through rapture" mingles Romantic ideology and aesthetic repose within the cosmopolitan sensibility. Rehearsed here are the stirrings of Melville's own cosmopolitan rhetoric: the "flashings-forth of the intuitive Truth," the transmutation of those shared bursts of genius into the cosmopolitan "shock of recognition [that] runs the whole circle round," and the American articulation of that genius in "the still, rich utterances of a great intellect in repose."[22]

American cosmopolitanism extends into the internationalism of James, Eliot, the Lost Generation, Nabokov, Pynchon, Vonnegut, and others. And yet its presence in American letters largely dissolved after the Civil War, playing second fiddle to America's drive toward regionalism.[23] As Oliver Wendell Holmes conceded, "identification with a locality is a surer passport to immortality than cosmopolitanism."[24] This failure may derive from a vacancy in the ideal, which Melville's contemporaries also sensed. In *Representative Men* Emerson pairs Napoleon and Goethe as two inadequate halves of one cosmopolitan soul: One rose by "hands and head," the other was "the type of culture, the amateur of all arts, and sciences."[25] But Napoleon's imperialism gave the lie to his early promise of universal law. He was not a gentleman but "an imposter and a rogue . . . deserv[ing] the epithet of *Jupiter Scapin,* or a sort of Scamp Jupiter" (*RM,* 250). Or, to translate further, a sort of godlike confidence man. Goethe fares better, in faint praise. "A philosopher of . . . multiplicity," this "Ur-Writer" possessed "a manly mind, unembarrassed by the variety of coats of convention with which life had got encrusted" (*RM,* 267). As with the little emperor, something is missing in the cosmopolitan spirit: Goethe is "artistic, but not artist" (*RM,* 279). The characterization prefigures Melville's complaint about the American cosmopolite Benjamin Franklin: He was a jack-of-all-trades and yet "everything but a poet."[26] Emerson's cosmopolite spreads himself too thin, and the resulting transparency reveals a disturbing vacuity.[27] Scratch a cosmopolite and you find a knave.

In midcentury America the good name of Cosmopolite had degenerated to signify little more than "wanderer" and "dabbler," or "intellectual vagabond." Any tourist could be cosmopolitan, including the "independent 'business man' " James Boardman[28] or the international merchant Vincent Nolte, or even the Bible-beating trickster Lorenzo Dow, each of whom used the *nom de plume* Cosmopolite or Citizen of the World. The cosmopolitan figure was so similar in behavior to the con man as to be confused for one, and herein lies the cultural ambivalence that appealed to Melville.

The cosmopolitan was morally ambiguous from the start. He is as indeterminate ethically as he is politically. Too easily adaptable to "flux," he inevitably falls prey to cultural relativism, for to do as the Romans or Parisians or Londoners do is to be so tolerant as to lose sight of one's native loyalties and private identity. Voltaire rejoiced in this liberty when, in a letter to Mme. Du Deffand, he wrote: "In London I was an Englishman; in Germany a German, and with you my chameleon coat would soon take on still other bright colors."[29] Voltaire's coat is tailored to cosmopolitan minds in "continual flux," but the price of this supreme adaptability is an identity diminished by its versatility. If he can be anyone, he is no one at all, a man without allegiance or creed. And without a clear sense of self there is no restraint upon self-delusion or the deception of others. Moreover, like the humbug Professor Bibundtucker, who professes "a most cosmopolitan spirit,"[30] he is as much a supreme Romantic ironist as a Voltairean shape-shifter.

Transplanted into the American wilderness, where a detachment from religious, political, or regional affiliation challenges the line between savage and civilized, the dubious cosmopolitan acquired an even more dangerous character. As a lover of all nations and creeds, he is, paradoxically, suspect because of the pluralistic company he keeps. On the frontier, multifarious meant nefarious. In *A Tour on the Prairies* (1835), Irving emphasized the cosmopolitan's shape-shifting potential in Tonish, a Creole "vagabond" and "liar of the first water." "Without creed, without country," this scampish "Gil Blas of the frontier" is the anarchic extreme of the cosmopolitan ethic. Melville sensed as much when he called the swift and shifting current of the Mississippi the "all-fusing spirit of the West" and a "cosmopolitan and confident tide" (*CM,* 9). What had passed in Europe as a benevolent tolerance became in nineteenth-century America a suspicious lack of any creed whatsoever. The flip side of the "indifference" or lack of prejudice that Crèvecoeur admired in Americans was a dangerous indifference to principle. In the New World, the cosmopolitan was more chameleon than gentleman, more satirist than humorist.

Even the dictionary reflected the New World shift from amiability to deceit. Noah Webster's definition (1828) of "Cosmopolitan" places Johnson's "homey" denotation third behind two curiously negative entries: The cosmopolitan "has no fixed residence" and is "nowhere a stranger." The citizen of the New World appears to be a vagrant, the kind of vagabond that Goldsmith derides. Nor is he, in positive terms, a *friend* to all, but merely not a stranger. In claiming that Cosmopolite is "nowhere a stranger," Webster underscores the figure's "unfixed" nature even as he hopes to dispel his "strangeness." Protesting too much, the definition gives the impression that, despite Johnson's domestic "at home in every place," the cosmopolitan is rootless, shifty, and strange. Portraits of self-styled cosmopolites confirm the dubious depiction. In particular, two American cosmopolites shaped the expectations of readers of *The Confidence-Man*.

Vincent Nolte: "True" Cosmopolite

Few will recognize the name of Vincent Nolte. Born in 1779 in Italy to German parents, he was throughout his long career a merchant, financier, caricaturist, medallionist, and raconteur. He hobnobbed with Napoleon, Andrew Jackson, and other luminaries; speculated in markets on both sides of the Atlantic; made fortunes and lost them; entertained Europe with his caricatures; and endured injury and insult for his unpardonable behavior, but somehow escaped catastrophe. He died an American.

Nolte did not style himself a cosmopolitan, but a reviewer of his memoirs, entitled *Fifty Years in Both Hemispheres,*[31] testily complained of his pranks and gall, using him to define for readers of *Putnam's Monthly* "the true cosmopolite."[32] Written by Donald MacLeod, the review, entitled "The History of a Cosmopolite," shows how Melville's contemporaries responded to the cosmopolitan figure. Moreover, MacLeod's rendering of Nolte closely resembles Melville's treatment of Frank Goodman, suggesting that a year before he began composing *The Confidence-Man* Melville had before him if not the inspiration for his character, then surely a name to give him—the cosmopolitan.[33]

Certainly the most distinctive feature in Nolte's personality was his problematic humor. Outwardly genial, he harbored an inner disdain for those he met. No one escaped Nolte's ridicule: not his Uncle Otto or his mother, not the Hamburg Senate, and not Queen Victoria, who imprisoned him for depicting her highness as a duck. His caricatures got him "his face slapped, his shoulders caned, his back spit upon" (HC, 328). In professing (according to MacLeod) a "sportive but yet kindly humor," Nolte would have us believe that his cosmopolitan personality is governed by a genial aesthetic whereby human follies are tenderly exposed through the lambent glow of a ripe sensibility (Nolte, 16). But his account of another cosmopolite, the flamboyant John James Audubon, whom he first stumbled upon in 1811 at a small inn near Juniata Falls, belies any profession of amiability.

Like anyone who came within range of Audubon, Nolte immediately recognized the ornithologist as "an original throughout." He reports that Audubon introduced himself as "somewhat cosmopolitan; I belong to every country" (Nolte, 177). And as odd as the self-characterization may seem, it is not at all off the mark. Given his French and Spanish heritage, his outlandish, multinational, half-savage, half-civilized manner of dress, and his travels throughout Europe and the territories, the marksman-painter held legitimate claim to a cosmopolitan identity. He was a jack-of-all-trades but also a rogue, whose most puckish scam was luring his rival, the French naturalist Rafinesque, into a canebrake, which he then set on fire.[34] A British reviewer who scoffed at Audubon's scientific credentials reported that he "could draw the long bow as well as many of the Americans."[35] In short, the artist was a self-promoter, liar, and con man, which is to say a "cosmopolite."

Audubon's line—"I am somewhat cosmopolitan"—must also be read in the context of what Nolte gives us beforehand. At first, Nolte presents Audubon as archly regional and barely literate: " 'Hi emm an Eenglishman, becas hi got a Heenglish wife' " (Nolte, 177). So much for cosmopolitan sophistication. Is the more elegant Nolte spoofing the rustic Audubon's pretensions, or is this odd mixture of dialect and good diction meant in some way to derogate all cosmopolites, Nolte himself included? We know that the two did meet, for Audubon also notes the encounter in his journal,[36] but exactly who said what to whom cannot be substantiated.

Although the review Melville read does not allude to the Audubon encounter, the passage is one of many that corroborate Nolte's more "sportive" than "kindly" humor. Reviewer MacLeod detects in Nolte "an eye considerably keener for faults than for virtues." He satirizes rather than than enlightens. And while this keen eye makes Nolte incapable "of being humbugged," it also creates in him "a too general irreverence, incredulousness and distrust" (HC, 326). Just as *The Literary World's* defense of gullibility condemns the incredulity of those who too readily seek to discredit alleged confidence men, so too does MacLeod discern in Nolte a wit more alive to defect than to benevolence.

MacLeod was clearly skeptical of Nolte. For him, cosmopolitanism was a valid ideal, not the soft soap of international business. This much he had made clear in his autobiographical novel *Pynnshurst* (1852), whose protagonist is a world-traveling young scholar of "all customs of all countries."[37] Nolte is surely Pynnshurst's moral opposite, but MacLeod will not lower himself to Nolte's practice of caricature to set us straight. He forswears invective for the false cosmopolite by ironically proclaiming him "true." In effect, he forces us to determine for ourselves Nolte's real character. As with Melville's Goodman, it is as though we are being tested or teased.

MacLeod's opening definition of a cosmopolitan predictably echoes Johnson and Goldsmith:

> A Cosmopolite has no country in particular, but makes himself at home in all. As he easily unlearns prejudices, he as easily adapts himself to the most varied practices. . . . He is never astonished at anything, for he has paid periodical visits to France since 1793. . . . He is accomplished—a bit of an artist in music, painting and literature—knows many languages pretty well.   [HC, 325–26]

But MacLeod quickly registers doubts about the cosmopolitan's subversive relativism:

> In forgetting his prejudices, he is apt to forget his principles: in becoming cosmopolitan, he generally loses love of country. He is passionately addicted to scandal. . . . He is disposed to caricature . . . he is not troubled by modesty. . . . He reverses our common law maxim, and supposes every man to be guilty until he has proved him to be innocent.   [HC, 326]

Unprejudiced hence unprincipled, the cosmopolitan has no dominant passion except himself. His many cultures suggest no culture at all; he does not share any of the predictable patterns of discrimination that make one culture distinct from another. But his worst flaw is the ungenial presumption of human iniquity. With this blanket misanthropy in mind, we conclude that if he hates all with comic abandon and can do everything, he may do his worst. He may be a con.

To keep this question continually up in the air, MacLeod only hints at Nolte's duplicity. He sustains his ironies to the end, balancing belief and incredulity toward Nolte's extravagant claims. This is as much to establish his own cosmopolitan fairness as it is to announce cosmopolitan malice. Mixing fact and lie, Nolte's memoirs ring true just enough so that one is as much inclined to marvel as to disbelieve. MacLeod does not want to appear so gullible as to accept Nolte at face value and yet so uncharitable as to scoff. Lacking the necessary evidence to expose Nolte for the charlatan he must be, amiable MacLeod plays along with Nolte, passing the creature on to us to challenge our gullibility. He delights in Nolte's uncanny ability to encounter great men at great moments (Napoleon at Waterloo, Jackson at New Orleans, President Madison during the Kentucky earthquake). Few have ever been in the right place at the right time so often. But, at the same time, MacLeod makes light of Nolte's pretensions without necessarily denying his veracity. One sample of this strategy tells of Nolte's problems on the eve of the Battle of New Orleans:

> It was exceedingly improper on the part of Congress to declare war with Great Britain, just as Nolte had taken and furnished his house; but Lord bless you, Congress is always doing something. The fact is, that the war was declared, and our friend had only time to make a hundred thousand dollars or so, break a leg, arrange the affairs of the Bank of New Orleans, fight a duel . . . and arrange preliminaries for a second . . . when General Jackson came furiously down upon Louisiana and put a stop to all amusements."   [HC, 328]

MacLeod's observations about Congress (Lord bless you) and Nolte's wheeling and dueling as "amusements" benevolently suggest that all this may be humbug. And later, in cataloguing the cosmopolite's alleged acquaintances, the reviewer puckishly includes Amerigo Vespucci and Mehemet Ali (HC, 330). MacLeod relishes a good lie and would continue to partake in the fun; "but pardon me," he flippantly intrudes, "I am not to write the whole magazine *this* month" (HC, 329). By restraining his own inflationary prose, MacLeod deflates Nolte's self-inflations. He puts a stop to all amusements. In the process, his simple reporting of Nolte's improbable "life-panorama" becomes a send-up of cosmopolitan versatility.

MacLeod's ironic pose is an effective defense against being taken in by Nolte's "facts." Other reviewers, too easily duped, were not so lucky. In arguing that the mercantile trade is an "art" for which "genius," not mere "love of money," is the "leading motive," one reviewer seriously proposed Nolte as an exemplary master of "the useful arts" of business.[38] Any excesses found in the memoirs were lamely attributed to Nolte's old age.[39] Certainly MacLeod saw more deeply into and through Vincent Nolte, but it is a sign of this Knickerbocker's amiability that his ironies do not degenerate into sarcasms or ridicule. Rather, his flippancies contain his rage over a generation that would confuse business for art and an operator for a true cosmopolite.

In the end, MacLeod's ironies leave much unsaid. They provide no reaffirmation or redefinition of cosmopolitanism. Has MacLeod introduced Nolte to illustrate just how low the traditional cosmopolitan character has sunk, or does he, more deeply, admit to the inherent inadequacy of cosmopolitanism itself? MacLeod's silence keeps the matter unresolved. Although Melville makes Goodman the ironic moral center of his novel, he sustains throughout *The Confidence-Man* a relentless ambivalence. Melville's narrator forces us continually to reconsider Goodman's values and intentions. Like MacLeod's ironies, Melville's cut both ways, for there was more dramatic effect to be gained by keeping readers in doubt and forcing them to play along.

Lorenzo Dow: Citizen of a World to Come

Complicating the reader response to the citizen of the world is the fact that Americans also knew a religious dimension to cosmopolitanism. Indeed, Goodman—in his naïve yet cagey search for faith and in his fatuous but sincere millennialism— resembles various religionists who as self-styled citizens of the world superimposed a cosmopolitan vocabulary onto their beliefs. Principal among these figures in both America and the United Kingdom was the itinerant preacher Lorenzo Dow (1777– 1834), popularly known as "the *eccentric* Cosmopolite," who may have preached to more souls than George Whitefield and whose publications sold in the tens of thousands.[40] Although a "true believer," this evangel (also known as "Crazy Dow") was equally renowned for his witty deceptions in luring the faithless to the fold as well as his land deals, libels, and court cases.

It was not unusual in Melville's day for cosmopolitanism to be defined in religious terms. Just as the traditional European citizen of the world looked forward to an age of political tolerance achieved through the eventual dissolution of all nation-states, the more saintly cosmopolitans prepared for the "second coming" by preaching against sectarianism. For these millennial cosmopolites, a respect for all creeds parallels the secular love of cultural dissent, just as the anticipation of a New Jerusalem with its institution of divine government mirrors the goal of world government. The shared end of universal brotherhood in the religious context derives, then, from revelation and Christ's providential return rather than from cultural relativism or any humanistic impulse.

Two types of religious cosmopolitans emerged at the turn of the century: the benevolent nonsectarian and the evangelical millennialist. Both tended to be Masons and Arminians, for Calvin's elitism found no quarter in the rationalist's sensibility or the evangelist's populism. But ultimately the two factions had little else in common. The benevolists were simply devout humanists, more at home with secular cosmopolitans than with their evangelical kinsmen, whose sense of a prophetic "other world" actually promoted an inverted consciousness.[41] As if to explode the cosmopolitan myth of worldly brotherhood, the millennial cosmopolites saw themselves as homeless and estranged. Instead of being "nowhere a stranger," they insisted that like Christ they were strangers in every place. For them, church denominations are illusory factions beclouding the path to one true, all-embracing belief. Thus Dorothy Ripley, an itinerant Quaker from England, proclaimed herself a "citizen of this world, but going above to the NEW JERUSALEM."[42] During the first half of the nineteenth century, scores of evangelists bore the Word in fields and camp meetings throughout the United States, Canada, and Great Britain. Their message and style were as familiar and popular then as today, and they had names like Father Vredenburg, Daddy Turck, Joseph Thomas, and (fittingly) John Strange. But only Lorenzo Dow, "the eccentric Cosmopolite," was recognized everywhere. His life and thought (recorded in countless memoirs, tracts, and pamphlets) reveal the radically unstable nature of the millennial cosmopolite.

Born in 1777, Dow was a New England consumptive who, despite opposition from family and clergy, persisted in becoming a circuit preacher. Having dreamed that John Wesley had beckoned him to preach, Dow was convinced of his calling, but the Methodist establishment would not condone his unlearned enthusiasm. Reluctantly, he abandoned all formal religious ties to develop his own mode of circuit preaching. Hitching his wagon to his own star paid off. He became popular, then notorious, then celebrated, then wealthy—yet not without hard work and deception. The hard work came in constant travel and endless preaching; the deceit (elixirs, con games, land schemes, word play, and lies) was mere stock in trade. Dow crisscrossed the Eastern part of North America on horseback repeatedly throughout his forty years of preaching, traveling from four thousand to eight thousand miles and conducting up to four hundred prayer meetings annually. He was the first itinerant to preach in Alabama and was instrumental in importing the camp meeting from the South into New England, and thence to England and Ireland. Apparently his conversion of the latter proved unsuccessful, although he incited a riot or two.[43] A prominent if not always respected figure, Dow was an enthusiastic preacher, a sharp wit (akin to Franklin or Paine), and a strident Arminian who found the doctrine of election not only un-Christian but also undemocratic (Dow 177). In his final years, he was an ardent Jacksonian.[44]

Dow's calling card was his eccentricity. He cultivated his public character as well as Barnum. Gaunt, poorly fed, and homeless, he was obsessed with punctuality and (it is alleged) never missed an appointed sermon. Perpetually enjoying ill health, he encouraged rumors of his imminent death, knowing that few would pass up the opportunity to see a preacher die. He ungraciously bolted down graciously offered food, rode borrowed horses to death, then walked, then insisted on being carried, without thanks, to appointed prayer meetings. Dow's oratory was rustic, anecdotal, and sarcastic. According to S. G. Goodrich ("Peter Parley"), "he often took scraps of text, and extracted from them, by a play upon words, an unexpected argument or startling inference."[45] Lewis Gaylord Clark, longtime editor of *The Knicker-bocker* and no religious extremist, provides an example of such wit. Once jailed for defaming a recently deceased man of wealth, Dow promised on the day of his release to preach upon another "rich man who died and went to ＿＿＿." He stopped himself, making a pretense to censor his sermon for fear of being sued again. The sermon turned out to be about Christ, a "rich" man who went to heaven. Dow's rhetorical gambit struck an ironic blow for tolerance that Clark and other "old fogies" (as Clark liked to call himself) would remember for decades.[46]

With his long beard and shabby appearance, Dow looked like something out of the Judean wilderness and was likened to John the Baptist (Goodrich, 210). But despite appearances, he became a "rich man" himself, living off land speculations (which often landed him in court) and income from a dubious patented elixir eloquently labeled "Family Medicine." Moreover, he drew large royalties from his many publications, including the numerous editions of his journal, *History of Cosmopolite*. (MacLeod later cribbed the title.) After his death in 1834, multiple printings continued to provide a comfortable living for his second wife, Lucy, until her death thirty years later (Setters, 257).

If Dow's manner was eccentric, his antisectarian and millennial beliefs were no less paradoxical, especially given his cosmopolitan identity. For Dow, apocalypse was a reality: "These are the last days of troublesome times" that will lead to the "fall of Babylon" and the rise of "Divine Government" (Dow, 326). Drawing from Isaiah, he foresaw that " 'all nations shall flow unto [God's house],' and then 'the wolf and the lamb shall dwell together,' " and that "the earth shall be of one heart and one mind" (102). The Eccentric Cosmopolite's advice in preparing for the New Jerusalem was "to excel in love" instead of "striving for a party" (328), and to worship in "a republican meeting house" that is "free for all denominations" (173). According to Dow's biographer, the preacher "sneered at the idea of each church [being] the only true one. A variety of denominations was advantageous . . . for it prevented any one body from coming into undue power and showed, with each schism, that the search for truth was going on" (Setters, 219–20). Dow held to his antisectarianism to the end. His epitaph reads: "[A Christian] is a slave to no sect, takes no private road but looks through nature up to nature's God."

References to American evangelism in *The Confidence-Man* abound,[47] and they suggest a deeper connection between Melville and the millennial movement during the author's formative years than we have surmised.[48] But what is rhetorically significant is that because of Dow's Cosmopolitan reputation, Melville was able to assume and build on his audience's association of cosmopolitanism with Dow's eccentric mixture of larceny and faith. Melville and Dow share the notion that the cosmopolitan is a "stranger" and that he resembles a confidence man or is, more aptly, "a trickster for God."

Dow did not accept Webster's 1828 definition of a "cosmopolitan" as "one who is nowhere a stranger." In fact, the opposite was true. Invoking familiar scriptures, he continually refers to himself in his journal as a stranger. In Ireland he found himself "a stranger in a strange land." A favorite text throughout his career (as with other itinerants) was "I was a stranger and ye took me in." Dow similarly contradicts Johnson's notion of the cosmopolite as being "at home in every place," for the eccentric Cosmopolite considered homelessness to be his and every man's lot: "The foxes have holes, and the birds . . . have nests, but the Son of Man hath not where to lay his head."[49] Johnsonian domesticity was not possible for such Christlike aliens as Dow. But more, his necessary estrangement from mankind is the cause of further abuse. In a tract on "American Character," Dow bitterly complains of the harsh reception of strangers in most frontier towns. If we take Dow seriously, the "abusing, insulting, blackguarding, swindling, cheating, imposing upon, and ridiculing" that he endured are the favored sports among American villagers. They expect mischief from a stranger and greet him with preemptive strikes. Heaped upon Dow's professional loneliness is his unjust expulsion from the family of man. Dow's alienation hints at the ultimate failure of the secular cosmopolitan ideal. Because of his antisectarian and cosmopolitan mission, Dow must travel; because a traveler, he is a stranger; because an alien, he is effectively denied the welcome accorded a cosmopolite. By necessity an outcast, he may shed the stigma of stranger and be "at home" everywhere but only in a world *to come,* not in *this* world.

Melville too explores this paradox in cosmopolitanism. He uses the word "stranger" more than sixty times in *The Confidence-Man,* almost exclusively in reference to one or the other of his principal con men. The mute is "in the extremest sense of the word, a stranger." Although Goodman proclaims that "no man is a stranger" and that "the principle of a true citizen of the world is to return good for ill" (*CM,* 132), he is himself called a stranger on several occasions. His toughest intellectual opponent in the novel is Mark Winsome, who directly contradicts his cosmopolitan sensibility—"where in this strange universe," the cool mystic asks, "is not one a stranger?" (196). Winsome's disciple Egbert, a "brother stranger," sends the otherwise controlled Goodman storming off the stage by refusing to be companionable. Since virtually everyone Goodman meets (especially Charlie Noble) is called "the stranger," Melville's self-styled cosmopolitan is clearly a "stranger in a strange land," despite his insistence to the contrary. As with Dow, Goodman's ideal collapses, for one cannot be a true citizen of the world in a world composed of strangers.

But it would be naïve indeed to take Dow and Goodman as merely oxymoronic hybrids (cosmopolitan strangers) or innocent victims of a failed ideal, for both are keenly aware of the rhetorical value of their own paradoxical being. Alienation is the preacher's lot, and prophets, both "true" and "false," from John the Baptist and Christ to today's televangelist on the skids, know the mileage to be gained by flaunting that burden. Suffering legitimizes the preacher—*and* it lures a crowd. The consumptive (or perhaps just asthmatic) Dow, perpetually on the brink of death, never denied himself the rewards of public suffering. The histrionic Goodman also suffers the rejection of those he hopes to convert (especially Egbert). Because of their ulterior motives, both cosmopolitan proselytizers use their mixture of alien aspect and cosmopolitan gesture to sweetly seduce us toward belief. By his very presence, such a *stranger* challenges our apathetic being. He confronts us with an invitation to trust him and yet reminds us of the necessity to doubt. He obliges us to "leap" but teases us with the possibility of a fall. In short, the cosmopolitan's cultural being, his "strangeness," becomes a rhetorical device that awakens us to the problem of faith and, therefore, our own humanity.

Goodman relishes his catalytic role. But easily enough, dilemmas arise out of his cosmopolitan rhetoric: Can a bold and crafty stranger truly make us believe? Both Dow and Goodman force themselves upon us *as strangers* in order to stimulate belief. They seem to say, "If you take me in, you can take God in and make the first step toward New Jerusalem." Indeed, out of our initial doubt may spring even deeper belief. But such a rhetorical ploy, when perceived as mere rhetoric, will destroy belief, and one's means quickly negate one's end. *Taking in* a stranger may lead to our being *taken in*. Even a dullard will shy away from a godly messenger who talks like Barnum and dresses like Harlequin. Goodman's "eccentricities" can entice crowds; his wit can trap them; but ultimately this cosmopolitan, because of his inveigling, creates as much doubt as belief. The same is true of Dow.

More than any other preacher of Melville's day, Dow epitomized the con man preacher. For some he was "an eccentric genius" (Dow, 236). His manner, like his white apparel and (in later years) his "long flowing patriarchical beard," was "entirely *sui generis*."[50] But his eccentricity was as much "calculated" (Goodrich, 199) or "designed" as it was "constitutional." Like a satirist, he preached with "biting sarcasm and strong mother-wit" (Dowling, v). As one observer put it, Dow was "an original, and self-sustained man, [who] would handle more than the rhetorician's tools."[51]

Dow loved to diddle his flock toward salvation. He began his career with a con game. After failing to make converts on his first circuit, the aspiring preacher learned from his superior of the ominous prediction that he would surely die if he did not improve his numbers. "Accordingly," he remarks with uncharacteristic understatement, "I was therefore resolved to do my endeavors to get a revival" (Dow, 44). It is, of course, God's prerogative "to get a revival," but Dow had no qualms about manipulating a revival into existence, if it would save his life. In later years his method was "to ensnare [backsliders] into a promise" to pray for two weeks, at which time he promised he would return to the community. Dow's "ensnaring" and "second-coming" tactics were highly effective wherever he found "religion to be low," and, needless to say, he never found it very high. Always the showman, Dow would ensure the reappearance of his audience by promising to "preach from the word of the Devil" (Dow, 60). Curious spectators, frontier doubters, and ruffians expecting a lurid exposé were perhaps disappointed but perhaps also edified to find him drawing his text from the holy scriptures recounting Satan's temptation of Christ.

Savior or swindler, Dow remained popular well after his death and throughout Melville's most productive years. One editor's excessive but telling observation is that Dow's life and words had become "part of the history of mind" (Dowling, iv). To be sure, his legend persisted even up to the Civil War, for in 1861 a "Lady" claimed to have received "communications from the Spirit World, given by Lorenzo Dow" (Setters, 259). Four volumes of anecdotes, analects, and sermons were also collected around this time (289). He eventually entered the popular consciousness as an archetypal comic Yankee. In various tall tales, the legendary Dow is called upon to use his divine powers to solve crimes, and invariably his applications of common sense and showmanship root the criminal out. In one episode, entitled "Raising the Devil," the Yankee appears as Satan to expose an adulterer; in another, he puts hot coals in a metaphysician's boot to convince him that reality is not merely "the force of imagination."[52] Either in legend or in reality, this early Elmer

Gantry manipulated men unto God—just as the sometimes satanic, always scampish Goodman attempts to coerce men into an act of confidence.

"Was Lorenzo Dow, in truth, a man of piety, savingly converted to God, or not?" one observer asked. In the end, Dow's contemporaries generally concluded that he was a "Godly and useful man" (Dowling, iv, viii). But they always voiced strong reservations. S. G. Goodrich is a case in point. Although a "sincere and religious" man, Dow's character "is not to be commended, for infidelity thrives upon foibles, eccentricities, artifices, and vulgarities, in one who assumes to be a preacher of the Gospel. Such things may catch a few thoughtless minds, but the reflecting . . . will be apt to point to them as evidence that religion is the offspring of ignorance and fanaticism, played upon by charlatans and pretenders" (Goodrich, 208n). An "eccentric" wit and "ensnarer" of men, a presumed charlatan and pretender, Dow reinforced for Melville's contemporaries the tacit cultural assumption that a frontier cosmopolitan was as shifty as the wilderness he roamed. Given such associations, Melville surely recognized that he could enhance his readers' doubts about Goodman by dressing his metaphysical scamp up as a millennial cosmopolitan.

Herman Melville: "Diogenes Masquerading as a Cosmopolitan"

Did Herman Melville know of Lorenzo Dow? Ample evidence suggests that he did.[53] Recently emerging information adds further confirmation. Melville may have written a parody, not of Dow, but of the magazine essayist Elbridge G. Paige, who went by the pseudonym "Dow Jr." Paige wrote scores of what he called "Short Patent Sermons" for the *New York Sunday Mercury,* many of which were reprinted in book form as late as 1850. The sermons are short indeed, and comic, although they are clearly intended to edify. Paige's publisher speaks of Dow Jr.'s style as a "mingling of humor and pathos" that "teaches the misanthrope to look with a more cheerful eye." Like his namesake, Dow Jr. possesses "original humor and genuine wit." The fact that Paige borrowed Dow's name suggests that Americans continued, decades after Lorenzo's death, to associate the name "Dow" with a certain brand of witty and pragmatic religiosity. Paige's publisher, however, makes it clear that Dow Jr. never "allowed himself to speak irreverently of religion," implying, of course, that his namesake may have offended certain stalwart audiences.[54] Donald Yannella contends that a parody of Paige, entitled "A Short Patent Sermon," appearing in *Yankee Doodle,* may have been written by Melville.[55] If the attribution holds, then Melville's awareness of Dow Jr. would have presupposed a knowledge of the life of Lorenzo Dow and the tradition of comic religiosity associated with America's version of the cosmopolite.

Literary attributions aside, the most important point to be gathered is that Melville knew the European cosmopolitan tradition and knew his readers would be sensitive to its cultural ambivalences. But rather than deride the Cosmopolite, Melville saw in the figure a reasonable solution to America's comic debate. It allowed him to propose the "genial misanthrope" as a new comic type, deliberately inverting the benevolent misanthrope previously associated with amiable humor. And it gave him the opportunity to challenge his readers to make sense of this archly ambivalent figure, and hence come to terms with their own radically imbalanced national identity. As improbable as the genial misanthrope may seem as the moral center for Melville's last novel, he is nevertheless the central ironic point upon which all questions of morality in the novel are focused. Is he benevolent or evil, a simpleton or confidence man, a schizophrenic dysfunctional imbalance of both or a subtle synthesis of sincerity and deceit? Although no audience can expect reliable guidance from Goodman to answer these questions, readers can, by playing along with Goodman's own genial misanthropy, learn to endure the necessary twistings of doubt and to rise beyond personal, regional, factional, and national identity to a comic, all-embracing, "all-fusing" vision. By reading Goodman closely, we become cosmopolitan ourselves, better able after our reading experience to live amiably and yet guardedly in doubt, with "indifferent eyes."

When Melville began to write, his cosmopolitan sensibility was never far removed. He "essayed" upon the ideal, trying it out in various works. *Typee* records young Tommo's experiences as a rover and vagabond, one tempted by a cosmopolitan relativism and yet finally repulsed by its social, psychological, and sexual implications. The more mature Ishmael, who characterizes himself as one who was "ever dusting his old lexicons and grammars, with a queer handkerchief, mockingly embellished with all the gay flags of all the known nations of the world" (*MD*, xv), is able to use a cosmopolitan sense of genial desperation more effectively to frame and control Ahab's dangerous, solipsistic isolation. But only in *The Confidence-Man,* through the agency of Goodman's genial misanthrope, is Melville able to give equal voice to both the promise and the threat of the cosmopolitan in a way that effectively mirrors the reader's own ontological dilemmas. Like Goodman, Melville plays the amiable cynic, a "Diogenes masquerading as a cosmopolitan," and by so doing he is able to contain selfhood within a remarkably flexible comic pose, one that is supremely detached yet always ready to "take a part, assume a character, stand ready in a sensible way to play the fool" (*CM*, 133). For Melville, the cosmopolitan was not only the means by which he could enliven the moribund vestiges of amiability; it was the rhetorical means by which he could realize his aesthetics of repose.

II

RHETORIC AND REPOSE

7

The Anxieties of Humor

Melville's first book is really three. Or rather, one must read *Typee* with triple vision. *Typee* is unique in the Melville canon, first because it is one of the few texts for which extensive manuscripts exist. Second, it is the only Melville book to go through several significant editions during the author's life, so that the changes from one edition to the next provide a fascinating record of Melville's writing process. And third, one such edition, the heavily expurgated "American Revised," affords a special glimpse at Melville's anxious interaction with his earliest audience. *Typee* is as much an event as it is a text. In stressing the creative phases of this event, a trifocal reading of *Typee* reveals the anxieties of that creation. Melville had seen "strange and romantic" sights during his four years at sea; he had witnessed political horrors; he had exposed himself to liberated sexual practices—aboard ship, in port, on the islands—that few could reconcile with Victoria's world. He had become an enthusiast for other worlds. And he had messages: Primitive life was not savage but amiable; imperialists were forcing islanders to commit savageries that allowed Westerners to call them savage and rationalize their extermination; missionaries were destroying Eden in the name of God. Just as he was coming to see what it was he wanted to say, Melville was also rushing to make his mark in the literary world. He had appalling messages, but a public to please. He added chapters at his British editor's insistence; he sacrificed others for America. Melville was also learning his craft: how to dramatize, how to transform experience into art, how to transcribe another culture, how to translate himself for readers. To gain a fuller sense of the triple "event" of *Typee*—its inchoate ideologies, emerging aesthetics, and experimental rhetoric—we must know the way Melville created it, from manuscript to first edition to revised. Reading *Typee* three ways illuminates how an American forged ideology out of real and aesthetic experiences in the midst of the literary marketplace.

In desiring to please and yet appal, Melville set *Typee* before his audience with more than the usual anxieties that accompany the first book of a young writer. The anxiety is explicit in his Preface. Speaking in the third person as if to distance himself from the perpetrator of his strange book, he presented himself as a truth-teller, "trusting that his anxious desire to speak the unvarnished truth will gain him the confidence of his readers."[1] Finding inaccuracies buried in Melville's "unvar-nished truth," Charles R. Anderson pointed out years ago that Melville had var-nished this material a good deal,[2] and the newly discovered manuscript now reveals that he also revised heavily to enhance drama, not fact. Indeed, Melville was offering under the aegis of John Murray's nonfiction "Colonial and Home" series a book that was effectively a fiction.[3] The facts of Melville's jumping ship are indisputable, but the Romantic particulars—the leg wound, his tense "incarceration," the cannibal feast, Fayaway—are too good to be autobiographical. Murray, who knew a fiction when he read one and hated them all, had his doubts but accepted Melville's book on the condition that he add three chapters of "real" facts concerning native customs. Even so, and after several reviewers suggested that a common sailor could not possibly write so well, Murray continued to doubt Melville's authenticity, requiring evidence from him of his tours at sea (*Log,* 200–201). Murray and his readers would not abide a humbug, for what good are words if they do not reflect that which is practical, unvarnished, true. Contrary to these conventions, Melville was already seeing fiction (varnish and all) as the principal avenue to truth. Most certainly, Melville's fundamental anxiety was that he was publishing false goods and knew it.

Having attacked the political and religious establishment with unqualified candor, he knew his truths would bite more than persuade—hence the anxious rhetoric of the Preface. Melville is sincere yet fatally presumptuous. He "trusts" that "his anxious desire to speak" will win our "confidence." His earnest passion will prove his veracity; we shall be persuaded by his desire to persuade. Only God's Fool would presume that rhetorical reliability is won by the insistence upon it. But in defense of Melville, the fact that he calls his "desire to speak" *anxious*—not "eager" or "earnest" but "anxious"—clearly suggests that this speaker was not so naïve as to forget how the recipients of unwanted truths slay the messengers of truth. Audiences bite back, as Melville seemed to know. And in the case of *Typee,* they did.

Melville's Preface is a nervous prolepsis lining up defenses in anticipation of attack. There is, for instance, the admission that he has been careless of specific dates but scrupulous with the Polynesian language; the disclaimer that he will not even attempt to explain "the origin and purpose" of taboo; and the lengthy insistence that despite being "rather hard on a reverend order of men," he respects their missionary goals if not their practices. As such, the book is merely a sailor's yarn designed to relieve "weariness" and "excite the warmest sympathies" with "no feeling of animosity" (*T,* xiii–xiv). But let the record show that Melville did intend attacks, direct and satiric; that his disingenuous denials did not fool the evangelical press; and that harsh reviews constrained him to make expurgations so extensive that they obviated his proleptic paragraph on missionaries. It too was cut in the revised edition, because the attacks it referred to had been cut. A fine line separates a book that will cause a stir and sell from one that may cause a stir and ruin a reputation. Melville was walking that Al Sirat, and this also contributed to the anxiety of his debut.

But that was the least of his worries. What he had not included in his Preface— not as a disclaimer, not even as a whisper—was any mention of the book's sexual theme. Melville had written a compelling description of island life, a political *cri de conscience* against Imperialism, and a castigation of American evangelism, but he had also written the story of a young man's sexual adventuring. That story is submerged in the fabric of the narrative, hinted at only in the prefatory admission that Melville has something "strange and romantic" to tell, but it is undeniable that at sea and during his virile twenties, Melville saw and did much. His Fayaway was based on experience and dreams as tense as reality.

Melville makes no allusion to his sexual theme. And what he does *not* do in this anxious preface suggests an overall rhetorical strategy for the book. In highlighting the political and religious controversies, Melville created a red herring that would distract hostile readers from the book's more compelling sexual message. If the factual content of *Typee* legitimized the book in Murray's eyes and, like motes of dust, irritated the eyes of religious reactionaries, it also submerged the sexuality of the book's fiction. Whether or not Melville fully understood this strategy as he wrote, the novel partakes of the tactics found in the literary confidence game, which like Poe's and Thorpe's tales contain messages about sexuality within ostensibly social or political arguments. Small wonder, then, that Melville concludes his nervy preface with the con man's insistence upon "unvarnished truth" in gaining the readers' confidence.

Just how effective Melville's rhetoric was can be ascertained from his book's reception. While Melville consented to broad political and religious expurgations, the more narrowly delimited sexual expurgations were far less invasive. For the most part, Melville's sexual theme was undiminished by censorship. Fayaway and all that she represented remained intact. Melville had enough supporters in the liberal establishment (both Knickerbockers and Brook Farmers)[4] to counter the religious reaction, and in supporting Melville throughout his career, they frequently invoked the name of Fayaway, fair remembrance of Melville's sexual desire. Even Melville's greatest detractor, William Oland Bourne, who condemned Melville as a "traducer of missions," acknowledged the author's "lively . . . often graceful . . . attractive . . . personal adventure."[5] Bourne's later parody of Melville's lush style betrays his own attraction to Fayaway, the sensual center of Melville's novel. Nineteenth-century Americans made *Typee* their favorite Melville work.[6] Although expurgations did not allow them a full view of the novel's politics, readers nevertheless had direct access to its heart—the fiction of Tommo's sexual growth.

Melville's model of restraint in treating his political, religious, and sexual themes was Washington Irving. At first glance, Melville and Irving share only the most superficial aspects of amiability. Politically, Melville was far more radical than Irving, both the sharp-tongued Tory of *Salmagundi* and the conciliatory conservative of "Rip Van Winkle." For Melville, revolution was not an event to endure; it was, as with Hazlitt, a logical extension of one's good nature. If Irving resorted to nostalgia and arabesque as a release from progress, Melville recast that pastoralism into a primal present, Eden here and now. Nevertheless, Melville borrowed from the "grasshopper" Irving three aspects of the amiable vision and style. He adopted an aesthetics of repose. He used the picturesque to fuse nature's coeval truths (geniality and "demonism"), and he invested these elements in an evergreen Langstaff (Tommo) who contains satiric impulses and excessive self-involvement within good-natured humor. But more than Irving, Melville depicts the necessary failings of his amiable hero; Tommo's fragile psyche lacks the vocabulary of a marginalizing ethic that can sustain a vital balance of civilization and savagery. In particular, he cannot adapt to Typee's repose; he fears its oblivion, the threat of cultural assimilation through sexual interaction, and the horror of conversion implicit in cannibalism. To give life to Tommo's ethical anxieties, Melville exercises Tommo's geniality beyond the Irving model, spreading his character out into a prismatic array of genial poses, which taken together amount to a Hazlitt-like critique of amiability's instinctual preservative nature, its whimsy, idealism, humanity, and also perilous limitations.[7]

Tommo poses as an amiable rebel, benevolent social idealist, domestic lover and brother, and false genialist. But most problematic is Tommo's uncontrollable whimsicality: He is prey to sudden, inexplicable, and instinctive shifts in mood and thought. And it is finally this rover's instability, or vagabondage, that keeps him from sustaining what Milton Stern calls a "border-crossing eclecticism"[8] or the higher sensibility of the cosmopolite. Most telling is the unpredictable way Tommo changes his mind. Here is a young genialist who forthrightly declares independence from despicable Western authority and violence, who falls in love with primitive life and grows from adolescence to sexual maturity, but who suddenly, violently, and ironically races back to the civilization he condemns. It is the story of a radical's unexpected reactionary reversal. Tommo rationalizes the "horror" of his reversal by pleading loneliness and a revulsion for cannibalism. But these are flimsy arguments, given Tommo's earlier defense of native customs, and Tommo's last-minute rationalizations reveal his whimsicality to be a failure of conscience.

Typee seems a mess, remarkable more for its contradictions than for narrative control. Those looking for Jamesian polish take *Typee* to be an engaging but finally formless literary beginning. More recent critics have found elements of cohesion in its play within the travel genre, its narrative development, its deliberate deconstructions, and even its expurgations.[9] In truth, the formal problems of *Typee* cannot be dismissed, but if *Typee* is a mess, it is a revealing one whose tensions are as contrived as they are pathologically unavoidable. Melville's adventurous past and cultural anxieties are conjoined with his immediate anxiety of addressing his first audience. Just as Tommo dances nervously "on the marge" of two cultures, desiring and reviling both, so too does Melville in his debut hang about the entrance to the literary marketplace. Tommo's ambivalence toward Typee's liberality projects Melville's worrisome desire to both embrace and criticize his Western readers. Thus, one set of anxieties hearkens to another, and the fictionalized sailor's vagabondage and rejection of Typee allegorize the artist's bid for acceptance. Melville's first problem was how to gain his reader's confidence.

Reliability and the Amiable Rebel

Gaining narrative reliability is not an easy trick for an author who in the course of his tale shows himself to be a deserter, a social renegade, and philanderer, as well as an anti-imperialist and, worse, an antimissionary. Some will applaud the liberal; others abhor the libertine. Melville's problem is to make Tommo's rebellion seem logical, natural, unavoidable, and righteous. He solves the problem by bringing both admirers and doubters under the umbrella of his whimsy. Tommo is an amiable rebel whom we are inclined to follow, but only so far as his whim affirms acceptable behavior and grows beyond itself toward a consistent vision. Finally, Tommo's transcendence beyond whim is never fully achieved. His arguments are always on the verge of becoming unhinged; they are digressive and anecdotal, pointedly satiric but then sentimental; they move in and out of control. Even so, Tommo's shipboard rebellion, as it was originally published, is finally no real threat to conventional mores. But readers of the expurgated *Typee* would not have been so readily convinced, for the American revised edition substantially mars Melville's rhetorical ploys.

Melville's tactic in making Tommo's rebellion credible is to present his act as a return to, rather than destruction of, picturesque domesticity. He does so by establishing the moral validity of land, precisely the opposite ploy of Ishmael's water-world rebellion. Tommo is no Bulkington declaring an open-sea independence. The land is the sensual repository of his being. Nor is he like the *Pequod*'s crew, loyal to his captain's obsessions. He has mutiny in mind from the start: To him land is freedom, the sea, tyranny. "Six months at sea!" he declaims in amazed disgust. "Oh! for a refreshing glimpse of one blade of grass—for a snuff at the fragrance of a handful of the loamy earth" (*T*, 3). Tommo shapes these details into a moral landscape of repose: "some green cove . . . sheltered from the boisterous winds" (5). In contrast, the ship, whose imprisoning bulwarks are painted in the "vile and sickly hue" of institutional green paint, is a mocking substitute for green fields. For Tommo, the sea is a barrier to self-awareness.

Melville's second tactic is to sensualize his ontological equations—to make the land not only mind but flesh—by making Tommo's rebellion a response to unconscionable violations of the genial spirit, in particular, human eating codes. I make these last three words purposely ambiguous to stress the novel's testing of the distinction between the codes humans use when they eat (foodways) and the code of eating humans (cannibalism). On board ship, humans endure a certain cannibalism in the way they are made to eat under the thumb of an autocrat, and later on, island cannibalism forces Tommo to reconsider paradise. Melville comically turns this problem into a submerged political observation. The pigs on board the *Dolly*, themselves deprived of food, have chewed the firewood bark, and the crew has in turn chewed up the pigs. All that is left is Pedro, an emaciated cock, who struts the decks lonely and confused. It is the captain's chicken, and he is saving it for himself. As the cook sagely surmises, Captain Vangs will not touch land for provisions until this last shred of fresh meat is gone. Only when Pedro is eaten will the Captain himself begin to suffer privation and head the *Dolly* for port. The crew can fight this injustice or submit. Not surprisingly, they endure privation and eye Pedro not as a source for their own nutrition but as an absurd barrier to freedom bolstered by the dietary whims of their tyrant captain. The irony of starvelings equating their "deliverance" with the Captain's ingestion of a bird allows Melville to couch an attack upon the vicious indifference of authoritarianism within the traditional gustatory imagery of geniality. But the attack is also upon the crew. So deeply bound are they to a hierarchical system that they perversely choose to starve rather than rebel. It is the absurdity of a slave's logic.

Ripening the irony of the situation are two comic inversions on the symbology of chickens. Pedro, through his namesake St. Peter, recalls an earlier conjunction of chickens and betrayal, the disciple's failure to acknowledge Christ as the cock crowed. In this context, Pedro represents the crew's failure to acknowledge their own power of political salvation and to see beyond their chains. This sense of the betrayal of the revolution by the masses is also found in Pedro's resemblance to Chanticleer, once the symbol of a new dawning revolution, now an enfeebled impediment to freedom and a symbol of oppression. If Pedro (just another starveling "doomed . . . to meet the fate of all thy race") is a feathered version of us all, then our fellow biped is as much a human as a feathered sacrifice, and the logical extension Melville encourages us to make is that given an oppressive society, the cannibal impulse is a perverse fact of political survival. We shall eat each other, not our masters, to achieve the illusion of freedom. We find in Pedro, then, the degree to which modern revolution has degenerated, for "the People" (as Melville would later call them in *White-Jacket*) would gladly sacrifice a fellow being to appease an oppressor. Tommo seems only half-conscious of the political significance here, for he, like his mates, concludes: "I wish thy throat cut . . . for oh! how I wish to see the living earth again!" (*T*, 4). The irony for Tommo is that he will exchange this symbolic maritime cannibalism for the "real" cannibalism among the Typees.[10]

Tommo's apparent failure to "get" the full political meaning of his own anecdote allows Melville to couch one of his deepest attacks upon the democratic masses in the form of jolly humor, or what Rosenberry calls the innocuous "jocular-hedonic" style of laughter.[11] The Pedro Affair is just a genial joke on a chicken, not us. Melville's strategy of distancing himself from his impercipient narrator worked, for while editors later had the author remove more obvious but less threatening attacks upon the French and British, they kept poor Pedro and all that he implied about the American mob intact. Tommo's later witticism equating the French slaughter of 150 islanders as an "effort at reform" (*T*, 7), for instance, lacked (despite its delightful understatement) the restraint of such narrative distancing. Its satiric jab cuts beneath the easy target of the always attackable French to the more sacred clan of reformists at home; moreover, there is no genially rendered symbolic chicken in which to contain the venom. The sarcasm cut, and therefore it was cut in the American revised edition, but the subversive Pedro survived. The cuts editors obliged Melville to make trained the author in the patterns of reader response. He learned the kinds of laughter that audiences would endure. The cuts in Chapter Four amplify that lesson.

Here is Tommo's most concerted defense of his desertion. To assure us that his revolt is neither harmful nor anarchic, he uses two modes of discourse: the formal declaration of independence[12] and the less structured amiable digression. By pairing rational and whimsical modes, Melville rests upon tradition and yet proposes to wander Cockloftily, although not so whimsically as to be irrational. But in fact the digression gets the better of his rationality. Wandering too far, he initiates (like Langstaff) a critique that prompted editors to cut.

Tommo's declaration of independence from Captain Vangs is structured on the familiar Jeffersonian model. He begins with the principle that revolution is not disobedience but the natural abrogation of an already broken social contract. Moving to "particulars" (as does Jefferson), he lists the captain's "arbitrary and violent" abuses and failure to "remedy . . . or alter his conduct." Tommo's revolt sounds rational, but the self-serving use of Jefferson strikes at the heart of the conflict between private will and national unity. Tommo resorts to a communitarian document to justify a personal revolt; he proposes a secession just as a nullifier might argue for Southern independence. Tommo's revolt lacks any sense of common cause. Of course, with Pedro in mind, Tommo has little faith in the collective efforts of the masses. A ship's mutiny is out of the question, for as Jefferson tells us, people will suffer rather than revolt "while evils are sufferable," and, as Tommo cynically presumes, his shipmates would in fact betray Tommo's plans for mutiny simply to gain personal favor from the captain. Tommo will not jeopardize his life, fortune, and sacred honor to set others free; he will seek a private independence; he will jump ship. Tommo's personal secession at sea seems to endorse nullification at home. But this modification of the nation's principal revolutionary document is more pastoral retreat than political dissolution, a fact enhanced by Tommo's shift from rational discourse to amiable tall tale.

Tommo exaggerates not to dupe the reader but to establish his genial sensibility. He transforms serious privations into elegance. "Delicate morsels of beef," he claims, that are cut in the galley "on scientific principles . . . and carefully . . . stored away in barrels [afford] a never-ending variety in their different degrees of toughness"; "the choice old water" is casked like wine; the petrified bread resists "decay or consumption" (*T*, 21–22). Not only is the food of "high" quality, it comes in high quantity; one dines on this seafare forever. Moving from sarcasm to tall tale, Tommo relates the case of one whaler that never touches port but sails endlessly with "three pet sharks" in tow. He supposes that "she is still regularly tacking . . . off Buggery Island, or the Devil's-Tail Peak" (23). In all, Tommo's whaling contract is simply not gentlemanly; it demands abrogation. To certify this good judgment, he reports ("on my faith as an honest man") that like the tall tale whaler the *Dolly* is still at sea. This digression has the earmarks of flapdoodle, and Tommo self-consciously cuts it off with, "But to return to my narrative." Nevertheless, in comically rendering the ship's privations, he portrays himself as conscious of injustice but not driven to sullen anarchy. He is a happy slave who deserves manumission because of his comic ability to stretch the facts in harmless ways. Hence we give assent to his flimsy self-justifications and ready ourselves to give him our confidence.

But Tommo loses control of this digression, and his amiable strategy falls apart. On the surface, his next step makes good sense: He will alert us to the alleged ferocity of the Typees so that we may recognize the risks he takes in jumping ship. In substituting cannibal fangs for Captain Vangs, he precludes accusations of cowardice. But his digression on the *causes* of native ferocity complicates our response. After recounting the unjustified torching of island villages by retreating British forces, Tommo asks, "Who can wonder at the deadly hatred of the Typees to all foreigners?" (*T*, 26), and "thus it is that they whom we denominate 'savages' are made to deserve the title." In short, European aggression in creating native retaliation has "exasperated" islanders "into savages"; if anything, we are the savages (27). Travelers to the Pacific are, for instance, themselves "denominated" vipers, cold-blooded robbers, kidnappers, and murderers, and yet report back home of the "diabolical heathens" they have betrayed (26–27). Suddenly Tommo's attempt to win an audience becomes the occasion to deplore Western practices. As Melville's commentary evolves into invective, audience alignment weakens. Now Tommo's amiable revolt is part and parcel of the islanders' more violent repulse of Western authority. Editors expressed their dismay at Tommo's "ungenial" ideological plunge by cutting the entire passage, as they did his next gambit.

Tommo attempts a rhetorical recovery. Native ferocity, he continues, does in fact exist apart from justified retaliations, and it has served to discourage the various tribes of Nuku Hiva from ever leaving their separate valleys. The threat of intra-island violence induces tribal seclusion. This sends Tommo on a new, unexpected whim: the "delightful sensation" of plunging into one of Typee's secluded glens, the meeting place of French and native potentates. This in turn triggers a further whim: the comparison of the French Admiral du Petit Thouars in his richly brocaded uniform with a native chieftain's "nakedness of nature" (*T*, 29). In the final leap of this digression, Tommo asks: "May not the savage be the happier man of the two?" Melville moves away from Langstaffian invective to a reposeful and Evergreen retreat, which allows him to transform direct accusations of Western treachery into a more palatable or even innocuous "questioning" of civilization's values. Tommo asserts the amiability of his retreat by concluding with insouciant flippancy:

> I can recall even now with vivid distinctness every feature of the scene. The umbrageous shades where the interview took place—the glorious tropical vegetations around—the picturesque grouping of the mingled throng of soldiery and natives—and even the golden-hued bunch of bananas that I held in my hand at the time, and of which I occasionally partook while making the aforesaid philosophical reflections.   [*T*, 29]

In framing the "throng of soldiery and natives" both as a Wordsworthian recollection and as a "picturesque grouping," Tommo sets himself physically apart and philosophically above both sets of "savages." Both cultures are contained within the bounds of memory, art, and humor; Tommo would have us forget his earlier political diatribe, just as he physically distances himself from the two clashing cultures. And just as this framed conclusion begins to materialize in our minds, Melville dissolves the fabric of his creation by amiably trivializing the scene as so much banana-munching philosophy. What began as a hurried retreat from unsavory truths resolves itself in a tranquilizing digression through cool groves and comic fancies.

Clearly, Melville's original rhetorical gambit was to expose a political truth and then quickly temper the little satire with a return to repose. For those who read *Typee* in the first English or first American edition or who read it today in its restored, critical edition, this complex comic manipulation remains intact and provides clinching evidence of Melville's maturing humor. But those who read *Typee* in the revised American edition—as did most readers in Melville's day—were deprived of this evidence, for the entire scene—outburst, retreat, and transcendence—was expurgated.[13] If Tommo's attempt to damper satire fails at this point, it nevertheless underscores the strong impulse toward amiability in Melville's writing, and in particular the manifestation of that impulse in a picturesque mode that crystallizes Tommo's complex mental state.

Tommo's Picturesque

Two moments, on sea and land, clarify Tommo's picturesque perspective. One of the most striking passages in *Typee* is Tommo's early description of the sea:

> The sky presented a clear expanse of the most delicate blue, except along the skirts of the horizon, where you might see a thin drapery of pale clouds which never varied their form or color. The long, measured, dirge-like swell of the Pacific came rolling along, with its surface broken by little tiny waves, sparkling in the sunshine. Every now and then a shoal of flying fish, scared from the water under the bows, would leap into the air, and fall the next moment like a shower of silver into the sea. Then you would see the superb albicore, with its glittering sides, sailing aloft, and often describing an arc in his descent, disappear on the surface of the water. Far off, the lofty jet of the whale might be seen, and nearer at hand the prowling shark, that villainous footpad of the seas, would come skulking along, and, at a wary distance, regard us with his evil eye. At times, some shapeless monster of the deep, floating on the surface, would, as we approached, sink slowly into the blue waters, and fade away from the sight. But the most impressive feature of the scene was the almost unbroken silence that reigned over sky and water. Scarcely a sound could be heard but the occasional breathing of the grampus, and the rippling at the cut-water. [*T*, 10]

The progression from sky to swells to depths and the rolling contrasts of blue and silver, of glittering form and shapelessness, of sunshine and evil, is the kind of masterful literary containment that made readers doubt Melville's freshman status. The supple imagery recalls Irving's iconic vista of the lordly Hudson in "Rip," and yet the ominous footpad shark (prelusive emblem of the "universal cannibalism" in *Moby-Dick*) suggests a violence far more subversive than the regions of passive decay found in Irving. In Tommo's picturesque, bright and dark play tensely upon the thin surface of the sea that separates them. Just as glittering fish break that surface in their unexpected flights, so too may sharks draw us down.

But still more distinctive in Melville's *chiaroscuro* is the silence. This silence is not, however, a return to the "general languor" of the ship he has experienced just before this picturesque vision. It is a new awareness of Nature's voicelessness. Exhausted by his sleep of consciousness, Tommo has awakened to "the beauty of the scene"; he has been revitalized. His listless physical repose has been transformed into a fuller mental repose made tense by the "footpad" shark.

Tommo's picturesque grows only to the degree that he can sustain this tense repose. After his escape, Tommo finds numerous opportunities in the Typeean landscape to recapture his aesthetic awakening at sea. Caught in a Polynesian version of a Louisiana canebrake, he blunders through a forest of impenetrable bamboo; it is a claustrophobic nightmare of "perplexities" (*T*, 39) registering the uncertainty of his rebellion. And yet after gaining higher, open ground, and after a night of rain, and after waking to a swollen leg, Tommo pushes aside a branch near his bed

of leaves to discover that he has been "unconsciously reposing" on the verge of
a precipice overlooking the valley of Typee. It is his first "glimpse of the gardens
of Paradise" (48). Nightmare becomes Eden. As with the sea vision, the scene
offers astonishing picturesque contrasts: heights and long vistas, "dazzling" white
huts against distant blue waters, and "small cascades" amid the "universal ver-
dure." Echoing almost precisely the wording of his earlier seascape, Melville adds
that "there was nothing about the scenery more impressive than those silent cascades, whose slender threads of water . . . were lost amidst the rich herbage." "Over
all the landscape," he concludes, "there reigned the most hushed repose" (49).

On land, Tommo's awakening mixes pain and awe. His eye is dazzled, yet his
leg throbs. The pain embodies his canebrake doubts and emergent sexual anxiety.
He thinks he may have been bitten by a "viper," and the valley lies before him
like a woman's "bosom," its two surrounding ridges converging like legs at a
bushy point precisely where Tommo has slept. But the symbolic sexual pain is lost
in the "spell" of "those silent cascades," whose erosive power is hushed by
distance. Just as Rip sits mutely before a scene of beauty and decay symbolic of
America's monarchic past and democratic future, so too does Tommo muse over
a scene prefiguring ecstasy and doubt. Throughout all this, the companion Toby,
"still slumbering" as if captive to unconsciousness, reminds us of Tommo's richer,
wakeful repose.

At sea and on land, Tommo's silent picturesque accommodates both his deepest
anxieties and his highest sense of repose. Although the shark's implied cannibalism
and the valley's submerged sexuality are barely articulated, their presence is felt
enough to give the "unbroken silence" and "hushed repose" of each scene an
edginess that questions the possibility of uniting awareness and repose. Accordingly,
all that "Typee" represents (landscape, culture, and text) is suffused with the tension
between intelligence and indolence. On the one hand, the island is the Utopian
realization of Christian benevolence. On the other, its "great business" is sleep,
and the life of its people little more than an "often interrupted and luxurious nap"
(*T*, 152). Tommo's distrust of repose as "mere slumbering" eventually leads to
his violent reaction against Typee, but not before he explores the amiable aspects
of island life. His evolution from fear to geniality to violence characterizes his
precarious mentality "on the marge" between clashing consciousnesses, and gives
Typee its strained sense of a perpetual "picturesque moment." What finally disem-
powers Tommo is his inability to transform his picturesque sensibility into a cosmopolitanism that includes both Western and Polynesian cultures simultaneously.
Some sense of why Tommo fails is evident in the way he tries to transform Typee
rhetorically into an amiable Eden.

Tommo's Amiable Eden

Melville's promotion of Typee as a utopian extension of European benevolism
founders on the hidden shoals of Tommo's expanding sexuality. In *Typee*, the *pi
pi* is home. Although lacking a hearth, it resembles a large "Verandah" (*T*, 81)
or piazza, the symbolic porch upon which Melville later investigated the picturesque

in his tale "The Piazza." Tommo's adoptive family is a Shandyan unit. The aging Marheyo is paternal, warm-hearted, yet noted for such "eccentricities" (84) as converting Tommo's abandoned shoes into a necklace. He also possesses "the warmth of hospitality evinced by an English squire" (96). His wife Tinor is an industrious Dame Van Winkle to the extent that she manages all domestic affairs, but in paradise there is "never . . . a termagant or a shrew" (85); thus she exhibits only the "kindliest heart." Fayaway, that "child of nature" virtually unblemished by tattoo (although more on this later), dresses in the "summer garb of Eden" (86–87), i.e. a leaf girdle only, and is as patient and loving as any country maid. If these be cannibals, Tommo crows, they are a "humane, gentlemanly, and amiable set of epicures" (97).

But the impediment to this good-natured domesticity is the island's sexual practices, including polygamy and bachelor promiscuity. Several chapters after reading of "affectionate" Tinor's homespun virtue, we learn in the heavily expurgated Chapter 26 of her affair with a "comical looking old gentleman" who takes "various liberties with the lady" as her husband "good-naturedly" looks on. Equally problematic (if we take its later expurgation as indicative of negative reader reactions) is Tommo's understanding that the Typee home inverts the Turkish seraglio, allowing married women a harem of husbands. Instead of registering proper Victorian outrage, Tommo criticizes his Western readers for being "scarcely amiable and forbearing enough to submit" to such redefinitions of matrimony (*T*, 191). Typeean mores, then, reveal the limits of Western tolerance, implying the need for a more open sexuality. Tommo would expand geniality to encompass what Victoria would forbid.

Typee is a land of love-making and "perpetual hilarity" (*T*, 126). There are no monkish, lachrymose, and repressed bachelors here. In fact, the male's sexual license is almost sacred since their "Ti," or "Bachelor Hall," is located on taboo grounds. King Mehevi spreads his royal seed indiscriminately, "romping in a most undignified manner" with young girls who later bear offspring that are reduced versions of himself, sans tattoos. Moreover, Tommo has observed the king and a fifteen-year-old lad "making love at the same time" with one girl. Tommo's own participation in this kind of "romping" is undeniable. He sanctimoniously notes that he has only held hands with Fayaway and never put his arms around her uncovered shoulders. And yet he lets slip that "I have more than one reason to believe that tedious courtships are unknown" in Typee (191). The coy phrasing is a winking admission of his own cocksmanship. Despite Melville's restraint, his audience was not ready to see him extend the genial spirit to include bachelor promiscuity, and needless to say these passages were also snipped in the revised edition.

In all, Melville's extension of amiability into Eden was only marginally successful. But the sticking point was not so much Tommo's sexuality as the accusations of cannibalism and finally Tommo's failure to convince even himself of native amiability. In Chapter 17 Melville's rhetoric, based on cagey deflections and amiable whimsicalities, largely withstands editorial expurgations. But as Tommo comes closer to understanding the peril of his incarceration in Chapter 27, his more serious rhetoric (marred, too, by censorings) turns upon itself.

The Rhetoric of Tommo's Humor: Success

Chapter 17 signals the beginning of Tommo's acceptance of the "general repose" of native life (*T*, 127). Toby has escaped; Tommo is alone with Fayaway. He is not so much imprisoned as "kept," and as he abandons Western constraints, his leg pain subsides. Typee becomes his Happy Valley beyond the "world of care and anxiety" (124). Whereas he had been enduring "a kind of apathy," he now "experience[s] an elasticity of mind" (123). This "altered frame of mind" permits him to see the island culture in a "new light" (126). Unfortunately, in shining that light on Typee at the expense of Western "self-complacen[cy]" (124) and "the thousand self-inflicted discomforts of refined life" (125), Melville once again risked censure. By placing cannibalism beside the brutal "death-dealing engines" of "enlightened" Europe, he exposes our own "civilized barbarity," and his over-heated critique was expurgated along with other too-satiric passages.

But Melville also managed to get even more devastating commentary contained within amiable pronouncements on Typee's "perpetual hilarity" past censorious editors. Instead of singling out hypocritical missionaries, he focuses on a more generalized bogeyman—money—the absence of which ensures island felicity. In Typee, he notes, there are

> no foreclosures of mortgages, no protested notes, no bills payable, no debts of honor . . . ; no duns of any description; . . . no destitute widows with their children starving on the cold charities of the world; no beggars; no debtors' prisons, no proud and hard-hearted nabobs in Typee; or to sum up all in one word—no Money! [*T*, 126]

The passage is modeled on Gonzalo's idealistic greeting to the New World in *The Tempest* (II, i, 152–61). Since Shakespeare's own source is Montaigne's essay "On Cannibals,"[14] Melville simultaneously alludes to the essayist's amiable defense of native life. By the same token, the simultaneous allusion to Gonzalo is subtly designed to link Tommo's Polynesian Eden to Shakespeare's brave New World.

Given his sources, the "new light" Tommo sheds here in genializing his cannibals is not so new. What *are* new, however, are the adjustments Melville makes to adopt the familiar model to his peculiar rhetorical situation. Whereas Montaigne and Shakespeare reject Western society *in toto* (no magistrates, commerce, letters), Melville more cautiously attacks the easy target of the "almighty dollar." His rejection of money diverts attention from his previous (eventually censored) attacks on missionaries and offers up a social culprit that even pious evangelists would join in vilifying. Once Melville establishes money as the root of all evil, he can easily conclude that moneyless Typee is evil-free. Melville co-opts the very audience of religionists he has earlier offended.

But Tommo's innocuous rant has a deeply penetrating sting when properly perceived. Carefully embedded in the lull of Melville's incantatory "no"'s is an image—"children starving on the cold charities of the world"—that punctures Western philanthropy. Readers, nodding in easy assent over the rejection of mortgages, bills, and duns, nodding too over Melville's reposeful rhythms, may inadvertently swallow, with the attack on money, the corrosive implication that charity damns the very souls it stoops to save. While casting the money-lenders out of Eden with one hand and thereby gaining Christian approval, Melville exposes with the other the radical disempowerment inherent in Christian charity. A sign of Melville's rhetorical success is that although some minor editorial tinkering was done on this line for the revised edition, no one cut the passage.

Melville's concluding gambit is to contrast legends of native violence with scenes from a benevolent utopia in which "all was mirth, fun, and high good humor [and where] Blue devils, hypochondria, and doleful dumps, went and hid themselves" (*T,* 126). No violence unsettles this Eden. Tommo further deflates our doubts with a burlesque of Typeean warfare. Posing as a callow lad, he pretends to be secretly disappointed that allegations of "diabolical malice" are "nothing more than fables" (128). Hoping to find "a cut-and-thrust tragedy" in Typee, he cries with mock regret over having to endure the "genteel comedy" of island life. When a small battle between Typees and Happars does in fact disrupt this repose, Tommo heightens the humor to mitigate the violence. We discover that after the "obstinately contested affair," the number of "killed, wounded, and missing" amounts to nothing more than "one forefinger and part of a thumb-nail" (*T,* 130). The Lilliputian war is more like a "country dance." Finally, the fear of native violence is simply trivialized, and Western warfare quietly deplored.

The only flaw in Tommo's otherwise successful strategy is Melville's failure to sustain full control over his earlier, more strident social critique. His eruptions over Hawaiian missionaries remind us of Irving's Salmagundian barbs, but with a significant difference: Whereas Langstaff's satires are instinctive and cannot be helped, Tommo's are the purposeful digressions of a polemicist with an axe to grind. We can forgive Irving's eccentric for his cranky reactionary indiscretions, because his apologist Evergreen excites our own genial spirit into doing so. But Tommo has no Evergreen—only the malcontent Toby—and with no genial foil to keep him in good countenance, Melville's attack stood without apology. So, for the American audience, it was cut. But despite this setback, Melville also artfully deceived his censors into accepting deeper attacks on Christian Charity and warfare. Melville's rhetorical victory lay in his ability to modulate from satirist to humorist.

. . . And Failure

Chapter 27 marks a second intellectual awakening for Tommo, but it is a problematic growth in which his confidence in the Typees is diminished even as he tries to convince himself of their innocence. Whereas earlier, his mental "elasticity" sheds "new light" on social concerns and trivializes the legends of Typeean violence, here Tommo attempts a more philosophical defense of cannibalism. But for Melville's earliest readers, the episode fails.

What puzzles Tommo is how "heathens! savages! ay, cannibals!" can achieve social order without established laws. The answer lies in the culture's assumption of humanity's "tacit common-sense law" or the "indwelling . . . universally diffused perception of what is *just* and *noble*" (*T,* 201). It is our unalienable "fraternal feeling" (203) found in both the "uncultivated" and the "enlightened mind" that promotes order in Typee. Any debasement of this inherent benevolence derives largely from society's "arbitrary codes" and, in particular, the Western notion of property, which Polynesians vaguely acknowledge in their lives but never to the extent that it becomes an infringement of other people's right to "borrow." The islanders "held their broad valley in fee simple from Nature herself," knowing nothing of Western crime. It is a benevolent arrangement, which has been ruined, however—and Tommo cannot resist the barb—by the French. Apparently, Melville's sarcasm at this point inspired his editors to reduce these Rousseauan ruminations—some thirty lines—to nine deliberately innocuous words: "There are no rogues of any kind in Typee" (365). Also blasphemous were the suggestion that islanders demonstrated more benevolence than Christians and Tommo's sardonic observation that the "higher estimation of human nature" he had gained in Typee was eroded by his subsequent tour of duty on a man-of-war (203). Melville's strategy is to establish the innate benevolence of Typee's inhabitants so that in later paragraphs readers will be more receptive to the logic of their cannibalism. Ontology prepares us for anthropology. But expurgations (induced by Melville's untamed satiric impulses) destroy the subtle fabric of his argument.

In opening the chapter, Melville "essays" in Montaignean fashion upon benevolence and cannibalism. He places the "savage" before us as a mirror of our degeneracy. The islanders are more rational, more amiable than we. They "form one household" bound by "the ties of strong affection"; and the proof of this superior domesticity lies in the fact that Typee women are not forced to work. Feminine leisure—a sign of rank and privilege in the West—is a right on the island enjoyed by plebe and patrician alike. Moreover, Melville concedes that Typeean violence, while it may exist, does not violate the true spirit of benevolence, for it is never internal or "domestic" but is directed entirely against rival tribes or foreign provocateurs.

Anticipating a rejection of cannibalism, Melville draws upon the mediating structures of William A. Jones's "Familiar Philosophy" to harness his readers' revulsion. His ploy is to characterize Western responses to cannibalism from two comically deflated and mutually untenable extremes, necessarily forcing amiable readers toward a judicious middle ground. But eventually this leads to trouble. At one end are those idealists who find the legends of savages luring travelers into fleshpots so ludicrous as to discount allegations of cannibalism as a mere "popular fiction." At the other end are those cynics who "firmly believe that there are people . . . with tastes so depraved that they would infinitely prefer a single mouthful of material humanity to . . . roast beef and plum pudding" (*T,* 205). Neither position obtains in truth, and Melville hopes we shall see that while cannibalism is no fiction, neither is it the depraved reality one might suspect. Seeking middle ground, for "Truth . . . loves to be centrally located," amiable Melville reaffirms the amiable notion that amiable cannibals practice only upon slain enemies. Given Melville's later view in "*Mosses*" that Truth is as elusive as "a scared white doe," his insistence upon placing Truth so schematically between extremes suggests a kind of special pleading, or at least a willingness to serve up the "enigma" of cannibalism to meet the tastes of an audience habituated to a diet of benevolence and middle truths. It all seems too neat; his comic ploy backfires.

Part of the problem is that the expurgations of native benevolism at the opening of the chapter severely weaken Melville's strategy. The initial evidence of universal domesticity is calculated to undercut our fears of the cannibal "enigma." If the Typees "form one household," they will not eat one another, or us, their white brothers and sisters. With this thought in mind, readers are prepared to be persuaded in later pages by Tommo's familiarizing logic. The opening genializes the natives, but the Revised edition, in substituting for these felicitous facts the bland over-statement that there are "no rogues" in Typee, radically disables readers from apprehending Melville's logic. Indeed, the denial of rogues puts us on the lookout for rogues. In sum, Melville's little satiric attack on the French instigated a wholesale slaughter of his opening gambit in the expurgated edition, which seriously under-mined his concluding ploy.

But even with the opening restored (as it is in most twentieth-century editions), Tommo's rhetoric is doomed to fail: By attempting to explain away a primitive horror, it only heightens the dramatic tension surrounding Tommo's incarceration. Tommo's rationality can place cannibalism in an amiable context and reduce its fearfulness by defining the limits of the practice, but it cannot explain *why* the practice exists, nor can it protect us from the realization that as *enemies,* not brothers and sisters, of the Typees, we white invaders are, in fact, perfect candidates for ingestion. In short, all of Tommo's rhetoric cannot keep him from becoming, in his captors' eyes, an enemy to be slain then eaten.

Thus, we sense a mindfulness within Melville's benevolent assertions that "hor-rible and fearful" cannibalism is, in fact, "to be abhorred and condemned," and it is this cognizance that withers the confidence of his final line—"still I assert that those who indulge in it are in other respects humane and virtuous" (*T,* 205). There is a chill in this genial, too-urgent insistence that opens a chasm between Tommo, the defender of cannibals, and Tommo, the captive; and the growing tension between his rhetoric and his self-interest anticipates his own violent escape from the island culture. Tommo can mount, if left uncensored, a reasonably persuasive campaign to win his readers' respect for Typee; he can even convince us of the rationality of the cannibalism in this genial culture; but the grim irony is that he cannot convince himself.

In demonstrating Melville's largely successful attempts to cast Typee as an ami-able Eden, we find not only the author's versatility in adopting the amiable mode to his rhetorical needs but also his careful attempts to build from one amiable pose to the next a growing dramatic tension. This comic progression in voice dramatizes Tommo's paradoxically tense repose; it converts his earlier picturesque visions of blue seas, footpad sharks, and muted cascades into a fragile psychological state. Comparing expurgated passages to those Melville was allowed to retain gives us some sense of what elements in the author's rhetorical strategies succeeded in the marketplace. Wherever Melville compressed social outrage within an amiable frame, his words were not cut. Satiric eruptions against Western powers and mores, however, prompted excisions that, as in the case of Chapter 27, severely weakened Melville's rhetorical thrust. In turning from editorial expurgations to Melville's actual manuscript, we learn just how conscious Melville was during his creative process of the need to contain his enthusiasms within humor.

8

Typee in Manuscript

The *Typee* fragment, a working draft manuscript covering Chapters 12–14, is thirty sheets of long blue paper crammed with words on both sides. To casual readers, the scribbled revisions are chaos; to scholars, they are the verbal equivalent of a fugue. If writing is a fluid process of composition destined never to be completed and prematurely frozen into print, then this manuscript of Melville's is sweet music indeed. In places we find the flowing melody of unimpeded thought rushing to be set confidently into words; elsewhere is the staccato of false starts, erasures, fresh starts, and cancellations. There are shifts in language and voice, and modulations of humor and insight. In piecing together Melville's revisions, we see the the many Prufrockian decisions and indecisions of word choice he entertained, from which we may infer the rhetorical strategies he developed to control himself and readers. Reading Melville in manuscript is a chance to retrieve moments of growth; it is our closest link to his creative process and rhetoric.[1]

The manuscript of Chapter 12 reveals Melville's modulations of amiability and gothicism, his shaping of fact into drama, and his molding of an aesthetics of repose. Chapter 13 records the emergence of a narrative voice and Melville's quandary over how to tell a story. We also discover how a single, ambivalent letter can crystallize the relevance of that quandary. Finally, a single deleted sentence in Chapter 14 affords us a glimpse at Melville's trials and errors in forging his political and religious ideology.

Drama and Restraint

In its printed form, Chapter 12 is an exciting exploration of Tommo's volatile frame of mind during his first contact with his alien captors. It begins with his first exposure to the naked girls of the island and leads to the growing gothicism of the Taboo groves and its bachelor retreat of the Ti. Here, Toby and Tommo eat *poi-poi* and smoke, drowsing off into a sleep that is abruptly shattered by a midnight ritual. Both sailors assume that they are about to be eaten, but the natives have in fact prepared a feast for them, not of them. By morning lurid gothic fears have vanished, and a procession of natives leads them to Marheyo's genial home. In all, Tommo's early sexual stirrings are diverted and his gothic fears of a cannibal death are dramatically purged, leaving him suddenly bereft of cultural anxiety and warmly enfolded in the arms of his country squire of a host. Good humor subsumes anxiety and fear.

Tommo's first encounter with Typee girls occurs at the stream, when Kory-Kory forces the sailor to strip to the waist in order to bathe himself, while equally undressed girls "sport" about him in the water. Earlier, Tommo has "felt infinitely sheepish" and "exceedingly shocked" by similar sights—although his reaction is pointedly more moderate than that of the "immeasurably outraged Toby" (*T*, 77). Later, of course, Tommo loosens his modesty through Fayaway's ministrations, but in Chapter 12 his Victorianism has not dissolved, a point Melville is careful to emphasize. In the initial stages of composition, Melville has Tommo offer only the Cooperesque comment that he felt "somewhat embarrassed by the presence of the female portion of the company." But some time after completing his working draft, perhaps even as late as the galley stages, he added the following:

> and feeling my cheeks burning with bashful timidity, I formed a primitive basin
> by joining my hands together, and cooled my blushes in the water it con-
> tained. [89]

Melville's intention here is to intensify Tommo's embarrassment and impress upon us the young man's relative state of innocence. He may, as well, have hoped to placate more inhibited readers by representing the blushes that they themselves may feel. Ironically, this very passage which Melville added to establish Tommo's modesty, which was printed in the first English and American editions, was expurgated in the American Revised edition. Presumably a burning cheek (like the word "virgin") suggests more passion than modesty. Some blushes burn too hotly.

Once Tommo has cooled down, he retires to a rock to engage in his favorite sport of voyeurism. Crippled by his leg pain, he watches "young girls springing bouyantly into the air, and revealing their naked forms to the waist" (*T*, 90). Originally, Melville had made this participial phrase into a full clause by adding a sirenic comparison: the young girls springing buoyantly

> looked among those green mossy rocks like so many mermaids sporting in the
> billows that washed the sea weed covered sides of their [treacherous] mossy lurking
> places[2]

The passage, while not canceled in manuscript, was eventually deleted before publication. Melville tinkered with the image, replacing the word "treacherous" with "mossy" in order to tone down the threatening sexual promiscuity inherent in the image of "mermaids sporting." This he did despite the seemingly unintended repetition of "mossy." Perhaps, however, the repetition *was* intended to give the passage an insistent sensuality suggestive of a female's genitalia. In fact, we cannot tell for sure whether Melville's tinkering is meant to heighten or damper the sexuality of the scene. We can surmise, however, that the legendary sexuality of mermaids alone was enough to make Melville think better of his comparison. At this point he would not have Tommo's blushes complicated by thoughts of sexual gratification. Moreover, the deletion eliminates any hint that Tommo's future sexual encounters may be taken as sirenlike seductions. Whatever the reason for the deletion, its effect is that Tommo is left more the wide-eyed innocent than the leering sailor he seems originally to have been.[3]

As Melville moves Tommo from sportive waters to the darker recesses of the Houlah grounds, he complains of his difficulty in sketching the spot "as vividly as I recollect" (*T*, 91). An abundance of cancellations and sentence recastings in manuscript verify that difficulty. Melville was eager to explore the meaning and "feel" of his past sexual experiences in Polynesia but also anxious not to offend his audience. For one reason or another, and through various agencies—his editors or himself—the suggestive passages of the watering hole were later excised even after they had been toned down. But as Tommo moves past sensual waters on to sacred groves, Melville transforms sexual desire into more acceptable symbolic expression. In retrospect, the lesson learned is that his audience preferred its sensuality packaged in lurid gothicisms rather than naked waists, mossy places, even blushes. The manuscript version of the first descriptive paragraph in this scene (91.6–17) shows Melville struggling to find the right words to intensify the scene's gothic mood without crossing too far into excessive horror. The result is a dark picturesque, and in revising to ensure this effect, Melville instinctively resorts to his aesthetics of repose: He pushes his description into gloom—his initial "*deep* shadows" become ominously "dark" in revision—but he also pulls the language back into light, making his potentially threatening pagan scene more solemn and controlled. Here, Melville's tinkering results in a masterfully precarious and uncensored passage.

Initially, as the manuscript shows, Melville intended an abrupt, journalistic opener to his paragraph: "It was the sacred groves." The line directly announces the theme of piety, sewing together such following words as "consecrated," "cathedral-like," "hallowed," and "religious." Melville also tinkered with his lighting, changing the bland phrase "perpetual twilight" to "solemn twilight" in order to enhance the sacrilizing leitmotif. But Melville presses deeper in secondary revisions. He cancels his topic sentence altogether, replacing it with, "Here were situated the Taboo groves." The sentence structure is less dramatic, but the word "taboo" radically reorients the paragraph toward the exotic and forbidden. Sacred piety is dissolved. Accordingly, an image of "rude" and "rustic altars" appearing later in the manuscript paragraph suddenly takes its exit when revised to its final, more savage, printed version "idolatrous altars."

Not all changes are so direct. Melville alters "the sombre genius of pagan worship" first to "horrid genius" and then to "frightful genius." The pulsing of these successive adjectives from the complacent "sombre" to a too-threatening "horrid" then back to the measured jolt of "frightful" reveals an artist's attempt to inject discrete doses of fear into his toned-down gothicism. One instantaneous revision at the end of the paragraph suggests that his artistic restraint was virtually instinctual. Concluding with an image of "putrefying" sacrificial relics, Melville first contemplates the phrase "recent bloody sacrifice" but interrupts himself in mid-thought, canceling "bloody" even before he can complete the word. All he writes after "recent" in the initial stirring of his creative process is the first half of "bloody," only the three letters, *blo*. This half-word is summarily stricken the instant it is written, and Melville completes the phrase with the word "sacrifice." What was finally published was not "recent bloody sacrifice" but merely "recent sacrifice," with no hint of blood.

Comparing Melville's first intention ("bloody sacrifice") to his final reading ("sacrifice") provides a fascinating glimpse into Melville's creativity. With the canceled half-word in manuscript, we see the full lurid sensuality of fresh blood enter the artist's mind; we see Melville beginning to register the thought in ink on the page. But we also see his immediate realization that the sanguinary image would stain the well-poised tension between sacred and uncanny feelings that he had been striving to create. In striking over *blo,* Melville canceled his initial flashing-forth and toned down his most lurid impulse even before his hand could fully record the thought. In confirmation of this moment of instinctive restraint, we also find in the manuscript that sometime after writing his first draft Melville inserted on a separate slip of paper an image of *vegetable* offerings (breadfruit and coconuts) in various stages of "decay." The most likely explanation for this afterthought is that Melville wanted his putrefying sacrificial relics to be purely vegetal, not carnal. Thus, again, Melville's revisions, both at the initial moment of creation and upon later reflection, divest his text of any hint of bloody sacrifice, excessive carnality, or even cannibalism from Typeean paganism. Such restraint keeps revulsion from undoing our fascination with the sacred, savage rites. It also prepares us for the comic inversion of Tommo's deepest fears of cannibal feasts to follow.

A final example of another virtually instantaneous revision confirms the toning-down process inherent in Melville's aesthetics of repose. In comparing the "solemn twilight" that reigns beneath the trees to a "cathedral-like gloom," Melville first concluded this thought with a routine dependent clause: It is a gloom, he wrote, "that hung over the place & bathed every object." The wording, however, was vague and rhythmically inept; he canceled the clause. Keeping the notion of an overhanging gloom in mind, he wrote quickly to keep pace with a flood of new words that flowed without the false starts and revisions that had previously thwarted him. "Cathedral-like gloom" gives birth to the word "sombre," and suddenly the central image of his paragraph seems to write itself:

> The sombre genius of pagan worship seemed to brood in silence over the place,
> breathing its spell upon every object around.   [Leaf 3]

As noted, "sombre" was eventually changed to "horrid" and then "frightful," but at the moment of creation, "place" and "every object" remained anchored to his initial thought. Somehow, the words "genius" and "brood" spring from "cathedral gloom." And yet the key word added in this sudden expansion is "silence": It is the mode through which "genius" expresses itself; it is an eerie pagan mysticism recalling earlier silences in Tommo's sea and land picturesques. It is the silence of a heightened repose over gothic fear. The sacrificial yet sacred scene, the horrid-frightful light, the carnal then vegetal putrefaction—these are the highly sensual details Melville transformed into a silent picturesque to bring his readers to the margins of forbidden thought, to contain the unthinkable bloody sacrifice.

Melville's next descriptive sketch in Chapter 12 is our first exposure to the "Ti." This all-male enclave combines church, armory, and gentleman's club. Having cleansed himself beside naked girls and having made his *rite de passage* through gothic groves, Tommo has withstood sensuality and fearful silence; he is ready for a feast. But is this a celebration or the fattening of a sacrificial lamb? At this juncture, neither Tommo nor Toby registers any fears. They lapse into "drowsy repose." Here is what Melville first wrote to describe the scene:

> The repast concluded, a pipe was lighted, which passed from mouth to mouth [and under its soporific influence the chief & Kori-Kori were in a short time slumbering beside us.]   [Leaf 6]

It is a routine sequence leading to innocent sleep. There is no tension. "From this," Tommo continues, "I awoke." But in revision Melville expands the paragraph to dramatize the anxiety of Tommo's repose. The bracketed clause above is canceled and replaced with the following:

> and *yielding* to its soporific influence, the quiet of the place and the [sh] deepening shadows of approaching *night* my companion and I *sank* into a kind of *drowsy repose,* while the chief and Kori-Kori *seemed* to be slumbering beside us.   [my emphasis]

The inclusion of "yielding" suggests a resistance to a sleep that is as unavoidable as "approaching night." "Sank" carries, too, the inevitable pull of unconscious-ness. Added to this is the ominous fact that the islanders "beside us" only "seem" to be sleeping. The false start "sh-" for "shadows" is quickly changed to "deep-ening shadows" to enhance the fearful inevitability of the "drowsy repose." Finally, Melville changes the opening of his next paragraph from the original "From this, I awoke" to the more explicit "I awoke from an uneasy nap." In a few deft strokes, Melville the reporter becomes Melville the dramatist.

The implications of these revisions are clear. At some point after his initial composition of this paragraph, Melville realized the dramatic potential of Tommo's "nap" and the opportunity it afforded him to introduce the double-edged dilemma of repose: its genial ease, its sinking unconsciousness. We see him shaping "un-varnished facts" into fiction and using humor as an aesthetic restraint to create both fusion and repose. This appears most directly in the following comic scene, when Tommo quickly perceives that he and Toby must confront a throng of torch-bearing "demons," including the cannibal king Mehevi, who cautiously approaches with the amusingly ambivalent words: "Tommo, Toby, ki ki! (eat)." Here, timing is everything. The immediate concern is over the verb "eat" and whether Tommo and Toby are expected to be the subject or direct object of that verb. Such a marvelous difference there is between the eaters and the eaten. We await a reaction from either of the sailors, but Melville purposely delivers a description of Mehevi that comically delays their response. Initially, Melville composed two full sentences: one recording Mehevi's surprise at finding the two awake, the other speculating that Mehevi's cautious approach was due to his "fear of disturbing our slumbers." The second line, by reinforcing Tommo's assumptions about the good nature of savages, clearly defuses the carefully built comic ambivalence, for if Mehevi is so indulgent of their rest, he is not likely to be a murderer. Moreover, the sentence ineffectually prolongs the pause between Mehevi's "eat" and Toby's comic re-action: "Ki ki, is it . . . well, cook us first, will you?" In cutting the excessive second line, Melville sharpened the timing and tension of his comic scene, thus more effectively fusing humor and fear.

Soon enough, the sailors learn that they will not be eaten and that the dish they are served is not "baked baby" (as Toby presumes) but pork. This little comedy dramatizes the mental states that civilized man experiences when facing the primitive. Our laughter becomes a purging of our doubts about paradise and its repose. But the comic purgation is never a complete cessation of awareness. As we laugh with Tommo over his initial misconception of the word "eat," we are not fully relieved of our suspicion that we are among cannibals, that the pork in fact may be baby done rare. Thus, like Tommo, readers are suspended in humor between awareness and ease, and as Melville's manuscript manipulations indicate, this tense repose was indeed the artist's studied intention. The conclusion of Chapter 12 provides final testimony to this fact.

Chapter 12 ends with a heavily revised section relating Tommo's procession from the sacred Bachelor's Ti back to Marheyo's family home. The gothic fears, the feasts, and the tense repose are over. No longer on Taboo ground, Tommo returns to the village led by males and cheered on by young women. The chapter beginning with titillating sexual pleasures and a repressed vision of mermaids promises to end on a similar note of heterosexual delight; the night of fear and apprehension dissolves in the dawning of Polynesian sensuality. But this promised return is only partially realized. To be sure, Melville's first intention was to recast the nubile girls of the stream into wood nymphs from classical mythology. The following passage, originally the chapter's penultimate paragraph but deleted from the printed version, sets the scene:

> This picturesque procession carrying along such glorious specimens of tropical vegetation moving with wild chants through the sylvan defiles of the valley might have been taken for a throng of the ancient devotees of Ceres wending their way with votive offerings towards the altars of the goddess. [Leaf 10]

Once again, the passage modulates between the sacred (devotees, votive, altars, goddess) and the exotic (wild chants). The "glorious specimens of tropical vegetation" also defuse any lingering thoughts of carnal sacrifice, while the comparison of Polynesian rituals with Roman paganism roots the alien practice in an accessible classical tradition.

But the mythological references also draw Melville back to native sexuality. He continues in manuscript:

> As we proceeded along our way, bands of nymphs darting from the surrounding groves, hung upon our shirts, and accompanied us with shouts of merriment and delight, that almost drowned the deep notes of the recitative.

Melville preserved most of this passage in print, altering only the word "nymphs"— a logical extension of the preceding Roman allusions—to the more innocuous "young girls." But as carefully written as the Ceres paragraph is in familiarizing the exotic, it remains an expression of paganism—objectionable still to the overly "evangelized" among Melville's readers—and it recalls the water nymphs, mermaids, and mossy stones of Tommo's even more objectionable bath. It had to go.

Moreover, Melville felt compelled to do more than compare one set of pagans to another. To legitimize his natives, to "civilize" these savages and make their practices compatible with our own, the author moved beyond Roman myth to modern amiability. Accordingly, he dropped the "picturesque procession" of Ceres completely, dropped at the same time his young girls and nymphs, and proceeded to lard his conclusion with almost excessive infusions of geniality:

> On approaching old Marheyo's domicile, its inmates rushed to receive us; and while the gifts of Mehevi were being disposed of, the superannuated warrior did the honors of his mansion with all the warmth of hospitality evinced by an English squire who with a heart like a mastodon's regales his visitors at some fine old patrimonial mansion in the country.

Melville's belaboring of "old" (even to the tacit invocation of genial Lamb's "superannuated man"), as well as his emphasis on mansion, domicile, and the near ludicrous image of a Polynesian squire, demonstrates the lengths to which Melville was willing to go in depicting Tommo's amiable island mentor. One expects an Allworthy or a Shandy to peek from behind a palm. Some indication of the author's awareness of his excess is found in his eventual deletion of Marheyo's "mastodon heart"—an odd image best saved for a book about whales.

Melville's rhetorical strategy in Chapter 12 is to arouse, frighten, and then relieve readers through a progression of scenes that inevitably solemnify the amiability of Tommo's Eden. The manuscript offers palpable evidence of the author's intricate modulations of voice and idea to make this strategy work: his toning-down of sexuality, his balance of gothic and sacred, his intensification of humor and dramatization of doubt, his attempts to "genialize" the savage mind. In sum, the working draft of Chapter 12 shows us an artist inventing and then shaping words—amplifying generalities here, reining in excesses there—so that sexual matters and alien fears may be registered but contained largely through humor. In effect, Melville made language conform to his aesthetics of repose. In Chapter 13, however, aesthetic restraint is more self-conscious, demonstrating the author's increased awareness of himself as a fiction maker.

Finding Voice: Transcription, Transformation, and Translation

Setting out in Chapter 13 for medical supplies, Toby is wounded by a band of rival Happars and chased back to Typee Valley, where he relates his adventure. The servant brother Kory-Kory responds with a remarkable oration against the Happar tribe that leaves Tommo exhausted and amused. In a sense, the two scenes demonstrate different ways of telling a story. But the structural pairing of Toby's serious narrative and the native's comic harangue implicitly demeans Polynesian culture at the moment when Melville is attempting to deepen our respect for his captors. In its printed version, Kory-Kory's "eloquence" is another comic trivialization that renders the alleged cannibals harmless while indicting the Happars of that crime. But the manuscript tells more. Originally Melville had planned to lampoon his Man Friday, which if published would have compromised Polynesian language and culture. Melville's deletion of this burlesque, along with other revisions, provides intriguing glimpses of Melville's wrestling with the differences inherent in the transcription, transformation, and translation of experience into words.

Let's begin with Toby. The working draft manuscript reveals that Melville first transcribed Toby's narrative in a stiff, discursive tone and that in revising he transformed the too-literary prose into the rhythms of dramatic speech. For instance, Toby's phrase "Quite elated *at the close vicinity* of the Happars" is changed to "Quite elated at being so near the Happars" (*T,* 101). The leaden pretense of "My first impulse was immediate flight" is happily changed to Toby's impulse "to run for it." And so on. Interestingly enough, two passages Melville labored over but then deleted record his apparent reluctance to conceal the obvious fact that these are not the actual words of a Tobias Greene that have been meticulously transcribed but Melville's own words, revised for dramatic effect. Melville's first apologetic passage was clumsy and was duly canceled:

> As I cannot remember the words made use of by Toby in this occasion, I shall accordingly relate his adventure in my own language[,] tho' in the same[,] putting the words in his mouth.   [Leaf 15]

His second attempt is more fluid:

> Though I cannot recall to mind anything like the precise phraseology employed on this occasion still for the sake of unity I shall permit my companion to rehearse his own adventures in the language that most readily occurs to me.

Although this version is not canceled in manuscript like its predecessor, it too never made it into print, and with good reason: It unnecessarily diminishes the excitement of Toby's coming narrative while calling attention to its fictionality. Nevertheless, the attention Melville paid to his apology reveals his serious concern for his role as a writer.

In both versions Melville wants to transcribe or quote Toby, but poor memory makes this impossible. With Montaigne's argument that a good liar must have an excellent memory in mind, Melville's admission of a memory lapse paradoxically enhances his reliability, because, while attuned to the larger matters of the heart, he forgets the little details. Ironically, the failure to remember forces Melville to invent (simulate) words that create the facts. Failing to *transcribe* literally, then, he must *transform* Toby's experience into language. But here, the two versions of Melville's apology vary. Whereas the author first tells us he will use "my own words" to relate Toby's adventure, he subsequently allows Toby to tell his tale "in language that most readily occurs to me." In the first instance, Melville proposes simply to substitute his words for Toby's forgotten lines; in the second, he implies that he will devise language that is appropriate for a particular character in a particular circumstance. On the one hand, Melville is ventriloquizing for Toby; on the other, he becomes Toby. Thus, in shifting from indirect to direct dialog, Melville must in fact endure a sea change, a momentary psychological transformation of himself.

Clearly, the young writer is stretching his muscles, testing the limits of his new profession and craft. His first instinct was to relate Toby's narrative in Tommo's voice, to maintain the tone of a reflective enthusiast that pervades the entire novel.

But he quickly decides to invent a voice for Toby, to "permit [him] to rehearse his own adventure," and this readily explains such revisions as the shift from "immediate flight" to "run for it." Only the manuscript reveals Melville's urge to move beyond fact into fiction and the degree to which he can already do what he will have his confidence man do: don a mask, assume a role, play a part.

Melville's reticence in making his transformation is fascinating. Initially he feels a deep obligation to expose himself, to admit to readers that what they are about to read is a necessary fabrication. His assumption is that, unless apologized for, his fictionalizing will undermine his narrative reliability. To placate readers, he makes his transformation of reality "for the sake of unity," suggesting that whatever is lost in terms of our faith in Melville's exact reportage, he will regain in our appreciation of a voice commensurate with Toby's dramatic circumstances. The dilemma he was forced to recognize, of course, is that no unified rendering of experience can be literally factual; all narratives are fabrications; indeed, unity itself is a fiction. And yet readers like John Murray, who demand facts, also expect a unified narrative that requires inventions that are like fact. Realizing, then, that his apologetic passage would only call attention to his necessary fictionalizing of fact, Melville dropped his apology altogether. As it now stands, Toby's narrative evolves seamlessly out of Tommo's, and readers are none the wiser.

The deleted apology is our earliest record of Melville's self-awareness as a fiction writer and of his anxiety at addressing an audience. This little aesthetic epiphany takes on richer meaning in the second half of chapter 13, when, in describing Kory-Kory's harangue, Tommo is obliged to do what he could not do with Toby: transcribe the native's words. What he attempts, he says in a deleted passage that is later repeated and retained in print, is a "literal interpretation," and his word-for-word translation of Polynesian sounds into English equivalents suggests that Melville favored precise linguistic renderings. Here, he will report objectively and not fictionalize, and that objectivity is meant to establish Melville's anthropological respect for Polynesian language. But the manuscript shows that at the same time Melville became caught up in a comic invention that burlesqued Kory-Kory to the point of savage ridicule.

As it now stands in print, Kory-Kory's oratorical explosion is the outburst of an enthused servant taking pains to repeat the obvious. He gesticulates wildly, running in and out of the hut, and at one point illustrates his meaning by pretending to eat "the fleshy part of [Tommo's] arm." Such "gibberish" gives Tommo a headache, and the printed chapter ends. It is a comic parallel to Toby's more frightening version. But in manuscript Melville derides Kory-Kory's "eloquence," stating that the native would have used the standard rhetorical signposts (firstly, secondly, etc.) "had he been anything other than the illiterate barbarian that he was." The derogation is surprising since Melville typically refers to the Typees as "islanders" or "natives," carefully reserving the negative term "savage" for certain dramatic moments, and never calling his captors "barbarian." The term seems out of place, and though Melville does not cancel it in manuscript, it was later deleted along with the rest of his excessive burlesque. Melville's further criticism that "any millstone might have comprehended" the islander's meaning also violates the amiable stricture against ridiculing the harmless, and in the published version this particular phrase was revised to the less graphic but more respectful line, "It was impossible not to comprehend" (*T*, 103).

Melville's largest deletion is an earlier version of his concluding paragraph to Chapter 13. Instead of ending with Tommo's headache, he further mocks Kory-Kory's "gibberish":

> he reminded me of a man with his mouthful of chicken spluttering, choking, & spitting the bones out in every direction. Such a horrific [clucking?] merciless jargon never surely was heard before. [All these mad sounds seemed to be served up in a hasty kind of fricassee] It might have been denominated a fricassee of vowels and consonants [coated] with a spice of cayenne. Heaven defend me from such another infliction! It gave me rheumatic pains in every joint in my body. What it all meant I could not for the life of me conjecture without the speaker was employing the occasion to enlarge upon the transitory nature of all human enjoyment & the vanity of terrestrial expectations.   [Leaf 20][4]

The description is comic enough, appealing to an amiable mind drawn to gustatory joking. The image of language as a fricassee would be a palpable hit in any other book about pagan savages, but in his Preface Melville had emphasized his fidelity to Polynesian language, promising to render its "beautiful combinations of vocal sounds" far more accurately than had previous South Sea writers. Obviously, the "spluttering, choking, and spitting" of Melville's fricative fricassee would have to go, and with it went the slightly more respectful references to Kory-Kory's putative enlargements upon transitory pleasures and human vanity, an uplifting coda to a generally demeaning comic attack. In toning down the burlesque, Melville preserves our growing regard for the island culture. If these "amiable epicures" are worth emulating socially and morally, then their language merits serious attention. It deserves objective translation, not ridicule. In his revisions and the final printed version of this section, Melville seems, in fact, to have forfeited broad humor for a treatment of Polynesian that is *literal*.

This last word has become a textual crux in Melville studies since the manuscript's discovery,[5] and a brief digression on it before we conclude will help us confront the complexities of knowing Melville's mind and rhetoric.

Because of the peculiarities of Melville's hand, it is impossible to determine whether, in discussing Kory-Kory's harangue, the author wrote that he would supply a "literal" or "liberal" interpretation. The "L-Word" that Melville actually wrote appears twice in manuscript, and in both cases the "t" (if that is what it is) is uncrossed and may be taken as a "b." Readers will instantly appreciate that the minute orthographic difference between the words "literal" and "liberal" results in two radically distinct readings, for in matters of interpretation, a liberal translation is worlds apart from one that is literal. In effect, the two possible readings are virtual antonyms. A gamesome Melville inspecting his own manuscript would have delighted in the confusion created by the simple omission of the crossing of a "t": A word intended to convey a precise meaning seems thwarted in that mission by the very nature of its orthographic form. Words are therefore hieroglyphic and inherently, inscrutably disposed to multiple meaning. But audiences do not read in manuscript; they read print, and these hermeneutic penetrations are lost on readers, for on a typeset page all "t"'s are crossed and no "t" looks like a "b." Obviously,

Melville intended no ambivalence when he wrote his "L-Word"; he meant one word only at the moment of creation, and one would like to assume that printed versions of his "L-Word" would clarify precisely what meaning he intended. The problem is that the authoritative first editions contain both readings.

Melville's first editors, both British and American, were the first to confront the problem. They printed Kory-Kory's Polynesian "gibberish" ("—ah! nuee, nuee, nuee!") along with Melville's translation ("ah! heaps, heaps, heaps"). Between the two, we find the following linking phrase: "Which, *literally* interpreted as before, would imply." That is, they read the "L-Word" as "literal." This, it would seem, ought to settle the matter, for in proofing galleys, Melville had every opportunity to get his L-Word right in print. But in the Revised American edition (also inspected by the author), the linking phrase was changed to "*liberally* interpreted." Although the revised edition is known for its unwanted expurgations, it also contains legitimate and desirable authorial changes. Assuming that Melville, in fact, authorized this particular revision, modern editors of Melville have followed this last reading, printing "liberally" instead of "literally" as the standard text. This decision, however, was made fifteen years before the discovery of the *Typee* manuscript, with its utterly ambivalent hieroglyphic "L-Word," and presumably editors will now want to reconsider their "liberal" reading in light of the "literal" evidence.

Their reconsideration might proceed as follows. Melville's original printers set their type not from the working draft manuscript we inspect here but from a fair copy drawn from that manuscript by either Melville or a relative. Quite possibly, the fair copyist crossed Melville's "t" and the printers printed what they saw: "literally." Quite possibly, too, the fair-copyist perpetuated the "L-Word" dilemma by not crossing the "t," leaving it to printers to print what they thought they saw: again, "literally." But when *Typee* went into its Revised edition, Melville asked or allowed "literally" to be changed to "liberally." Of course, that change may have been a typo Melville simply missed.

With this in mind, we can imagine at least three equally valid scenarios to explain the full course of textual variation. Melville may have intended his L-Word to be "liberally" in the working draft and fair copy, but the word was misread by his first typesetters as "literally" only to be *corrected* by Melville back to "liberally" in the Revised edition. Or Melville may have intended "literally" at all of the early stages, both in manuscript and in print, only to change his mind in the Revised edition and have the word *altered* to "liberally." Or "literally" may have been intended all along, only to be *corrupted* to "liberally" through a typesetting mishap in the Revised edition. Textually, then, "liberally" may be Melville's correction or alteration or a typesetter's corruption.

While manuscript evidence neither confirms nor denies the Northwestern–Newberry decision to print "liberally," it does force us to consider more carefully the rhetorical strategies implied in the choice Melville had to make between "literally" and "liberally," for overall, if Melville intended a change to "liberally," the decision would seem to be ill-advised; "literally" is the better word.

To be sure, the case for "liberal" is appealing if only for its typically Melvillean ramifications. Consider the metaphysical nature of translation itself. Can one ever render one language into another literally, submitting one word as a precise equivalent of its foreign counterpart? Must not *translation* necessarily involve a careful *transformation* of words that can only approach but never fully achieve literal equivalency? Given that words in a Platonic or Romantic framework are fated merely to represent, not create, reality, and given as well what Tommo finally discovers to be the seemingly unbridgeable chasm between the civilized and the primitive mind, translation can only be a transformative, not a transcriptive, act, a fictive process, a liberation, and hence something that must be done "liberally." Given, too, Melville's earlier wrestling in manuscript over Toby's narrative, we know that the author was particularly conscious of the inevitability of his own fictionalizing transformations. But we also know that his "liberal" fictionalizing of Kory-Kory's harangue had gone too far. Whereas Melville's transformation of himself into Toby succeeds as a flowering of the creative self beyond his actual being, his recasting of a native into an "illiterate barbarian" would suggest the writer's failure to transcend cultural barriers. As we shall see in the next chapter, this failure to adopt a more cosmopolitan sensibility is Tommo's ultimate undoing. But in mid-novel, Melville seems intent upon preserving Tommo's potential to understand his alien captors, if only to enhance the seriousness of his retreat from Eden. Thus, "literally" is a viable indeed persuasive reading.

As already noted, the manuscript shows Melville's rejection of his too-liberal transformation of Kory-Kory. In cutting the Polynesian burlesque, Melville reined in his comic creation. Although the idea of "literal" interpretation may run counter to his growing metaphysical views, it squarely met his rhetorical need to render Typeean culture with respectful objectivity. To provide only liberal translations would be to suggest that Polynesian language is incomprehensibly silly and imprecise, meriting only the loosest of renderings into the Imperial Queen's more effective tongue. Melville surmised that a sign of a culture's relevance lies in the degree of care taken in rendering its language "literally." In choosing to be literal with Kory-Kory's language, then, Melville not only made a further enactment of aesthetic restraint but encouraged his readers to become more endeared to the inhabitants of his amiable Eden. In short, Melville will not ridicule Kory-Kory; rather, he will allow us to delight in the native's enthusiasm, sincerity, and eccentricity. Although this gives Tommo a headache, this is not a result of too-liberal effusions on his part but rather an attempt to grasp his respected friend's "literal" meaning.

Forging Ideology: Melville and "Little Henry"

Thus far, the manuscript has afforded us penetrating glimpses of Melville's creativity: his dramatizing and comic restraint, his visions and revisions, and his transformations. This is the artist at work, forging language into voice. We can also glimpse the curious route Melville takes in the forging of his liberal ideology. Already we have seen that, in letting his comic spirit fly too freely, Melville had experimented with a damaging lampoon of Kory-Kory. The fact that the author eventually rejected the ridicule may confirm our faith in his good sense, but it does not erase the fact that he entertained the burlesque in the first place. Moreover, had Melville begun with a fully formed notion of Kory-Kory's linguistic and cultural respectability, he would not even have considered such ridicule. Thus, the most immediate force that drove Melville to write was not so much the earnest desire to promote an idea but the pleasure of putting words down on paper. For him as for any writer, writing precedes ideology, and meaning waits on creation. The fascinating case of Melville's deleted reference to the famous Sunday School tract *Little Henry and His Bearer* also suggests that when he wrote *Typee,* the author's ideological support of native culture had only partially solidified.

The deleted passage I refer to appears just after Toby's departure. Tommo's leg pain intensifies, and he allows Kory-Kory to carry him about the valley and especially to the nymph-laden stream for morning and evening baths. The pain reflects Tommo's sexual repression in contrast to the innocent liberality of his companions Fayaway and Kory-Kory. But Melville had trouble finding an appropriate image to express the odd dependency implied in Kory-Kory's carrying of Tommo. At one point in the text, he compares the piggy-back duo to Sindbad's bearing the Old Man of the Sea upon his back (*T,* 90); however, he never develops the idea beyond this brief mention. Perhaps the disparate ages and roles of the Arabian Nights characters did not gibe with the more fraternal relationship between Tommo and Kory-Kory. Perhaps the author simply wanted his own depiction to stand on its own, uncomplicated by any announced association to the rich tradition of the man-carrying-man image that dates back as far as the *Aenead.* But the manuscript shows that Melville toyed at some length with an image drawn from his own culture, in particular the Sunday School Movement of early-nineteenth-century England and America.

The image comes from one of the most popular Sunday School tracts of Melville's youth. In its earliest draft, the eventually deleted passage in question reads as follows:

> Oftentimes when borne by him [Kory-Kory] through the shady paths of the valley
> I have thought of the picture of ''Little Henry & his Bearer'' which usually decorates
> the title page of that pleasing and popular religious tract.   [Leaf 26]

The pamphlet *Little Henry and His Bearer* was written in 1814 by Mrs. Mary Martha Sherwood.[6] Appearing in more than one hundred editions by 1884, it was as well known in its day as *Uncle Tom's Cabin.*[7] It is the story of an English lad orphaned in India and raised by a negligent relative who allows his moral and religious training to be conducted by a Hindu servant named Boosy, whose principal function is to ''bear'' the child from here to there.

Appearing in most editions of *Little Henry and His Bearer* is an illustration of the turbaned Boosy carrying Henry about the jungle. The pamphlet itself is a shameless piece of missionary propaganda. The sickly Little Henry is too angelic for this world, but when a proper nanny comes to take care of him, he quickly learns scripture and abandons Boosy's heathenism. With the help of his nanny, Little Henry realizes that the true goal in his short life is to convert Boosy to Christianity. ''India,'' says the precocious little imperialist, would be a very good country, if the people were Christians. Then they would not be so idle as they are now; and they would agree together, and clear the brushwood and build churches to worship God in. [Sherwood, 181]

Little Henry soon dies, but not before he converts Boosy away from his "foolish" and "satanic" ways. Sherwood's cloying tale argues forthrightly for missionary work and ends with a direct appeal to "Little Children in America"—"whenever any measure is proposed for the benefit of the heathen; . . . think how Little Henry . . . would have done, and *go and do likewise*" (196).

Chances are Herman Melville first read Sherwood's tract in his mother's church during the 1830s, and like thousands of other "little children in America" he may have fallen for a time under the spell of its narrow sentimentality and evangelism. Perhaps he had hoped that God might call him to emulate Little Henry. But Little Herman grew to despise the missionary Mrs. Sherwoods of his day; all of *Typee* attests to that. Nevertheless, the lessons of youth die hard, and it is a curious tribute to the popularity of *Little Henry* that, even as Melville was composing his stridently antimissionary book, he automatically turned, and apparently without irony, to a promissionary tract to illustrate Kory-Kory's carrying of Tommo. Melville was not as yet so advanced in his quarrels with God and America that he was able to reject *in toto* the preachings of his early days.

Eventually Melville dropped the reference to *Little Henry,* and rightly so, but the sequence of compositional events that led to the deletion provides a fascinating insight into how a writer can write in spite of himself, how he can write the wrong thing and then correct it. In an image from the frontispiece of *Little Henry,* Melville found an apt and popular depiction of an innocent Westerner borne by a caring native and infidel. What did not occur to Melville at the time of composition—and he revised the passage twice before deleting it, suggesting that he held on to the imperialist image for some time—was that the allusion to Little Henry and Boosy would be taken as a positive endorsement of the missionary movement, that it would imply Tommo's duty to convert, not emulate, the heathen Kory-Kory, just as Henry converted Boosy. Captivated by a vibrant visual image, Melville allowed himself to be duped, for a while, by the very "forces of civilization" he hoped to counteract. Eventually Melville dropped the unsuitable passage.

Melville's play with *Little Henry* reveals the complex interactions of ideology, emotion, and cultural symbol. Melville's four years at sea had exposed him to French imperialism, American evangelism, Victorian puritanism, and Polynesian taboo; the voyage had altered his life and confirmed his adolescent suspicion about the repressive nature of Western culture. Melville's voyage had exposed all this, but in writing it down the author embarked upon a new voyage of self-discovery that was as liberating as his initial sea changes.

Consider once again the scene in Chapter 14 that Melville wanted to convey. His young hero, disabled by cultural doubt and sexual anxiety, finds himself twice a day the voyeur of a dozen Polynesian nudes. He is charmed and yet appalled by their lack of inhibition. His leg pains him more, and yet he does not object to being carried in the arms of an older island male to see this daily natatory event. Into this highly charged scene of sexual and cultural relativism, Melville experiments with an image from Sunday School, an image of black men bearing white but also one of innocent, sexless Henry happy to die in the cause of converting shameless heathens over to Our God. Melville would not have entertained this image if he had begun his book with a firm understanding of his antiWestern and antimissionary ideology. Rather, his ideology was growing during and perhaps even because of the process of composition. As an evolving social critic he could see directly to the heart of religious hypocrisy, but he still retained the Sunday School images of his youth. In writing out the Little Henry passage, Melville was registering his own innocence and lingering imperialism and evangelism; he was clinging still to a sexless and patriarchal vision, but in finally rejecting the passage, he was bidding farewell to what Huck Finn calls the lies of Sunday School, and for that matter the sexual sterility of a Western civilization that presumed to Christianize an Edenic society already more Christian for its primitivism than the cultivated West. Melville had yet to earn his liberal credentials. Accordingly, we must read *Typee* with a sense of how it was written—as not so much a unified text paralleling a cultural conflict as the narrative of an artist making up an ideology as he wrote.

Like the ''L-Word'' affair, or any of Melville's fascinating manuscript revisions, the case of *Little Henry and His Bearer* illuminates a crucial moment in Melville's creative life: the first stirrings of the writer toward transformations of voice and ideology. At the heart of Melville's rejection of Little Henry is an implicit psychological concern that overrides the political, that is, Tommo's fear of conversion, both religious and cultural. It is the anxiety of ''going native'' that infects Tommo, especially as *Typee* comes to its dramatic, reactionary conclusion. Tommo's radical ambivalence toward conversion is also tied to his developing sexuality, an issue we shall explore in conjunction with several anxious forays Melville made into the rhetoric of deceit.

9

Tommo's Rhetoric of Deceit

Typee is an amiable novel with an amiable voice but a most unamiable end. Hobbling down to the shore, Tommo is permitted to search for Toby, who he thinks may have returned with a group of sailors to rescue him. Two reckless acts seem out of character. Taking a bolt of cloth from a boat, he tosses the material to Fayaway as if to pay for services rendered, saying with frantic self-righteousness, "Here, woman, cover yourself." Next, he makes a sudden dash for freedom. This sparks a ferocious mêlée, turning the shore (that marginal territory emblematic of Melville's balanced repose) into a battle scene. Pursued beyond the breakers, Tommo shows no reluctance to commit an act of "horror" (*T*, 252) by pitching a boathook at the warrior Mow-Mow, who sinks in agony. In an instant, Tommo has resumed the hypocrisies of the West: the violent reaction against the "other," the shame of sexual freedom, the betrayal of a brother. Tommo's amiable Eden dissolves like a dream, the stuff for more tranquil future reflections.[1]

Tommo's sudden unmasking and retreat pose significant problems for Melville's amiability. Tommo's benevolism may be taken as a naïve delusion, encouraged by islanders hoping to sustain his commitment to their culture. That is, Tommo has been duped by his own geniality. Or Tommo's retreat may be a nose-thumbing at readers who have too readily accepted his benign South Seas Romanticism. In this case, Tommo's geniality is a calculated sham. Either way, *Typee* is a literary con game. Both readings have their appeal. Fayaway aside, the Typees are competent humbugs who are not above duping an eager-to-be-duped Tommo. They have the humor, the motive, and the victim to play a confidence game. Conversely, Tommo might be our con man. Although his "altered frame of mind" unites him to the islanders, he discloses that his "only hope was to induce the natives to believe that I was reconciled to my detention in the valley, and by assuming a tranquil and cheerful demeanor, to allay the suspicions which I had so unfortunately aroused" (*T*, 144). He reiterates this strategy as his narrative closes: "I did all in my power to appear composed and cheerful" (231). Playing the happy captive, Tommo is the first of Melville's "false genialists," a type later developed with Oberlus in "The Encantadas," loathsome precursor to more appealing confidence men. Tommo's duplicity forces the question: If he dupes the Typees, might he not also dupe the reader? Perhaps there is more method than caprice in Tommo's sudden escape.

In some respects *Typee* resembles the tall tales of Poe and Thorpe. Tommo persuades us to embrace the savage mind, but once we are about to accept that sensual world, he suddenly disengages, leaving us alone with our freshly adopted beliefs, puzzling Hamlet-like over the shrunken heads of these gentle islanders and wondering why Tommo has ironically turned to the despised West for deliverance. As with a hoax, we find ourselves drawn to beliefs that our narrator has already abandoned; eating the dust of Tommo's sudden retreat, we cling to the idea of native benevolism as though it were not the false goods it seems to be. We have been had.

It is tempting to recast *Typee* into the mold of *The Confidence-Man*. But Tommo is not one of Poe's "pacer" intellects, nor is he Frank Goodman, for his shifting poses, especially the last desperate reversal, lack the calculated control of a cosmopolitan sensibility. More like Goodman's victims Roberts and Pitch, he is at the mercy of his own unpredictable instincts, both demonic and genial. He exhibits all the mental fatigue of one in culture shock; he is an amiable intellect in retrograde, an exhausted Romantic. In this regard, Tommo is all the more "sincere" for his sudden reversal. He is reliable because he is flawed, and this allows us to explore the tragic limitations of his geniality. But *Typee* does not repudiate amiability. In fact, for us to feel the irony and despair of Tommo's finale, we must come to share with him an authentic belief in the Eden he tragically rejects. We feel his loss only to the degree that we value the amiable paradise he forfeits. *Typee* is not about the failure of Eden but about Tommo's inability to sustain the vital tension between benevolence and awareness that his Polynesian sojourn actualizes. It is about the failure to hold the picturesque moment.

To take Tommo as the dupe of con men cannibals trivializes his precarious psychological state, but to elevate him to the status of a cosmopolitan con man suggests a wisdom he clearly does not have. Still, Tommo engages readers in hoaxes. We find Tommo teasing, exaggerating, lying, mocking, and posing; and his isolated lie works lead us to his deepest cultural anxieties. With varying degrees of rhetorical success, Tommo plays the roles of sexual Prometheus, religious revivalist, and vagabond rover. In Chapter 14 some of Melville's most sophisticated indirections submerge the issue of Tommo's sexual maturation within an ostensibly political framework. Chapter 24 provides a less successful rhetoric of deceit in which Melville attempts to tease yet mollify religious readers. Both chapters address Tommo's slowly emerging fear of cultural conversion. Finally, in Chapter 18 Tommo's symbolic consummation with Fayaway and subsequent jealousy of the cosmopolitan Marnoo reveal his failure to move beyond physical love to higher realms of art and beauty that transcend all cultural differences. To grasp why Tommo adopts his histrionic poses, we must examine the root of his pathological fear of conversion.

Tattoo, Taboo, and Cannibalism: Forms of Conversion

One of the more vexing questions about the Typee natives is why they insist upon keeping Tommo. Since Melville does not reflect on this, we assume that the simple-minded islanders treat him like a fetish. In fact, the natives are not so naïve. Tommo's intrusion threatens their political autonomy, and his departure would compromise their hermetic independence. His presence is imperative. The covert reasons for Tommo's captivity help us to understand why the natives must convert him and why Tommo fears conversion.

The Typee valley is remote. While other tribes of Nuku Hiva have fallen prey to the French, the Typees remain sovereign because of their inaccessibility. They trade with Europeans, but only on a distant beach (*T*, 74). When Tommo and Toby arrive, not by closely guarded paths from the sea but by a presumably impassable mountain route, King Mehevi is understandably agitated. His rear defenses have been breached. He and others continually interrogate the two about the "Franee" (79). Tommo is amused by this infantile curiosity, but clearly Mehevi fears that Tommo may be the vanguard of a Western incursion. To release him would be to risk the betrayal of Typee. Thus, for the sake of their autonomy, the Typees must hold Tommo captive; to ensure his captivity they must make him one of their own; and to assimilate him, they must keep him happy. The sailor, then, is handsomely treated and even allowed a controversial dispensation of taboo so that he may court Fayaway in an otherwise forbidden canoe. But he is never let out of their sight. He is free in Eden, but not free to go.

Tommo's resistance to conversion reflects his desire for an independent, cultureless identity, but it also bespeaks his failure to understand the dilemma he poses for his captors.[2] Obsessed with his personal condition,[3] Tommo is dangerously insensitive to Typeean politics. He is pulled by two mutually exclusive alternatives. He lives "on the marge" between two worlds, each with its own coordinated dispensation of repression and repose: the West with its excessive authority and yet civilized control, and Polynesia with its liberation and yet deadening somnolence.[4] Both require a total conversion to their gods. Tommo has no desire to assimilate these cultures; rather, he is fatally resistant to both. He cannot abide the West's power and hypocrisy; he will not submit to Typee's "perpetual hilarity." Unlike the cosmopolitan Marnoo, who is "at home" in both worlds, he can find no middle ground. He fails to achieve an enlivened cultural marginality, which is the ethical extension of his own picturesque aesthetic. Of course, the Typees will not allow him a picturesque, cosmopolitan synthesis; they would convert him entirely to their sleep of reason. Tommo's blindness is in failing to see that their intransigence is fundamental to their political survival. Three "mysteries"—tattoo, taboo, and cannibalism—manifest Tommo's fear of cultural conversion.

Tommo's two most pronounced fears—the tattoo and the cannibal—seem reasonable. No one relishes being eaten; and while tattoos may be tempting to some, relatively few get one. In most cultures, the tattoo is a colorful scar recording a rite of passage; it is an emblem of one's identity and often a flag of one's sexuality.[5] In Typee, tattooing is the culture's great art. The design of a spreading Artu tree drawn upon Marnoo's back, for instance, unites his flesh with nature itself. Tommo is both attracted to and repulsed by tattooing. Married women, he observes, are routinely tattooed on their right hand and left foot (*T*, 190). Sexually active girls are encoded with three small dots on each lip and a thin three-inch band of "delicately executed figures" on the "fall of the shoulder" (86). Tommo is clearly drawn to the sexual implications of tattoos but quickly compares them to military epaulettes, the very decoration that he has derided in Chapter 4. Melville's odd diversion distracts us from the fact of Tommo's sexual awareness. Tommo's ambivalence toward tattooing involves a deeper anxiety in knowing himself. Richard Ruland puts this ambivalence in a religious context when he argues that Tommo resists the disfigurement of the "face divine" in tattooing as a submission to an "unreflecting life."[6] But Ruland too readily accepts Tommo's convenient commitment to Western religious values at this point. From the Marquesan point of view, facial tattoos have less to do with religion than with social identity. They are a sign of certain clan affiliations but are also as unique and personal as one's fingerprints or signature. Indeed, when coerced to sign their names to documents, Marquesans invariably sketched their facial tattoos.[7] For Tommo's captors, facial tattoos are not a disfigurement but a celebration of one's family, rank, and Self. And Tommo's resistance is based on his awareness of this fact.

For him, tattooing signifies one's irreversible induction into island culture. This fact is made explicit in Chapter 30, when Mehevi and "some other savages" repeatedly pester Tommo into submitting to a tattoo. "[T]hey were resolved," Tommo notes, "to make a convert of me" (*T*, 220). For Mehevi, a tattoo would put his family mark on Tommo and would, in proclaiming the sailor's sexual affairs among the women, secure his continued presence and eventual allegiance to the culture. Mehevi knows that this mark of cultural conversion would also compromise Tommo's reliability among Typee's Western enemies. Similarly, Tommo's claims to resist tattooing out of respect for his Christian "face divine" is merely a bid to stabilize his rhetorical relationship with his more pious readers. He keeps hidden the sexual and social implications, for to resist tattooing as a sexual rather than religious marking would be to admit to his promiscuity, a fact he prefers to reveal only in subtle hints. Like his earlier "military diversion" tactic, Tommo uses religiosity to deflect our attention from his sexuality.

But Tommo's resistance is even more problematic, and it is tied to the "taboo Kannaka" Marnoo. Marnoo's taboo status assures him the freedom to travel among warring tribes; it is emblematic of his cosmopolitanism. He is one of the few adult men who have no facial tattoos, a fact that further reinforces the notion that tattooing establishes one's tribal affiliation. If Tommo himself is to sustain his own precarious life "on the marge" between two cultures, he must resist total conversion either way by refusing a facial tattoo. Thus he proposes a compromise. A facial tattoo, which clearly inhibits social interaction with the West, is out of the question, but he will assent to the tattooing of his arms above the wrist. This is a token acceptance of the Typee community, one that he can cover up at will with his Western sleeve. It is a convenient bid for Marnoo's cosmopolitanism. But Mehevi, who can ill afford another interloping Marnoo, will not accept the plan. He cannot trust Tommo to be a true cosmopolite, giving equal favor to both cultures and betraying neither. He wants all of Tommo or nothing.

The desire to enjoy a cosmopolitan taboo status triggers in Tommo worse fears: the revulsion for cannibalism. As noted, Tommo goes to great lengths to show that the ritual eating of human flesh is performed exclusively upon slain enemies. Moreover, enemies are not slain *to be* eaten but are eaten only if they *happen* to be slain.[8] It is purely a symbolic act, and rationally Tommo should have no fears. He will not be eaten alive, or killed for food, for the natives do not cannibalize for nutrition. He is not a Happar or Frenchman, so he is not an enemy to be slain.

As long as he remains an ally, he will be safe. But Tommo quickly flounders in canebrake doubts after he stumbles upon evidence of a cannibal rite executed upon slain Happar tribesmen. While such an act should not threaten him, his revulsion is unavoidable and heightens his curiosity over a package that has hung for some time in the Ti. It contains, he accidentally discovers, three shrunken heads. Understandably, it is the head of a white man that bothers him. What enemy was this? Is this Toby? The thought triggers a chain of logic. If this is Toby's head, he must have been slain as an enemy and secretly eaten. Toby became an enemy because by leaving the valley, he necessarily compromised the valley's security. He had to be slain because he would betray to Europe the inland route to Typee, a betrayal that would eventuate in the culture's destruction. Moreover, Toby had to be eaten because the cannibal act would both physically and symbolically force Toby to do what he had refused to do: become a Typee. The act of physical digestion, then, constitutes a *total* cultural conversion. Quite literally, one culture consumes another. This is not a metaphysical conversion; it is purely metabolic.

Rationally, Tommo should have no fear, but symbolically he has every reason to run. Whether the shrunken head is Toby's or not (and it is not), Tommo knows that, by reason of his desire to escape and the false geniality he uses to cover up that desire, he is a secret enemy of the Typees. The more he knows that he is their enemy—that he shall betray them—the more he fears their finding him out. Ironically, his leg wound grows along with his secret fears. Since his legs are his only means of escape, the pain he feels becomes as much the symbol of his repressed guilt for betraying the Typees as it is a symbol of his sexual liberation.[9] Tommo now sees that the Typees, too, know his secret. Although this logic is not articulated explicitly in the text, the connections are clear: Tommo's resistance to the symbolic act of tattooing may inspire the Typees to take an even more irreversible symbolic action. They will eat him and convert his solid flesh into theirs. As Ruland so nicely puts it in a different context, they "want to devour his identity," not, we should add, to co-opt his virtues and strengths as they would a valiant enemy's, but to dominate and consume them, to convert them metabolically into themselves.

Tommo balances the tensions of sexuality and cultural conversion with varying degrees of success. In Chapter 14, tall-tale manipulations help him transform the energy of his sexual growth into a symbolism of fire. It is a *tour de force* of comic containment. By contrast, Tommo's attempt in the heavily expurgated Chapter 24 to assuage religious readers backfires when his rhetoric of deceit devolves into a parody of revivalist oratory that undermines his own liberalism and alienates readers. Caught between the rock of his antimissionary stance and the hard place of his slowly emergent fear of conversion, Tommo is finally unprepared for any cosmopolitan assimilation of the two cultures, and his misplaced resentment of Marnoo in Chapter 18 attests to this moral failure.

Tommo Prometheus

Chapter 14 marks a crucial moment in Tommo's sexual development. The chapter relates Toby's escape, Tommo's depression, Fayaway's consolations, and Kory-

Kory's making of fire. In manuscript, Melville called this fire-making scene a "Promethean operation," but he eventually dropped the allusion to Prometheus, perhaps because Kory-Kory is more creator than thief of fire. Still, the association is worth retrieving, for Melville's artful transformations of Tommo's sexual fire fantasy into political realities are no less than Promethean.[10]

Let's look at this celebrated scene in the context of Tommo's overall sexual growth. Tommo's sexuality is first expressed almost exclusively as a puerile fixation on bodily functions, rude exposures, and titillations typical of the repressed adolescent male. His sexual joking suggests a Rabelaisian burlesquer in arrested development. He delights in the near rape of a pretentious missionary wife who sets herself among the natives as a model of propriety. So overly dressed is this white goddess that the islanders cannot determine her sex, and in seeking "to pierce the sacred veil of calico . . . in the gratification of their curiosity" (*T*, 6), they strip her. Melville's sly response to this anecdote (later expurgated) was that the "gentle dame was not sufficiently evangelized to endure this" (7). Obviously, the laughter is directed more against missionaries than against women, but Tommo too readily delights in the "innocent" little rape. His satiric exposure of hypocrisy, inextricably linked to the humiliation of a woman, also exposes his own barely repressed sexual energy.

Even more graphic is the sexual joking played on the French. Hoping to impress the American commodore, a French officer pays a visit, bringing the King and Queen of Nuku Hiva in tow. The royal pair have been overdressed in Western plumage to befit their rank, but their tattoos ludicrously belie their nobility. The king, for instance, has a dark band imprinted across his eyes like a pair of goggles, "and royalty in goggles," says Melville, puckishly hinting at monarchical blindness, "suggested some ludicrous ideas" (*T*, 8). But this concealed attack upon imperialism becomes more graphic when the Queen compares her tattoos to those of an old tar. Bending over, turning around, and throwing up her skirts, she "display[s] the hieroglyphics on her own sweet form" (8), which puts the "polite Gauls" in retreat. Melville's "moonshot" humor "ends" Chapter One, a shocking "catastrophe" (to use Melville's term) made all the more amusing by the wordplay in the second syllable of that word. Here, sexual exposure is not forced upon the female but is, in fact, interpreted as a rear attack on the French. We know the hieroglyphics of her moon. Unfortunately, so did Melville's audience, and the entire section was cut.

As with the missionary "rape," Tommo's adolescent longing takes the form of comic sexual attack. But with Fayaway Tommo matures. He relates to women as companions, not projectiles, limiting the expression of affection, he tells us, to "innocent" hand-holding and massage rather than the exposure of sexual parts. Tommo's heterosexual growth also runs concurrently with a shift in his homoerotic affections. The adolescent who has lived for more than a year on ship among other males has necessarily grown attached to men. Probably a sexual virgin, he is appalled by the debaucheries of his mates when they reach the islands. He also is drawn to the darkly handsome Toby. But once the two reach the Typee Valley, Toby's function as a homoerotic friend diminishes as Fayaway claims center stage. And once Toby is physically removed from the scene, Kory-Kory (Fayaway's brother and Tommo's devoted "bearer") takes his place. As primitive replaces Western friend, Tommo's new male bonding with brother Kory-Kory is an acting-out of his desires for the sister Fayaway. Indeed, his sexually charged description of Kory-Kory's fire-making ritual is a masturbatory fantasy and a symbolic anticipation of sexual consummation with Fayaway. Moreover, the energy of this sexual fantasy is directed away from personal gratification and transformed in subsequent imagery into a higher meditation on the art and politics of fire. Tommo becomes, then, a sexual Prometheus, bearing the light of creative fire as a sublimation of his desires for making life. Rhetorically, the amiable transformations operate much like a hoaxy tall tale in which anthropological detail and political critique hide the bold exposure of Tommo's sexuality.

The first step in this process is Tommo's ambivalent farewell to Toby. When Toby leaves for good, Tommo plunges into Fayaway's arms. He alternates between despair over Toby's apparent desertion and remorse for imputing such a betrayal to a loyal friend who, he fears, may have in fact been murdered. In manuscript Melville attempted to intellectualize Tommo's unbalanced mental state:

> But with the inconstancy of a desponding mind that speculates in the dark as to the causes that have produced the misery under which it languished, I would often experience the most bitter remorse after indulging in these reflections & again would seek to *peirce* [sic] *the mystery* that hung on the sudden disappearance of my comrade. [Leaf 24][11]

Melville cut this modicum of "dark speculation." Presumably, its emphasis on the gothic mechanisms of bitterness and guilt detracted from the love story he wanted to establish. The omitted passage prepares us "to peirce the mystery" of Toby rather than the delights of Fayaway. Instead of researching the "causes" of masculine misery, Tommo will show us its feminine cure.

Quite possibly, too, Melville sensed that the reference to "mysteries" might unnecessarily draw attention to the Promethean mysteries he was about to create. The tactic of his lie work throughout Chapter 14 is to deflect attention from his growing sexuality. By transforming physical acts into scenes of symbolic sensuality and cultural critique, he amiably teases his most percipient readers, but the mention of "mystery" threatens to alert even the most obtuse of readers. There was too much of a wink in the wording "to peirce the mystery," and Melville was not willing to risk the exposure of his carefully contained joke. Like Poe in "Rue Morgue," he was taking no chances. And with good reason. The material he was about to present was as sexually loaded as any reader of the day was likely to find. Melville's further manuscript revisions reveal a pattern of restraint that is both a containment of the climactic masturbatory material in his hoax and a form of self-censorship designed to obviate invasive editorial cuts. All evidence indicates that his rhetorical manipulations worked.

Tommo's attraction to Fayaway registers the expansion of his sensuality beyond the early self-indulgent puerilities. He is not attracted to the blue-eyed, brown-skinned Fayaway simply for her "extraordinary beauty" (*T*, 108); he loves her for her "intelligence and humanity." More than any other islander, she empathizes with Tommo's loss of home. He senses that she worries that somewhere "brothers and sisters'' despair of ever seeing him again. ''[R]eposing full confidence in her candor and intelligence''—in manuscript Melville almost wrote ''*superior* intelligence''—Tommo cradles himself in Fayaway's uncovered bosom. She holds him, fans away insects, and in a ''gesture of pity . . . murmur[s] plaintively 'Awha! Awha! Tommo' '' (108). This is the kind of mothering no lonely sailor could possibly reject. But as Fayaway continues her ministrations, Tommo's adolescent self-pity blossoms into a fuller sensuality, evident in a fairly steamy passage:

> Every evening the girls of the house . . . would anoint my whole body with a fragrant oil, squeezed from a yellow root, previously pounded between a couple of stones, and which in their language is denominated ''aka.'' And most refreshing and agreeable are the juices of the ''aka,'' when applied to one's limbs by the soft palms of sweet nymphs, whose bright eyes are beaming upon you with kindness. [*T,* 110]

Here sensuality is everywhere on the verge of bursting into graphic detail. The concise description of how we get ''aka'' (the squeezing of a root and pounding of it between two stones) seems ejaculatory. No wonder Kory-Kory is sent away during ''this luxurious operation.'' Melville toned down the passage for publication. He removed a suggestive phrase concerning the sweet nymphs as they ''rise with one another in the ardor of their attentions.'' He had originally wanted some form of the word ''delight'' to appear as a substitute for either ''agreeable'' or ''kindness,'' but he thought better of this and retained the more blasé terms.

But these self-censorings are minor compared with the cutting of a passage that likens Tommo's rubdown to the scandalous affairs of harem life. Melville wrote, then removed, the following:

> Like Captain MacHeath in the opera I could have sung ''Thus I lay like a Turk with my doxies around'' for never certainly was effeminate ottoman in the innermost shrine of his seraglio attended by lovelier houris with more excess of devotion than happened to me on these occasions I have mentioned. Sardanapalus might have experienced such sensations but I dout whether any of the Sultans ever did. [Leaf 27]

Whether Melville's full-body massage rivals the ''sensations'' of MacHeath, mad Sardanapalus, or any Sultan, the references clearly emphasize the illicit nature of the scene that is barely latent in the ''aka'' root description. Melville cut this passage before less tolerant readers would have the chance to do him the honor, and take with it the rubdown scene. As luck would have it, what Melville did print was in fact only partially expurgated. The word ''whole'' in ''anoint my whole body'' was cut as was the entire sentence alluding to the ''sweet nymphs.'' Apparently Melville's editors knew something was foul, but they left the ''aka'' root untouched. They failed to see anything suggestive in the technical description. After all, how could such bare facts be dirty? Melville would use the same tactic of secretly sensualizing routine native procedures, but even more successfully, in what follows.

This is the climax of Melville's lie work. Just as Thorpe's readers, deluded by their need for myth, fail to see Jim Doggett's comic self-exposure, Melville's readers, immersed in the technical details of this fire-making ''lesson,'' are made to overlook Tommo's masturbatory fantasy. Transcribed below is the entire scene, including passages (numbered here and placed in brackets) Melville cut from his manuscript.

> Often he was obliged to strike a light for the occasion, and as the mode he adopted was entirely different from what 1[I had been led to suppose it was among savages, I shall here record it for the benefit of Europe & posterity & incidentally for the comfort of those who may hereafter get lost in the woods at night & be desirous of building a fire.] I had ever seen or heard before, I will describe it.
>
> A straight, dry, and partly decayed stick 2[denuded of the bark] of the Habiscus, about six feet in length, and half as many inches in diameter, with a smaller bit of wood not more than a foot long, and scarcely an inch wide, is as invariably to be met with in every house in Typee as a box of lucifer matches in the corner of a kitchen cupboard at home. 3[Having said thus much in brief introduction, I here take Kori-Kori by the hand & introducing him to the reader I have no doubt but that the former is perfectly willing to go through the Promethean operation for his particular gratification.]
>
> The 4[savage] islander, placing the larger stick obliquely against some object, with one end elevated at an angle of forty-five degrees, mounts astride of it like an urchin about to gallop [Leaf 28] off upon a cane, and then grasping the smaller one firmly in both hands, he rubs its pointed end slowly up and down the extent of a few inches on the principal stick, until at last he makes a narrow groove in the wood, 5[which running from him to an abrupt head, where] with an abrupt termination at the point furthest from him, where all the dusty particles which the friction creates are accumulated in a little heap.
>
> 6[Like a locomotive on the start Kori-Kori] At first Kori-Kori goes to work quite leisurely, but gradually quickens his pace, and waxing warm in the employment, drives the 7[slender] stick furiously along the smoking channel 8[in which it plays], plying his hands to and fro with amazing rapidity 9[that blends them apparently into one. The perspiration starting from his pores threatens to extinguish as soon as it shall appear the feeble spark that he is endeavoring to elicit.—But now he attains his climax—he pants gasps, his eyes protrude from their sockets with the violence of his exertions.] the perspiration starting from every pore. As he approaches the climax of his effort, he pants and gasps for breath, and his eyes almost start from their sockets with the violence of his exertions. This is the critical stage of the operation; all his previous labors are vain if he cannot sustain the rapidity of the movement until the reluctant spark is produced. Suddenly he stops, becomes perfectly motionless. 10[—it is like the instantanious cessation of a steamer's paddles.] His hands still retain their hold of the smaller stick, which is pressed convulsively against the further end of the channel among the fine powder there accumulated, as if he had just pierced through and through some little viper that was wriggling and struggling to escape from his clutches. The next moment a delicate wreath of smoke curls spirally into the air, the heap of dusty particles glows with fire, and Kori-Kori almost breathless, dismounts from his steed. [Leaf 29]

Not a line of this scene was expurgated in the American revised edition, and part of the reason is that Melville was willing to tone it down before going to press, to push the overt sexuality out. Thus, he removed "denuded of the bark" [2], the playing of the slender stick in its channel [7,8], the blending of hands and stick into a Donne-like singularity, the protruding eyes, and the explicit reference to "*his* climax'' [9] rather than ''the climax of his efforts.'' Also removed are the locomotive [6] and steamboat [10] metaphors. Melville even changed Kory-Kory from a ''savage'' to an ''islander'' [4] to civilize the Promethean operator, although he discarded that pagan allusion as well, along with the word ''gratification'' [1] since the author had earlier established a sexual association with that word in describing the missionary ''rape'' (*T,* 6) and ''the unholy passions'' of his former shipmates ''and their unlimited gratification'' (15).

Despite these self-censorings, the sexual nature of Tommo's description is more powerful because of the excisions. What remains in the printed version—the convulsive exertions, the perspiration, climax and dusty particles, the stick, steed, and viper—is enough to convince us that Tommo has expressed his sexuality deftly, embedding it within what he purports to be dutiful cultural reportage, the kind of factuality his publisher wanted. Any more hints of sexual ''gratification'' than these remnants would have risked a too-easy detection of the hoax. Melville even diverts us from sexual innuendo with a typical amiable ploy: By casting Kory-Kory's sexual mounting as a lad's ''gallop[ing] off upon a cane,'' he encourages us to take the scene as a Shandyan's riding of a hobbyhorse. This infantilizing of adult behavior, like some of Jim Doggett's puerilities, is a safe, traditional, Irvingesque coverup of sexual longing.

Of course, it may be argued that the author's lie work is *too* deeply embedded, that the joke is consciously made to be undetectable, and that just as an undetectable hoax is no hoax at all, this Poe-ish sort of private joke reveals more about the author's pathology than about his rhetorical strategies. After all, critics trained to detect sexual double-entendre (to the amazement of freshmen) have only recently exposed this particular ''hoax.'' Given that it has taken readers more than a hundred years finally to ''get'' the joke, we might claim that Melville intended his censorings to repress his sexual feelings so completely that the few hints that were printed must have unconsciously slipped out. This raises the important rhetorical question of whether Melville intended to *conceal* rather than artfully *contain* Tommo's sexuality. The answer, it seems to me, is the latter, and support for that lies in the single word, pierce.

We have noted that Tommo transfers his affections from Toby to Fayaway and that Kory-Kory's ''operation'' is, in fact, a fantasy fulfillment of Tommo's sexual desires. We have also noted that Melville originally intended to emphasize Tommo's desire ''to peirce the mystery'' of Toby, but deleted the idea and its phrasing to focus more upon Fayaway. We now find that the lost word ''peirce'' (on Leaf 25) returns at the end of Tommo's fantasy (on Leaf 29). Kory-Kory has reached his climax and in the tense sexual repose that comes at this point—he is ''perfectly motionless''—his ''stick . . . press[s] convulsively against the further end of the channel among the fine powder there accumulated, as if he had *just pierced* through and through some little viper that was wriggling and struggling to escape from his clutches.'' How do we account for the transformation of Melville's canceled ''peirce'' in manuscript to the finally printed ''pierced''?

Throughout the novel, Melville casts Toby as the impenetrable ''other'' in Tommo's civilized life; he is a moody mirroring of Tommo, an unpredictable *doppelganger,* the kind fancied by Hoffmann and Poe. Thus, Tommo's desire to ''peirce the mystery" of Toby's sudden departure is a longing to penetrate the mysteries of Toby's alien being and to grasp the meaning of their male bonding. But Melville forestalls this ontological penetration and turns Tommo's attention toward a Polynesian alternative. As a primitive substitute for Toby, Kory-Kory offers Melville the means to resolve Tommo's problems of alienation, sexual ambivalence, and arrested metaphysical introspection through symbol. In Tommo's fantasy, Kory-Kory "pierces through and through" just as Tommo had once desired to "peirce" Toby and just as he now wishes to penetrate Fayaway, who, unlike cold Toby, "deeply compassionates" his alien condition. Thus, Tommo imagines a symbolic transference of his affections from the impenetrable male to a more accessible, quite penetrable female by means of the heavily submerged sexual activity of an otherwise sexless friend and brother (Kory-Kory). But if this is the deep meaning of Melville's sexual joke, it is one that could be detected only through our awareness of the deleted manuscript passage concerning Toby, a deletion Melville purposely made.

One possible reading of all this is that in cutting his first use of the word "peirce," Melville intended to *conceal* the connection between Toby and Fayaway via Kory-Kory, probably because he wanted to eradicate what appears to be Tommo's homosexual longing for Toby. But such an interpretation would deny us a much more fluid set of ideas. To begin with, Melville does not shy away from homoeroticism in *Typee* either with Kory-Kory or later on with the androgynous Marnoo. Therefore he is not likely to conceal what he has elsewhere exposed. It seems more probable that Melville deleted "peirce" in order to save the powerful term for later use; he did not want to dissipate its impact by its repetition. If this means the reader loses the retrospective hint that Tommo may have desired to "peirce" Toby sexually as well as metaphysically, then so be it. With Toby out of the picture and no lingering hint of possible psychological introspection, Melville could move to the broader implications of the Tommo–Kory-Kory–Fayaway ménage.

More meaning, both theological and metaphysical, could be achieved by emphasizing heterosexuality. The image of the piercing of the viper, for instance, is a kind of male mutilation or self-wounding over Tommo's residual homosexual anxiety. But given the theological implications of snakes in paradise and Tommo's early assumption that his leg wound is due to snake bite, the viper image more aptly suggests Tommo's triumph over the guilt of his impending sexual liberation. It is his slaying of a little dragon of homosexual anxiety. Moreover, the piercing of the viper "through and through" can be read not only as an impaling of the snake but as the using of the snake as a symbolic mechanism for penetration. That is, it is an instrument *through which* or *with which* consummation is achieved; Tommo "pierces" Fayaway "by means of" the phallic viper. With either reading of "through," the overall message is one of aesthetic control over sexual expression. Notice that the "wriggling and struggling" viper—like those in the Laocoön or like the wrestling of Jacob's angel or like the serpentine words we find Melville scribbling on the page—is finally grasped and controlled. The power of the snake is "clutched" and contained, and the product of these sexual exertions is "a delicate wreath of smoke"—an artful transformation of the writhing snake—and, of course, fire itself. Thus, in one Promethean operation, Melville accommodates sexual and religious guilt, nature and art, fantasy and reality, light humor and deep penetration—all by means of tall-tale rhetoric.

Further comic containments are to be found. In a coda to his fiery joke, Melville coyly diverts our attention away from sexuality altogether and toward the politics of fire as a means of comparing the distribution of light and warmth in Typee to that in the West. Because Typeans do not see any utility in sharing a perpetual flame, each must make new fire as the occasion demands. Tommo's first step is to suggest that the Polynesians establish "a college of vestals," who as keepers of a communal flame would obviate the arduous task Kory-Kory must otherwise repeatedly perform whenever fire is needed. Melville eventually discards this idea for two reasons, one unstated and the other hinted at in another deleted passage. On the one hand, Tommo obviously enjoys the sexual symbolism of fire-making, and since a college of vestals is made up of zealously guarded virgins, the "expediency" (Melville first wrote "propriety" on Leaf 29) achieved through such an establishment would be a cold comfort considering the barrier it would pose to sexual freedom. But Tommo spares himself from having to make this point by intimating another more ribald reason that Typee could have no College of Vestals: The island has no virgins. Of course, Tommo is too much the gentleman to say this openly; rather he makes his point indirectly when he "courteously beg[s] to be excused" from articulating what would be taken as "a slanderous aspersion on the fair fame of the gentle damsels of the vale." Even this sly indirection was too obvious for Melville, and he cut the line, leaving his readers with an even more oblique reference. All that remains in print of Melville's objections to the College is that there "might, however, be special difficulties in carrying this plan into execution" (*T*, 112).

So buried is this joke in the final printed revision of the last sentence that readers lacking access to the manuscript are not likely to comprehend Melville's joke concerning the island vestals.[12] And yet Melville kept the teasing remnant as if to lure readers into creating meaning of this shell of a joke. We are meant to work back through the argument to retrieve the humor that the sentence implies. What "special difficulties" would there be in assembling a group of virgins on this particular island? The more active reader will stumble over this problem, pause to reflect on the status of virgins in Typee, and in recollecting the open promiscuity of male and female youths eventually extract Melville's wry meaning, just as the reader of "Big Bear" must reinspect details in order to determine Jim Doggett's squatting posture. Even more active readers, with the newly acquired understanding of the impossibility of finding virgins in Typee, will continue to retrace the path of images a short step back to Kory-Kory's exertions and thereby gain a quiet confirmation of the sexual nature of Tommo's "special difficulty." In doing so, one finds in Kory-Kory's symbolic love-making the "cause" for the lack of virgins on the island. Thus, "in some dim, unsuspected way" (to quote Ishmael), we are meant to uncover Melville's buried humor, and the fact that the author leaves us a trail of clues again suggests not so much a concealment of truth but a measured containment of meaning that ripens our reading experience. By retrieving Melville's humor, we are made to piece together his sexual theme and participate in the construction of meaning.

But that is not all. Melville's next and concluding paragraph is designed to submerge all innuendo entirely by converting the fire-making ritual from its sexual symbolism to an occasion for a political moral. Even here, however, the author insists upon toning down explicit references to politics. Melville's point is a simple observation about comparative domestic economies. Although a Typeean parent must labor hard to make fire, his children enjoy the abundance of nature, eating and learning effortlessly. "A poor European artisan," however, can strike fire instantly and repeatedly with his Lucifer matches, and yet "is put to his wits' end to provide for his starving offspring" (*T*, 112). As it stands in print, Melville draws no conclusions from this comparison. Civilized life—Melville originally punned by calling it "en*light*ened" life—has instant light but is careless of its children; it is a heartless hearth. For the "savage," however, light is labor-intensive, although nature freely provides all other needs. Neither social structure is particularly secure. One prospers through the artifice of technology (and here the lost image of light-bearing, art-giving Prometheus takes on added meaning); the other, through the whim of nature's providence. Only when we reflect back upon the sexual implications of light do we sense a more pointed criticism. The mechanical "instrumentality" of the Lucifer suggests a debased sexuality of the civilized man: He is no match for the savage. Unlike the primitive fire-maker, who enjoys a direct and elemental attachment to his symbolic craft, the "European artisan" is removed from this deeper aesthetic experience. He is a mechanical lover and artist. True art makes its own fire; it creates light just as sex creates life.

As the published text stands, Melville only implies a rejection of civilized life, leaving it to his readers to transform the implications of his comparison into a conclusion. But originally he had intended a far more explicit argument and a call to arms. In manuscript, we find this deleted finale:

> This single practical illustration is, I insist upon it, worth volumes of learned disquisitions of the nature & theory of the respective pretensions of the various forms of social life & accordingly commend it to the consideration of all the political economists & public spirited philosophers who are engaged in putting to rights this most imperfectly constituted planet of ours. [Leaf 30]

In one sentence, the author manages to attack the pretensions and imperfection of the European sphere as well as condescend to its presumably heretofore misguided economists and philosophers, all in a fist-thumping tone. This overly insistent passage threatened to unhinge the quiet campaign of indirection that Melville had already waged. His tactic was to contain Tommo's scandalous sexual development within the safe confines of a fiery symbology, which in turn became the basis for a measured political comparison. To raise his comparison to a call for political action, "a putting to rights" of Western flaws, and to "insist upon it" would have been to risk inciting a negative reaction from readers. In short, Melville was censoring himself to contain political excesses and preserve his rhetoric of deceit for those readers prepared to see through his lie work and pierce the mystery of his Promethean hoax.

A measure of Melville's success in "putting this one over" is the light amount of expurgation he was forced to make in Chapter 14 of the American revised edition.

A further measure of this success can be discerned in passages that failed to pass the censor. In Chapter 24, Melville found himself cut to ribbons when he allowed too easily detected rhetorical ploys to be printed.

Baffled Scientist and Con Man Revivalist

If the inclusion of all requisite structural elements in a tall tale were enough to ensure rhetorical success, then, by all accounts, Chapter 24 should succeed, for it bears all the earmarks of a classic. We find, for instance, a gentleman (Tommo) "objectively" reporting the antics of rustic clowns (in this case, the native priest Kolory and Kory-Kory). Here too is the careful establishment of the narrator's reliability paradoxically coupled with clever warnings of a hoax (two extended references to "humbugs"). We find, as well, a sequence of comic anecdotes that build to an anticlimax and the author's attempt to transform worldly objects (a mummified canoe rower) into a dubious metaphysical dimension. But rhetorical structure is nothing without effective execution.

Melville plays both the "baffled" scientist and the con man revivalist in order to invalidate earlier Polynesian researchers and to lure destabilized readers toward a sense of Typeean spirituality. But as a comic evangelist, Tommo infantilizes the natives while insisting disingenuously upon a religious revival. The shift to sarcasm is the kind of strained humor of a Poe hoax that deconstructs itself rather than assimilates disparate factions. Liberal readers are confused, and conservatives put off. Indeed, Melville's rhetorical failure anticipates Tommo's reactionary breakdown.

The initial gambit of the hoax is successful to the degree that Tommo's manner balances social criticism and cultural relativism, while at the same time it allows Melville to contain his anxieties about his "varnishing" of the truth. Tommo secures his audience's confidence by admitting that Typee religion baffles him. In travel writing, where any day-tripper can play the expert, such honesty is refreshing, and given the inscrutability of taboo, Tommo's bafflement is credible. Indeed, it invites us to puzzle along with him. Moreover, since the Typees are heedless of the reasons behind their rituals, we are poised between ignorance and pretense: We do not understand Typee, but at least we know we do not understand. Tommo proposes, then, an armchair quest, and if we fail to "unbaffle" ourselves, we shall not be harmed by that failure.

But Tommo also insists that previously published accounts of Polynesian religion are fraudulent, and this aggression upon a missionary stronghold upsets his genial mode. Tommo proposes two reasons for what he calls the "unintentional humbuggery" of his predecessors in the field. First, such "learned tourists" visited the island for only two weeks at a time, keeping all the while to their ships. Second, they depended too heavily upon the tales of "old South-sea Rovers," noted for stretching the "long bow." Although he clearly states that his precursors have been duped, the blame is transferred to the salty humbugs who have duped them "unintentionally." At worst, the credulous missionaries appear naïve. Thus the charge of humbuggery is minimized. Melville's discussion of how a humbug is perpetrated is a risky gambit, for he, in fact, is a humbug.

In contrast to his predecessors, Tommo claims that he resided "for months" among the natives, implying, of course, that he was no tourist. But scholars have long known that Melville spent only three weeks in the valley of Taipivai, so it is clear to modern readers, if not to Melville's contemporaries, that he was willing to risk a lie to inflate his cosmopolitan credentials, even as he exposes the lies of others. Moreover, Melville stretches the long bow himself as he analyzes why old sea "rovers" will exaggerate. "A natural desire," he remarks, "to make himself a consequence in the eyes of strangers, prompts him to lay claim to a much greater knowledge of such matters than he actually possesses" (*T*, 171). Surely Melville (whose next title, *Omoo*, means "Rover") saw himself mirrored in the roving liar he depicts, for as a writer publishing for the first time he too was eager "to make himself a consequence in the eyes of strangers." Given his disingenuous protestations of presenting the "unvarnished truth," he knew full well that he was open to charges of humbuggery. Melville's further characterization of the returning tourist, who "having had little time, and scarcely any opportunity to become acquainted with the customs he pretends to describe, . . . writes them down one after another in an off-hand haphazard style" (*T*, 171), is also a self-portrait. Scholars have also known that *Typee* was accepted for publication on the condition that Melville add several chapters on the *facts* of native customs. Melville had little time to compose these discussions, and he relied hurriedly and heavily upon secondary sources to "acquaint" himself with the customs he was supposed to have known first hand.[13]

Clearly, the humbugged tourists and their humbug sources are as much a rendering of Melville's actual condition as an artist as they are a caricature of those we are told we cannot trust. Melville weaves his own anxieties about truth-telling into Tommo's bluff rhetoric. These secret winks warn us of a brewing hoax; thus in one bold conversion of anxiety into rhetoric, Melville asserts his credentials while hinting that he is a liar. Unfortunately, these tactics were lost on most of Melville's American readers, because the entire two-page prelude was expurgated in the revised edition, apparently to remove Melville's withering dismissal of missionaries who have "exaggerated the evils of Paganism, in order to enhance the merit of their own disinterested labor" (*T*, 169). Once again, what Melville had fashioned with subtle pen strokes was hacked out with a cleaver.

Having carefully composed these narrative tensions, Tommo proceeds to the heart of his hoax, a scene that (if it works) should affirm a liberal view of native life while it accommodates the missionary's requirement of "true" spirituality. Melville links these two readerships by showing conservatives that native nonchalance is a form of repose that is itself a sign of grace. Their benevolence, like their repose, is immanent, and the incomprehensibility of their rituals is a measure not of darkness but of ineffable enlightenment. In a sense the genial bafflement Tommo repeatedly expresses becomes the proper response to the unknown, and in this regard Tommo takes his cue from the care-less Typees. Tommo does not "pry" into their rituals because the islanders themselves do not pry; they are, he asserts, "either too lazy or too sensible to worry themselves about abstract points of religious belief" (*T*, 171). In short, the repose of faith among these natives is so natural that it is not an issue; their indolence is wisdom, and they are free to "repose implicit faith" in whatever gods they choose. There is an Edenic serenity in not having to know the roots of religion, but this tempting belief, while favorable among amiable benevolists, aggravates evangelists, for whom repose is only the side effect of a hard-fought resurrection.

To accommodate conflicting factions, Tommo focuses upon a scene of "peculiar charm" (*T*, 173). It is the sacred mausoleum of a mummified chief who sits in a canoe rowing toward death. Tommo is captivated by the "stillness" and "calm solitude" of the temple. His images are so vivid, they transport him from his New York study back to Typee. "I see them now" (172), he claims, breaking narrative unity to entertain his rapture. He projects himself into Kory-Kory and envisions a "Polynesian heaven" where one "reposed through . . . eternity" with abundant fruits and rivers of coconut milk. These are the "realms of bliss" that await the "impatient" mummy.

The mummy is an early version of the multi-interpretive "doubloon" in *Moby-Dick*. Here, the only interpreters are Tommo and Kory-Kory, but as their readings pile up, the rower becomes (for us) susceptible to the ultimate ironic interpretation: Like Thorpe's Bear or Poe's Ape, it is a phantom, planted amid truths in order to dupe us into a deep thought that annihilates reality.

Kory-Kory's amusingly pragmatic reaction to the rower unsettles Tommo's Romantic notions of death. One expects from him a sense of awe or longing for the nether regions. And when asked if he would join the mummified chief, Kory-Kory offers up a "smart-sounding" proverb, which Tommo reverently wishes he could "penetrate." In true hoaxing fashion, Tommo delays the disclosure of the proverb's deep wisdom just long enough for our tension to seem foolishly wasted, for Kory-Kory, whose attitude is "with bliss on earth, why hurry heaven?" says nothing more than "A bird in the hand is worth two in the bush." For Tommo, this "wisdom" is "discreet," "sensible," and "shrewd," but the impact on the reader of this anticlimax undermines the profundity of island repose. Kory-Kory is a Polynesian Franklin with little grasp of spirituality, and Tommo's inference is a comic misconstrual.

Tommo's attempt to meet this deflation with his own inflated protestations of native faith only draws our attention more to the mummy hoax. Addressing the effigy, he offers his own "wisdom":

> Aye, paddle away, brave chieftain, to the land of spirits! To the material eye thou makest but little progress; but with the eye of faith, I see thy canoe cleaving the bright waves, which die away on those dimly looming shores of Paradise. [*T*, 173]

Not only is this florid prose as false as Kory-Kory's proverb is flat, but Tommo misses his own point, for, in asking us to shift from the "material eye" to the "eye of faith," he hopes that *Kory-Kory* and all islanders are conscious of their spiritual longing. But Tommo's sentence structure clearly indicates that he shifts not only from material to spiritual eyes but from Kory-Kory's to his own. It is *he*, not the native, who sees with the "eye of faith." Thus the crucial point of *native* spirituality is lost on Tommo's increasingly skeptical audience. Enraptured by his Romantic idiom, Tommo is more baffled than he realizes.

Kory-Kory's mummy initiates a mare's nest of ironies. Is Tommo sincere, in which case he seems a blind fool idealizing a spiritless culture? Or is he trying to pull the wool over the eyes of religionist readers who, he hopes, will be duped into a more liberal view of native life? If the latter, does not the contravening evidence of Kory-Kory's materialism pose a stumbling block fated to unhinge even the most sincere defenses of pagan spirituality? If the former, is not Melville, then, suggesting through Tommo's faulty argumentation the first anxious hint of his disintegrating doubt about Typee's Eden? To some degree, both readings are valid. Tommo is a sincere character unconsciously anticipating a reversal of his idealism as well as the knowing agent of an author trying to tease yet appease the more religious in his audience. As such the doubloon-like mummy serves Melville well in destablizing an adversarial audience. Melville adopts the pose of a revivalist and pushes the fragile hoax into burlesque,[14] but by the same token in pushing too far, Melville's hoax falls in upon itself.

Tommo's short-lived and ineffectual career as a revivalist begins with a series of comic anecdotes designed explicitly to demonstrate the childishness of Typeean religion. The ploy recalls Melville's earlier infantilizing of native warfare in order to undo their reputation for ferocity. But here, the process simply derides without redeeming the Typees. They treat their icons as toys, so religion is like playing dolls (*T*, 176). Melville's one coup in all this is that in describing Kolory's prowess as a fortune-teller, the author hints that the priest may be a "vile humbug" (176), and it is only a small leap for us to draw the profane conclusion that Western religion is humbug, too.

If religious readers placed themselves too far above this comic priest to see a mirroring of themselves, the happy result was that no one bothered to expurgate the slur. But when the author later relates Kory-Kory's abuse of a decaying wooden idol that inadvertently slides onto his back, and when in the next paragraph Melville obliquely puns by calling Kory-Kory "back-slidden" in religion, censors began to snip. It was not, however, the allegory of Kory-Kory's finding himself weighted down by a rotten religion that offended, but rather the sarcasm in the concluding paragraph. The following was dropped entirely from the revised edition:

> In truth, I regard the Typees as a back-slidden generation. They are sunk in religious sloth, and require a spiritual revival. A long prosperity of bread-fruit and cocoa-nuts has rendered them remiss in the performance of their high obligations. The wood-rot malady is spreading among the idols—the fruit upon the altars is becoming offensive—the temples themselves need rethatching—the tattooed clergy are altogether too light-hearted and lazy—and their flocks are going astray. [*T*, 179]

The drastic reversal in Melville's affections for Typeean life is too severe to be taken seriously. His once indolently wise natives are now "sunk in sloth"; his sacred rower is now nothing more than one of many "wood-rot" idols. In addition, the parodic revivalist's diction—with its breathless dashes and incremental repetition—draws attention to the fact that Tommo is merely playing a part. This sudden breach in Tommo's sincerity breaks the listless pattern of comic anecdotes concerning native religion and shocks us into the recognition that Tommo is laughing at our laughing at the natives. *We* are the "back-slidden," and it is our temple that needs "rethatching." Instead of concluding his hoax, as might Thorpe, on a note of silence that deepens the ambiguities of his reveries, Melville exits braying in an unfamiliar tongue and with his thumb to his nose. There is not even the silence of the sacred groves where "sensible" natives sleep; there is only the clamor of ranting sarcasm. Melville's promising hoax degenerates into satire. No one is fooled; no artful assimilation of opposing views is achieved.

In Chapter 14, we found striking evidence of rhetorical success primarily because Melville was able to submerge sexual, aesthetic, and political ideas within a unified and amiable symbology. In a sense, Melville's anxiety over his sexual theme found a perfect outlet in the symbolic structure of his fire-making hoax. Tommo, too, is not encumbered at this point by his later fear of cultural conversion. Just as a good hoaxer believes his own lies, he is free to indulge in fancies that won't bite back. But Chapter 24 suffers from conflicting intentions that circle, entrap, and frustrate Tommo. Launching upon an impossible mission to mollify the "reverend order of" missionaries, he first lures readers toward an idealized view of native spirituality. Failing this, he attempts to lure religionists a step closer to accepting him by depicting himself as one of them, a revivalist. But instead of bringing the opposition to him, he finds himself drawn closer to them. Such is the peril of play-acting and of Tommo's unstable cultural marginality. In converting others to Typee, he finds himself on the brink of converting himself back to the West by way of a camp meeting.

Tommo's rhetoric fails, then, because he panics at the recognition of his incipient apostasy from his insistent benevolism. Worse, he discovers that he likes the part he is playing. It is this panic that triggers the sarcasm that in turn belies his pose. In playing his part "to the life," he has become the converter he loathes—whether it be the Western missionary or the Polynesian tattooist. One might argue that Tommo's role-playing is therapeutic psychodrama designed to exorcise his fear of conversion. But even here the therapy fails, for Tommo does not assimilate and thus control the character he plays; rather the character gets the best of him. Melville runs from his religionist readers and in his flight comes to doubt his own idealism. In the space of a few chapters, he will find himself racing from the Typees as well, on the beach, on the marge, running back to home and mother.

Rover and Cosmopolite

Melville's failure to dupe us in Chapter 24 is as revealing of his anxieties as his success in Chapter 14 is of his rhetorical control. The disparity between these two literary con games leads us back to the overwhelming problem of the sudden breakdown in the final chapters of the book. Why does Tommo abandon the amiable world he has taken such great pains to construct and defend? Why does Melville allow his narrator to forsake the principles he preaches? The answer is that both author and character cannot help themselves. As an inheritor of the amiable tradition, Melville had available to him a set of "humours" characters, including the genialist, misanthrope, con man, and various composite figures, such as the surly philanthropist, the genial misanthrope, and the cosmopolitan. Only the last lays claim to full self-awareness. The others are emotional "rovers" who live at the mercy of their unpredictable instincts, either to find benevolence or to seek out self-destructive truths. The essence of cosmopolitan repose, however, lies in the controlled containment of the latter instinct by the former, a balance I associate with cosmopolitan containment. In *Typee,* Tommo fails to sustain this state of repose, for at the end his deepest doubts unexpectedly emerge and he instinctively flees: Impulse denies reason, benevolence, and amiability. He is little more than the erratic and impulsive rover who first penetrates the island.

That much is true of Tommo. But Melville's dilemma as author goes deeper, for the pathology of his character infects his narrative control. The first-person format allows Tommo, as developing character, to intrude upon Melville's more stable and retrospective "implied author." Later in his career, Melville would try to solve this problem by moving on to third-person forms, but in his first book the problem of giving a reliable narrative voice ascendency over an unreliable character was only beginning to emerge as Melville's most significant aesthetic hurdle. In some way the instinctive fears that the Typee experience had triggered in Melville had not been fully assimilated in him even as he "tried out" his experience in the writing process in Upstate New York. Perhaps Melville's inchoate desires to marry and build a family at the time he wrote his book contributed to his character's impulsive rejection of Typee. Whatever personal causes deflected his rhetoric, it is worth reminding ourselves of the success of Melville's narrator in containing satiric outbursts within good-humored bounds and of the solid manuscript evidence that such a balance was indeed Melville's intention. Thus, if Melville seems to stumble, it is more a factor of the difficulty of his project than of his freshman status as a writer. But in the end, Melville's geniality falters because he cannot make Tommo distance himself from the instinctive "knowledge of the demonism of the world"; Tommo shouts down the rationality of his amiable voice. His inability to rise above the rover status is best revealed in Chapter 18, with the culmination of his sexual development with Fayaway and the severe limits of that growth manifested in his problematic association with the island cosmopolite Marnoo.

Thus far, we have recorded two phases in Tommo's submerged sexual progress: his adolescent fixation on female exposure and his deeper sensuality expressed in the sexual fantasizing of the fire-making scene. In Chapter 18, the consummation of Tommo's relationship with Fayaway, although expressed symbolically, signals Tommo's sexual maturation. In a sense the scene, which involves Fayaway's full bodily exposure to Tommo, may be taken as a regression—just more ogling. But in fact Tommo puts what he sees to serious, not burlesque, use and thus moves beyond adolescent snicker to a transcendent yet highly sensual view of female beauty. Once again, Melville's submergence of sexuality through symbolic indirection proved rhetorically successful. Not only did the American revised edition remove only two relatively inconsequential lines, but major portions of the arousing scene were reprinted in New York and London journals. When readers recalled Fayaway in later years, it was Chapter 18 that they most readily recollected.

And with good reason: The scene is powerful. Tommo begins with a sensuous description of the lake reminiscent of Chapter 14's water, wood, and Turkish imagery. It is "a lovely sheet" of feminine water surrounded by the masculine "shaft of the cocoa-nut tree," which droops and waves like harem "ostrich plumes" (*T*, 131). Here, Tommo tests his natatory skills against the girls'. Failing to catch them, he is both mystified and aroused. He feels like a "cumbrous whale attacked on all sides by a legion of sword-fish" (134). The languor and phallic attacking coming from the sportive water-nymphs no doubt pique Tommo's masculinity, stimulating him to escalate the foreplay. He gets a boat.

The ploy seems clever enough. As a sailor, he is a master of ships and can flatter himself that he shall impose his maritime skills over the submarine dominion of these mermaids. Symbolically, the shaft-like canoe suggests his phallic control of the "lovely sheet of water." But there is a catch. Canoes are taboo to women, and when he puts his bark in the water, the nymphs are departed. Ever the resourceful Yankee, Tommo beseeches Mehevi for a dispensation of this "[r]idiculous" and inexplicable zoning law. Granted his variance, Tommo loads his canoe with all manner of suggestive comestibles—stripped young coconuts, phallic yams, sticky poi—as well as two pipes. Whereas before, Kory-Kory labors hard to produce fire for Tommo's single-pipe, autoerotic fantasy, now Fayaway and Tommo can smoke together in their taboo craft, making fire together. Melville's diction links the two scenes, for just as Kory-Kory's exertions produce a flame that begins with "a delicate wreath of smoke" (111), so too does the smoking Fayaway give "forth light wreaths of vapor" (133).

Tommo and Fayaway's subsequent "manoeuvres" on the lake further suggest that the scene is a physical enactment of Tommo's earlier fantasy:

> As I turned the canoe, Fayaway . . . seemed all at once struck with some happy idea. With a wild exclamation of delight, she disengaged from her person the ample robe of tappa which was knotted over her shoulder (for the purpose of shielding her from the sun), and spreading it out like a sail, stood erect with upraised arms in the head of the canoe. [*T*, 134]

At first the scene may seem playfully innocent, at best only vaguely suggestive with both the word "erect" and the image of Fayaway's ballooning sail implying the phallic cause and feminine effect of impregnation. But Melville's parenthetical explanation of Fayaway's robe reminds us of certain facts, which lead inevitably to more explicit images. The parenthesis is required because normally Typee women wear their robes just below the breasts. (Tommo later tells us that he fashions a dress for Fayaway beginning even lower at the waist.) Thus when Fayaway stands in the canoe, she is modestly half-covered, but when she disrobes she is fully nude facing Tommo, who is seated with paddle in hand only a few feet away. "We American sailors," Tommo continues, "pride ourselves upon our straight clear spars, but a prettier little mast than Fayaway made was never shipped a-board of my craft." More than just Fayaway is now standing erect.

But the masculine joking over the "pretty little mast" that Fayaway's exposure has made of herself and in her partner's pants is carefully deflected in the next paragraph:

In a moment the tappa was distended by the breeze—the long brown tresses of Fayaway streamed in the air—and the canoe glided rapidly through the water, and shot towards shore. Seated in the stern, I directed its course with my paddle until it dashed up the soft sloping bank and Fayaway, with a light spring, alighted on the ground.

Here the sexual symbolism does not focus upon the expenditure of male autoerotic exertion but rather on heterosexual union. And more, the beauty of Fayaway's "happy idea" takes her beyond human intercourse. As a mast she unites the manmade canoe to the winds of nature. As a sail she captures the breeze of the spirit. Nude before Tommo, she dissolves into the landscape. Her *jeu d'esprit* is free, open, and whimsical: utterly sensual, utterly imaginative. Thus the heavy sensuality of the scene is transformed into a transcendent union of male and female, water and wind, art and nature, "craft" (both of sea and art) and imagination.

Further evidence that this scene consummates the desires of the fire-making fantasy is found in a correspondence between two symbolic details. When Kory-Kory completes his exertions, his stick is "pressed convulsively against the further end of the channel" (*T*, 111). It is an "abrupt termination." Fayaway's lake, we find, lies near the "termination of a long gradually expanding gorge" toward which trade winds blow. Thus, it is toward this vaginal channel that the phallic canoe sails, "until it dashe[s] up the soft sloping bank" and deposits Fayaway on the sand. Each scene, then, climaxes at a convulsive or abrupt terminus. Although these details clearly tie the two scenes together, Melville goes further in Fayaway's case. Here he does not need to deflect the sexual power of fire into a domestic and political commentary. The sexual fulfillment becomes an end in itself, pure joy and delight, the comic exuberance of Beauty. Instead of sweaty exhaustion, Kory-Kory (observing all this from the shore) "now clapped his hands in transport, and shouted like a madman" (134). Tommo has come of age.

Chapter 18, *Typee*'s central chapter, marks Tommo's fullest sexual development. He has moved beyond anxious adolescent debasements of women, jocular exposure, and autoerotic fantasy to an understanding of sex as liberating, expressive, and transcendent. Having made this *rite de passage,* he is by all accounts ready for the next step, marriage and procreation. At this, however, both Melville and his creature Tommo balk. Tommo's fear of conversion extends, through the implied sexuality of tattoos, which he abhors, to the very sexual activity that he has been joyfully sharing with Fayaway. Mehevi allows the canoe taboo to be abrogated to effect Tommo's broader and deeper commitment to the Typee valley. He will ensure his valley's sovereignty if Tommo stays with Fayaway. Thus, the more Tommo is sexually liberated, the more likely he is to be converted wholly to Typee. Perhaps he will even accept a tattoo.

But elsewhere, Tommo begins a campaign to discredit Typeean domesticity. "[D]ear, good, affectionate old Tinor" (*T*, 85), the epitome of maternal domesticity in Chapter 12, becomes in Chapter 26 the paramour of an older gentleman whom she services as her husband looks on (189). At best the island's solid, amiable domesticity is now little more than a scandalous free-for-all. This kind of illicit behavior, Tommo coyly repeats, is like Typee religion: a puzzle and a mystery (189, 190). But such bafflement is designed to provide Tommo a way out of his commitment to Typee. If, despite his own philanderings, he appears baffled and finally shocked over these marital practices, he can then adopt an uncharacteristic superiority over the natives and reject their amiable sexuality when, like its religion, it suddenly becomes too restrictive of his freedom. Tommo will exploit Polynesian sexuality for his own ends but will avoid Mehevi's insistence upon his conversion to Polynesian family life, even if this means a betrayal of his earlier notions of the superiority of Typeean domesticity. In effect, he is arguing quite hypocritically that he cannot settle down in Typee because, after all, the Typees themselves do not settle down. In this manner, Tommo can imperialistically exploit and be free of the natives, while Melville, by allowing his character to modify his love of island life, can seek to assuage religionists already convinced of Polynesian immorality. He shall become a pious rover.

Moreover, Melville has other rhetorical problems to resolve. *Typee* is dedicated to Lemuel Shaw, the oldest and best friend of Melville's deceased father and Melville's future father-in-law. Although Herman did not marry Elizabeth Shaw until 1847, they had known each other since childhood. The young sailor returning from four years at sea had his eye on his future bride even as he was writing and editing *Typee* for the revised American edition. In short, a decided first among equals in Melville's general audience was the Shaw family—father Lemuel and daughter Elizabeth. Given these associations and the tensions they bear, Melville's handling of his sexual theme had to be particularly delicate. He had to present himself to the father as sufficiently experienced and emotionally stable and to the daughter as sexually attractive. Not only does the blushing but sexually active Tommo come across as a capable mate, but in the later chapters he is scornful of extramarital practices. He has sown his oats and has loved the ladies, but he is ready for marriage, and a proper Boston one at that.

It is generally and rightly assumed that the bulk of the expurgations of the American Revised edition were imposed upon Melville. Some, however, were initiated by the author himself, and with an eye toward toning down expressions concerning marriage that might unsettle the Shaws. For instance, in a short paragraph disavowing any "flirtation" with married Polynesians, Tommo slyly concludes: "Married women, to be sure!—I knew better than to offend them" (*T,* 191). In the revised edition this passage was cut. No evidence exists to tell us for sure who authorized the cut, but considering the fairly innocuous nature of this routine sarcasm against the institution of marriage and given the religious and political nature of earlier cuts, it seems an unlikely candidate for an editor's excision. But in Melville's mind, the line protested too much against illicit liaisons. Fearing that the sarcasm might backfire and indicate the opposite to the Shaws—that he did have affairs with *married* women in Polynesia—he himself ordered it cut. In short, he would not risk offending Elizabeth even by teasingly denying he would ever offend the in-stitution of marriage. A second excision might also be Melville's. Originally writing "I have more than one reason to believe that tedious courtships are unknown in the valley" (191), the author may have cut the introductory clause, which playfully implies his own, too-numerous sexual couplings, again to avoid the censure of the Shaws.[15]

While all this is purely speculative, it reminds us of the complexities Melville faced in addressing his varied audiences: publishers and missionaries, politicos and domestic citizens, his family and even his bride-to-be. Whatever Melville's rhetorical anxieties may be, Tommo's sexual anxiety is clear. He has learned the beauty of sexual liberation from the Typees, but now he wants *back* to the culture he has fled; a natural enough conversion, we are led to believe, but it also means a failure to sustain a marginal existence between two cultures. In a sense, the sudden flight toward "Home" and "Mother" is a yielding to the uncontrollable instinct of Western geniality, the safety of the parlor. But in failing to moderate this instinct even as he does in fact moderate Typee's indolent repose, he projects himself as the mere rover he elsewhere derides.

The rover syndrome is not new to Tommo. During their escape, Tommo and Toby operate almost exclusively upon whim. Such an amiable attribute would be amusing were it not so obvious that they have little comprehension of their reversals. To begin with, Tommo characterizes his double in almost stock terms as an eighteenth-century "benevolent misanthrope" or surly philanthropist, to use Melville's term. Toby is a classic man in black. He has dark hair, complexion, and eyes. Outwardly, he is "a strange wayward being, moody, fitful, and melancholy" (*T*, 32), possessing a "quick and fiery temper." And yet he is "a big-hearted shipmate" who may never laugh but smiles a great deal and engages in "dry, sarcastic humor." Toby is by all means the American cousin of Goldsmith's Drybone. Tommo, however, senses that this melancholiac is "the very one" to be his partner in escape. The pairing is hardly expected except to the degree that opposites attract, and that Tommo senses an inner similarity to Toby's deeply conflicted personality. Little wonder, then, that Tommo characterizes his attraction to Toby as "reckless."

Tommo is invariably the optimist playing off Toby's innate pessimism. Thus, one emotional extreme agitates another, but considering the exigencies of their flight the two rovers need a single-minded consensus they are incapable of achieving. Tommo looks into a chasm and insists upon a descent: "there is something to be seen here" (*T*, 44–45). Toby's caution at this point is pathological—"If you are going to pry into everything you meet . . . , you will marvelously soon get knocked on the head" (45). A few pages later, the sailors reverse roles. Toby proposes that they take their chances and descend farther into the valley, and Tommo holds back, stating that "it was impossible for either of us to know anything with certainty" (51). Toby's reversal to optimism convinces him that the Happars they think they are about to meet must be good, for it is "impossible that the inhabitants of such a lovely place . . . can be anything else but good fellows" (56). As Toby's skepticism disintegrates, he falls prey to the most jejune of assumptions. As with Drybone, Toby's moody exterior represses rather than balances his genial instincts, so that his optimistic tendencies are not properly tested by the world and manifest themselves only in moments of ill-advised eruption. In all, Tommo's unguarded geniality and its darkly mirrored inversion in Toby's overly guarded geniality are characteristic signs of their unstable vagabond mentality. They rove up and down an emotional scale just as they rove the seas.

As a more fully assimilated figure, the cosmopolite Marnoo is Tommo's ethical superior. He appears only twice in the book, once in Chapter 18 as an extension in beauty of Fayaway and later during Tommo's escape. Although Tommo never achieves Marnoo's higher sensibility, Marnoo is nevertheless instrumental in effecting Tommo's release. His power, therefore, suggests his ideality.[16]

Marnoo is never directly called a cosmopolitan—Melville would not tie the term to a character until *The Confidence-Man*—but the portrait is undeniable. Marnoo is a cosmopolite by reason of taboo; that is, he is allowed to travel unharmed among hostile tribes and islands. In his own words, "me go every where,—nobody harm me,—me taboo" (*T*, 139). Like other "tabooed Kannaka" (Melville explains), he is an "interpreter" who facilitates "barter" (74). Thus he exhibits in his lowest functions the mercantile aspect of the nineteenth-century version of the citizen of the world. But Melville clearly expands Marnoo's qualities to include all that is benevolent, beautiful, sage, and even heroic in the ideal eighteenth-century cosmopolite.

Like Vincent Nolte, Marnoo entertains the natives with comic caricatures of everyone present; but more, he is "one of the most striking specimens of humanity . . . ever beheld" (*T*, 135). Marnoo's "matchless symmetry" makes him a "Polynesian Apollo," better than the Greek original, for his dark skin and warmth of expression transform "the marble repose of art" into life. Art and life are further conjoined in Marnoo's splendid tattooing. Down his spine is the trunk of the Artu tree branching about the shoulders, so that from behind he seems "a spreading vine tacked against a garden wall" (136). Elsewhere (but not on the face) he is illustrated with an "infinite variety of figures." Front and back, in profile and stature, this illustrated man is a breathing work of art, not stone or canvas, but flesh and figure, a supple fusion of man and nature through art. Moreover, Marnoo is politically and rhetorically "versatile," modulating the manner of his address to the crowd from the "voice of a prophet" inveighing against the French to a good-humored "bantering style," which "filled the whole assembly with uproarious delight." Finally, he is referred to ten times in seven pages as "the stranger," the term characteristically applied in Western culture to cosmopolitan figures. In all, Marnoo incorporates various patterns associated with the citizen of the world. He is worldly, versatile, and artful. He is, indeed, art itself: prophetic, good-natured, humorous, and manipulative.

Although admiration for Marnoo suffuses his description, Tommo's first reaction to the island cosmopolite parallels the standard cultural response to such figures: He thinks he is a confidence man. Marnoo does, in fact, string Tommo along, pretending at their first encounter to ignore the sailor and not to know English. Marnoo also proves himself to be an operator when he concocts various deceptions later on to help Tommo escape. But at this point, Tommo sees Marnoo as a particular kind of con man, the roué or "sad deceiver among the simple maidens of this island" (*T*, 138). Marnoo's capacity for this kind of deception is never dramatized; thus Tommo's dubious speculation, coming as it does on the heels of his own amours with Fayaway, is itself a "sad" projection of Tommo's careless philandering. Indeed, he accuses Marnoo of the crime he will commit, the loving and leaving of Fayaway. This self-aggrandizing attack upon a moral superior, who will by his good nature condescend to be Tommo's savior, ironically reveals the distance Tommo has yet to go in his sexual, social, and aesthetic development. He flees from love, beauty, commitment, freedom, and repose. He remains a mere rover, not a cosmopolitan.

As an artist, Marnoo is an interpreter and transformer transcending both aesthetic and social realms; he is in some sense the artist Melville was striving to become; he is most certainly the ideal Tommo fails to recognize. Physically, Tommo goes as far as one can in extending his sexual desires beyond the merely jocular and carnal to a deeper sense of beauty. But spiritually he fails to grasp the fuller function of Beauty that Marnoo projects: the harmonizing of disparate social groups by means of the divine mechanism of taboo or aesthetic restraint and the transformation of man and nature into Art. In short, Tommo is only beginning to see the necessity of conversion, not forward into Typeean life or back to the West, but rather a conversion to a third state that remains forever both worlds at once, forever marginal. If in the presence of Marnoo he gets cold feet and runs, casting his boathook at Mow-Mow's throat, we can take heart that in calling his aggression a "horror" he recognizes the betrayal of his retreat.

Moreover, we can draw a deeper significance, for Tommo's problems in accommodating primitive and Western cultures, in adhering to his logic of cultural relativism and to the "unvarnished facts" of native custom, in transcending Typee's mysteries, and in adopting Marnoo's cosmopolitan sensibility, allegorize Melville's own anxious situation in accommodating the separate "cultures" of audience and self. He wrote and revised, continuously, to meet, instruct, inflame, cajole, and appease a variety of audiences, including editors, publishers, liberals, conservatives, family, and future family. He was, like a "true cosmopolite," attempting to be "at home" with all readers and a stranger to none. But he was writing for himself as well, attempting to get to know the new artist within him: to forge a complex ideology that chastens without rejecting the West, to establish reliability and narrative distance, and yet to reconstruct the sailor he once was. In building his text rhetorically, he was also shaping it to his own emergent political and sexual ideas. It was an ambitious balancing act, a struggle for self-expression and yet containment.[17]

If *Typee* is a problematic text—and like all of Melville's books, it is deliciously so—it struggles at cohesion rather than stumbles before it. And for Melville, no other relationship between art and experience could obtain than that which is the product of an intellect struggling to capture repose while tensely situated "on the marge" of two worlds. In *Moby-Dick,* Ishmael advances upon Tommo's picturesque, pushing it toward a more politically viable cosmopolitanism, and improves upon his precursor as both a more stable character and a more reliable speaker. And yet the most exciting structural feature of Melville's whaling masterpiece is that, once at sea, it perpetually pushes beyond the limits of a unified first-person narrative. Melville was itching to explore new narrative stances, and with Ahab he was able to experiment with a more fully conceived dramatic mode.

10

Ishmael: Sounding the Repose of If

Moby-Dick is a tragedy staged within a comedy, and a drama contained by a meditation. Just as Ishmael projects Ahab out of himself, and Ahab projects the white whale, so does Ishmael's redemptive geniality frame the demonic impulse that informs Ahab's dramatic conflict with Moby Dick. This framing technique, which draws upon gothic and tall-tale formulas,[1] is most directly felt in the rhythmic alternations in the narrative between disintegration and coherence, the pulse of Ahab's "unsmoothable . . . seam" (*MD*, 488) and counterpulse of Ishmael's "one seamless whole" (492). With these alternating periods of tension and repose, we feel wrapped in the tides of the author's unfolding consciousness, in which seamless vision and fracturing realities enact a circular discourse. For Ishmael that circularity—and circles more than whiteness are the novel's dominant symbol—is a comfort; for Ahab, despair. Melville gives the more solid beat in this rhythmic give-and-take to Ishmael's repose, and finally this recurring comic beat is the narrative's organizing principle.

Ishmael is Melville's central character because he is the most "marginal." Drawn toward the vortex of the *Pequod*'s suction, he floats "on the margin" of that maelstrom, buoyed up by Queequeg's coffin. He is a part of the action and yet detached. Situated now between past experience and the present, recreative act of his narrative, he will write it all out; his marginal status symbolizes the artist's condition. Ishmael also writes out himself. Like Montaigne, he "essays," wandering whimsically and seriously through actions and ideas, landing now and again upon the essential "facts" of his being.[2] *To essay.* In its original sense, the essay is the record of intellectual discovery, an *attempt* at truth, a trial run. *To essay. To try.* This writing process extracts meaning out of experience, including writing itself. For whalers, "trying out" means the rendering of oil out of blubber, the discovery of an essence within the carcass. *To try. To know.* What Ishmael learns far more than Ahab is that knowledge is utterly experiential; knowing exists solely in essaying, the trying out of self and idea. It is forever contingent, hence marginal and picturesque; always unpredictable, hence comic.

Melville himself is marginally situated between two ways of writing. The tragic and *dramatic mode* tries out a conflict of ideas through the staging of allegorized characters. The comic and *lyrical mode* tries out meaning through meditations upon symbols. In one mode Melville stages Ahab's inability to wrestle knowledge out of experience; in the other he exposes Ishmael's failures and successes in his picturesque wanderings. Both act out an experience of doubt, and both allow Melville a transcendence of self. Indeed, the experiment with drama, through the formal elimination of the first-person voice, assisted Melville's aesthetic self-effacement, for he could stage a "theater of the self" without personality. In the final chapters of The Chase Melville drops lyricism and drama altogether. Word and action fuse, and the personalities of Ishmael and Ahab dissolve into the currents of the text. The novel's "framing" and "essaying" end in a moment of dynamic repose.

Ishmael confronts two problems congruent with the novel's lyric and dramatic modes. The first deals with the dangers of human associativeness. Ishmael finds that to know himself, he must know others, in particular that Queequegian "other"—both princely and primitive—that lies within.[3] Contrary to Ahab's self-sovereignty, Ishmael is cosmopolitan. But human viciousness impedes this liberal vision; thus Ishmael must learn to withstand the likes of Ahab and his crew. He does so by showing how the genial spirit can grow out of the demonic. Ishmael's second problem is the epistemological and rhetorical crisis of how we know what we know and whether that knowledge can be voiced. Since meaning is not inherent within an object but derives from our experience with the object, Ishmael acts out the process of "essaying" meaning out of fact; he "poeticizes." By pressuring fact into symbol, Ishmael solves his epistemological problem: His creativity is knowledge. But since voice shapes creation, Ishmael's personality-driven poetics threatens to dissolve into solipsism. Ahab dramatizes that point. He cannot rest easy with essaying; he must break through fact to the animating spirit he thinks exists within. As he fails to realize that such a spirit is actually located within himself, in his creativity, his attempts to know are self-destructive.[4] A crucial aspect of Ishmael's repose is that his genial instinct enlivens but also controls his instinct to become the demonic; he can play within a world of symbols that Ahab would destroy.

Perhaps the deepest puzzle posed by Melville is why Ishmael is blessed with a creative instinct and Ahab is not; why one survives and the other self-destructs. Is it a matter of nature's unequal dispensations; is it the vagaries of social or familial nurturing that switch Ishmael on but Ahab off; is it a sexual wound that decrees the difference, or is impotence merely a further symptom of Ahab's failure, not its cause? Given one's unwilled instincts, personality is happenstance. Ishmael simply survives; Ahab destroys. But if character is only instinct, then Ahab's tragedy will strike us as merely mechanistic and Ishmael's humor as mere whim. Both characters possess a sufficient degree of self-control that neither is a mere automaton of geniality or despair. Ahab's madness is self-reflective. Ishmael's self-conscious marginalism lifts him above Stubb's slumbering repose. His detachment gives relevance to his whim and restraint to despair. Ishmael and Ahab, then, are projections of Melville's battling instincts, palpable agents of his sublime flashings-forth and creative containments.

Ishmael's Initiation: Narcissist and Cosmopolite

Moby-Dick begins in comic crisis. Our principal speaker is caught in the trammels of an excessive addiction to himself. We are amused by the instinctive morbidity that lands him in coffin warehouses. Full of the hypos, he chooses whaling over "pistol and ball" for therapy. The speaker tells us to call him Ishmael, but is this command an invitation or a coverup? And what of the label? Is "Ishmael" a loser, outcast, orphan, wanderer, "isolato"? Like Tommo, Ishmael roves at the whim of his instincts, which are as unpredictable as they are creative. He finds himself "bringing up the rear of every funeral" or at the Battery where "meditation and water are wedded for ever" (*MD*, 3–4). Here is a "metaphysical professor," and yet "here is an artist": Ishmael lives both roles. Eventually he holds the latter above the former, but in "Loomings" (ch. 1) he is still more Narcissus than either. Here is an egoist.

Ishmael is not entirely lost; his good humor impels him toward cosmopolitanism. But losing his self-indulgence, he naïvely embraces philanthropy, thus exchanging one problem for another. Ishmael's humor is guided more by chance than by reason; it is (to concoct a Melvillean phrase) a thoughtful thoughtlessness, for he pursues an idea to the edge of despair and then whimsically reverses himself. It is more reflex than intelligence. When he stumbles into a tavern called "The Trap," he discovers "a negro church" whose minister preaches "the blackness of darkness" (*MD*, 10).[5] His physical comedy counters this Ahabian theme with the accidental thought that an obsession with darkness is a mental "Trap." Later, in contemplating the difference a pane of glass makes between the frozen outer world and the toasty climate inside, Ishmael compares the window to his eyes and the warm parlor to "this body of mine" (10). But the brief metaphors of self-involvement expand into politics. Ishmael contrasts the freezing homeless with the protected elite, ending with a withering attack upon the philanthropist who "only drinks the tepid tears of orphans" (11). Just as Ishmael instinctively "backs out" of the Trap of darkness, he thrusts directly to its cynical heart. He is that marginal pane of glass that simultaneously looks out and in.

Or at least that is his potential. At this point, Ishmael's humor finds no picturesque moment; it pushes him erratically in or out, but nowhere between instinctual urges. The memorials to drowned sailors in the Chapel "gnaw upon all Faith" (*MD*, 36). But soon enough faith itself gnaws back as "a jackal [that] feeds among the tombs [gathering] from these dead doubts . . . her most vital hope" (37). Ishmael's whims batter his psyche, pushing him to the brink of nihilism and back. "But somehow I grew merry," Ishmael concludes, thumbing his nose at death and Faith, giving three mindless cheers for whaling and his eternal soul. As long as the whims of that soul can counter every depression with a cheer, Ishmael's geniality will serve him adequately. But there is no repose in this dependency. Faith in the redemptive value of one's alternating instinct is as flimsy as Ishmael's naïve faith in immortality, and his suspicion of inadequacy urges him toward a cosmopolitan religion. Nevertheless, Ishmael must be conned into this new faith, and Melville structures Ishmael's growth so that the sailor's ontological whims are transformed into a more stable vision through the energy of a comic and sexual growth. Ishmael is not only conned; he is seduced.

Peter Coffin's conning of Ishmael to bunk with Queequeg is one of the richest veins of humor in *Moby-Dick*. From the moment he planes a bench to "soften" it as a bed, he is pulling Ishmael's leg, converting his fears of darkness into a desire for the primal experience of it. Ishmael hotly insists he is "not green" (*MD*, 18), and he won't be teased by Coffin's obscure remarks about his bedmate's selling his head, a point Ishmael takes figuratively and erroneously to mean that the individual in question is mad. When Coffin explains the literalness of the head peddling, Ishmael is further conned into thinking that the peddler must be a sailor like himself—"the landlord, after all, had had no idea of fooling me." No green lad here. But the real con is that Ishmael will not be bedding down with anyone so familiar as a lunatic, salesman, or white sailor, but rather a cannibal prince.

Coffin's seduction is as sensual as it is comic. He puts Ishmael and Queequeg in the bed he and wife Sal used on the night they were "spliced." Much room there for "kicking about." The sexual joking continues when Ishmael inspects his roommate's poncho. It is shaggy, thick, and damp with a slit for the head to pass through. Ishmael is modeling Queequeg's "cassock," made (as we learn in ch. 95) from the skin of a whale's penis, which Melville calls the vestments of a "bishoprick." Standing before the mirror, dressed in these phallic canonicals, Ishmael reacts with slapstick horror, tearing himself out of the garment so quickly as to give himself a kink in the neck. Eventually Ishmael's subconscious aversion to the dimly perceived sexuality of the moment melts into a universal acceptance of sensuality. No longer the fool of his own reserve, the rejecter of Negro churches, and choirboy adulator of the redemptive soul, he subsequently admits into his bed the "wild cannibal" owner of the comically obscene poncho; he loosens mind and body, and Coffin's seductive con game ends: "Better sleep with a sober cannibal than a drunken Christian" (24), Coffin tells him, and Ishmael wakes up, teased out of anxiety and wrapped in Queequeg's arms.

Ishmael's love for Queequeg is a sensual rendering of his new cosmopolitan religion. There is no doubt that here as elsewhere Melville essays homosexuality,[6] but the final rhetorical effect of Ishmael's love-making is to take readers beyond gendered sexuality toward a pansexual embrace of humanity. No longer trapped by narcissism, the white sailor weds black in a bed made for all: He sleeps with Peter Coffin and Sal as well as Queequeg. Further intratextual associations illuminate the essaying of these powerful sexual ideas.

"The Cassock" (ch. 95), which replays Ishmael's anxious modeling of Queequeg's poncho in "The Spouter Inn" (ch. 3), is a coda to "The Squeeze of a Hand" (ch. 94), which relates the method by which whalemen squeeze globs of congealed sperm oil back to a liquid state. It is a lubricious process, and masturbatory.[7] In squeezing sperm, Ishmael discovers "a strange sort of insanity." This is not the catatonic autism that nineteenth-century psychologists attributed to onanism,[8] but rather altruism, for in squeezing sperm Ishmael also squeezes his fellow laborers' hands. Moreover, Ishmael does not report just any erotic fantasy:

> Would that I could keep squeezing that sperm for ever! For now, since by many prolonged, repeated experiences, I have perceived that in all cases man must eventually lower, or at least shift, his conceit of attainable felicity; not placing it anywhere in the intellect or the fancy; but in the wife, the heart, the bed, the table, the saddle, the fireside, the country; now that I have perceived all this, I am ready to squeeze case eternally. In thoughts of the visions of the night, I saw long rows of angels in paradise, each with his hands in a jar of spermaceti. (416)

Ishmael's onanistic dream registers the full shift from narcissism to the "attainable felicity" and angelic domesticity of a cosmopolitan geniality. (It is as well the comic prelude to Ishmael's ethical distancing from Ahab in chapter 96, "The Try-Works.") Returning to "The Spouter Inn" (via the poncho-cassock imagery), we find that Ishmael's and Queequeg's homosexual love (their hugging is a squeezing) is a "possible" (productive and creative) love. As cosmopolites, they make that love into a domestic (heterosexual) religion of wife, table, hearth, heart in contrast to Ahab's useless impotence. In all, the fact that Ishmael's initial comic horror in "The Spouter Inn" over the phallic poncho becomes an expansive comic acceptance in "The Cassock" signals the degree to which Ishmael has grown in his sexuality beyond sterile bachelor whim and hypo to fertile "felicity."

The phallic poncho is at the center of more essaying that connects two widely separated chapters: "The Counterpane" (ch. 4) and "The Blanket" (ch. 68). In the latter, Ishmael's meditation on the whale's skin promotes a marginal sensibility. Just as the whale maintains a uniform body temperature in every climate, humanity, too, must "remain warm among ice [and] live in this world without being of it" (*MD*, 307). This is crucial advice for the artist, who, in converting experience into expression, must find a critical distance from selfhood. This formal restraint also prefigures the "attainable felicity" found in "Squeeze" and "Cassock." Moreover, the blanket of skin, a sheath that preserves felicity, is explicitly compared to "a real blanket or counterpane; or, still better, an Indian poncho slipt over [one's] head" (307). The recurring phallic "poncho" now partakes of the philosophizing of "The Blanket," so that Ishmael's sexual growth becomes analogous to his growing metaphysical confidence. The comparison to a "counterpane" only re-inforces this connection, for it beckons back to "The Counterpane" (ch. 4) in which Ishmael awakes beneath Queequeg's tattooed arm and the multicolored bed-cover. Beneath the skin and sheets is a sensual rendering of Melvillean repose. These verbal linkages stress Ishmael's poetic ability to transform his marginalizing wisdom into the melting exuberance of sexually charged cosmopolitanism.

The reader's retrospections circling from "The Blanket" back to Ishmael's "wed-ding" in "The Counterpane" are only one phase of Ishmael's essaying. He has other "phantoms" to pursue. The pressure of Queequeg's arm reminds him of an episode in his youth, when he was caught "trying to crawl up the chimney." Given the phallic associations in "I and My Chimney," the hint is that young Ishmael has been caught "playing with himself."[9] Forced to spend midsummer's day in bed, he lapses in and out of sleep, his arm (like Queequeg's) hung over the coun-terpane, and he dreams of a phantom hand holding his. The word "phantom" recalls Ishmael's concluding vision in "Loomings" (ch. 1) of "endless processions of the whale, and, midmost of them all, one grand hooded phantom, like a snow hill in the air" (7). And this "procession" of whales prefigures the "rows of angels in paradise" that conclude the masturbatory dream in "A Squeeze of the Hand." Similarly, the "hooded" phantom (Moby Dick) prefigures the warmly covered whales in "The Blanket." These early "phantoms" are germinous seeds projecting Ishmael's deepest sense of a sexual being, coming from Melville's first use of "phantom" (also in "Loomings"): "the ungraspable phantom of life" or the reflection of Narcissus in his pool. This phantom of Ishmael's problematic self is "the key to it all" (5).

Melville's essaying combines ontology and phallic joking to redefine the words phantom, blanket, poncho, and self. The "ungraspable phantom" is at first Ishmael's impulse to define life in terms of himself. But this phantom becomes hooded, phallically contained as with a blanket, counterpane, or poncho. In turn, it becomes the hand-holding phantom in Ishmael's childhood and the phantom pressure of Queequeg's love in Ishmael's adulthood. Solipsism evolves into the life-affirming phantom of humanity. This is not a Manichean flip from darkness to light. Ishmael's racy humor fuses both the demonic and the genial. The row of masturbating angels— the image is daring but undeniable—recalls Queequeg's phantom "squeeze" and the pressure of a hand after Ishmael's pubescent chimney exploit. The boy's "self-abusing" hand is now the guiltless phantom of life he always thought it was despite his stepmother. No more the narcissistic pleasure of self-indulgent autoeroticism, the grand hooded phantom of one sperm whale called Dick is now the sensualized image of human interdependency. Thus, comedy and insight are wedded. Ishmael now becomes a willing participant in Coffin's "skylarking." He will play along with the comic seduction: "A good laugh is a mighty good thing. . . . And the man that has anything bountifully laughable about him," Ishmael concludes, "be sure there is more in that man than you perhaps think for" (29). He speaks as much of himself as of Coffin. Born laughing into his counterpane world of sexual brotherhood, he has discovered a new sensuality that contains his former, sullen self. Dissolving the windowpane barrier between self and other, he gives Queequeg entry and celebrates the counterpane birth of his repose.

Queequeg is Ishmael's model: his "calm self-collectedness of simplicity [that] seems a Socratic wisdom." He is "entirely at his ease; preserving the utmost serenity; content with his own companionship; always equal to himself" (*MD*, 50). This equanimity is infectious: "I began to be sensible of strange feelings. I felt a melting in me. No more my splintered heart and maddened hand were turned against the wolfish world. This soothing savage had redeemed it" (51). Queequeg's savage repose replaces the jackal. Keeping to the Golden Rule, he turns "idolator" (52) and later claims to belong, with Queequeg and everyone else, to the "First Congregational Church" (87), a happy transformation of Calvinism into a "great and everlasting" cosmopolitan religion. Ishmael's conversion is complete. Not only can he be "social with a horror," but he can bed, wed, and redefine a horror into a religion of repose.

But Ishmael trades one greenness for another. His liberal rebirth is more perilous than his former repressed state, and his continued naïveté makes him an easy mark. Peter Coffin is his particular nemesis. In directing him to a Nantucket inn Coffin offers a bewildering list of larboards and starboards that ends with the snapper: "ask the first man [you] meet where the place [is]" (65). It is a shaggy dog con. In another episode Ishmael expects to gain the 275th "lay" (i.e., that tiny fraction of the profits) as his portion for sailing the *Pequod,* but Peleg and Bildad play a good captain–bad captain con, parlaying their initial offer of a 777th lay up to a still unacceptable 300th, which Ishmael accepts despite his expectations of better. Finally, the most telling con is self-inflicted. When Elijah's "ambiguous, half-hinting, half-revealing, shrouded sort of talk" arouses Ishmael's suspicion, he rejects the prophetic derelict as a "humbug" (94) as if proudly exposing a con man. In fact, the thrice-diddled Ishmael only diddles himself, for Elijah's warnings are true. Ishmael's new self-confidence is as much a trap as any excessive absorption into the "blackness of darkness." His knee-jerk cosmopolitanism primes us for a dramatic disintegration in "Midnight, Forecastle" (ch. 40).

Ahab has just challenged his crew to hunt Moby Dick (ch. 36), and in successive chapters (37–39) he, Starbuck, and Stubb soliloquize while the crew make merry. It is all a staged play. The lights dim; a storm brews. The sailors, an assemblage of all nations and races, gather to dance away their sexual desires. They want girls, and all the world's a *ball*, an Old Manx Sailor remarks with a triple pun on globe, dance, and copulation. The sensual intensity peaks when a Maltese sailor imagines the white-capped waves to be dancing women. "There's naught so sweet on earth," he claims, " . . . as those swift glances of warm, wild bosoms in the dance, when the over-arboring arms hide such ripe, bursting grapes" (176). Little else in Melville is so sexually graphic as this glimpse of female nipples.[10] And yet the aroused crew, heated by dance, become hotter still when a chance remark concerning the black sky piques black Daggoo's racial sensitivity, which in turn ignites a Spanish sailor's "old grudge" of racism. In a lightning flash (or is it Daggoo's teeth? the Spaniard taunts) a fight breaks out and the cosmopolitan "ball" disintegrates into a racial brawl. The "ring" of brotherhood becomes a boxing "ring," one that God made, says the Manxman, to circumscribe Cain and Abel.

In "Midnight, Forecastle," Ishmael's cosmopolitanism meets a fierce antithesis. The homosexual love that loosens Ishmael is superseded by a heterosexuality that undermines the foundations of cosmopolitan ideals. Racism seems the inevitable consequence of sexuality; it comprises the instinctual mechanisms that deny a fusion of self and other. Not until we meet Pip do we find a way out of the vicious ring that delimits Ishmael's cosmopolitan ideal. For now, there are more immediate ontological and rhetorical problems for Ishmael to resolve.

Knowledge and Voice

As a cosmopolite, Ishmael is no more certain of who he is, or what his narrative function is. After the curtain descends on "Midnight, Forecastle," Ishmael regains narrative control in chapter 41 ("Moby Dick") claiming: "I, Ishmael, was one of that crew" (179). But to which crew does he refer? We naturally assume that, returning on the heels of the dramatic set piece, Ishmael includes himself among "that crew" of rioting sailors. Thus his implied complicity in the brawl suggests a failure of cosmopolitan conscience. But as we read further, it becomes clear that Ishmael refers to "that crew" which, in "The Quarter-Deck" (ch. 36), swears its oath to hunt the white whale. This scene, as fully dramatic as "Midnight, Forecastle," projects a crew united against evil, not divided in evil against itself. The ambiguity over the antecedent of "that crew" in chapter 41 leads us to suspect that Melville initially composed chapter 41 to follow directly after chapter 36 but that he inserted the dramatic set piece (chs. 37–40) in between, causing the identification of Ishmael with the Quarter-Deck crew to become confused with the Forecastle crew. Presumably, Melville simply failed to see that his insertion muddles Ishmael's moral alignments, for the added emphasis on Ishmael's loss of narrative control announces his problem of voice.

Ishmael is still green. Not everyone, he learns, loves Queequeg or Daggoo. At midnight we witness the breaching of a "wolfish" world that is neither narcissistic nor cosmopolitan, but tribally exclusive, sexually violent, and politically chaotic. Ishmael's most immediate problem is establishing an identity out of the conflict of his new ideal and these unanticipated human realities. Father Mapple is only a tentative model for that voice, for his injunction, "Woe to him who seeks to please rather than to appal" (*MD*, 48), contradicts Melville's message in *"Mosses"* that the poet must both please *and* appal. Mapple's noisy histrionics designed to captivate an audience—wise Queequeg leaves in mid-sermon—suggest his failure. Proclaiming a delight that is higher than any woe is deep, he ends humbled by his inadequacy; and Ishmael leaves in silence.[11] Ishmael is more teacher than preacher, but to become both cosmopolite and poet he must rise above conventional learning.

Godly Games: Historicism and Symbol

Ishmael sees through what Mapple has *not* said: that knowing God's truth is impossible, for God is always changing; that the nature of truth is change itself. But rather than appal his audience, Ishmael develops a "careful disorderliness" (*MD*, 361) that changes with the fluidity of truth itself and keeps step with the mental dance of appalling sublimity and the pleasing picturesque. This experiential rhetoric is rooted in the inductive and empirical processes of symbolism. But to reach that stage, Ishmael wages a Cockloftian war against authoritarian structures, in particular those academic barriers to truth known as History, Science, and Philosophy. Melville's comic deflations are interspersed throughout the largely dramatic chapters 24–54: "The Advocate," "Cetology," "The Mast-Head," "Moby Dick," and "The Whiteness of the Whale." The first three touch upon whaling practice; the last two on a particular whale and the cause of our fear of that whale. As a rhetorical unit, the five chapters take us deeper into the monster at the heart of the tall tale.

Although Melville borrowed from Beale, Macy, and Scoresby, the structure of "The Advocate" is his.[12] Ishmael establishes the credibility of the whaling industry by arguing from cosmopolitan principle: "I freely assert, that the cosmopolite philosopher cannot . . . point out one single peaceful influence, which . . . has operated more potentially upon the whole broad world . . . than the high and mighty business of whaling" (*MD*, 109). Like Tommo, Ishmael is "all anxiety to convince," and his anxious tone corrodes our confidence. The presumed cosmopolitan effects of the "high and mighty business of whaling" seem a bit tall. As a "peaceful influence" in international commerce, whaling stands as an alternative to war. Melville prefers the whale ship's slippery decks "to the unspeakable carrion of those battle-fields from which so many soldiers return to drink in all ladies' plaudits" (109).[13] Whaling ships are also the pioneers of the South Pacific. But while they open new markets, they are also the vanguard of imperialism. Drawing upon Obed Macy for this observation,[14] Melville has Ishmael naïvely remark: "If American and European men-of-war now peacefully ride in once savage harbors, let them fire salutes to the honor and the glory of the whale-ship, which originally showed them the way'' (110). Has Ishmael forgotten what Tommo knew: that Polynesian ''peace'' was achieved at the expense of native blood? The only hint that his remark may be ironic is Melville's subsequent overargumentation: Edmund Burke is hailed as the chronicler of whaling; Benjamin Franklin (the cousin by marriage of whaling men) somehow becomes the genealogical source of a line of whaling nobles; the constellation Cetus apotheosizes the entire industry. If the feeble claim for whaling's peacemaking does not cave in on itself, these irrelevancies surely deflate Ishmael's entire project. We suspect a burlesque on Macy's politics, and yet the irony is so fully submerged as to lose its bite. Ishmael is bidding for credentials with the partisans of Manifest Destiny at the expense of his cosmopolitanism.

The same corrosive whimsy is used with the Art History of whales (chs. 54–56) which ends with fatuous praise for whales depicted in folklore and constellations. Similarly, ''The Affidavit'' (ch. 45) uses Natural History to confirm whaling migration patterns, but this disintegrates into the irrelevant assertion that Procopius' legendary sea-monster was a sperm whale. With each application of politics, economy, law, art, and nature, Ishmael retreats from history into legend and myth, invariably puncturing the fragile authority of historical fact. Like Irving in *The History of New York,* he tests the limits of history. But Ishmael's doubts about the reliability of historicism is not a denial of meaning. Rather, it is a redefinition of what a usable fact is and a new means of capturing the essence of Ishmael's past experience. The personal ''fact'' of Ishmael's remark in ''The Advocate'' that ''a whaling ship was my Harvard College and Yale'' legitimizes his academic deflations. For him, institutional learning is a barrier to direct experience. Myth and legend (whether in Cetus or Procopius) do not, however, attempt any retrieval of the past but are an imaginative reenactment of universal impulses that transcend time.[15] Ishmael's corrosive whimsy, despite its confusing politics, is the comic fire that melts historicist presumption into a fluid poetics. It is his first step toward symbolic thinking. But Melville has bigger fish than history to fry. In ''Cetology'' and ''The Mast-Head,'' he deflates both science and philosophy.

For many freshman readers of *Moby-Dick,* ''Cetology'' is the call to abandon ship. It is longer than any preceding chapter; it has no Queequeg, Stubb, or Ahab; it is pedantic in the worst way; it is study hall. In fact, my high school text of *Moby-Dick* obligingly omitted ''Cetology'' altogether. Those who slog through the chapter recall it with masochistic pride, wearing the reading of it like a red badge of courage, another book they had to read. The irony is that ''Cetology'' is a burlesque of all that these readers would want to see burlesqued: latinate scholarship, relentless classifications, tedious books and more books. Perhaps the parody is too close to reality and the jokes too much in need of explanation. Nevertheless, the humor teases us out of the most superficial expectations (that science accounts for all phenomena) and into the organic structure of experience (that science and art are necessarily incomplete).

Actually, Melville's jokes are not so appalling. Ishmael goes to risible lengths to prove that the whale is a fish. Although whales are equipped with a distinctly mammalian sexual apparatus and horizontal flukes, which require an up-and-down propulsion rather than a fish's side-to-side wriggle, Ishmael will not be deceived: The whale is a fish. Granted it is an odd fish: ''a spouting fish with a horizontal tale," a fish with penis and breasts that suckles its "spawn." Some fish. Even pre-Linnaeans would not insist on this madness, but Ishmael has an authority. The whale is a fish because Charly Coffin of Nantucket says so, and thus "this fundamental thing [is] settled" (*MD,* 136). Ishmael classifies whales by their "externals" as though he were too anxious to attempt a fuller anatomy of inner systemic realities.

This reluctance to anatomize frames Ishmael's more familiar second joke: his bibliographic system of classification. Again, Melville stresses surface over structure. He will not determine the *mass* of a whale, which would measure the reality of its substance, but rather its "volume," which unlike mass varies with size and shape.[16] A pun unites whales to bibliography because, of course, they both possess "volumes." And just as Ishmael avoids the invisible and yet more reliable measure of mass for the superficial reckoning of whales by their volume, so, too, does he assume that the best measure of a book is its size and shape (the space it occupies) instead of the weighty substance of its ideas. Ishmael uses a false system to classify falsely defined whales by their most deceptive, volumetric feature. The final twist is that this bibliographical system must be jury-rigged in order to work. Ishmael divides whales into Folios, Octavos, and Duodecimoes because, while these kinds of books (based upon the way a single sheet of paper is folded to create separate pages) represent decreasing sizes, they all retain the same rectangular shape. Quartos, which naturally follow Folios in diminished size, are eliminated from the system, Ishmael explains, because their square *shape* is out of proportion with the other rectangular book sizes. The logic here is that since all whales have the same shape but come in varying sizes, the Quarto classification is out of place. But even a child can see that "by its externals" the square-nosed sperm whale is smaller and radically disproportionate to all other shovel-jawed whales. If ever there was a Quarto whale, it would be the Sperm. Either there is madness in this method or a certain Mozartian playfulness, with unsystematic leaps within the system—"a godly gamesomeness," as Melville puts it toward the end of "Cetology."

On the surface, Ishmael's classification lampoons academic systems. And yet his obsessive chromaticizings go beyond burlesque. The structure is symbolic, not scientific. By denying the whale its mammalian status, he makes that "fish" into an alien "other," but ironically this chop logic only calls attention to just how human-like this "fish" really is, especially in sexual terms. It breeds and nurses like men and women. Furthermore, by illogically prioritizing the Sperm Whale above larger whales,[17] Ishmael necessarily pushes language beyond exposition and into creative symbolism. He implicitly redefines "volume" to mean not merely "space," or even "book," but rather "the capacity to create." Ishmael describes the Sperm Whale through the etymology of its odd name: sperm. The Sperm Whale comes first in the system because the male's "quickening humor" (ancients thought whale oil was semen) initiates creation. (Granted, the female gamete is also in attendance, but this does not fit Melville's phallocentric joking.) As if to legitimize the false prioritizing of the Sperm Whale, Ishmael places the "sportive" Huzza Porpoise (a sperm whale in "miniature" with its "godly gamesomeness") at the end of his system so that the two are the symbolic alpha and omega of creativity and the sires of gamesome thought. The system speaks volumes.

The incompleteness of Ishmael's system is itself a symbol of the necessary incompleteness of creation. Significantly, the comic act of giving priority to symbol over fact, of ignoring orders of classification or bending animal description to fit preexistent forms, is the very cause of incompleteness in Melville's jury-rigged cetology. Incompletion is not simply a consequence of symbol-making; it is inherent in the process. Ishmael begins his chapter with the assumption that "any human thing supposed to be complete, must for that very reason infallibly be faulty," and he ends by comparing his system to the Cologne Cathedral. Both "erections" (the pun here unavoidably recalls the sperm whale's "quickening humor" and the Huzza Porpoise's sportiveness), like all "grand ones, true ones, ever leave the copestone to posterity" (*MD*, 145). Ishmael protests that he lacks the "Time, Strength, Cash, and Patience" to finish his cetology. In fact, as with any symbolic structure, he has no control over the completion of a symbol. The finishing touch (the meaning) is left to readers (posterity), who by reading supply interpretations and thereby regenerate the creative process on their own. The brilliance of the too-often ignored chapter called "Cetology" is its demonstration of the comic foundations of symbol.

With "The Mast-Head" (ch. 35) Ishmael turns from science to the perils of philosophical meditation. The humor remains jaunty—Ishmael flatly warns businessmen to steer clear of absent-minded mystics such as he—but it increases in seriousness when, perched upon the masthead, he imagines himself so entirely at one with the universe that he "loses his identity." Here, marginal Ishmael caught "by the blending cadences of waves with thoughts" becomes "enchanted" by this mystic sensibility but imagines, too, how a little slip will send him to the deck below—"and your identity comes back in horror" (159). His warning to all "Pantheists" dramatizes the precariousness of repose, in which self-awareness vies with transcendence. Unlike White Jacket, whose fall from the mast engenders the birth of an artist, Ishmael's imagined fall depicts the trap of metaphysics wherein the Self is as much deadened by the prospect of Nothingness as it is enlivened by the momentary glimpse of full Being. The philosopher's identity is death, and the only voicing of this knowledge is the "half-throttled shriek" as one falls. There is no artful transformation of experience here; thus philosophy without art, like idea without action, is useless.

Ahab's frustrations in "The Sphynx" (ch. 70) demonstrate the art-less philosopher's dilemma. The sea is calm. For Ishmael this repose is "an intense copper calm" which he transforms into a "yellow lotus" that "unfold[s] its noiseless measureless leaves upon the sea" (311). Ahab, however, cannot poeticize: This is "a deadly calm," a repose out of which no symbol can emerge. The sphynxlike whale head has seen sorrow (drownings, piracy, murder), but it will not speak "one syllable." Ahab reckons that a meaning lurks here, for all physical objects have their "cunning duplicate in mind," but man remains as mute as nature. For Ahab, the "linked analogies" of mind and nature are "far beyond all utterance" (312). Ahab cannot voice the silence in "a still rich utterance of a deep intellect in repose." Nor can he conclude that one must rise above self-consuming philosophy. With two whale heads suspended one on either side—one is Locke, the other, Kant— the *Pequod* is a programmatic balance of experience and ideality, but sitting low in the water, it cannot move. A better balance is achieved by throwing both "thunderheads'' overboard; ''then you will float light and right'' (327). Thus Ishmael seeks a marginal relation to philosophy; he knows its direst potential but will contain it within the ''copper calms'' of his art. He must free himself from philosophy as he does from history and science.

While Ishmael's academic deflations obliterate the barriers that prevent our most direct experience of the whale, they leave no alternative system of knowledge; history defers to myth and legend; science is mere surface; philosophy, death. It is time for a renaissance, and on the heels of the intellectual chaos of ''Midnight, Forecastle,'' the chapter called ''Moby Dick'' signals that rebirth. Here it is again that Ishmael wills himself back into his narrative. ''I, Ishmael, was one of that crew'' (179). As noted, the problematic line suggests a confused identity, but in the context of the previous comic deflations, it is a confusion Ishmael resolves in the full expression of the symbolic process found in the following chapter, ''The Whiteness of the Whale.'' Characteristically, Ishmael stumbles upon his creativity; it is the final serious act in the comic essaying of his being.

In ''Moby Dick'' there are no bombastic legalese, punning leaps, or false analogies, but rather the empiricist's insistence upon seeking out the cause of an effect. Ishmael reclaims the historicist's reliability not by discounting ''wild rumors'' associated with the malign ubiquity of the Sperm Whale but by piercing to the foundations of fear in the whaleman's contact with the sea. And by penetrating Ahab's vengeance, Ishmael unites both science and philosophy into a discipline of psychology. With this new philosophy of mind, he can investigate the mechanisms whereby idea becomes incarnate through Ahab's ''transference'' of all hate onto Moby Dick's white hump. He can measure the ballistics of Ahab's ''hot heart's shell'' as it explodes upon that hump, and he can descend into the basement of his heart—like a tourist winding down to the ancient ruins beneath the Hôtel de Cluny— to find Ahab's sane dissembling of his mad motives (185–86).

Despite this rebirth of intellectual vigor, Ishmael does not solve his initial riddle. He has determined what Moby Dick means to Ahab, but what it is to the crew, ''all this to explain, would be to dive deeper than Ishmael can go'' (187). He might in ''some dim, unsuspected way'' attempt an account, but the mental exhaustion of so much deflation and regeneration has left him bewildered and mute. But for every despondency over the impenetrability of the whale, there is invariably a subsequent affirmation that the whale *can* be known. This Ishmaelian two-step recurs throughout the book. In ''The Prairie'' (ch. 79), the whale's brow simply cannot be ''read'' (347). But in ''The Nut'' (ch. 80), Ishmael takes the whale's spine as a line of vertebrae, each a miniaturized skull and brain, or nut to crack, the combined force of which shapes the whale's hump, ''the organ of firmness or indomitableness in the Sperm whale.'' Thus a meaning emerges: The ''great monster is indomitable'' (350). Whereas the vain physiognomy of ''The Prairie'' leads to doubt, the penetrating symbolism of ''The Nut'' bears fruit. Similarly, ''The Whiteness of the Whale'' is the upbeat of an Ishmaelian two-step that begins with the exhaustion of ''Moby Dick.'' Here, Ishmael's resolve returns; he will ''dive deeper,'' for ''explain myself I must.'' Before, he imagined ''in some dim, unsuspected way'' (187) that Moby Dick might seem a demon; now, he shall re-essay the fear of the white whale ''in some dim, random way'' (188). The self-quotation signals an indomitable will to break his writer's block. But the research into whiteness is neither dim nor random. Ishmael builds a hypothesis out of facts and pushes to "the hidden cause" (192) of fear. Rejecting folk myths that link whiteness to death, he inverts his earlier progression into myth and legend. He becomes a scientist, not the Linnaean classifier of "Cetology," but a Montaignean empiricist. And as such he is a symbolist voicing the invisible lines of causation that impinge upon an effect. Finally, science is tied to poetry and rhetoric, for theories, like symbols, are words designed to explain and convince.

Toward the end of chapter 42, Ishmael reaches a critical impasse with his reader that clarifies the point:

> But thou sayest, methinks this white-lead chapter about whiteness is but a white flag hung out from a craven soul; thou surrenderest to a hypo, Ishmael.
>
> Tell me, why this strong young colt, foaled in some peaceful valley of Vermont, far removed from all beasts of prey—why is it that upon the sunniest day, if you but shake a fresh buffalo robe behind him, so that he cannot even see it, but only smells its wild animal muskiness—why will he start, snort, and with bursting eyes paw the ground in phrensies of affright? There is no remembrance in him of any gorings of wild creatures in his green northern home, so that the strange muskiness he smells cannot recall to him anything associated with the experience of former perils; for what knows he, this New England colt, of the black bisons of distant Oregon? (194)

To convince the reader that these details are not "hypos" but an *objective* encounter with fear, Ishmael creates a symbol out of the common experience of the colt's fear of the robe. Thus a poetic act extends scientific pursuit. Ishmael concludes that the root of fear is not whiteness but "the instinct of the knowledge of the demonism in the world" (194) that it represents. But these words, like any theory, lack substance unless they are tied to concrete incarnations defining a circle of causality.

> Thus, then, the muffled rollings of a milky sea; the bleak rustlings of the festooned frosts of mountains; the desolate shiftings of the windrowed snows of prairies; all these, to Ishmael, are as the shaking of that buffalo robe to the frightened colt! (194)

Ishmael's creative awakening in "The Whiteness of the Whale" is not so much the discovery of the instinctual knowledge of demonism as a new means of talking about it. Like Jim Doggett, who turns from rhetorical con man to poet in the face of his unhuntable bear, Ishmael turns from burlesquer to symbolist as he abstracts meaning from experience.

But the chapter is not over. Ishmael anatomizes the process of symbolism itself. He has pushed beyond the colt to demonism, but that symbol is only a word, and beyond the word is an unexpected zero that negates the symbolism itself. Whiteness is "the visible absence of color" and "the colorless, all-color of atheism"; it is the harlot Nature's "mystical cosmetic" covering nothing (195). By essaying his symbol to its farthest reaches, Ishmael goes beyond fear and demonism to a leprous nihility behind "all visible objects," and here the circular chain of linked analogies breaks; the symbol implodes into a black-hole singularity whose meaninglessness is unvoiceable. Ishmael's discovery of a voice through symbolism is both an answer and a further problem. His art is the means and material by which he may contain the sublime; it is, however, a rhetoric as fragile and empty as a bubble. Once again, Ishmael verges on the entry of a "Trap."[18]

Finding Voice: Ishmael's Genial Desperation

Ishmael cannot "prove" the existence of an objective reality. Instead, he does what any artist would do; he finds a rhetoric that will allow him to withstand the alternations of faith and doubt that his investigations of reality perpetually induce. For Ishmael, that rhetoric is a voice of genial desperation. The philosopher becomes the artist. For philosophical critics, this artist's resolution of metaphysical dilemmas is doomed to a failure that only accentuates the impossibility of voicing the voiceless. But Melville presumes a certain degree of failure in any enterprise and settles instead for the rhythmic pulses of aesthetic failure *and* success. Ishmael's voice of genial desperation is necessarily picturesque, full of doubt and yet also of repose. It comes after his "First Lowering" (ch. 48). A squall separates Ishmael from the *Pequod*. In the aftermath, Queequeg (like "hope in the midst of despair") holds up an "imbecile candle" as signal, but to no avail (*MD*, 225). At dawn, having given the boat's crew up for lost, the *Pequod* crashes out of the mist, nearly killing the abandoned sailors. It is an episode of humor, irony, and repose.

Stubb, "one of those odd sort of humorists, whose jollity is sometimes . . . curiously ambiguous," opens the scene. He makes a "religion of rowing" (like Hawthorne's "religion of mirth"), and his ministry is "so strangely compounded of fun and fury . . . that no oarsman could hear such invocations without pulling for dear life, and yet pulling for the mere joke of the thing" (219). "Take it easy . . . and burst all your liver and lungs!" (223) saith this preacher in a tone that is both a fulfillment and parody of Melville's aesthetics of repose. Stubb's manner inoculates Ishmael. In the subsequent chapter, "The Hyena," Ishmael considers the absurdity of his near-disastrous rescue as evidence that "this whole universe [is] a vast practical joke," and death seems "only sly, good-natured hits, and jolly punches in the side bestowed by the unseen and unaccountable old joker." Ishmael's "odd sort of wayward mood," like "odd" Stubb's easy fury, grows into a "free and easy sort of genial, desperado philosophy" (226). It is a "cool, collected dive at death" (228), a comic control of horror. Ishmael's "genial desperation" arrives on the heels of "The Whiteness of the Whale" and just before the resolvent meditations of the cetological chapters. This crucial placement emphasizes a resurrection of Ishmael's humor. Green Ishmael acquires a sudden ripeness after his first lowering; he is ready to play along with death.

Ishmael demonstrates his self-containment through a picturesque symbology of circles.[19] His ethical response to the vacuity found in "The Whiteness of the Whale" is to skirt around the sublime; he will encircle it and bring it to repose. Although we find plenty of literal circles in this symbology, Ishmael also engages in various circularizing processes, such as the continuous rounds of frustration, acceptance, and calm in his cetological chapters; a circular sequencing of ease leading to fury, and fury to ease. These alternations are manifested in one scene in which little white Flask perches on black Daggoo, who is "giddily" balanced "with a cool, indifferent, easy, unthought of, barbaric majesty" (221) on the loggerhead of a wobbling boat. Here, the whiteness of the whaler Flask, by itself, is ineffectual, but in conjunction with Daggoo's darker substantiality, the two are a suitably precarious symbol of cosmopolitan value. As a racially abused but noble "bearer," reminiscent of Tommo's Kory-Kory and Little Henry's Boosy, Daggoo dominates in this picturesque interdependency, suggesting a momentary triumph over the alienating sea. It is as though the awe-ful symbol of whiteness has been stoppered up in a little flask and kept aloft in Daggoo's hands.

The circularized interdependency of Flask and Daggoo reappears in "The Line" (ch. 60). A chapter on lines is an unlikely source for Melville's circularities. But a ship's lines are pliable, and in Ishmael's hands infinitely so. "There is," he tells us, "an aesthetics in all things." In a whale boat, the harpooner's line is coiled in a tub and laced fore and aft between the rowers so that when a whale is struck, the line whizzes like "ringed lightning" out of the tub and around the rowers. Designed to acquaint readers with the probability of Ahab's demise, the line grows beyond its plot function into a circularizing symbol of terror and repose: The "graceful repose of the line, as it silently serpentines about the oarsmen before being brought into actual play . . . is a thing which carries . . . true terror" (281). The line unites potential and kinetic energies: stillness and action. But its aesthetic relevance lies in its ethical effect upon the crew. Ahab has no pliancy and would straighten all lines: His ambition is grooved to iron rails; he is scarred with a straight line from head to toe; he charts the globe with migration lines; he is killed by a line of rope. Ahab runs afoul of the whaleboat's line, and soon enough he is hanged by what he cannot bend. But the oarsmen survive through Ishmael's pliant aesthetic. Like Flask and Daggoo, who maintain "a certain self-adjusting buoyancy and simultaneousness of volition and action" (280–81), they acquire a "self-adjusting" poise between the calm center of repose and the disastrous circumference of universal chaos. They epitomize Ishmael's genial desperation.

Ishmael finds aesthetic comfort in circles even to the degree that he shapes certain sequences of chapters so that they have a resolvent circularity in their argument leading readers into the problems of politics, sex, and philosophical awareness and then back out again. Readers, too, must adopt a "self-adjusting buoyancy" to keep up with the flip-flopping. We learn from our circularizing reading experience how to balance center and circumference in a tense repose that is characteristic of Ishmael's marginal picturesque vision. A sequence of five circularizing chapters (85–89) shows the process.

"*Inland There I*": *Ishmael's Picturesque*

"The Fountain" (ch. 85) may be Ishmael's most picturesque meditation. Like "The Whiteness of the Whale," it seeks whether the cause of the whale's spout is water or vapor. Ishmael will not ride the whale and risk his life to make the necessary investigations, but scientific method saves him; he will "hypothesize": The spout is mist. The Cockloftian logic he enlists to support his claim is that since the whale dives deeply, it must be profound, and since the heads of profound thinkers always emit a "semi-visible steam," the deep diving whale's emission must be vapor. Moving from pun to poetics, Ishmael envisions the "conceit" of a whale whose spout is "glorified by a rainbow." And moving next from poetry to scientific fact, he concludes that since rainbows only appear in mist, not water, the whale's spout can only be vapor. Pun, poem, proof: The fact is settled. But Ishmael essays the allegorical meaning of his new knowledge. The vapor is doubt; the rainbow, heaven's intuitive hope. From allegory, he ranges into symbolism and ethics: "Doubts of all things earthly, and intuitions of some things heavenly; this combination makes neither believer nor infidel, but makes a man who regards them both with equal eye" (374). Ishmael's symbol recalls the fusion of rainbow and thunder in "The Enviable Isles." As with that poem, anxiety and faith are placed at a distance so that the artist's position "on the marge" (and with "equal eye") reinforces his picturesque perspective.

But the whale's other end, "The Tail" (ch. 86), possesses such terrifying power that Ishmael's confident voice in "The Fountain" is gagged. "The more I consider this mighty tail, the more do I deplore my inability to express it." Once again perched in the mast-head (its linear verticality forbids circularizing), he alternates between seeing hell and heaven in the tail, and finally lapses into fruitless relativism: "it is all in what mood you are in; if in the Dantean, the devils will occur to you; if in that of Isaiah, the archangels" (378). Ishmael's symbolizing fails; the tail yields no knowledge, only the self-reflexive subjectivity of mind. The peace, silence, and understanding of an "equal eye" are alien gestures that whales share with whales, but never with humanity. "Dissect him how I may," Ishmael concludes, "I know him not, and never will" (379). In the space of a chapter and the flip of a tail, Ishmael's two-step is upon us again. Picturesque fusion disintegrates into epistemological despair.

But Ishmael insists upon a sensual resolution. In "The Grand Armada" (ch. 87), perhaps the most dramatic visualization of Melville's circle imagery, Ishmael witnesses in a circling pod of whales the primal functions of creation and human savagery. Within the "circumference of commotion" and at the "innermost heart of the shoal," Ishmael finds "an enchanted calm" populated by a "crowd of reposing whales" (387). Queequeg is first to spot the birthing of a calf and its upwardly spiraling umbilical cord as it tangles in the murderous lines of the waiting fishermen. Ishmael is alive to the scene: "Some of the subtlest secrets of the seas seemed divulged to us in this enchanted pond. We saw young Leviathan amours in the deep" (388). The shush of sibilants hushes the image of lovemaking and birth, and excites Ishmael to an inner meaning: "[A]mid the tornadoed Atlantic of my being, do I myself still for ever centrally disport in mute calm; and while ponderous planets of unwaning woe revolve round me, deep down and deep inland there I still bathe me in eternal mildness of joy." But a frantic whale flailing several detached harpoons creates a circular saw in the pool, "wounding and murdering his own comrades," frightening away the "submarine bridal-chambers and nurseries," and panicking the whales at "the margin" of the once "serene lake." "The long calm" is over (389); the whaling begins.

The catastrophe argues that repose is mere illusion, and the "inland" calm just a dream. But Ishmael's symbolism does not deconstruct as in "The Whiteness of the Whale"; it is destroyed by an external mechanism, one that converts living tissue into cash. Melville's political message in "Grand Armada" is clear. The machine in Ishmael's garden exposes the horror of industrialism and imperial democracy.[20] But Melville's title subverts this reading. As a Grand Armada, the large lumbering whales recall the oversized Spanish galleons of Philip II on their fatal mission to invade England and reimpose feudal Catholicism upon a new, bright, and energetic people, or so the myth of British national virtue would have it. By this logic, the whalemen, who sail easily among the galleon whales, are associated with the heroic British. Thus our sympathy for unjustly butchered whales is seriously compromised by the unavoidable associations of those whales with the "justly" defeated Spanish. Melville's title flatly contradicts the chapter's dramatic content, and this irony hampers any confident political reading of the chapter as an attack either on the whaling industry in particular or on capitalism in general. While Melville was surely inclined to sanction the general attack, he could not, after repeated ennoblings of whaling life, sanction the particular. He cannot reconcile the primal serenity of the whales with the industrial butchery of the whalers; his "equal eye" squints. Melville relies on sexual joking to work himself out of this bind. Rather than try to deny the whaleman's obvious complicity in a vicious and imperial capitalism, he focuses on the pod of whales to assess its social structures. He distracts readers away from industrial horrors by subsuming elements of human aggression into cetacean sexuality. By this route a disturbing political contradiction is transformed into the complexities of love. Successive chapters show the way.

In "Schools and Schoolmates" (ch. 88), Ishmael discovers different kinds of pods. There is the harem with its single bull, a kind of mutual assistance arrangement; there are pods of aging bulls, penitent of former amours; and there are the pods of young males, "rollicking" collegians committed "forever" to one another until they find separate harems and then never associate again (393). Male bonding is only a prelude to betrayal. If a female is struck by a whaler, her companions run to assist, but if a male is struck, all "friends" depart. Self-indulgent, rapacious, and unprincipled, the male whale mirrors the piratical, capitalistic whalers (cf. Paul Jones in *Israel Potter*). Rather than continue with the bloodiness of whaling, then, Melville relocates its violence into the sexual practices of whales. The symbolic transference of the butchery of capitalism from a human realm into the thinly veiled discussion of male whales creates a comic allegory that allows us to assume we are speaking only of whales, not men. But in the next chapter Melville's two-step kicks in, for we are never far from political reality.

In "Fast Fish and Loose Fish" (ch. 89), matters of attachment and betrayal among whales are reduced to the legalistic formulae of possession among humans. A whale is a fast-fish when attached by line to a whale boat or symbol of ownership, the waif-pole. A whale is a loose-fish when the tie is severed. This commodification of whales carries with it an immediate sexual connection, for Melville uses a case of adultery and divorce to illustrate his legal point. Inevitably, the chapter reforms sexual possession back into political aggression. A husband divorces his adulterous wife, but when she remarries, he wants her back. According to law, she is now someone else's "fast-fish" (the "subsequent gentleman's property"), and the former husband cannot "re-harpoon" her (397). The reduction of affection to a "gentleman's property" is designedly vicious, and Melville pushes the point of possession back to an unpinning of American capitalism and imperialism. Possession is not half the law, Ishmael maintains; it is "the whole of the Law." What ensues recalls the careful rhetoric of Tommo's rant in *Typee* against money:

> What are the sinews and souls of Russian serfs and Republican slaves but Fast-Fish, whereof possession is the whole of the law? What to the rapacious landlord is the widow's last mite but a Fast-Fish? What is yonder undetected villain's marble mansion with a door-plate for a waif; what is that but a Fast-Fish? What is the ruinous discount which Mordecai, the broker, gets from Woebegone, the bankrupt, on a loan to keep Woebegone's family from starvation; what is that ruinous discount but a Fast-Fish? What is the Archbishop of Savesoul's income . . . seized from the scant bread and cheese of hundreds of thousands of broken-backed laborers (all sure of heaven without any of Savesoul's help) what is that globular 100,000 but a Fast-Fish? What are the Duke of Dunder's hereditary towns and hamlets but Fast-Fish? What to that redoubted harpooneer, John Bull, is poor Ireland, but a Fast-Fish? What to that apostolic lancer, Brother Jonathan, is Texas but a Fast-Fish? And concerning all these, is not Possession the whole of the law? (397–98)

The text moves quickly from the veiled allusion to Southern slavery to a series of "alien" tyrannies (tithes, peerage, Ireland). Once the reader is lulled into the presumption that injustice is largely European, Ishmael unloads his snapper: America's unjust claim on Texas. Possession becomes a dirty antonym of freedom: "What are the Rights of Man and the Liberties of the World but Loose-Fish?" (398). Finally, Melville manages to have his fish and eat them, too.

Ishmael proposes a circular interdependency of possession and freedom in sexuality, politics, and art that draws us back to the problematic chapter that initiated this comic sequence of transferences.[21] When he notes that America in 1492 was a loose-fish until Columbus made it fast for Spain, we reflect, in Melville's new idiom, that "The Grand Armada" now symbolizes Spain's attempt to make England its fast-fish. But now the specter of Spanish conquest recoils onto American politics, for in the course of centuries Mexico's Northern reaches (once held by Spain, then Mexico, and now the United States) "will" become loose again. In prophesying a redress for the sins of the Mexican War, Melville also atones for the commodified wife at the opening of chapter 89. The politics of gender implied in the harems and bachelor pods of chapter 88 not only hark back to the earlier aggressions of industrial whaling but now promote a more individualized application. The woman as Fast-Fish is like Mexico waiting to be free.

Ishmael pushes further. He includes himself as well as the reader in the circle of associations. The "thoughts of thinkers" are Loose-Fish, free and unwaifable, which the "smuggling verbalist" tries vainly to make fast with words. The process of writing (the converting of ideas into object words) is an attempt to gain possession of thought, idea, and the ideal; but it is a problematic form of empowerment, for it necessarily enslaves thought at the moment of expression. Tying idea to word destroys the looseness of thought and hence the thought itself, even though that thought cannot be glimpsed without waif-pole words. Melville's whaling terms amplify the dilemma of voicing the voiceless. Writers harpoon readers with words.

Moreover, our reading is both our acquisition of and enslavement by the writer's words; we are taken over when we take up someone else's writing. Thus "you, reader" are "but a Loose-Fish and a Fast-Fish, too" (398). In giving Melville's famous conclusion a rhetorical twist, we recognize how a "line" can draw us back, through images of bonding and bondage, sexuality and politics, generation and destruction, to the beginning of the sequence of chapters under discussion, back to "The Fountain" (ch. 85), so that ultimately the problems of possession and freedom, and of knowledge and voice, are, like the interpenetrating images of rainbow and dark mist, part and parcel of the interdependency of faith and doubt.

In a sense Melville has not only articulated his notion of living with "equal eye," he has induced readers to participate in the necessary circularity of that vision, thus enacting on their own the ultimate aesthetic interdependency of creative writer and creative reader. Chapters 87–89 are palpable evidence that the whale can be "known," or at least encircled. For the ideas of freedom and possession connect cetological sexuality and social behavior to human politics and our sense of gendered being. Melville's circle-making rhetoric challenges us to make the link. What might have been a too-sentimental melodrama in "The Grand Armada," clumsily propagandizing against Capitalism, becomes in the subsequent chapters a more effective seduction of readers into an awareness of imperialism as it seeps into the bedroom, the act of reading, and thought itself. Once we concede that readers are loose-fish continually in jeopardy of becoming fast, we can all the more deeply feel the anxiety of freedom and the perils of restraint in politics as well as sexuality and art. If we take whales; if we take Texas then Mexico; if we take wives and slaves; if we take words for ideas; how shall we avoid being taken ourselves?

By humanizing whales and linking their behaviors to the fabric of civilized life— our history, laws, science, and philosophy—Melville creates a new culture beyond that which he has spoofed, and a new sympathy between reader and brute. We are the monster whales; they are we. And what befalls them shall inevitably befall us. In the end, Ishmael's admission that he cannot know the whale is only a temporary ploy, encouraging readers to catch with equal eye the very knowledge he coyly pretends he cannot grasp.

Pondering Repose

Ishmael finds voice through lyric meditation. Its tone is genial despair; its structure, the circle; its vocabulary, picturesque. Ishmael's ethics operate in a morally dynamic arena "on the marge" between faith and doubt; his aesthetics (equally marginal, equally picturesque) is one of tense repose. Despite its whims and reversals, indeed because of them, Ishmael's voice is, in the Irvingesque manner, reliable and sincere. But it is in the nature of his essaying that, once found, his voice will be lost, then lost and found perpetually. It is an enactment of the voicelessness of the universe. Ishmael's circular rhetorics demand as much tension as repose. Indeed, the two define each other. "Nothing exists in itself" (*MD*, 53), Ishmael tells us: Warm defines cold; the savage, our civility; the "other," our selves. There is no idea without an expression of it; no language without the threat of silence; no geniality without despair. We are "like the one warm spark in the heart of an arctic crystal" (54). Ishmael's heroism lies not only in enduring the alternations of these moods, instincts, and states of being, but also in his boundless comic energy in voicing them. Ahab's heroism lies in his tragic awareness that he can have none of this. He is broken on a wheel that Ishmael loves to spin.

The most forceful articulation of Ishmael's ethical if not dramatic dominance is in "The Gilder" (ch. 114). Just as such chapters as "The Blanket" may be said to "replay" an earlier episode ("The Counterpane"),[22] "The Gilder" replays in title and structure " The Doubloon" (ch. 99). But this is not the standard interpretation. In their annotations, Mansfield and Vincent take "the gilder" as a person who gilds or covers lesser metals with gold foil. They argue that such "gilding" links Ishmael's revery in chapter 114 concerning nature's ability to hide its "tiger heart" back to Ishmael's conclusion some seventy chapters earlier in "The Whiteness of the Whale" that nature "paints like the harlot."[23] But Ishmael is not gilding in "The Gilder." He is offering us a moment of mystic transcendence as if it were a golden coin of wisdom or a Dutch "gilder" hidden away in a coffer. Like a doubloon. The golden scenes of natural tranquility depicted at the beginning of "The Gilder" are not images falsely painted by nature; they are true gold fruitlessly enticing Ahab toward an optimistic vision: "But if these secret golden keys did seem to open in him his own secret golden treasuries, yet did his breath upon them prove but tarnishing" (492). Ahab is something of an inverted alchemist whose ironic "secret" is in turning gold into base metals.[24]

What clinches the notion that "The Gilder" is a coin and not deceptive gilding is that the chapter's structure recapitulates the structure of the novel's only other "coin" chapter, "The Doubloon." Here, Ahab uses a gold coin both rhetorically to inflame his crew and symbolically to reveal the limits of his solipsism. As each character soliloquizes successively upon the coin's design—peaks, flame, and tower, and cock, valley, and stars—we glimpse the fatality of subjectivism. "The Doubloon" suggests the inevitability and danger of symbolic thinking. "The Gilder" is similarly structured but with fewer speakers and a different effect. But before analyzing the chapter's relevance to Ahab and Ishmael, we must consider a pair of quotation marks.

Up until the 1988 Northwestern-Newberry critical edition of *Moby-Dick,* readers have assumed that the major speech in chapter 114—it includes a cycle of life imagery ending with "manhood's pondering repose of If"—belongs to Ishmael. Although the paragraph introducing it prepares us for a speech from Ahab, and subsequent speeches by Starbuck and Stubb have similar preparatory introductions, the "Repose of If" speech lacks the appropriate set of quotation marks around it to earmark it as Ahab's. Editors Hayford and Parker had suspected two decades earlier that this was a typographical omission, for neither the first American nor the English editions have a set of quotation marks around the speech. Thus there is no substantive variant in the textual history of *Moby-Dick* to warrant an emendation. The only argument for adding the punctuation, which effectively reassigns the speech to Ahab, is based on narrative context. Thus Hayford and Parker refrained in their 1967 Norton critical edition of *Moby-Dick* from making the admittedly speculative change. But their 1988 edition does make the change so that Ahab now speaks what generations of critics have taken to be Ishmael's lines.

Textually, the change is daring; contextually it is necessary. Without the quotation marks, Ahab is excluded from a chapter that promises his "tarnishing" breath. Moreover, the subsequent speeches from Starbuck and Stubb—they, "too," speak up; the adverb implies a previous speech from Ahab—seem carefully ranked below their captain. But again, without the quotation marks, there is no captain speaking, only Ishmael. With them, Ahab resumes his place in an order prefigured in "Knights and Squires" and the three soliloquies (chs. 36–38) prelusive to "Midnight, Forecastle." And we immediately see a parallel to "The Doubloon," in which a meditation by Ishmael is followed by a series from Ahab, Starbuck, Stubb and five others. Granted, this replayed lineup is truncated in "The Gilder": Only Ahab, Starbuck, and Stubb speak; Flask, the manxman, Queequeg, Fedallah, and Pip, who follow these three in "The Doubloon," are excluded in "The Gilder." But this truncation only serves to sharpen the focus on the major characters' positions—doubt, faith, and comic indifference—as the novel reaches its climax.

With "The Gilder" as a replay of "The Doubloon" and with "The Repose of If" speech assigned now to Ahab, we see a loosening of Ahab's egoism. In effect, Ahab begins to sound more like Ishmael. Of course, for some this is the obvious consequence of putting Ishmael's words in Ahab's mouth. But the textual reassignment makes the narrative richer, reminding us that Ishmael is the voice that frames all his characters, that Ahab is a projection of Ishmael, and that his use of an Ishmaelian vocabulary indicates a temporary fusion of sensibilities (a Dantean mind glimpsing Isaiah). Moreover, the melding is precisely the artistic engagement Ishmael has been talking about in his own properly assigned meditation that introduces Ahab.

Ishmael begins. He experiences the sea as though it were the "filial, confident" land, but he is also conscious that the sea's "velvet paw . . . conceals a remorseless fang." This Mast-Head revery achieves a momentary artistic transcendence in which "fact and fancy, half-way meeting, interpenetrate, and form one seamless whole" (*MD*, 492). This "mystic mood" is the artful fusion Ahab fails to reenact, for the Ishmaelean language in Ahab's mouth cannot sustain a full voicing of faith *and* doubt. He insists upon doubt alone. Ishmael uses Ahab to purge himself of his own dalliance with nihilism, a corrosive doubt that would otherwise disintegrate his carefully balanced repose. If Ahab speaks Ishmael's lingo, it is only for a moment, and Ahab's failed plagiary only anticipates his demise.

Ahab's Ishmaelian speech is as follows:

> Oh, grassy glades! oh, ever vernal endless landscapes in the soul; in ye,—though long parched by the dead drought of the earthy life,—in ye, men yet may roll, like young horses in new morning clover; and for some few fleeting moments, feel the cool dew of the life immortal on them. Would to God these blessed calms would last. But the mingled, mingling threads of life are woven by warp and woof: calms crossed by storms, a storm for every calm. There is no steady unretracing progress in this life; we do not advance through fixed gradations, and at the last one pause:—through infancy's unconscious spell, boyhood's thoughtless faith, adolescence' doubt (the common doom), then scepticism, then disbelief, resting

at last in manhood's pondering repose of If. But once gone through, we trace the round again; and are infants, boys, and men, and Ifs eternally. Where lies the final harbor, whence we unmoor no more? In what rapt ether sails the world, of which the weariest will never weary? Where is the foundling's father hidden? Our souls are like those orphans whose unwedded mothers die in bearing them: the secret of our paternity lies in their grave, and we must there to learn it.   (492)

The circularity of human consciousness is Ishmael's salvation but Ahab's hell. Ahab can desire the eternal mildness of life; he accepts that "calms [will be] crossed by storms"; and he even recognizes the "mingled, mingling" of sensibilities that contribute to "manhood's pondering repose of If." What Ahab cannot endure is the cyclicity of mentalities in which this moment of maturity is not as a culmination, but only one of several recurring phases of perpetual development.

Ahab has stolen these phases from Shakespeare's Jaques, the sullen comic of *As You Like It*. Earlier in "The Doubloon," Stubb has also fashioned a twelve-stage cycle based on the Zodiac. In a sense, Ahab's speech is a double replay, first of Jaques then of Stubb, but it is not so mordant. Jaques ends his seven stages with "mere oblivion"; Stubb his twelve with a sailor's drowning "sleep." But Ahab's "final harbor" is an unfound place where the foundling shall find a father. Ahab is a pathological denier of ontological nothingness. Whereas Ishmael confronts and contains the idea of there being "naught beyond," Ahab presumes a *something* beyond at which he may shake his fist. For all his rage, Ahab remains a believer, desiring contact with a sovereign father. He is Isaac and Jacob, playing Faust but searching for the bosom of Abraham. Thus he imagines death sentimentally, not as oblivion or sleep but as a safe haven.

Melville turns Jaques's linear stages of consciousness into a circle and strikes at the heart of Ahab's frustration. The first six stages—unconsciousness, thoughtless faith, doubt, skepticism, disbelief, and pondering repose—are not a straight line but "gradations," which when completed we are forced "to trace the round again." That is, we relive our earliest phases of development so that our consciousness is a constant replay of selves. Jaques and Stubb suppose the kind of "steady unretracing progress" from beginning to middle to end (birth, maturity, death) that Ahab's linear mind would like to see, and when Ahab projects beyond the six-phase cycle to a seventh (his harbor), he demands an end to the turning. He envisions the stable land placing boundaries around an oscillating sea. Ahab's speech is the authoritarian's willful denial of the perpetual Ishmaelian alternation of moods; it is a line's envy for a circle. Ahab wants to put a Godlike frost on mutability. If he could freeze the cycle at its ripest stage in a permanent "repose of If," he would be satisfied, but the paradox is that this moment of tense repose is necessarily unstable— its ripeness is only the prelude to rot—and that awareness can be known only through the continual experience of *retraced* gradations: thoughtless faith and doubt. Ahab does not fear oblivion but rather this endless reliving of successive mentalities, the exhaustive questioning or "if-ing" in relation to Being.

Ishmael's lyric expansions have reached their full measure: He has become Ahab, and in letting Ahab speak in the manner of Ishmael we glimpse the chasm that separates the linear philosopher from the circularizing artist. But Melville is not done. In the last two sections of his novel he moves beyond Ishmael's personality to the voiceless drama of Ahab (chs. 106–32) and farther on the narratorless conclusion of pure action (chs. 133–35). The character who has philosophized and poeticized, who has doubted and discovered, is virtually dead in these final sections. By transforming lyrical meditation into drama, Ishmael plays all parts; he becomes all "others." Ironically, this loss of personality (Melville's aesthetic goal) entails a necessary surrender of dramatic centrality to Ahab, a submission of transcendent vision to the experience of a single human being, a turning from comedy to tragedy. Only the short but significant "Epilogue" admits a final comic containment. But Melville's treatment of Ahab is dramatically problematic. The captain seems a self-parody in the later chapters, a con man who cons himself and a misanthropist who willfully resists the persistent hand of Pip, the mad clown of genial cosmopolitanism.

11

Ahab: Personifying the Impersonal

In "The Candles" (ch. 119) when Ahab bellows out his mastery over the "speechless, placeless power" of the corposants (St. Elmo's Fire), he dramatizes the absurdity of his being: "In the midst of the personified impersonal, a personality stands here" (*MD*, 507). Ahab's speech comes at a chiastic moment when Ishmael's and Ahab's rhetorical paths cross: Loquacious Ishmael has silenced himself into an objective reporter, reducing his contribution to parenthetical stage directions, while Ahab noisily struts and frets the boards. The crossing of these personalities marks the spot that allegorizes Melville's problem in voicing the voiceless. Here, Ahab's defiance of the "speechless" and Ishmael's silence "meet and mate." Melville's misuse of personification accentuates the issue. By having Ahab address the corposants as "you," he imputes a consciousness to the electricity, and a meaning. They are the embodiment of an impersonal universe. But the corposants are balls of static, things not persons, although Ahab insists they are personifications. Ahab has it wrong. What is Melville up to?

Perhaps Melville lacked the critical vocabulary to designate the precise poetic function Ahab is using—call it allegoresis or reification. One might excuse Melville: Ontology not language is the issue here, and the word "personified" allows him the dramatic wordplay on "personality," an artifact of Being. But Ahab's willingness to sacrifice precision for a witticism, strains the moment, affecting our reading of him. In "The Sphynx" (ch. 70), Ahab tells us he cannot articulate the "linked analogies" and "cunning duplicates" connecting mind and nature. And here, as the novel reaches the climax of Ahab's intellectual development, Ahab's misnomered attempt to personify the impersonal, proves indeed the futility of his poetic gesture. In "The Open Boat" Stephen Crane provides a successful objective correlative for his impersonal universe with the image of a temple at which one would like to throw stones but cannot because, in fact, there is no temple. The strategy is to erase the very image he has labored to produce, leaving readers to wander about in the vacuum. Making a symbol and breaking it is one way to voice the voiceless. Ishmael, for instance, fills the void with artful objectifications (call them whalifications) that reduce the threat of nothingness by their very gamesome transcendence of self-involvement. But Ahab fills his void with person, person, person. The triple usage lacks playfulness and is symptomatic of Ahab's solipsism.[1] He is not poetically essaying the symbol of "personality" but insisting that the universe must have a personality, and one that he shall command, as if his wit will give him dominion over the "naught beyond."[2] Ahab's troping is a hopeless self-aggrandizement. Whereas Ishmael would have "subtilized" the corposants, Ahab makes scenery out of them and makes a scene of himself. In earlier appearances, Ahab's dramaturgy is cunning and convincing. But here at the end it is stagey, theatrical, and false. The misuse of personification signifies Ahab's creative failure. His wordiness calls attention to Ishmael's silence.

In erasing Ishmael's personality just as Ahab is exposing his own, Melville explores the margins between Ishmael's lyricism and Ahab's drama. While Ahab claims dominance by giving personality to the Impersonal and then presuming (with frontier braggadocio) to outtalk it, Ishmael abandons personality altogether, as if that erasure were itself the enactment of an impersonal universe. Ishmael hides himself away in these chapters, but only to assume the higher role of the novel's secret dramatist. Accordingly, his power increases as his presence diminishes. Ishmael not only reports Ahab's thought but becomes them or, rather, Ahab's words and actions become the embodiment of Ishmael's thought as if Ishmael's varied lyrical speculations are given roles to play: Ahab, Stubb, Starbuck, Pip. Although quiet, Ishmael is never far away or out of control. In moving from lyricism to drama, Melville surrenders the narrator's voice to the actor's "business," so that characters and events may seek their logical end in destruction leaving voiceless Ishmael alive. Ishmael does not surrender his pragmatic Platonism to Ahab's one-sidedness. His meditations from "The Whiteness of the Whale" (ch. 42) to "The Try-Works" (ch. 96) proclaim his aesthetic restraint: He will not stare into the "fire," for it will invert him. He knows that the fullest essaying of symbol leads to white, blinding annihilation; he can never fill the ungraspable void.[3] Instead, he will have Ahab act out the direct consequences of such essaying. Through Ahab he comes as close to knowing oblivion without any irrevocable experiencing of it. He will "play along" with death. The act of becoming Ahab is itself a self-oblivion, the loss of himself within an "other." He uses Ahab as a way to essay a consciousness that would if endured by himself destroy him. Thus, by *impersonating* Ahab who tries to *personify* the Impersonal, Ishmael achieves a palpable, dramatic version of that impersonal. Ahab's insistent misuse of "personification" helps us penetrate to the deep structure beneath his often shabby histrionics. Our awareness of this strategy comes in crucial moments of replay when we see Ishmael as a ventriloquist and puppeteer putting words into Ahab's mouth.

"The Candles" is one such replay, for it rechews arguments Ishmael has made thirteen chapters earlier in "Ahab's Leg." A few lines after his personification speech, Ahab taunts the corposants' inability to know their lineal roots and therefore know themselves. The key to Ahab's argument is "genealogy": Humans have one and yet know they cannot fully know it, but the Impersonal by its infinite nature is never-ending and "unbegun," and therefore has no definable genealogical source at all. Ahab pins his superiority on this paltry point as one might pity a dog for its lack of color vision. He assumes that consciousness is transcendent and that linked analogies between personal and impersonal consciousness exist. Given this link between subjective and objective minds, he presumes that as with human consciousness the Impersonal must know its genealogical status. Thus, the infinite is no better off ontologically than finite Ahab. But the fallacy of this argument lies in its forced and over-reaching personification. Ahab first humanizes the infinite and then sympathizes with its self-ignorant power: "Oh, thou foundling fire, thou hermit immemorial, thou too hast thy riddle, thy unparticipated grief" (*MD, 508*). Obviously, Ahab's sympathy is just a self-projection. The "foundling fire" is the foundling Ahab seeking the mystery of his paternity in "The Gilder" (ch. 114); the "hermit" is the reclusive captain of the early chapters. The fire's "riddle" also has a link to Ahab, and here the reader begins to experience a sense of *déjà vu*— a feeling that this scene replays an earlier episode in which Ishmael shares a "secret" about Ahab's leg. By returning to "Ahab's Leg" (ch. 106) we find a bit of knowledge that Ahab labors through his wordiness in "The Candles" to drive into his unconsciousness. And by comparing the two chapters we glimpse the causes of Ahab's pathology.

In "Ahab's Leg," a groin wound occasioned by the snapping of Ahab's ivory leg is "the direct issue of a former woe" (*MD, 464*). That woe is, of course, the initial loss of his leg to Moby Dick, but it is also hinted—through Ahab's subsequent depression, through the implied coverup in the inadequacy of Peleg's "bruited reason" for Ahab's seclusion, through the "muffl[ing] up the knowledge of this thing from others," and through Ishmael's admission of having "unwittingly" divulged a "secret"—that some "deeper part" of Ahab has also been wounded. The implication is that Ahab has been castrated.[4] Ahab's thoughts on his broken ivory leg, while not explicitly sexual, are indirectly related to his impotency. He compares generations of grief and joy. Just as one grief generates another and their lineage can be traced, so too with joy, except that even the highest joys are rooted in some earthly pettiness, while "all heart-woes" (grief) have a "mystic significance," a heritage in heaven. Tracing the "genealogies" of human grief back before Eden, Ahab concludes that grief preexists humanity, that it is inherent in Being, and since Being precedes God, "the gods themselves are not forever glad." The comfort Ahab takes here in a genealogically proven consanguinity of grief in man and God is the same genealogical argument replayed later in "The Candles."

There are, however, two fundamental differences between the scenes. I have related Melville's genealogical argument in "Ahab's Leg" as if it were solely Ahab's, but this is not entirely true, for Ishmael does all the talking. Ahab speaks only in indirect monologue, and the genealogical rhetoric is shaped entirely by Ishmael's interpretive voice. Melville wants us to see this distinction, for he repeatedly adds the otherwise uncharacteristic tag phrase "Ahab thought" throughout the speech to remind us of Ishmael's penetration into Ahab's mind and hence his controlling intellect. Moreover, no quotation marks are used here, so that Ishmael transforms rather than merely transcribes thoughts. The genealogical argument is as much Ishmael's as Ahab's. But in "The Candles," Ahab speaks the same argument for himself with no Ishmael in sight.

Ishmael's complicity in the earlier chapter reveals a second difference. In "Ahab's Leg," the idea of castration is only suggested through tortuous prose, as if Ishmael surreptitiously leaks the sexual cause of Ahab's anxiety. Ahab does not know that Ishmael has intuited this knowledge. Knowing more about Ahab than Ahab at this point also places us above the captain, and our foreknowledge of Ahab's "secret" lends dramatic irony to Ahab's projection onto the corposants in "The Candles." Our discovery of Ahab's sexual loss in "Ahab's Leg" shapes our response to his "riddle [and] unparticipated grief later on." We assume the role of an analyst observing a patient's unconscious sublimation of his deepest wound.

The corposants themselves add a deeper irony. As balls of static, they are merely "pale fire" but one that Ahab addresses as a "flaming self," as though they were a source of energy, not just a harmless side effect. Ahab confuses this impotence with Nature's omnipotence; thus they represent Ahab's loss of true creative fire. And, while he thinks he is "acting," in both the moral and the creative sense, he is, in fact, merely "acting out," unconsciously projecting his secret impotence. With the key words "genealogy" and "riddle" from "Ahab's Leg" recurring now in Ahab's speech, we reckon the irony of Ahab's unconscious dramaturgy. He is not personifying, defying, or dominating at all; he is merely playing the psycho-drama of his hidden sexual wound.

In "The Symphony" (ch. 132), Melville stages a last-minute recognition scene in which Ahab doubts his free will—"what cozening, hidden lord and master, and cruel, remorseless emperor commands me. . . . Is it I, God, or who, that lifts this arm" (*MD,* 545)? It is neither Ahab nor God but Ishmael who pulls the strings that lift that arm. Ahab is the puppet not of fate but of a dramatist on ship who intuits Ahab's unconscious anxiety of sexual dysfunction and dramatizes that knowledge in "The Candles." Ahab is a projection of Ishmael's instinctual demonism. Rhetorically, Ahab's dramaturgy substantiates Ishmael's status as creator of the world of *Moby-Dick* and further ensures Ishmael's credibility. Later on, in *The Confidence-Man,* Melville creates a more coherent drama—one unlinked to a first-person narrator—that permits only the rarest of authorial interventions and results in a more directly felt sense of doubt and being.[5] But in *Moby-Dick* Ishmael's lyric and dramatic control remains a constant certitude.

Of course, Ishmael's excellence as a dramatist depends upon his convincing us that Ahab is as much a plausible reflection of ourselves as he is a stage mechanism. Ahab's tragic vision must be as valid as Ishmael's in order that the tension of sensibilities may be perpetuated. Melville's dramatic mode must be played for its verisimilitude as well as for its Shakespearean theatricality, so that it is as vital as Ishmael's lyricism. Ahab's tragic self-ignorance—his nobility and yet theatricality, his philosophical integrity and yet foolish consistency, his cunning and yet lack of creativity—emerges most clearly when we recognize him as a failed confidence man.

"What Cozening, Hidden Lord and Master"

In chapter 10, we entertained the view that as a framed narrative *Moby-Dick* shares a great deal with the tall tale. On the surface this seems implausible, for while Ishmael may be the knowing gentleman situated in new territory, digressing in serio-whimsical fashion, Ahab is no frontier clown. But, to borrow from Peleg, Ahab is not without his comicalities. His outrageous stumping of the deck, his claiming for himself the doubloon meant as a reward for the crew, his charts and augur holes, his phallic wound—these are the eccentricities of the eighteenth-century man in black. Still, if he is not an obsessive clown, Ahab is most assuredly a schemer and trickster. He hides his obsession to make his madness seem sane, and he cons his crew. In playing along with Ahab we appreciate his manipulations of too-conscientious Starbuck, indifferent Stubb, and mediocre Flask. The crew are his dupes. Like Poe's most adept hoaxers, Ahab promotes a transcendental frame of mind that, once adopted, will ensure the crew's allegiance to his quest. The hidden joke is that it also ensures their death, and the joke on Ahab is that he allows himself to be duped by that transcendentalism. His tragic flaw is that he believes his own con game. But if Ahab is too sober to be the comic con man, the humorless captain has his compensatory fools. Like Lear, Ahab is beset with clowns, probing his depression with sensible nonsense. Stubb and Pip are a chain of fools— one linked to the other and each linked back to Ahab—who serve as a *displacement* of Ahab's humor. Thus the frontier foolishness, the braggadocio, the joy and ease, the mystic redemptive symbolizing that we might expect from Ahab if *Moby-Dick* were a pure tall tale like "The Big Bear of Arkansas" have been projected onto Stubb and Pip, allowing Ahab a complex detachment from humor itself. Let's look first at Ahab's failure as a trickster and then at his potential realignment with humanity through his two fools.

Transcendental Trickster

Moby-Dick is not a literary con game in the tradition of Poe or Thorpe, because Ishmael is too sincere to dupe us, and in allowing us access to Ahab's mind he exposes the con man's strategies. We are never in any danger of being duped. Rather, Melville is content to dramatize the psychological necessity of a con man's duping of himself. One crucial strategy borrowed from Melville's hoaxy precursors is the manipulative misuse of transcendentalism. Like Poe's narrator, Ahab exploits his audience's desire for transcendence, but the tactic backfires. In contrast to Ishmael's pragmatic Platonism, Ahab's failure as a transcendental trickster is symptomatic of his own pathological desire for transcendence. Still, Ahab's skill as a con man is manifest.

"The Specksynder" (ch. 33) reveals Ahab's competence. Since whaling is a joint-stock venture (in that crew and captain own shares) and since whaling hierarchy is more egalitarian than naval command, Melville lacks the usual "outward majestical trappings" with which to dramatize his protagonist. Ahab's tragic superiority "must needs be plucked at from the skies, and dived for in the deep" (*MD*, 148). Intellect, not birth, is all Melville has to work with; hence Ahab's dominance derives from a "certain sultanism of his brain" made incarnate in an "irresistible dictatorship" (147). And to make Ahab's thought "irresistible" to crew and readers, Melville must show how Ahab bends sea "forms and usages" to meet his "more private ends," how he "sometimes mask[s] himself" and relies upon "external arts . . . more or less paltry and base" to maintain supremacy. Like Machiavelli's republican prince, whose high-minded goal of Italian unity is often effected through brutal acts, Ahab is a pragmatic idealist, a fusion of Lion and Fox, a metaphysician and a "masked" diddler in "external arts." And as with Prince Hamlet, who comes to know a villain's smiles well enough to gladhand two school chums before signing their death warrants, Ahab's greatness depends upon con man allurements that are "paltry and base."

Ahab's first opportunity to use his "external arts" on the crew follows soon enough in his Quarter-Deck speech (ch. 36). It is his best rhetorical moment, demonstrating a lightning flexibility of argumentation and facile theatricality. Only Starbuck sees through it. To a large degree, Ahab also recognizes the baseness, even the vanity, of his persuasive arts, and yet that cognizance only enhances our sense of his sultanic control. But when Ahab escalates his arguments beyond the mere promise of a gold doubloon to the insistence upon the transcendental necessity of his quest, his hoaxy rhetoric shows its fatal limitations.

Starbuck is outraged at Ahab's theatrical presentation of the doubloon, and when he unexpectedly identifies Moby Dick as the whale that took off Ahab's leg, Ahab is startled: "Who told thee that?" Up until this point, Ahab has been self-assured, "humming to himself" (*MD,* 162) and playing upon the crew's curiosity and greed. He hides his previous contact with Moby Dick. Starbuck's untimely question interrupts this gambit, but Ahab's reaction—a sudden outburst of emotion, a "tossing of both arms," and (remarkably enough) "a terrific, loud, animal sob, like that of a heart-stricken moose" (163)—is a self-exposure so immediate and sincere that the crew is further riveted. Starbuck sees through the theatricals; his allegiance will not extend to his captain's vengeance, and at this point Ahab's altered rhetorical aim becomes clear: to convince Starbuck that this "private end" of killing Moby Dick is a universal desire. He invites the mate to consider "a little lower layer." Ahab designs his pun to ensnare both Starbuck's spirituality and the crew's cupidity. On the one hand, "lower layer" suggests a transcendent truth beneath the material. On the other hand, in whaling parlance, a lower *lay* means a *higher* percentage of the ship's profit, so that Ahab implies his followers will acquire a monetary as well as a moral gain. Through the "economy" of his wordplay, Ahab neatly accommodates spirit and body, Starbuck and crew. But for the reader the pun also accents Ahab's histrionics. Buttonholing Starbuck, he nevertheless eyes the crew, carefully choosing his words to inflame their greed.

What follows conceals a flaw, which, like the hidden clue to a hoax, inevitably gives the lie to Ahab's base transcendentalism. Moby Dick, Ahab argues, is not a "dumb brute" but, like "all visible objects," is only a "pasteboard mask" that manifests a deeper "unknown but still reasoning thing" (164). The argument assumes the fundamental transcendental distinction between natural and spiritual facts, base actuality and sublime ideal, word and thought, practical understanding and Reason. But clearly Ahab does not match this ontology with a corresponding transcendental ethics or aesthetics. Rather than propose to escape the realm of natural fact through a poetic or creative act, which is itself a recapitulation of original creation, Ahab attributes the flaws of actuality (Moby Dick's malice) to ideality itself. He deduces a malignancy in Reason and proposes to destroy the mask (Moby Dick) as if to destroy the evil reason behind it. The logic is understandable, even if it inverts Emersonian optimism into the demonic, but the inversion is designed to convince the crew that their materialist venture is inherently spiritual. If we accept that whales are not whales but symbols and that the white whale symbolizes evil, then we can justify the destruction of that symbol and call it a spiritual act. It is the logic of genocide and holocaust.

Such is the "lower layer"—both monetary and imperfectly transcendental—that Ahab would have the crew accept, but it is a heterodoxy that the Quaker Starbuck would deny. To accommodate Starbuck, Ahab cuts through traditional transcendentalism to get at a presumably higher spirituality. Ahab's subsequent claim that he does not *care* whether the white whale is "agent" or "principal" is designed to deflect Starbuck's attention from Ahab's inverted Emersonianism, to underplay the blasphemous view of Moby Dick as the "principal" of evil. In effect, his deliberate dismissal of the agent–principal distinction reveals Ahab's attempt to transcend transcendentalism, to brush aside doctrine for the deepest ideality, even as he denies the inherent goodness of Being at the heart of transcendental thought.[6] All this is for Starbuck, but in the heat of his tortuous rhetoric Ahab lets slip his most fundamental philosophical anxiety, that there is no ideality at all: "Sometimes I think there is naught beyond, but 'tis enough." Ahab's rhetoric is really a coverup for his pathological fear of nothingness. Ultimately, Ahab's logic is insincere because, although he considers himself a theist and presumes a malicious God behind the mask of Moby Dick, he is an unacknowledged atheist. Ahab's revelation in "The Sphynx" that he can find no objective reality beyond the "linked analogies" of matter and soul, that there is no meaning beyond Self,[7] exposes Ahab's theism as a pasteboard mask concealing his atheism. Unlike Ishmael, who can endure a forthright disclosure of an "all-color, colorless atheism," Ahab denies Nothingness by inventing a God to battle. Theism is his resort from the nihilism implicit in his solipsism. But this jerry-built theism cannot contain his unconscious fear of nonexistence. It is released in his little slip ("Sometimes I think there's naught beyond"), and his instantaneous coverup ("But 'tis enough") only amplifies what he has tried to conceal from Starbuck, crew, and self.

What Ahab denies in his histrionic posturings, he admits in dreams. In "The Chart" (ch. 44), Ahab dozes in reposeless sleep shrieking out his "somnambulistic" night terrors. Ishmael argues that in sleep Ahab's soul and mind separate, the former becoming "horror-stricken" by the latter's thought, and its awareness of its dissociation from mind. For a moment this "self-assured, independent being" is shocked by the sheer vacuity of its independence. Without mind or matter, Ahab's soul is "without an object to color, and therefore a blankness in itself" (*MD*, 202). Here is the palpable psychological model of Ahab's "naught beyond." It is the same as the whiteness in Ishmael's symbology. But for Ahab, the revelation is an eruption of the unconscious; it is a demon of dreams, the same ungraspable phantom of *death* (not life) that momentarily emerges in the Quarter-Deck speech and is quickly put back to sleep with Ahab's peremptory self-denial, "But 'tis enough."

Ahab tells us that he is "madness maddened," that he is aware of his insanity. In the Quarter-Deck speech and the dream in "The Chart," however, his "madness" is not self-possessed but unbidden and uncontrollable. Unconscious fear and more conscious rhetorical desires shape Ahab's speech. On the one hand, his equation of all objects to pasteboard masks is meant to lure Starbuck toward a higher quest; on the other, Ahab inevitably draws himself into the equation so that whale, wall, and Ahab alike are mere pasteboard beyond which there is "naught." Ahab's rhetoric is as much a self-deception as it is a dissembling act of persuasion. Indeed, through Ahab Melville allows us a unique vision of the rhetorician's precarious sense of being, in which the "true" self discovers through consciously duplicitous masks deeper, unanticipated selves.

Starbuck's "stare" in response to Ahab discloses Ahab's forced reasoning and disingenuous theism. Ahab calls Starbuck "doltish" and must labor to win over the unwinnable mate. Ahab dons the new mask of a placating friend: "So, so; thou reddenest and palest. . . . I meant not to incense thee. Let it go." And next, a contradictory pose. Instead of proclaiming the whale as a universal symbol, he insists that a whale is only a whale, and the quest only routine. Starbuck's part is merely to "strike a fin." Rather than an Idea, the whale is now an object in itself, only a fraction, in fact: a disembodied "fin" detached from any higher meaning. Ahab has reverted to Starbuck's view of the whale as "dumb brute," but such meretricious pandering only belies Ahab's transcendental posturing and alienates Starbuck more. Arrogant and blind, he declares, "Starbuck now is mine."

Ahab's colossal misreading of Starbuck's stare is symptomatic of his inability to interpret the universal silence that Ishmael finds at the root of all being. Like the silence of "The Sphinx" and the blankness in "The Chart," it is inscrutable. He cannot abide the perpetual trying out of silence into meaning. Symbols are inert to him; they yield nothing reliable, and his interpretations are rigid, often dangerously false. Indeed, Ahab ignores some significant symbols and misreads others. He fails to detect a criticism of his rhetoric in the wind's "hollow flap" of the sails. Later he reads Fedallah's predictions of death as signs of his invincibility. A hearse at sea cannot exist, he insists; unless, as we learn, it is a metaphoric whale bearing the Parsee's corpse. A symbolist like Ishmael, who sees the world carved on Queequeg's lifebuoy coffin, can see hearses anywhere. Ahab's limitation as both a thinker and a confidence man is that he cannot expand his interpretive skills beyond self-absorption. No better sense of this poetic limitation can be found than in Ahab's lifeless use of an image Ishmael holds dear: the circle.

In "Sunset" (ch. 37), Ahab envisions the circular horizon as "the ever-brimming goblet's rim." His language is luxuriantly picturesque: The "warm waves blush like wine. The gold brow plumbs the blue" (*MD,* 167). But the goblet turns into an "Iron Crown of Lombardy," and the iron scrapes Ahab's steely skull. Crown becomes helmet, and "all loveliness is anguish." Reflecting back upon his galvanizing speech to the crew, Ahab envisions himself as "one cogged circle fit[ting] into all their wheels, and they revolve." Just as he has reduced gold to the base metal iron, the crowned king and helmeted soldier now becomes a metallic mechanism. The next, more familiar, image is a logical, leaden step: "The path to my fixed purpose is laid with iron rails, whereon my soul is grooved to run. Over unsounded gorges, through the rifled hearts of mountains, under torrent's beds, unerringly I rush!" Ahab's self-projection as a locomotive—he is "grooved" to straight, linear, and unbending "iron rails"—is the final deconstruction of the natural, golden, curving rim of the horizon he first envisions: The circle is broken and made straight.

Ahab dismantles language even more, hurrying to reduce his machine imagery into abstract geometry. In the conclusion to his soliloquy—"Naught's an obstacle, naught's an angle to the iron way"—Ahab reduces all impediments to hen-scratches and puns. Whereas before he has spoken of rims and cogs, he now speaks of "naughts" (a zero, or little circle of nothing), straight-line rails, and angles. The golden goblet of wine comes to this: a hieroglyphic of x's and o's. But given the context of his admission of "naught beyond" on the previous page, these markings support the irony of Ahab's conclusion: "Naught" (i.e., the problem of ontological nothingness) *is* an "obstacle" for Ahab. The complex Shakespearean pun allows Ahab's outward defiance (Nothing can get in my way) to become an unexpected admission of his fear of nihility (Nothingness gets in my way). The perfect line of Ahab's "iron way" is tied up in a naught.

Ahab's wit is cunning but lacks Ishmael's richer self-awareness. In "The Symphony" (ch. 132), Ishmael sees "the horizon" as the juncture where feminine sky and masculine sea meet and mate. In this replay of Ahab's sterile "Sunset," Ishmael transforms homoerotic energy into heterosexuality—"those two seemed one; it was only the sex, as it were, that distinguished them." Their "soft and tremulous motion [denote] the fond, throbbing trust, the loving alarms, with which the poor bride gave her bosom away." In contrast, this "immortal infancy, and innocency of the azure" plays ineffectually about Ahab's "singed locks which grew on the marge of that burnt-out crater of his brain" (542–43). Given earlier hints of Ahab's impotence, Ishmael's explicit sexuality urges us to see Ahab's physical sterility as homologous to his philosophical and aesthetic sterilities. Ahab's mind is itself a "naught," an extinct volcano "on the marge" of which dance the creative and procreative forces of life. If Ishmael, like *Mardi's* Lombardo, "creates the creative," Ahab "de-creates the creative." The rigid poetics of his "Sunset," as opposed to Ishmael's sexual dawn, destroys itself in the humorless wit and self-delusion of "Naught's an obstacle." In the end, Ahab's rhetorical expertise, while it may fool the crew, only signals a fatal blindness and inability to transform anxiety into art.

Ultimately, Ahab's mechanistic "decreativity" is part and parcel of his rhetorical failure as a transcendental trickster. The captain's final strategy in the Quarter-Deck speech is to turn from transcendental argumentation to pure theatrics. The gambit draws upon his misplaced fondness for technology (in this case electromagnetism) and his willingness to resort to humbug necromancy. Once again, circles play a prominent role.

Ahab has the crew "circle round" and lets drink "spiralize" in them; they "ring" him in. This encircling prefigures the "ring" of belligerents in the climactic "Midnight, Forecastle" scene that concludes the episode. One ring of destruction replays the other. Ahab's little theatrical game is to have his harpooners cross the detached metal shafts of their harpoons and, while grabbing the axis, to pretend—by "suddenly and nervously twitching" the crossed blades—that he is transmitting his "electric thing" into the others. Ahab "would have fain shocked into them the same fiery emotion accumulated within the Leyden jar of his own magnetic life" (*MD*, 165), but Starbuck with "honest eye" looks downward in shame, and even Stubb and Flask will not meet their master's eyes. The parlor game is an embarrassment, which even Ahab declares "vain." The practical-minded crew want rum, not voltage, and Ahab obliges with a round of grog. When shock therapy fails, a little nip always helps.

"The Quarter-Deck" has long been regarded as one of Melville's most memorable scenes primarily for its economy in establishing Ahab's relation to Starbuck, crew, and whale. But it is more. Or rather, it is *less,* for the high Shakespearean dudgeon is a subtraction from Ahab's tragic bearing. In content, Ahab's speech is both brilliant and flawed. But as with any prose rendering of a dramatic moment, we tend to miss visual details in the heat of the action. We disregard Ahab's ludicrous animalism: his flailing arms, mooselike sob, and horsey, dilated nostrils out of which "something" shoots. (Surely, this is the most repulsive image to be found in Melville, even though the author no doubt intends "something" drier and more ethereal than what might be expected.) We overlook, too, the comic reversals in argument—the naught, the fin, the hollow flap—the humbug with electromagnetism, and the resort to alcohol. In short, we refuse to associate the tragic captain with the far less noble melodrama of the tall-tale backwoodsman who hides behind a pasteboard mask of transcendentalism. The joke is not that the reader has been deceived into making a Lear out of a Doggett, but that in relying finally more upon theatrics than on words to ensnare his crew, Melville reveals just how "paltry and base" this Sultan can be. And worse, Ahab believes his own histrionics: that he has won Starbuck and Stubb and that the electric fire within him, despite his inability to transmit it to the crew, is a substantial link to the creative powers of the universe rather than the ineffectual static of parlor games.

Ahab's fascination with electricity is a misplaced desire for the true creative fire he lacks. In "The Try-Works" (ch. 96), Ishmael resolves to turn away from the bewitching power of such "artificial fire." This Promethean fire, emblematic of technological arts (*techne*), is an artifice for rendering fat into cash.[8] It also lures him toward a self-consuming misanthropy (*MD,* 422). Ishmael avoids disaster for himself and the ship by transforming this fire into a picturesque effusion.

> There is a wisdom that is woe; but there is a woe that is madness. And there is a Catskill eagle in some souls that can alike dive down into the blackest gorges, and soar out of them again and become invisible in the sunny spaces. And even if he for ever flies within the gorge, that gorge is in the mountains; so that even in his lowest swoop the mountain eagle is still higher than other birds upon the plain, even though they soar. (425)

The Catskill eagle is Ishmael's fluid accommodation of self, audience, and being. It traverses heights and depths and remains continuously engaged in flight. And like Lombardo, it discovers the essence of creativity when it becomes "invisible in the sunny spaces," self-less and yet suffused with the light of pure being. In occupying this sunny space Ishmael draws life from "the glorious, golden, glad sun," which in contrast to the try-works fire and Ahab's corposants, is "the only true lamp" (424).

Ishmael brands all other lights as "liars." But Ahab, entranced by the critical fires of his own Promethean defiance, would strike the sun if it insulted him. He fancies that, in controlling the lesser lights of industrial fire and electromagnetism, he can ensure a dominance of universal creativity. Like another "Modern

Prometheus,'' Victor Frankenstein, he confuses technology with creativity. When his worship of the corposants' pale fire nearly turns the ''panic-stricken'' crew to mutiny, Ahab blows out the harmless static on his harpoon and recaptures the crew's confidence. And when the corposants invert the compass, Ahab further galvanizes the crew. Relying upon high school science, he remagnetizes the needle, but not without ''going through some small strange motions with it— whether indispensable to the magnetizing of the steel, or merely intended to augment the awe of the crew is uncertain'' (518). The little con game convinces the crew, but Ahab's claim to be ''lord of the level loadstone'' only convinces Ishmael of Ahab's ''fatal pride.'' Finally, the flawed brilliance of Ahab as a transcendental trickster and metaphysical confidence man is not so much that he stoops to ''base'' theatrics but that he allows himself to believe they constitute his link to the fires of Being.

In the late dramatic chapters in *Moby-Dick* Ishmael steps beyond the wise ethics derived in ''The Try-Work'' to assume for a while the role of Ahab, and to ''try out'' vicariously the consequences of staring too long into the fire. It is ''a way [he has] of driving off the spleen,'' or more appropriately of safely investigating the dark potential of his Being, the demonic within him, the sunset as well as the dawn. He can inhabit the misanthropist's soul, feel his pride, taste his obsession, make his mistakes, but come away from death scot-free, and cured of the hypos.[9] Ishmael's cure comes in the release of himself, the letting go of his personality, the self-effacement implicit in playing along with Ahab's tragedy.

Some sign of redemption in Ahab from his pathological despair is that in performing his function as a confidence man, he too, like Ishmael can project himself into other characters. He can recognize the sober simplicity of Starbuck's domesticity, or the patience and endurance of the alcoholic blacksmith Perth. But more significantly, especially in terms of Melville's cosmopolitanism, Ahab has his fools, Stubb and Pip, fictive displacements of a redemptive humor that he cannot otherwise tolerate in himself.

Displaced Fools

As a version of the dark-suited misanthrope and frontier trickster, Ahab enjoys a rich double heritage in satire. And given the novel's framed structure, we would expect Ahab to be the central brooding satirist whose antidemocratic attacks would be contained if not ameliorated by the genial Ishmael's framing cosmopolitan vision. It is a wonder that Ahab is not more laughable. Melville has deprived Ahab of the humanizing humors that would make his satire palatable: the benevolence of Goldsmith's Drybone or the sentiment of Kotzebue's ''The Stranger.'' Overall, Ahab's satire is so fully attached to his ''ontological heroics'' that his politics (Machiavellian, monarchic, capitalistic) are merely a symptom of his egoism. In all, Ahab is the shell of a satirist; the cone of a nearly extinct volcano, erupting now and again upon the political scene, but not with any more specific satiric object in view than the demagogue in general or ''man in the mass.''[10]

Mirroring his picturesque sensibility, Ishmael's politics are based on a Kantian and cosmopolitan synthesis of associative and dissociative instincts. While the soul may persist in "keep[ing] the open independence of her sea" (*MD,* 107), it equally craves society. It is as fast as it is loose. Ahab's politics derive from a purely isolationist, not associative, ontology, and as a leader he ignores the responsibility of guiding the alienated crew toward cosmopolitan restraint. Melville's political goal is to reconcile these oppositions, to subsume the dissociative within the associative, and more specifically to bring egocentric leaders in line with the inevitable, cosmopolitical force of history.

It is a structural peculiarity of *Moby-Dick* that Ishmael and Queequeg, the two characters most capable of enacting a full cosmopolitan rebellion against Ahab's autocracy, are in fact removed from the action. The former's narratorial detachment and the latter's repose necessarily deprive them of this agency. Ishmael's genial desperation and sensual love for Queequeg are merely private discoveries that, while they symbolically prevail over Ahab, have no dramatic effect upon captain or crew. The cosmopolitan ideal is a universal religion that Ishmael keeps to himself. But this disempowerment of Ishmael and Queequeg makes comic sense, for if Ahab is to rediscover his associative instinct, his cosmopolitanism must grow logically out of his solipsism.

Melville's gambit in dramatizing the potential in Ahab for a cosmopolitical efflorescence is to let a set of fools act out for him a coalescence of humor and satire. Stubb and Pip are these displacements of Ahab's humor. Melville's model for this structure of displaced fools was Shakespeare, whose genial Falstaff and "mad" Edgar constitute comic visions that their "lords" are forced to keep at a distance. Melville's orchestration of Ahab's fools is connected to the plot, making this comic thread a crucial element in Ahab's dramaturgy. Moreover, Stubb and Pip represent, respectively, the failure and the redemption of geniality. Together, they conspire to bring Ahab back to a genial and cosmopolitan ideal and thereby promote Melville's politics of reconciliation. Thus Ahab's fools voice Melville's most prescient political statements concerning America, race, and national unity.

Ahab's growth toward a reunification with humanity must come from a recognizable version of himself. Pip is that seed of cosmopolitical regeneration. He possesses Ishmael's socializing humor and Queequeg's link to the primal self; moreover, his madness mirrors Ahab. This little Shakespearean clown-gone-mad appears at crucial moments as both a symbol of the persistence of geniality and a dramatic cure for the captain. That Pip is black and clearly embodies the political tensions in America after the Compromise of 1850 adds an immediacy to the general message, a warning against nullification. The fact that Pip fails to revert Ahab— his function in the novel's peripety is to try but dramatically fail—does not invalidate his cosmopolitan ideal. Indeed, his sane madness, like grass growing between paving stones, indicates the persistence of the human will to connect the energies of despair back into life. Pip emerges slowly. And Stubb, Ahab's other fool, is the comic instrument of Pip's alienation, which triggers Ahab's sympathies. Thus, Stubb plays midwife to Pip's regenerative "attack" upon Ahab. To know Pip, we must know Stubb.

Stubb: Pipe, Dream, and Confidence Game

In *Macbeth, Hamlet,* and *King Lear,* Shakespeare begins with ominous scenes of conflict. With no room for laughter, he sends in his clowns later, in mid-play, as lusty diversions, wise fools, or foolish foils. Melville, however, begins with a clown. Ahab first appears in a staged confrontation with Stubb: It is tragedian and clown from the start (ch. 29). The two are at odds; their bone of contention is repose. As the *Pequod* sails south, the January sky begins "to grow a little genial" luring the as-yet-unseen captain on deck. The days are like "crystal goblets of Persian sherbet, heaped up—flaked up, with rose-water snow" (126), and amidst this sweet mildness Ahab ("with a crucifixion in his face") almost cracks a smile. "Old age," however, "is always wakeful," and his relentless pacing distracts "his wearied mates, seeking repose" in their hammocks below decks. "With a certain unassured deprecating humorousness," Stubb vainly suggests that Ahab put his ivory heel in a "globe of tow" to muffle the noise, and for his inventiveness he is yelled at so violently that he later dreams he has been kicked, although Ahab never touched him.

Ahab's first dramatic scene—more comic than tragic—generates the novel's first two soliloquies: Stubb's mutterings in retreat, which culminate with his two new commandments of comic repose ("Think not" and "Sleep when you can"), and Ahab's symbolic rejection of his pipe. Given Melville's frequent equation of smoking with geniality and the fact that Stubb gets his name from his stub of a pipe, Ahab's tossing of his pipe overboard is as much a symbolic casting off of Stubb as it is a rejection of geniality. The pipe, says Ahab, "is meant for sereneness, to send up mild white vapors among mild white hairs" (129). Ahab's hair, though, is the "iron-grey" of anxiety, and when his pipe hits the water its meditative "vapors" turn to mechanistic steam. Stubb's dream is more complex. In retaliation for Ahab's "kick," Stubb kicks back, loses his leg, and continues kicking even though Ahab turns into a pyramid. A humpbacked merman intercedes, and when Stubb offers to kick him instead, he offers his posterior, which is full of marlin spikes pointing outward. The merman reasons Stubb out of anger, showing him that Ahab's ivory kick is more honor than insult. "Wise Stubb" rolls over into reposeful sleep.

The allegory involves a displacement of roles. As pyramid, Ahab becomes Moby Dick (who has a pyramidic hump) and the legless Stubb becomes Ahab. But here the loss of a leg is not the *cause* for revenge; it is its self-destructive *result*. In effect, the dream is Stubb's unconscious sympathy for and avoidance of Ahab's misanthropy. The protean merman extends Stubb's consciousness even further. With spikes and hump, he too is an incarnation of Moby Dick, but, unlike the previous pyramidic avatar, his comic wisdom tempers Stubb. Stubb's dream reveals Moby Dick to be both inscrutable destroyer and knowable creator. Stubb experiences a heretofore unacknowledged Ishmaelian "conscience." He moves from the passive "don't think" into a form of "sleep" so active that its dreams become poetic discourse, a symbolic acting out of Ahab and an artful resolution of Stubb's anger. In short, Ahab kicks Stubb from indifference into wisdom.

Ahab's and Stubb's encounter symbolizes the conflict between tragedy and comedy within the context of repose. Ahab asserts his wakefulness—the ivory leg is both noisy and noisome—onto the backside of pipe-smoking Stubb, and the result is the tense repose of a dream that transforms silence into meaning. Ahab's kick also transforms a mere second mate into a Falstaff, a sympathetic genialist awaiting the shock of his king's rejection. As with Hal and Falstaff, we cannot observe either Ahab or Stubb without an awareness that both acquire meaning through the tension of their contrast and yet moral interdependency. The two are dramatically and symbolically inseparable, and in Stubb's best scene he plays a confidence game that is a comic extension of his captain's manipulations.

In chapter 91, Stubb "issu[es] from [Ahab's] cabin" (403) with the go-ahead to diddle the French captain of the *Rose-bud* out of a cache of ambergris concealed within the rotting flesh of a blasted whale. Stubb succeeds because of a kind of politicized transcendentalism borrowed from his captain—that is, he exploits physical surfaces to find deeper "treasures"—but like Ahab he does so at the expense of cosmopolitan values. Indeed, the burlesque is the comic consequence of the tragic debasement of humanity found in "Midnight, Forecastle."

Stubb's con is a double diddle. The incompetent French captain of the *Bouton de Rose*, who has made fast to a rotting whale, does not know that the minimal oil to be rendered from the decayed blubber is not worth the horrific smell. The captain retires to the "fresh air" of his privy. Ironically, this former perfume manufacturer cannot sense beneath the stench the presence of ambergris, both a by-product of cetacean constipation and an ingredient in perfume. The captain's mate, a Guernsey-man, wants only to cut loose from the smell. Stubb's first diddle is to conspire with this French-speaking Briton to persuade the perfumer captain to let go. That task is easy: While Stubb hurls English epithets at the unsuspecting "Crappoes," the Briton straightfacedly "translates" the insults into more acceptable French arguments for the whale's release. In a sense, this is no diddle at all since the Guernsey-man does all the rhetorical work for Stubb, but prefiguring Tom Sawyer, Stubb lets his victims whitewash themselves. The second diddle is against the Guernsey-man, whose monetary loss is as great as his captain's and who should have "seen" through the smell for himself.

This routine game is fun enough. Stubb's victims are witless and deserving; Stubb prevails because of his instinctive penetrations. But Stubb's theft on cosmopolitan seas is reminiscent of Vincent Nolte's mercantile operations. Like Nolte, Stubb caricatures his victims as he diddles them; his "sting" involves no subtle rhetoric, nor does it bring victim or reader to any redefinitions of belief. Instead, it abuses the tradition of the Gam or "social meeting" between two whalers. According to Melville, gamming is exclusive to whaling, presumably because other ships—men-of-war, pirates, and merchantmen—lack the "godly, honest, unostentatious, hospitable, sociable, free-and-easy" spirit of whalers (240). Melville's fulsome characterization is in keeping with his general attempts to ennoble the whaling profession and to emphasize the contrast of Ahab's lack of geniality in cutting all gams short that yield no news of Moby Dick. But Ahab allows this gam to promote through his fool's false geniality a satiric attack on the Frenchman's impercipience. Stubb's flouting of fellowship, his abuse of the process of finding meaning beneath fact, and his commodification of hidden truth into profit constitute a comic subversion of the cosmopolitan *Rose-bud* crew. In effect, Stubb performs Ahab's comic "dirty work" for him.

In such scenes as "The Pipe," or the gam with the *Samuel Enderby,* depicting Ahab's sullen impatience with the tall-talking clowns Boomer and Bunger (ch. 100), Ahab's refusal to make merry is merely symptomatic of his pathological obsession. But here Ahab's operation through Stubb entails a perversion of his first mate's good humor. Not only has he, in dream, "kicked" Stubb into a higher consciousness, but he kicks him further into a cynical inversion of geniality. As a false genialist, Stubb enacts Ahab's secret satires, japing in a low-comic con game the cosmopolitan ideal that Ahab will not jape in person. Stubb's limitation, however, is his pragmatic rationality. He lacks the sympathetic madness that speaks to Ahab's flawed idealism. But if Shakespeare's Hal denies his Falstaff, so too does Lear embrace his Edgar. Melville adopts the second of these options through Pip, that link in the chain of displaced fools who brings humor, perverted through Stubb's confidence game, back in its more good-natured form to Ahab. If Ahab kicks Stubb, Pip kicks back. But between these events, Pip too must be kicked.

Pip: Castaway and Cosmopolite

Just as Stubb draws us into a satiric attack upon the futility of cosmopolitanism within a capitalistic world, so too does Pip, through the racial consciousness he represents, bring us to a submerged political commentary. And just as Stubb gets his kick from Ahab, so in turn does Pip receive a crucial transforming kick from Stubb. One displacement engenders the other—Ahab to Stubb to Pip. But Ahab exhibits an attraction to Pip that he never shows for Stubb; thus we recognize that a final comic displacement from Pip back to Ahab is, in fact, a tentative curative return of humor. It is as though the comic spirit, "cast away" with Ahab's pipe, winds its way, through various transformative stages in Stubb's jolly cynicism and Pip's mad sympathy, back to Ahab. Pip is Ahab's new Pip(e), a Platonic other half, the comic side severed from the tragic, black split from white, leaving both destructively fractionated without each other's integrative power.

Pip's first and only sane speech concludes "Midnight, Forecastle." Having just witnessed the racial violence of his mates, he deftly equates these "jollies" to the advancing "white squalls." The equation, "White squall? white whale," extends the argument: Moby Dick's malignancy is the reckless hatred in men, a political passion of the crew that Ahab, lost in his personal ontological definition of the whale, will not control. Through his neglect, Ahab shares complicity in the racial incident. Pip prays for mercy to the "white God aloft," knowing all too well that the most likely victim of fearless white men competing for the white whale is this reasonably fearful little black boy.[11]

Pip loses his mind just after the *Rose-bud* incident in "The Castaway" (ch. 93); he is a comic minstrel, and like the tuneful plantation "darky," he possesses a "pleasant, genial, jolly brightness peculiar to his tribe" (411). But Melville sedulously deconstructs this stereotype. He emphasizes Pip's "brilliancy," a trait both personal and racial. Pip's humor is not a slave's coverup but an emblem of the natural intuitiveness already witnessed in "Midnight, Forecastle." Melville knows his audience will resist the point: "Nor smile, so," he tells us, "while I write that this little black was brilliant, for even blackness has its brilliancy." Ishmael expects his smiling white reader to scoff at the impossibility of African intelligence. In order to break the stereotype, he poeticizes Pip's skin, comparing it to ebony and allowing the symbolic logic to work in us a moral transformation. Seeing Pip poetically allows Ishmael to transcend racism. He even admits the boy to his own private symbology of circles when he describes how in former times Pip's music "had turned the round horizon into one star-belled tambourine" (345). And yet Ishmael's final maneuver is to transform Pip from ebony to the deceptive luxuriance of diamond. The black's brilliant opacity becomes a fiery transparency. But this transformation is one of madness.

Pip's experiences have excited his "brightness" into something "luridly illumined by strange fires that fictitiously showed him off to ten times the natural lustre." It is as though an external light activates the cabin boy. That light is both Ahab and Ishmael. Melville elaborates the image, comparing Pip to the "purewatered diamond drop" that, given the artistry and "unnatural gases" (i.e. gaslights) of "the cunning jeweller," becomes "infernally superb . . . like some crownjewel stolen from the King of Hell." On the one hand, Pip's madness is a stolen jewel plucked from his captain's iron crown. At the same time it is merely the fictitious "effect" of some "cunning" author, Ishmael. Finally Pip is a fictive creature suspended between stereotype and a heightened reality, a dramatic effect defined by Ahab's alienation and Ishmael's mediating art. And though robbed through his madness of a dramatically effective personality, he nevertheless emerges (like Stubb's cryptic merman) as a symbol that can talk back to his creator. The final deconstruction of Pip's stereotype is that his language is no longer tuneful but absurd.

Pip's madness is generally associated with his accidental abandonment at sea. And there is no doubt that his isolation "drowned the infinite of his soul" or that in his loneliness he "saw God's foot upon the treadle of the loom," recognized his insignificance, and "spoke it." Nor is there any doubt that his "insanity is heaven's sense," that Ishmael's own later abandonment at sea replays Pip's (414), or that in voicing the voiceless indifference of God, Pip (like Ishmael) becomes a "cunning" speaker of truth. However, the agent of this ontological crisis is not the sea, but Stubb.

Pip was never suited to whaling, and when in an earlier episode he jumps out of a careening whale boat, Stubb forfeits the whale to rescue the boy. The mate makes no bones about the monetary loss, and Stubb's admonition is politically direct: "We can't afford to lose whales by the likes of you; a whale would sell for thirty times what you would, Pip, in Alabama" (413). In an instant, our brilliant jewel, "the loftiest and brightest" Pip, becomes a worthless slave. Flesh is cash. In keeping Pip "fast" to the boat, Stubb converts him into a "Fast-Fish," just as in chapter 89 slaveless Mexico became fastened to the imperial ambitions of the slave-state America. When Pip makes a second jump, Stubb does not return, and Stubb's projection of political worthlessness onto Pip becomes a psychological reality. Thus Pip's madness stems directly from the conscious commodification of him by his mates as well as his metaphysical abandonment, and his new "music," his sane-mad gibberish, necessarily fuses foreboding disharmonies of ontological nihility and inevitable political destruction for the American union.

But dramatically, Pip is the only effectual (although finally ineffective) means of luring Ahab off his destructive course and back to a cosmopolitical repose. By virtue of his blackness and his prophetic role at the end of "Midnight, Forecastle," Pip is a constant reminder of the crew's and Ahab's failure to find a social cohesion beyond their mutual greed and quest. His portentous conjugation of the verb "to look" at the end of "The Doubloon" serves a similar function. Unlike the others, he does not interpret the coin but embodies the process of searching they enact. His critique is that everyone is *looking* at the doubloon but no one is *seeing*. None of these lookers—Ahab, Starbuck, Stubb—breaks out of solipsism. Pip calls the coin the ship's navel—the omphalos of self-absorption—and jokingly reminds us that the consequences of unscrewing one's navel (i.e., excessive self-involvement) is that one's buttocks fall off. It is a jocular version of Ishmael's "Mast-Head" warning against too much meditation. But Pip's incantatory conjugation also implies a solution to this problem. By stressing finitive constructions over the infinitive, Pip recognizes that the quest for insight cannot be an idealized abstraction ("to look") but rather a comprehensive collectivity of mediating points of view (I look, you, he; we and they). The sanity behind the mad grammarian is not so much the verb he chooses—after all, to see is better than to look—but the cosmopolitan pluralism implied in what he does with the verb. Like Ishmael, he encompasses with "equal eye" the varied perspectives of Ahab, Starbuck, and Stubb. Pip's communal vision establishes his role, beyond Ishmael and Queequeg, as redeemer of the cosmopolitan ideal.

Pip's last scenes with Ahab revolve around the encounter with the *Rachel*, whose captain has just lost two sons to Moby Dick and who pleads with Ahab for aid in their rescue. Their disappearance replays Pip's abandonment and prefigures Ishmael's being bumped on the final day of the chase. Ahab, who in "The Gilder" wonders "where the foundling's father is hidden" and whose sympathies for this distraught father ought to be strong, is tempted but refuses. Nowhere do we find Melville's understanding of classical tragedy more acute than in this peripety. Ahab's doubts about his obsession entice us into an ironic anticipation of a reversal in which the inevitable catastrophe would be averted if only the protagonist would simply come to his senses, settle for "attainable felicities," and turn the ship back home. Ahab's choices are to join the *Rachel* in search of sons, to become the father he has lost, and to return to the family of man; or to fight Moby Dick. Pip intensifies the agony of this choice.

Three chapters previous to "The Rachel," Ahab notices Pip for the first time. He is appalled by those "creative libertines," the gods, who begat only to abandon the boy. (Given his rejection of the *Rachel*'s boys, we recognize a vicious hypocrisy in placing blame for Pip's abandonment on the "gods" when, in fact, the culprit is his own emissary, Stubb.) In striking at Ahab's "inmost center" (522), Pip's abandonment sympathetically coincides with the captain's deep-seated fear of nihility. Moreover, Pip's "gibberish" is by its parabolic nature an effective "voicing" of the voiceless power witnessed at sea. His mad tunes are a kind of silence, as impenetrable as the ocean: a sensible nonsense that means nothing and yet everything, because everywhere is nothing. Pip's disjointed poetry is a far cry from Ishmael's darkly good-humored symbolizing, and yet it is a language Ahab intuitively comprehends. And just as Ahab grows closer to Pip, so too does Pip's language become more accessible. Holding his captain's hand, he suddenly grows saner, proposing that the blacksmith should "rivet these two hands together; the black one with the white; for I will not let this go."

Ahab's acceptance of Pip plays upon our desire for a reversal, but along with these metaphysical and aesthetic longings is the compelling political allegory of the black boy leading the white man toward a cosmopolitan reconciliation of self, society, and nature. The ruination for America and the crew in "Midnight, Forecastle" appears to be on the mend. Pip has witnessed the attack on Daggoo; he has been the victim of Stubb's racism; he is the embodiment of social alienation. In taking Pip's hand, Ahab acknowledges that man's orphan status is not simply ontological but politically contingent. Ahab's fresh realization suggests a healthy confrontation with his dis-ease. Instead of fighting the gods, he might turn his attention toward fighting anomie, to which he as the captain of a capitalist enterprise has unwittingly contributed. Rather than exploit the racist passions of his crew, he could with the simple embracing of the black boy lead them toward harmony.

At least this is the comic reversal implied in the image of Ahab and Pip hand in hand. But after the *Rachel* incident, Ahab reverts to his indomitable isolationism. His dis-ease becomes itself a consciousness that replaces his very being, and he rejects Pip as a threat to that self: The boy is "too curing to my malady" (534). Pip persists in battering Ahab's heart; his ultimate argument is to tell Ahab that he can be used "for your one lost leg." In replacing ebony for ivory, Pip proposes to heal Ahab's physical wound (and impotence) through a symbolic integration of selves that is, again, both metaphysical and political. His blackness links his musicality to Daggoo's earthy self-balancing so that he is, in effect, the embodiment of a mediating Ishmaelian creativity, but one responsive primarily through a cosmopolitan merging of races, white leg beside black. Ahab, however, will not yield the sovereignty of his dis-ease. Earlier, in giving his instruction for a "complete man" (ch. 108), he has the carpenter position his own leg where Ahab's lost leg would be in order to demonstrate the phantom sensations that amputees often feel. He hopes to draw a parallel to the soul, but the carpenter is confused. Ahab is angered that such a clod is responsible for the crafting of his prosthesis, and he curses his "inter-indebtedness." Pip, however, intuits Ahab's longing for his leg as the desire for the completeness of his human consciousness and the revitalization of his potency. And as an artist rather than the rude mechanical carpenter, he is able to supply himself as a symbolic prosthesis, a representation of Ahab's lost creativity, so as to make Ahab, as Pip puts it, a "whole body" again.

The tragic irony that Melville heightens here is that Ahab is not willing to sacrifice the autonomy of his wounded and hermetic soul for Pip's "inter-indebted" humanism. Nor is he capable of adopting the poetic logic that would allow him to accept Pip's symbolic consciousness as a substitute for the physical leg. As he puts it to the carpenter, the soul is "an entire, living, thinking thing" that stands "*un*interpenetratingly" with respect to the corporeal self and mind (471). Ahab can perceive a "linked analogy" between himself and Pip, but he cannot merge the correspondent halves. His grief, as he puts it in "The Candles," is "unparticipated" (508). Pip's healing, recombinative, participative consciousness is finally for Ahab another pasteboard mask, a barrier to break through rather than a living symbol with which one might merge. The rejection of Pip is Ahab's failure to reintegrate, to poeticize, symbolize, and create.

It is also like a weaver's straightening of a thread gone awry. Melville puts his tragedy back on course. Abandoned for a last time while the crew chases Moby Dick, Pip (as instructed) occupies Ahab's cabin chair and imagines himself an amiable "host to white men" "pass[ing] round the decanters" (535). It is the fantasy enactment of what should have been the cosmopolitan gathering of sailors in "Midnight, Forecastle," but which ended in riot. His political meaning is that America's leaders must resolve the problem of race to avert the nation's looming civil crisis. But beyond this, and despite Pip's actual failure to win his leader over, there is the larger vision of the resilience of geniality to grow out of pain and to heal. In a dream, Ahab has "kicked" Stubb as if to project his wound upon that suddenly displaced fool. Stubb in turn "kicks" Pip (claps him in political and metaphysical irons), perpetuating the abuse, inflicting Ahab's and now Stubb's cynicism upon the black boy, and converting his brilliancy into madness. But Pip's humor persists, grabbing at Ahab's hand and leg, as though the misanthropy of Ahab's initial kick has now been fused through the successive returning kicks of his displaced fools with the resolvent, curative benevolence of Pip's geniality.

Although the tragic hero and displaced fools sink together, one final comic displacement concludes the novel. In precisely the same manner as in Pip's abandonment, Ishmael is bumped from his whale boat and left to float on Queequeg's coffin. With the "Epilogue" the meditative comedy that frames Ahab's tragic drama returns; Ishmael's voice regains control. And just as Pip is true to Ahab "as the circumference to its centre," the comic Ishmael (his picturesque vision still intact, enhanced by his symbolic link to Pip and the *Rachel* orphans) slowly revolves "on the margin" of the sinking *Pequod*'s maelstrom: alive, awake, yet calm, true to the tense repose of his resolvent circular vision.

Ahab's relation to his displaced fools is an allegory of the nation's comic debate. As a "self-consuming misanthrope," Ahab has divorced himself from all geniality. He is a trickster relying upon false wit and the false logic of an imperfect transcendentalism, a misshapen, humorless satirist who mocks the spiritual longings of the mass of men even as he finally discloses his own self-delusion. Such is the degenerative side of the demonic instinct, but the counterpulse of the genial spirit is manifested in Ahab's displacement of his satiric function upon his comic fools. The essence of Melville's allegorized debate is found in the series of comic transformations in which Ahab's rancor is transmuted into Stubb's indifferent jocularity, which is in turn inverted by the sane madness of Pip into regenerative geniality. Thus resolvent and cosmopolitan humor becomes the distillate of satire. Read in this manner, the succession of comic "kicks" acknowledges Melville's persistent faith in the ineluctable dominance of humor over satire.

On the Margin of the Maelstrom

Melville finished *Moby-Dick* under strained circumstances. After almost a year and a half, he contracted the Manhattan printer R. Craighead to set his manuscript in type before he had finished the novel. Melville found himself reading, correcting, and revising proofs while he was composing his conclusion. To facilitate productivity, he lodged with his brother in New York City, both to escape distractions of Arrowhead and to be closer to his printer. This was not the slow, grass-growing mood in which (he later told Hawthorne) a novel ought to be written. And yet these circumstances may have helped to alter his rhetoric, for in The Chase (chs. 133–35) all voices are dropped—Ishmael's lyricism, Ahab's dramaturgy—and language itself, like an agent of the impersonal, becomes a force in itself transforming word into pure action. Ishmaelian digression gives way to economical description, as in the unforgettable picture of Moby Dick rising from below the whale boats at first a "white living spot" then "magnifying as it rose" his "open mouth and scrolled jaw; his vast, shadowed bulk still half blending with the blue of the sea" (549). Dramatic encounters, such as Ahab's final dismissal of the too-jocular Stubb who "laughs before a wreck" (553), are few and brief. And Ishmael, who silently manages the pacing of description and dialog, claims no central mediating presence. He is a third-person observer—"the third man helplessly dropping astern, but still afloat and swimming" (569)—an object, like the characters, ship, and sea, not a personality, a silenced Pip perfectly positioned "to look."

In these chapters Melville's language is free of Shakespearean trappings. It is clear, confident, even cinematic, with Ishmael the impersonal camera. In the midst of the unfettered prose and intensified action is a recurrent emphasis upon repose linking the novel's two protagonists and their nemesis, two hunters and the hunted whale. Moby Dick glides with "a mighty mildness of repose in swiftness." But the whale's "quietude [is] but the vesture of tornadoes" (548); the image of his exterior calm hiding an inner fury is a con man's inversion of Ishmael's self-projection as a calm spot amid the tornadoed Atlantic of his being. The whale is similarly distinguished but in a variant key from Ahab, whose final self-reckoning on the third day yet again reveals an Ishmaelian potential. He sees his brain as a "calm" capable of God's repose—a "coolness and a calmness" of thought (563)—but finally, his is an unrealized repose, a deadness, "a frozen calm," the antithesis of Melville's own green, grass-growing calm of creativity, achieved away from the Berkshires' rolling hills, in the heart of Manhattan, with his printer's "devil" rapping at the door.

Ishmael returns in the "Epilogue" to close the structural frame. His voice is shriven of personality. It gathers up a set of familiar images—circle, margin, tempest, calm, coffin, isolato—into a brief symphonic poem. With sharks and sky-hawks muzzled, Ishmael drifts unharmed, on "soft" waters, himself an image of repose and an embodiment of the impersonal. "The drama's done"; the rest is silence.

The transcendence of self in *Moby-Dick* is the culmination of a remarkable experiment in narrative control and the aesthetics of repose beginning with *Typee*.

In his first book, Melville's picturesque and cosmopolitan visions are established but imperfectly dramatized leaving readers at times captivated, at times betrayed by Tommo's anxious and conflicted voice. With *Moby-Dick,* Melville set up a framed structure that could effectively fuse his conflicting impulses: tragedy within comedy, satire within humor, the con man within genialist, woe within wisdom, politics within sexuality, philosophy within art. He tossed genial and cosmopolitan ideals into the crucible of Ahab's misanthropic fire in order to transform them into Ishmael's more useful genial desperation. He developed a form of symbolizing, pliable and expansive, distinct from Ahab's deadening allegories, that allowed him "to essay" the whiteness of nihilism but brought him full circle into an affirmation of human creativity. With Ahab, Stubb, and Pip, he bodied forth elements of America's comic debate into a carefully contained political prophecy and critique upon the need for a cosmopolitan reaction to America's racist capitalism. He played with dramatic forms, assumed many voices, copied Shakespeare and invented him anew. In the end, *Moby-Dick* is a series of self-effacing narrative transformations, one framing and extending into the next: an ode on whaling and whales that we may call "Ishmael" encasing a play called "Ahab" giving way to the pure cinematic action of the chase that by its impersonal nature can take no name. These literary structures allowed Melville to push personality out of his voice, to lift expression beyond the impulses of geniality and demonism, beyond humor and tragedy, toward the voicelessness of the impersonal void.

12

Melville's Comedy of Doubt

The reviews of *Moby-Dick* were mixed, and given the months of composition, Melville had every right to be discouraged. Still, he could take comfort that journalists were learning how to read him. What impressed them was Melville's style. The reviewer for *Graham's* captured the essence of Ishmael's "careful disorderliness" (*MD*, 361) and genial desperation when he wrote that "the style is dashing, headlong, strewn with queer and quaint ingenuities moistened with humor, and is a *capital specimen* of *deliberate and felicitous recklessness,* in which a seeming helter-skelter movement is guided by *real judgment.*"[1] *Moby-Dick* was also a "capital specimen" of a verbal picturesque. The reviewer for *The Leader* wrote, "The book is not a romance, nor a treatise on Cetology. It is something of both: a strange, wild work with the tangled overgrowth and luxuriant vegetation of American forests, not the trim orderliness of an English park" (*D*, 26). The *Boston Evening Traveller* summed up Melville's mixed style in deliberately provocative words: It is "a sort of hermaphrodite craft" (*D*, 32), drawing upon the beautiful and the sublime, and yet occupying a middle ground distinct from either contributing "sex." Melville walked Simms's "Al Sirat," the thin creative line between two aesthetic realms. His style was "strange," said the *National Intelligencer* in Washington, in its "power to reach the sinuosities of a thought" (*D*, 68). All agreed Melville's "moral chiaroscuro" had "charm."[2]

But "The Whiteness of the Whale," which had taken the creative process of symbolism to its nihilistic extreme, exposed the pretenses of nature and even symbol itself. Art can "charm" us into thinking there is "*something* beyond," and this aesthetic belief is useful for our mental survival. But when aesthetic belief presumes the status of fact, our minds rigidify the illusion. Readers must live the fiction that meaning exists beyond ourselves but with an "equal eye" on the possibility of nothingness. Fiction, like religion, must make us "feel the tie" (*CM*, 183) between ourselves and Being; it must be a discourse between the "something beyond" and the "naught." Melville could achieve this comically, but only through a rhetoric more subversive than *Moby-Dick*'s. By exposing himself as the necromancer he is, he could (like Frank Goodman in *The Confidence-Man*) put readers in a condition of wonder not over the charming style created but over the detached charmer himself. By making language devoid of personality and fiction hoaxy, he could also disrupt the confident, amiable voice in his writing that was threatening to become too reposeful. He wanted to perpetuate the off-balance balancing of recklessness and "real judgment." He did so by killing Ishmael.

In the first half of his career, Melville fashioned a sincere voice that could place readers in the picturesque moment of tense repose between oblivion and awareness. But finding this Ishmael only provoked the need to lose him. *Moby-Dick* takes amiable humor to its height. Up on the masthead we listen to Ishmael's rapture; we follow his transcendent mood; we plunge with him into doubt. We survive through him. He is our culture's finest example of genial desperation, a wise man we often quote. And this is precisely the problem: Ishmael does all the work of meaning-making for us. Thus, at tale's end we shelve the exemplar just as easily as we quote him. Either way, Ishmael is alive only to the degree that he persists in our sentiment, which is to say he is barely alive at all.

In order to make fiction truly connect, Melville adopts a method of writing that kills off reliable speakers and makes readers wrestle out meaning for themselves. He created a voiceless voice that denied through its detachment the sincerity in amiable fiction but retained its amiable spirit, one that relieved readers of their dependency upon a personable authorial guidance. In doing so, he did not have to rely upon the sympathetic "spiritualizing nature" of such "refined" readers as the Hawthornes but embarked on the ambitious project of inducing creative bewilderment among all readers. No longer followers of Ishmael, Melville's readers would have to become Ishmaels themselves.

To rid himself of Ishmael's picturesque, Melville devised a compensating mode of literary dramatism devoid of wise, or even ironically wise, first-person speakers. "The Piazza" emphasizes this rhetorical shift.[3] An artist disillusioned by nature hikes into picturesque highlands only to discover a sterile and lonely setting. Nevertheless, he returns home rejuvenated, but his porch, once taken to be a "picture gallery" bench from which one might frame nature, is now a "royal box" from which the writer observes nature's pageant. Melville's movement away from the "Fairyland" of the picturesque to experiential drama prefigured in "The Piazza" required a full effacement of selfhood: the reduction of voice and symbol in favor of dialog and objective observation; the ironizing of the genial character and expansion of the confidence man type; and experimentation with third-person narrative.

The Confidence-Man dramatizes far more than *Typee* or even *Moby-Dick*. It silences the Ishmaelian voice finalizing the shift from picturesque to fictive drama adumbrated in *Moby-Dick*. It articulates the complex issues of America's comic debate and transforms the cosmopolite from a dubious cultural figure to a moral hero. It builds upon an elaborate setup and sting designed to free us of the habits of allegorical reading, and more than any other Melville work, it forces readers to play along in a comedy of doubt.

Melville's Reader: Partner, Victim, Participant

The reviewer for the London *Illustrated Times* did not much care for *The Confidence-Man;* in fact, it nauseated him. He did not know what the book meant, and, worse, he could not tell what it was—a "novel, comedy, collection of dialogues, repertory of anecdotes, or whatever it is." His colleague at the *Westminster Review* was able to locate a meaning in the book's apparent theme ("the gullibility of the great

Republic''), but he had to agree with the *Illustrated Times* that Melville's work was indeed "a sad jumble."[4] The assessment has proved prophetic, for critics still have no consensus on "whatever it is."[5] *The Confidence-Man* has been labeled allegory, "new Novel," comedy, picaresque, satire, romance, and even "picaresque satiric romance."[6] As if to encourage this critical comedy, Melville offers few clues of his formal design. At the end of chapter 14, for instance, his narrator announces that he will "pass from the comedy of thought to that of action" (*CM*, 71), suggesting that the book comprises, in the broadest sense, both satiric (or didactic) and dramatic (or mimetic) forms. Some jumble.

The modern critical impulse has been to read *The Confidence-Man* didactically as a social, religious, or philosophical commentary.[7] And the notion that Melville wrote a satiric allegory remains deeply embedded in the scholarly community, even to the degree that general studies of allegory often use the book as a crucial example of the form.[8] Although the case for allegory is valid, it is a reading of last resort. Since we cannot seem to find in this obdurate text anything truly mimetic, psychologically "real," or novelistic, and since the book seems more puzzle than representation, it is assumed to be veiled in allegory. Elizabeth Foster, for instance, observes that "the surface story is an aimless string of episodes, without tension, suspense, variation in pace, or climax." But when seen as an allegory—"when the allegory surfaces"—the book becomes "as formal as a fugue [and] richly patterned." As a "cipher" to be "decoded," it is "tight, ingenious, and rational."[9] Foster's orientation has persisted. Hershel Parker calls *The Confidence-Man* a "consistent" and "carefully structured allegory" with the Devil as the title character.[10] And recently, less satanic, more elaborate allegorical readings correlate the fiction's seemingly haphazard development to the growth of abstract human consciousness.[11] For these readers the entire novel is clearly a "comedy of thought," a comic allegory or satire.

Allegorical fictions develop along the lines of an external set of ideas rather than the probable and necessary forces inherent in human action. That is, plot and character are defined in terms more of an argument (social, moral, or otherwise) than of human desire. But this approach does not account for Melville's full effect.[12] To begin with, his unreliable narrator, not usually found in allegory, abdicates any responsibility for interpreting motives or guiding the reader through events. As a result, Melville's argument seems to disintegrate for lack of a resolute voice, and readers must float between "maybe yes" and "maybe no"; it all becomes a "carefully-constructed muddle," according to Lawrence Buell.[13] Moreover, as the novel progresses into its second half, social satire diminishes and our involvement in a human comedy expands; the allegorical opening yields a mimetic, darkly comic end.

The difference between these two halves is as dramatic as the broad disparity exemplified in the mute who opens the novel and the cosmopolitan who puts it to rest. Clearly an allegorical figure, the colorless mute (emblematic of ineffectual Christianity) engages our emotions only at a minimum. But the colorful and talkative cosmopolite, Frank Goodman, excites deeper sympathies. A flesh-and-blood character with dubious motives seeking confidence for either positive or malicious ends, he arouses our anxieties and, to use Wayne Booth's words, "force[s] the reader into thought about his own moral dilemma.''[14] To the degree that Goodman's story awakens us to our ''own moral dilemma'' of faith, *The Confidence-Man* is as mimetic as it is didactic. Moreover, despite assumptions to the contrary, the novel is equally dramatic in its focus upon the discovery of Goodman's real identity.[15] Ultimately, Melville's last novel is both puzzle and drama, not a jumble.

Melville blends comic thought and action as early as chapter 14, where his digression on fiction heightens the audience's involvement in the action. The merchant Roberts, who has been diddled twice already, and a Mr. Truman, who is about to diddle him again, stand poised, champagne in hand, when the merchant suddenly calls off all bets. As the two principals remain frozen on stage with lines of pain and wonder etched on their brows, Melville digresses on ''the queer, unaccountable caprices of [Roberts's] natural heart'' (*CM*, 68). The effect of this anticlimactic interruption is twofold. On the one hand, Melville tells his readers how to read or, more specifically, how we may empathize with Roberts, whose inconsistency derives from a ''natural heart.'' If our hearts are ''natural,'' we will know his dilemma well. On the other hand, the digression is a ''delaying tactic,'' intensifying dramatic suspense by forestalling the resolution of vital questions that have grown out of the action. Will Roberts clarify the nature of his doubt, expose Truman, and provide useful warnings for future victims of larceny (the reader included)? Will Truman reveal his motives or fabricate a coverup? Is confidence a wine-induced fantasy? Melville's interruption complicates both action *and* thought. It is as suspenseful as it is idea bound, as mimetic as it is didactic. Melville's well-crafted narratorial detachment at this point also creates a moment of tense repose.

The detachment, repose, and mixing of modes, sustained throughout Melville's larger drama, are best understood in the context of the evolving interrelationship of text and reader. In earlier days, Melville encouraged readers to become what Wolfgang Iser calls ''partners in a process of communication.''[16] When, for instance, Sophia Hawthorne found a ''subtile significance'' in *Moby-Dick*'s spirit-spout image, the author replied with emphasis that he did not ''*mean* it.'' The creation was hers: ''You . . . see more things, . . . and by the same process, refine all you see, so that they are . . . things which while you think you but humbly discover them, you do in fact create them''[18] (*Letters*, 146). Reading, because it is an act of seeing and refining, is an act of creation, a sharing in, indeed completion of, the author's dynamic creative process. Ishmael proclaims as much in his familiar declaration of independence from aesthetic completion—''grand [erections], true ones, ever leave the copestone to posterity'' (*MD*, 145). Posterity's readers, more than the writer, supply the copestone of coherence to a fiction like *Moby-Dick*.

But this symbiotic partnership between text and reader erodes almost entirely in *The Confidence-Man*. Although Melville invites us in the first half of the novel to create ''subtile significances,'' especially with its procession of confidence men and victims, the reader's ability at the end of the work to ''allegorize'' confidently is thwarted. The confidence man may be God, Devil, or Man, or any two, or all three. Eventually, the reader's mind short-circuits. Just as Melville's sentences at times collapse under the weight of too many nested subordinations, we are left confounded and confused. In chapter 18 a chorus of three gentlemen interrupts the drama with their confusion: Is the herb doctor a knave, fool, original genius, or all three, or perhaps an agent for the Pope? All three perspectives are mere "suspicions." But if "True knowledge comes but by suspicion or revelation," and it is a "wise" man who waits for suspicions to "ripen into knowledge," then our chorus of three, like the reader, must wait indefinitely for a deliverance from doubt, for their "triangular duel" ends "with but a triangular result" (*CM*, 92). There is no ripeness here, nor any "True knowledge." Melville does not invite us to supply a "copestone" to his fiction. We are not partners with his text. Like the chorus in chapter 18, we are victims.[17] It seems clear, though, that Melville's point is that we recognize our victimization, that we see ourselves throughout as the potential dupes of a literary confidence game, and that we share in the confusion. For in knowing our embattled status, we are better prepared to take up our own role in the game: either to storm off in anger or to hang on in confusion, or else to play along.

But all this is risky business for a dramatist. Unrelieved doubt or confusion is generally taken as a fatal flaw in any fiction, didactic or mimetic. To be sure, students of allegory like Angus Fletcher have convincingly demonstrated the form's capacity for fluidity and ambivalence in conveying "the action of the mind." But despite this potential for ambiguity, allegory's ultimate function is to purge doubt: It " 'carries off' the threat of ambivalent feelings." Moreover, "its enigmas show . . . an obsessive battling with doubt. It does not accept the world of experience and senses; it thrives on their overthrow, replacing them with ideas."[18] Unrelieved doubt among readers is equally problematic in mimetic fiction. As Booth observes, a consequence of the unreliable or "inconscient" narrator is that the author may be misunderstood.[19] The fate of irony is misreading and audience alienation.

This is a risk Melville was willing to take. In chapter 14 he argues that while nature is inconsistent, "experience is the only guide," and that, by logical extension, fiction is an experience that can guide us only to the degree that its "twistings" (no matter how confusing) parallel nature's. Thus, by inflicting upon his reader triple-layered suspicions and refusing to supply a trigonometry that will triangulate "True knowledge," Melville engages us in a process of doubt that mimics thought and life. He forces us to participate in the drama of passionate thought that his earlier characters from Tommo on have expressed in words. In short, Melville's fictive confusion, like all confidence games, has a moral function. It only remains to show how Melville combines allegory and humor to structure this complex reading experience.

Allegory and Breakdown

The Confidence-Man clearly possesses the trappings of allegorical plot, character, and setting. It works within a highly schematized time frame, moving from sunrise to midnight, with sunset occurring just as the cosmopolitan enters precisely halfway into the action. The aptly named steamboat *Fidèle* falls in the *narrenschiff* tradition; it is a ship of fools, a comic microcosm.[20] For those who take the confidence man to be a single, protean, and supernatural figure disguised as all of the novel's confidence men, the title character is typical of allegory, bearing such typically allegorical names as Goodman, Truman, and Noble. For Angus Fletcher, he is a "daemonic agent," or half-human, half-divine character "possessed" by a single idea and "act[ing] free of the usual moral restraints, even when he is acting morally." Moreover, Goodman engages in both Quest and Battle, the "radically reductive" patterns of action found in allegory, for his search for confidence progresses from one "debate" or "Socratic dialogue" to another.[21]

Fletcher observes that allegories display rhythmic, ritualistic plots (such as the pattern of repeated shipwrecks in *Gulliver's Travels*) and what he calls the "fractionated" character.[22] Briefly, the allegorical hero generates one or more doubles of himself, and the repeated actions of these "fractionated" or "partial characters" enhance both the rhythm and the symmetry of the plot, which accordingly engender the reader's expectations of allegory. Fletcher's ritualized patterns occur in the first half of *The Confidence-Man* but are sedulously thwarted in the second, leaving us vaguely suspicious of the author's reliability in fulfilling his promise of allegory. The failure of Black Guinea's prophetic list of confidence men to be fully realized illustrates the point.

Melville "fractionates" his con man in chapter 3 when Black Guinea lists eight "ge'mmen" who will vouch for his integrity. Through the first half of the novel, each gentleman appears in the order in which he is listed, and each is clearly an "avatar" or "fraction" of the con man. But the list of fractionated characters breaks down upon the cosmopolitan's entrance. Two of the predicted con men, one in a "yaller west" another in a "wiolet robe," do not appear. Some account for this lapse by noting that if the colors were interchanged, the resultant "wiolet west" might refer to Charlie Noble (who wears a vest) and the "yaller robe" to a minor figure in the last scene or even (because he wears a traveling robe) to the cosmopolitan himself, Frank Goodman. But if the men on Black Guinea's list are, in fact, the serial guises of *one* "daemonic agent," and if (through the rational emending of the text suggested above) Noble were admitted to that list, and if Goodman is, as many assume, *the* confidence man *par excellence,* then Goodman's and Noble's crucial encounter (chs. 25–35) would be logically impossible. Two "avatars" cannot occupy one stage at the same time. Even if the Devil could pull off this trick, it is unlikely that he would waste his time trying to talk himself into having a drink or giving himself a loan. Given the problems of Black Guinea's list, the allegory becomes dramatically absurd.[23]

In the final analysis, the nonfulfillment of Black Guinea's list leads to an arrhythmic, asymmetric, and incomplete fiction, one that is at best a problematic allegory. Whereas six confidence men in the first half of the novel follow each other in ritualized rhythm, only one suspected confidence man, the cosmopolitan, occupies the stage in the slower-paced second half. H. Bruce Franklin notes a number of crucial differences between Goodman and his allegorical predecessors, intimating that the cosmopolitan may not be one of those operators at all. He takes no money but, in fact, gives away two shillings; he exposes a confidence man, Charlie Noble; he grows in stature as the novel progresses.[24] By reason of Goodman's departure from the anticipated allegorical mold, the entrance of this cosmopolitan works against allegorical plot symmetry and form. The failure of Black Guinea's list is only one of many recurring patterns of breakdown in Melville's allegory. Nine other broken patterns contribute to an overall two-part structure in the novel. First, the structure.

Readers rarely fail to recognize that Melville's text is divided into two sections. The first half includes six confidence men (seven, if you count the mute) who engage in eighteen interactions with fourteen minor characters. But the second half follows only one man, the cosmopolitan, through five encounters with five inter-locutors. Whereas the first half leaps rapidly from one episode to the next, each spotlighting a single confidence man, the second half creeps through extended dialogues on friendship and confidence. To accentuate the bifurcation, Melville sets the first half mostly outdoors and in sunlight and the second indoors and in darkness from sunset to midnight. The two halves are as distinct as the many and the one, outside and in, day and night. Clearly, the text begs us to play one half against the other. The first encourages the reader to formulate empirical judgments on the nature of confidence men, and the second carefully disintegrates our confidence in those judgments. In a way, *The Confidence-Man* is Biblical in the deepest, typo-logical sense of that word. The novel's first half is an Old Testament that supplies the type of the confidence man; the second, New Testament half, the antitype. But in Melville's anti-allegorical fiction, the millennial cosmopolitan Frank Goodman of the second half is a purposely imperfect antitype of the prophetic con man type of the first, and yet this breakdown in the coherence between Melville's "Old and New Testaments" is the basis of a moral rhetoric of deceit that pervades this hoaxy novel. Although one's confusion in moving from the first to the second half of the novel creates a sense of betrayal, we are continually teased to read on in hopes that our cosmopolitan will be revealed as an inverted messiah and "new man" for the ages.

Melville's novel is a one–two punch, a confidence game complete with *setup* and *sting*. Each half of the novel is organized upon a single, dramatically compelling question. In the first we ask "What *is* a confidence man?" This is a relatively easy problem to solve: One merely observes. Here, Melville presents a complex but comprehensible world of knaves and fools; our task is to learn that world. We discern patterns of behavior that constitute a syndrome of larceny. By the time we reach the sixth Mississippi operator, the Philosophical Intelligence Officer, we have had our fill of pious pretenders, genial panhandlers, and enthusiastic faith healers. We know a confidence man when we see one. In the first half, then, Melville educates us to survive in the self-contained world of confidence men. Like the three gentlemen in chapter 18, we are bemused by our suspicions but secure in the knowledge Melville has passed along. Although a "True knowledge" of the con-fidence man's motives may not be possible, our suspicions are certain, for as each of the six confidence men enters, his larcenous behavior corresponds to that of his predecessors. Thus, even without a narrator, the reader is able to discern, within this hermetic world, a confident system of facts, relations, and knowledge. It is a little culture of awareness unto itself. Even the narrator's distant irony and circuitous language contribute to this process of familiarization. Melville conditions us to respond to the signs that identify the confidence man. He works upon our "demonic instinct" for seeking out iniquity. Although the world he portrays is duplicitous, even triplicitous, it is knowable, and the reader is trained to understand that world. Of course, Melville builds up this confident world only to tear it apart.

The second half challenges our reading skill. The second dramatic question that propels us to the end of the novel is whether Frank Goodman fits the syndrome. Given our conditioning, the solution should be easy. But our training fails us. As Goodman moves from scene to scene, our early expectations of nabbing yet another diddler dissolve. The signals of larceny are only partially transmitted. Here, Melville triggers the reader's opposing instinct for geniality. Having trained us to be wary misanthropes, he now teases our native longing for philanthropy, creating a tension over the issue of when Goodman will somehow slip and reveal his duplicity. But solid evidence never arrives, and the dramatic suspense grows until the last dim, anticlimactic scene. Our failure to identify Goodman conclusively as a confidence man forces us to reconsider our demonic expectations in light of our newly exercised geniality or, in a more radical mental leap, to doubt the efficacy of Melville's early signals and the validity of such correspondences in general.

Nine patterns of behavior (both ritualized and aesthetic) recur throughout the first half of the novel and condition the reader's responses to the second half. Three of these patterns bear directly upon the characteristics of the con men. To begin with the most obvious, a confidence man reveals his identity when he (1) initiates a *confidence game*. Such fishy propositions as the appeal to charity, the bogus stock deal, and the herbal panacea were as familiar to Melville's first readers as they are to us. Once a character plays a game, his guilt is confirmed, and by this yardstick Black Guinea, Ringman, the man in gray, Truman, the herb doctor, and the PIO man are all con artists. Equally suspicious, although less conclusive, is (2) a character's *shape-shifting* ability. Like any actor, a confidence man assumes many roles and is an excellent rhetorician who molds himself and his arguments to fit the needs of a particular audience.[25] A third pattern of behavior is that the six confidence men adopt (3) the benevolent mask of a *simpleton* (Black Guinea, PIO Man), *enthusiast* (man in gray, herb doctor), or *genialist* (Truman). Three more patterns hint that the confidence men are in cahoots. Melville links his characters to one another through (4) an elaborate network of *setups* in which one knave prepares a potential victim to be duped by another.[26] In the same vein, a confidence man will acknowledge the existence of other confidence men or (5) *confirm* their good will.[27] Furthermore, Melville uses (6) *physical resemblances* and *spatial linkages* to suggest a conspiracy.[28]

In addition to these six characteristics, we find three patterns in the narrator's treatment of the confidence men. A well-known pattern is (7) the *dual imagery* used in describing the sometimes angelic (mute, herb doctor) sometimes satanic (PIO man) confidence men. Moreover, Melville often introduces a new con man with a new chapter that begins with (8) *unidentified dialogue*. Chapter 19 is a case in point:

"Mexico? Molino del Rey? Resaca de la Palma?"
"Resaca de la *Tombs*."

Not until the middle of the chapter do we fully understand that the bitter response of the second unidentified speaker (soldier of fortune) to the first (herb doctor) refers to his crippling incarceration in New York City's prison and not to any heroic wound received during the Mexican War. Melville's use of unidentified dialogue generates a complex reading experience, which forces us to suspend judgment, read on, reread, and reevaluate.[29] Finally, when Melville does identify speakers, he often refers to them as either (9) *"the stranger"* or *"the other."* For the most part, this subtle stylistic pattern is reserved exclusively for the confidence men both early in the novel and late.[30] These nine features are part of the confidence man's talisman. But in the second half of the novel, the identifying emblem fails us; the allegory breaks down, and we must move from a confident, didactic, satiric mode into a comedy of doubt.

"Who in thunder are you?"

The speaker is Pitch, a skeptical Missourian, now moved to truculence by a series of confidence games. What has happened to him has happened before; it is a replay of a replay. Just as Roberts has been set up and stung by Black Guinea then Ringman then Truman, Pitch has endured the serial onslaught of the herb doctor and the PIO man. Now the reader anticipates the arrival of "Jeremy Diddler No. 3." Thus, it is with equal vehemence that the reader asks along with Pitch, "Who in thunder are you?" (*CM,* 132) when Frank Goodman enters the stage.

For Pitch, the issue is clear. Goodman is "another of them": a "metaphysical scamp" (136). And the reader, conditioned to recognize a confidence man's patterns of larceny, readily concurs. Goodman first appears as an unidentified speaker (pattern 8). Like those before him, his faceless rhetoric precedes any physical description. With "philanthropical pipe" in hand, he quickly assumes the role of a genialist (pattern 3), inveighs against too much "soberness," and invites Pitch "to tipple a little" (134). In this regard, Goodman bears a strong physical resemblance (pattern 6) to another genialist, the ruddy-faced confidence man Mr. Truman. Moreover, his geniality takes on a satanic flavor (pattern 7), for he loves man so much that he could eat the "racy creature" (133). Finally, like Melville's confidence men, Goodman is referred to as "stranger" and "the other" (pattern 9) five times throughout the scene (131, 136, 138).

On the other hand, Goodman does not appear on Black Guinea's list, nor is he "set up" (pattern 4) by any other earlier confidence man. He does not himself set up other potential victims, nor does he "confirm" (pattern 5) other confidence men. Thoroughly uncharacteristic of his predecessors are his *denial* of knowing another confidence man, the herb doctor (136), and his disparagement of the PIO man's ill-fitting coat (133). Goodman does not seem to be a part of any conspiracy of confidence men, nor does he attempt any confidence games. In fact, he is a miserable specimen of con artistry. He openly confesses himself an eavesdropper (133), admits to perpetrating a "little stratagem" (135) against Pitch, and revels openly in play-acting rather than insisting upon a certain sincere singularity of personality (133). Finally, Goodman, who eschews "Irony, and Satire" (136), is himself the victim of Pitch's ironic wordplay. When this cosmopolitan states his preference for Diogenes' sociable misanthropy over Timon's antisocial behavior, Pitch deliberately misconstrues the point, salutes Goodman as a fellow misanthrope, and exits triumphantly. Goodman plays the dupe; his presumed victim, the knave.

In all, Goodman's first scene leaves us confused. He follows some of the behavior patterns perfectly, some ambiguously, but many not at all. Our expectations thwarted, we warm to the possibility that Goodman is not a diddler but a true believer in man, seeking friendship amid a boatload of untrusting souls. Our instinct to expect the worst of Goodman—that he is the ringleader for the preceding confidence men, drumming up business for the following day, or that he is the One and Only confidence man, all others being himself in disguise—decreases. As Goodman progresses, Melville's novel acquires a new and forceful coherence. No longer a series of disjointed episodes, the comedy becomes unified by our search for the evidence that will prove or disprove Goodman's alleged infidelity. But at this juncture our thinking is so strongly set against Goodman that Melville's ambiguous signals introduce only a passing doubt. Goodman's next encounter enhances our admiration for the cosmopolitan.

The ten chapters of dialogue with Charlie Noble *should* reveal Goodman to be a confidence man. But in fact, we quickly perceive that Noble is our operator and the cosmopolitan his intended victim. Here, the comedy revolves around Noble's ineptitude and Goodman's ability to "con the con man."

Noble fits many of the most damning patterns of larceny. He attempts to "fuddle" Frank (174) by plying him with wine and cigars while refraining himself (pattern 1). He professes geniality (pattern 3), but, like his false teeth which are too perfect to be true, he harbors uncharitable moods. Having just eaten a "diabolic ragout" (169), he is associated with the Devil (pattern 7) and is as well a shapeshifter (pattern 2) comparable to "Cadmus glid[ing] into the snake" (180). But the most intriguing evidence against Noble is that he is referred to as "stranger" or "the other" more often than any other single character in the book (twenty-nine times), while the cosmopolitan, who has told Pitch that "no man is a stranger," is never in this scene called "stranger" and only twice called "the other" (142, 163).

In contrast, Goodman exhibits none of these questionable traits and grows from an apparent simpleton to a sage humorist fully capable of sparring with a sharp wit. Charlie Noble's opening gambit is to gain Goodman's esteem by inviting a vicious comparison between Pitch and the Indian hater, Moredock. In the following chapter we shall inspect the complex rhetoric of deceit that holds this famous section together, but for now it is enough to note that by reducing the surly Pitch to Moredock's level, Noble hopes to validate his false geniality and to grow in Goodman's esteem. But the cosmopolitan denies the existence of such depravity, calls Moredock a fiction, and warns Noble against "one-sided" views (175). Normally, such naïveté would only make Charlie's game easier, but Frank's good nature has its own self-validating "sting." As a "genial misanthrope," Goodman uses his benevolence to subsume a deeper awareness of iniquity. For him, humor is "so blessed a thing" that it can "neutralize" the "sting" of a "wicked thought" (163–64). By containing his own misanthropy (his awareness of Noble's duplicity) within a philanthropic heart, he can "play along" with Noble's scam. This balance allows Goodman his genial aspirations while guarding him against iniquity. By asking Noble for the very loan that Noble was intending to extract from Goodman, our cosmopolitan beats the confidence man at his own game, vanquishes his inept and false wit, and gives us a taste of "genial misanthropy."

How in thunder is the reader to take this frank, good man? His dramatic growth as a character necessarily subverts the criteria we have come to rely upon for discerning the confidence man. His "air of necromancy," instead of being sinister, is amusing in its outdistancing of the presumptuous Noble. He is a different order of operator, "a new kind of monster," a victim who fights back, with a new sense of confidence that succeeds where Roberts and Pitch before him have failed. And yet Goodman's ability to play Noble's game must give us pause. To what end does a genial misanthrope repress his misanthropy? Will he use his "wisdom" to guard against the likes of Noble, or is he capable of more offensive larcenies? If we invert his genial pipe, will we find a tomahawk? Such lingering doubts typify the reader's response to the second half of Melville's novel. When Goodman fails to conform in lock step to his predecessors, we must, like Sophia Hawthorne, "see" the character in new light, "refine" our expectations, and "create" a new understanding of his role. On to a fresh start, the reader warily anticipates who in thunder Goodman really is.

"Egbert, this is, like all of us, a stranger"

The speaker is Mark Winsome; Egbert, his disciple; and "this" is Goodman himself. Winsome hopes to warn the cosmopolitan that Noble is a "Mississippi operator" (196). And yet this mystic philosopher, a cross between "a Yankee peddler and a Tartar priest" (189), appears to be a satanic operator himself (pattern 7). He admits, for instance, to a curious desire to "change personalities" with a rattlesnake (190). He is a "metaphysical merman" (191) whose "tempting" discourse "bewitch[es]" Goodman (193). Just as Noble attempts to gain Goodman's confidence by disparaging his predecessor Pitch, he disparages Noble. It seems to be another replay in the works. And as with Noble, he (not Goodman) is referred to repeatedly (nineteen times) as "stranger" and "the other."

Winsome and Goodman are precise opposites. One is cool and transcendental, the other warmly genial; one a stranger, the other (to borrow the standard American definition of cosmopolite) "nowhere a stranger." Despite the evidence against Winsome, he is, in fact, too disinterested to be the confidence man he seems to be. Once establishing his doctrine of universal estrangement, he leaves all further discussion to Egbert, who reenacts with Goodman the scene in which Frank asks Charlie for a loan. Egbert will be Charlie, and Frank will play himself. It is the ultimate act of playing along, the ultimate replay. In the psychodrama that ensues, Frank-as-Frank resorts to numerous rhetorical ploys to get Egbert-as-Charlie to be friends. He creates a common heritage for the two—they are, he imagines, boyhood and college chums. He portrays himself as a business associate, a personal friend in need, and finally as a simple "fellow-being." In a sense, he addresses himself as all the victims who have preceded him on the *Fidèle*. But Egbert-as-Charlie will not budge from his cool insistence that a friend in need is no friend at all: "no man drops pennies into the hat of a friend. . . . If you turn beggar, . . . I turn stranger" (223). In this play within a play, Goodman as a humanist and dramatist takes many parts, each a projection of himself; he explores a full spectrum of human desire. Unlike Ahab, his histrionics deepen his humanity. Egbert is only a spokesman of another man's (Winsome's) one-sided principle. Goodman fails to win his point, drops his masks, and leaves enraged. Both defeat and rage are uncharacteristic of those confidence men we have already met. Indeed, it is the confidence man's victims who often stalk off in anger. Goodman, the victim of a harsh philosophy, has played his part for real. Egbert has only played a game (pattern 1).

This is Goodman's darkest hour. His humor and humanism have failed to dissolve stony distrust or enlighten blind orthodoxy. But out of these defeats, Goodman gains our sympathy. More of a knave-killer than a knave, he has not fulfilled the allegorical behavior that would label him a confidence man. In fact, he is the intended victim of various game players who bear more of a resemblance to earlier operators than he. Moreover, his simple-minded confidence has evolved into the more pragmatic notion of genial misanthropy. But, sadly, this sagacity is more effective as a safeguard against diddlers (Noble) than as a means for winning friends (Egbert). He is as ineffectual as the mute. But the novel is not over.

Thus far, in applying our understanding of con men to Goodman, we have moved from the reasonable suspicion that he is a con man to a willingness to accept the cosmopolitan as another Roberts or Pitch. But at the eleventh hour, when Goodman greets the barber, Melville turns the tables. Suddenly the larcenous signals flood in upon us. Chapter 43 begins with an unidentified speaker (later revealed to be Goodman) whose form might represent either an angel or the devil. By shifting point of view, Melville now refers to Goodman as "the stranger" and "the other" (225, 226, 229). Once the good-natured humorist, he is now a false wit, quibbling (in the manner of the PIO man or Noble) that a man's wig is not a sign of falsity, for it is genuinely "his" hair (in that he has purchased it) as if hair were a possession rather than a part of one's self. But most damning is that he finally plays a confidence game. Goodman persuades the barber to remove his "No Trust" sign by assuring him that if he is cheated, Goodman will compensate him against "a certain loss." Papers are signed; the sign comes down, and Goodman promptly refuses to pay for his shave. Amusingly, the insurer causes the client's claim.

In "shaving" the barber, the cosmopolitan reveals a duplicity we have come to deny. But the reversal does not prove Goodman is a diddler. Goodman has not, in fact, broken his contract. Paradoxically, his request for credit is the necessary act that validates the contract; it will convert promise into fact, if and when Goodman pays. It forces the barber to exercise the necessary emotion of confidence. Thus, an irresolvable comic question remains: Will Goodman make good on the "certain loss" he has perpetrated? Will he pay the debt and simultaneously redeem the loss? The barber knows; he replaces his sign. The reader—amused by the barber's absurd business predicament (which exposes how confidence is essential in the running of a market) and bemused by the larger moral dilemma it induces—continues to reserve judgment. Thus, all of Melville's episodes—the early introduction to the confidence man's varied patterns of behavior and the later inspection of the cosmopolitan in light of that pathology—lead the reader to the delicious anticlimax in which "True knowledge" of Goodman's identity should, with certainty, be revealed, but is not. It is a palpable experience of doubt.

Goodman rushes below decks to the gentlemen's cabin, where passengers sleep fitfully beneath a dying, smoky lamp. Here, the tension between allegorical satire and mimetic humor reaches a moment of febrile repose. "Dispens[ing] a sort of morning" in this dark "place full of strangers," the ebullient cosmopolitan now harbors "a disturbing doubt" (241, 240, 242). Melville has created a dramatic embodiment of his most striking image of picturesque ethics in *"Mosses,"* in which he likens Hawthorne's mirth to the "ever-moving dawn" that penetrates darkness and circumnavigates the globe. In both picturesque image and dramatic scene, humor draws its validity from the potentially degenerative philosophical doubt that it contains. Here are the particulars of the scene. Previously, the barber had quoted a scripture that condoned distrust and challenged Goodman's argument for confidence. Goodman has entered the gentlemen's cabin in search of a Bible so that he may check the barber's line. An old man points out that the scripture is from the Apocrypha and therefore lacks wisdom. The argument is specious, but Goodman is convinced, although he renounces wisdom altogether: "What an ugly thing wisdom must be! Give me the folly that dimples the cheek, say I, rather than the wisdom that curdles the blood" (243).

At this point, readers are left to endure a final round of "disturbing doubts" about the cosmopolitan's character. Why should a minor scriptural citation bother Goodman? If he is a confidence man, he should have no problem arguing around the quotation. If he is a genuine seeker of confidence, his sudden doubt would seem to belie his earlier expressions of bedrock faith. His equally precipitous relief over the line's apocryphal source is naïve, for the damaging wisdom would be no less wise because of its unauthorized source. In fact, the cosmopolitan has typically argued from "experience," not "authority." In all respects, Goodman seems out of character. The reader is left with yet another "triangular" conclusion: (1) Goodman's worry is an act, more histrionics to lure more victims; and yet (2) with no victims in sight at this late hour, these histrionics seem genuine; his own faith, having withstood the "curdling" onslaughts of Pitch, Noble, Winsome, and Egbert, has finally, sadly, begun to erode; and yet (3) his quick recovery suggests he may be a pious, "dimpled" booby, too easily reassured of his view of the world. Is Goodman a knave, a fool, or "quite an original"? The answer is past knowing.

But Goodman's apparent rejection of "ugly" wisdom takes on deeper meaning. His words resonate with the mediating language of the man with a weed: "There is sorrow in the world, but goodness too; and goodness that is not greenness, either, no more than sorrow is" (24). In *Moby-Dick,* Ishmael uses the same cadences to perform a similar triangulation: "There is a wisdom that is woe; but there is a woe that is madness" (*MD*, 425). And here Melville replays these chords but in a comic key. Goodness and sorrow can be tempered without greenness or madness. Thus, to survive in "a place full of strangers," one must combine folly and wisdom in such a way as to steer clear of what is too naïve (greenness) and what is too wise (disintegrative madness). It is the mediating moral stance of the genial misanthrope, the prophetic "new monster" that we shall inspect in the following chapter.

Our "disturbing doubt" about Goodman's motive is never resolved. When the old man asks the way to his stateroom, the cosmopolitan offers assistance: "I have indifferent eyes, and will show you" (*CM*, 251). Are these the eyes of a balanced sensibility that can penetrate darkness and genuinely lead the vulnerable masses, or are they the optics of a knave who spares no victim? Melville clearly intends to sustain the dramatic tension of this problem as long as possible, but we can discern, through Melville's reading of Plato, a tendency to favor the former position. The final cabin scene in *The Confidence-Man* can be read as a New World version of the allegory of the cave in *The Republic*. When the philosopher-king in that myth returns, as he must, from his above-ground vision of truth back to the dark, smoky, and fire-lit cave, he is at first blinded by the illumination he has just experienced. His eyes must adjust to darkness; but since he stumbles about in his temporary confusion, he is taken by the cave-dwellers to be a madman and a fool. Eventually, to use Plato's words, the returning philosopher must "accustom himself to behold obscure objects";[31] he must learn to see in darkness; he must acquire "indifferent eyes." Goodman is the cryptic philosopher-king, and the *Fidèle*, his cave. Melville's detached dramatization of Goodman's pragmatic Platonism forces readers to educate themselves about his growth. If we see him as a knave, we rattle the metaphysical chains that tie us to the cave. But if we reckon through all the patterns of behavior, fulfilled or unfulfilled, that he is an "original genius" then we may find ourselves capable of illumination, even as we begin to stumble in darkness.

What "may follow of this Masquerade" is not as important as what has happened to the reader. We have experienced the breakdown of an allegory and of allegorical ways of thinking. We have witnessed the disintegration of an empirical process, but the breakdowns have proven instructive. We have found patterns of iniquity keyed to a larger pattern of allegory, which we assume will be sustained throughout the novel; we have been forced to revise our assumptions when Goodman fails to conform to those allegorical requisites. But having once revised, we have learned that our original suspicions may be correct. Recognizing that the fictive process has been a con game, we are urged to play along, to turn this stiff comedy of thought and satire on American gullibility into a more fluid comedy of action revolving around our discovery of Goodman's identity and of our own condition as readers. In the final analysis Melville's initially victimized reader becomes once again a new kind of partner in creation. No longer just the seeing and refining reader discovered in the Hawthornes, we are participants in a drama of doubt. Inevitably, Melville's willful creation and deconstruction of norms pushes us beyond authority and certitude into a Mardian world of perpetual questioning. As Melville puts it in chapter 14, fiction is like a "true delineation" of old Boston; it should show us the "twistings of the town." Similarly, fiction succeeds only in the degree that it makes the reader twist. We play these twistings "to the life" (181). By removing himself from the narrative, by silencing the Ishmaelian voice and thus making our own doubt the central action of the novel, Melville has his participant readers taste the full ripeness of "manhood's pondering repose of If."

13

Comic Debates: The Uses
of Cosmopolite

The Confidence-Man begins with a dynamic vision of the West. Like Broadway, its opening image of the Mississippi is the cosmopolitan stage for all makes of man, foreign and domestic:

> men of business and men of pleasure; parlor men and backwoodsmen; farm-hunters and fame-hunters; heiress-hunters, gold-hunters, buffalo-hunters, bee-hunters, happiness-hunters, truth-hunters, and still keener hunters after all these hunters. Fine ladies in slippers, and moccasined squaws; Northern speculators and Eastern philosophers; English, Irish, German, Scotch, Danes; Santa Fé traders in striped blankets, and Broadway bucks in cravats of cloth of gold; fine-looking Kentucky boatmen, and Japanese-looking Mississippi cotton-planters. [*CM*, 9]

And the list goes on, pairing such opposites as Quakers and soldiers, Mormons and Papists, jesters and mourners. The West is an "all-fusing spirit" that contains "in one confident and cosmopolitan tide . . . that multiform pilgrim species, man."

Melville borrowed this opener from T. B. Thorpe's "The Big Bear of Arkansas." So well known was this tall tale that Melville's readers could not miss echoes of Thorpe's own cosmopolitan passenger list: "the wealthy Southern planter, and the pedlar of tin-ware from New England—bishop, and a desperate gambler—the land speculator, and the honest farmer—professional men of all creeds and characters— Wolvereens, Suckers, Hoosiers, Buckeyes, and Corn-crackers, beside a 'plentiful sprinkling' of the half-horse and half-alligator species of men."[1] Some of Melville's phrases—men of pleasure, men of business, backwoodsman, speculator, cotton-planter—are close enough to be plagiarisms of Thorpe, but his repetition of the "-hunter" suffix manifests an aesthetics of fusion not found in the rhetoric of "Big Bear."

More important, Melville drew upon Thorpe's tall-tale strategies. But unlike *Moby-Dick*, which co-opts the fantasy, theatrics, and framing of the genre, *The Confidence-Man* develops in abstract the ethical dimensions of geniality and misanthropy left dormant in the traditional tall tale. Melville's frontier, with its threatening social vacuum and yet potential for human fusion, is personified in Frank Goodman, whose cosmopolitanism is equally ambivalent. Here is the troubled satiric thrust of Teufelsdrockh, Bibundtucker, and Poe rolled together with the geniality of Irving, Hawthorne, and Thorpe. As we have seen, Goodman is essentially an idea trying to become a character. He is a Jamesean "ironic center" around which a groping, lonely, democratic crowd (like Thorpe's silenced throng) seeks an accommodation of doubt and faith. Understanding his cosmopolitan fusion of opposing humors allows us to see how this allegorical citizen of the world and con man grows into a psychologically complex citizen of America. Goodman is the novel's moral center because his comic cosmopolitan versatility induces us to "play along" within the perpetual suspension of ontological and ethical doubt incumbent upon the democracy.

Goodman's complex identity is as central to *The Confidence-Man* as Ishmael's to *Moby-Dick*. The crucial difference, of course, is that Melville chooses to have readers experience Goodman not as a first-person narrator, but as a dimly perceived player whose motives, as we have seen, are sedulously concealed. Melville does not in this book tell us what a true cosmopolitan sensibility is, nor does he provide us with a direct champion of that cause; rather, he encourages us to feel the conflicting passions of cosmopolitanism as we attempt to make out just exactly who or what Goodman is. In doing so, Melville subjects us to a new kind of fiction that places readers more deeply in the drama of playing out moral dilemmas. As Melville himself becomes less a presence as an author, the reader in the absence of Melville's authorial guidances and amid the resultant confusion achieves that tense form of repose in which certainty and doubt hold equal sway. Still, this new participant role requires readers to commit themselves to a genuine research into Goodman's identity. Early critics seeking to allegorize Goodman as a kind of ironic, shape-shifting Devil oversimplify and effectively remove Goodman from the realm of recognizable (and imitable) human beings. But Goodman is as much a person—indeed the novel's moral center—as he is an idea. And he is as much Melville himself as he is any allegorical or historical figure. To see into Goodman's cosmopolitan identity, we need to look more closely at a set of encounters that occupies the central section of the novel. In these chapters, Melville builds sympathy for Goodman by establishing credence for his new type of man, "the genial misanthrope." He does so almost methodically by exposing the inadequacy of first Pitch's false misanthropy and then Noble's false geniality. Only through the short but central fable of Charlemont does Goodman project a potential synthesis of these constituent values that can fulfill the cosmopolitan vision that Tommo denies and Ishmael so ardently pursues.

Pitch: The False Misanthropist

By the time Goodman appears, Pitch has been accosted unsuccessfully by the Herb Doctor and by the Philosophical Intelligence Officer, who has persuaded Pitch to hire, sight unseen, yet another young farmhand, even though his past experience with such boys has been abysmal. Pitch has been conned despite his professed distrust in man. As his dark and sticky name implies, he is a frontier counterpart of various men in black who have preceded him in the culture. Pitch is that brand of "humourist" Goodman calls a "surly philanthropist," for he "hide[s] under a surly air a philanthropic heart" (*CM*, 176). Like Drybone, he loves mankind not in the aggregate but individually and therefore assumes a gruff misanthropic demeanor to ward off those who would play upon his inherent good nature. Pitch is not a misanthrope at heart but adopts the pose out of a misguided sense of self-preservation. In fact, his outward misanthropy, like an unmended wall, provides little protection; it only deludes Pitch into a false sense of security that makes him all the more vulnerable.

Goodman's assessment of Pitch confirms our own earlier judgment of the Missourian, and a rare shift in the novel's narrative point of view makes the confirmation certain. To explain, we must backtrack. Throughout the novel, Melville depends upon dramatized dialogue for characterization; the soliloquizing of *Moby-Dick* is a rarity. We hear the outer expressions but rarely the inner workings of a character's mind. This severe detachment contributes largely to the reader's inability to determine with certainty who believes what. Melville knew that the narratorial alternative of exploring with omniscient scope and Jamesean precision the inner worlds of con men would also mean exposing their motives. As a consequence, readers would readily distinguish knave and dupe, and too easily presume a moral superiority of one over the other. Worse, they would fail to see the necessary similarity of the two. The effect would be to demonize the confidence men and reduce to a flat consistency the psychological inconsistencies of both knaves and dupes. The novel's impact on readers therefore depends upon the narrator's radical detachment. But with Pitch, Melville temporarily drops his practice of narratorial detachment and places us directly inside Pitch's mind, allowing us to penetrate to the root cause of his error. Because Melville lets us inside Pitch, we rightly assume that for once in this swampy novel we witness an unqualified truth concerning a particular character. And later, when Goodman reiterates the same judgment, we conclude that not only does the cosmopolitan substantiate Melville's inside view of Pitch, but he reveals Melville's guarded intent.

Leaning over the ship's rail to examine himself in the miasmal waters, Pitch ponders how the PIO man "left [him] in the lurch a ninny." What follows is the rare moment of dramatized introspection:

> But where was slipped in the entering wedge? Philosophy, knowledge, experience—were those trusty knights of the castle recreant? No, but unbeknown to them, the enemy stole on the castle's south side, its genial one, where Suspicion, the warder, parleyed. In fine, his too indulgent, too artless and companionable nature betrayed him. Admonished by which, he thinks he must be a little splenetic in his intercourse henceforth.   [130]

Pitch's response is logical but unwise. With the PIO man he has swung too far into benevolism; now he will compensate by feigning to vent his spleen. The reactive pose will not undo the diddle or cure his artlessness, nor will it prevent Pitch from becoming a dupe again. He would be better off as a genuine misanthropist, savoring his isolation and railing without exception against humanity. Instead, as a false misanthropist, he dons a mask of hatred and deludes himself into thinking his appearance of self-possession is real repose.

Later we shall inspect Goodman's confirmation of this victim's psychology. For now, let's look at the strategy that snared poor Pitch. Pitch suspects that the PIO man has conned him through the transcendentalist's "doctrine of analogies." The

PIO man has argued, to no one's real satisfaction except Pitch's, that just as the caterpillar "resurrects" into a butterfly, so too will naughty boys metamorphose into virtuous men. If surly youths like Augustine and Loyola could become adulthood saints, then by analogy we should not squash caterpillarian boys until the full flight and color of their manly Being is revealed. Pitch realizes that seeing his favorite philosophers used to flesh out this dubious analogy was the first factor to weaken his castle-like defenses against hiring boys. Such analogizing is "Fallacious enough doctrine when wielded against one's prejudices, but in corroboration of cherished suspicions[, it is] not without likelihood." Pitch recognizes faulty thinking but cannot resist analogizing himself. To him, the PIO man with his sly speech and sloping heels is "the flunky beast that windeth his way on his belly" (130). Of course, the operator is no more a snake or devil than men are butterflies, but just as Pitch will attempt to undo his error of benevolence with an error of the spleen, he will "stick" to the kind of chop logic he calls "punning with ideas" (124) that he formerly derides in the PIO man.

Pitch understands the punning nature of analogies, but he cannot resist the lure of transcendentalism. Instead of letting this philanthropic side loose in Shaftesbury's "free market" of wit, he tries to hide his softness for analogy within a castle keep and deny its existence. And when an artful punster like the PIO man breaks through, Pitch's philanthropic side is ill-equipped to withstand what Pitch otherwise knows is false. Like the reader Poe hopes to snare, Pitch is duped because of an uncritical commitment to a transcendental mode of thinking.

While complex in his psychology, Pitch lacks the breadth of the cosmopolite. "Clothed" not in the flags of all nations but "in the skins of wild beasts" (126), he is a secluded regionalist. Although his fifteen years of bad luck with hired hands has acquainted him with the "flowers of all nations" (117)—American, Irish, English, German, African, Mulatto, and Chinese—he rejects them all as "rascals." For Pitch, this diversity demonstrates one unifiying principle of deceit. Just as he is enamored of transcendental analogies, he scorns cosmopolitan ideals. Goodman's flamboyant dress and "boisterous hilarity" (183) represent precisely the antidote for Pitch's false misanthropy.

Pitch uncharitably supposes that this genial "stranger," who with legs crossed and pipe in hand is a picture of "indifference" and repose, is "the intelligent ape" of popular theater. The seraphic Goodman (130) ignores the offense, and proclaims himself instead:

> A cosmopolitan, a catholic man; who, being such, ties himself to no narrow tailor or teacher, but federates, in heart as in costume, something of the various gallantries of men under various suns. Oh, one roams not over the gallant globe in vain. Bred by it, is a fraternal and fusing feeling. No man is a stranger. You accost anybody. Warm and confiding, you wait not for measured advances. And though, indeed, mine, in this instance, have met with no very hilarious encouragement, yet the principle of a true citizen of the world is still to return good for ill—My dear fellow, tell me how I can serve you.   [132–33]

Pitch has reason to be suspicious, for Goodman's defining speech bristles with the encoded ambivalences inherent in the cosmopolitan ideal. His Goldsmithian good-nature disavows man as a true stranger; it breeds "a fraternal and fusing feeling" that further links him to Carlyle, Richter, and the Mountain Monologist of *Graham's Magazine*. But the sincerity of this "mature man of the world" comes immediately into question.

Given the con men who precede Goodman, we tend to read Goodman ironically. Like the cosmopolites Vincent Nolte and Lorenzo Dow, he will not serve man but serve him up. But as we have found, Goodman does not fit Melville's own behavior codes for the con man syndrome. Thus, the problem of Goodman's motives seems irresolvable. Although Melville's authorial detachment actually encourages an ironic reading, his refusal to provide any definitive moral valuation of Goodman also frees us to take the cosmopolitan at his word. Given the tendency to regard cosmopolites as a pragmatic mixture of the idealist and the con man, we are just as inclined to entertain Goodman's sincerity as his duplicity. An unstable irony always flips both ways. What finally prompts us to read Goodman *straight* is that he knows Pitch's mind as well as Melville would have us know it, and he gives Pitch advice that would prevent him from continuing to be a victim. Goodman's proposal "to serve" Pitch is useful and reliable.

Let's return to that rare glimpse inside Pitch's mind. The brief moment is unsullied by any ambiguity. Pitch is, to play with Goldsmith's term, a "machine" of scorn. He responds to the world, as Melville quietly interjects, in a "perverse way" (136) with a shield of misanthropy. Goodman attacks Pitch's perversity by showing him the "inconsistencies" of affecting "disesteem for man" (133). He counters Pitch's monomania with balanced oppositions: While "revelry may lead to inebriation," he argues, "soberness, in too deep potations, may become a sort of sottishness." And when Pitch holds to his own "too-sober view" because he "rate[s] truth . . . above untruth" (134), Goodman counters again by comparing such austere champions of "truth" to old boots left forgotten above the pie man's oven to "curl and warp." "This notion of being lone and lofty," he concludes, "is a sad mistake." Pitch does not take kindly to the metaphor, and, in response to Goodman's sociable invitation, he retaliates with a sarcastic tirade on loners: They are "worldlings, gluttons, and coquettes."

In conflict are not simply "Philanthropist and Misanthropist" but the rhetorical modes that constitute the comic debate. The satirist Pitch rails and defames. The humorist Goodman concludes that "irony is so unjust . . . something Satanic about irony. God defend me from Irony, and Satire, his bosom friend." As for the worldlings, gluttons, and coquettes, their "foibles," Goodman allows, do not commit the "awful sin of shunning society." In terms of his cosmopolitan ideal, Goodman embraces the amiable humorist's party platform. Acknowledging human venality, he does not commit Hawthorne's unpardonable sin of rejecting, as does Pitch, all humanity.

Of course, Goodman also behaves like a confidence man. His arguments for Pitch's joining society are quite possibly an overture to a confidence game. His offhand suggestion that Pitch surrender his watch recalls the gambit of William Thompson, New York's original confidence man of 1849. His disavowal of irony is precisely what a "Satanic" ironist would do to establish credibility. Indeed, as the ever watchful Pitch puts it, an open, naïve, anti-ironic pose is "a right knave's prayer, and a right fool's, too'' (136). But despite a tendency to agree that Goodman is out to con Pitch, we must also allow that in insisting upon the need for Pitch to socialize, Goodman is not so much knave or fool as a realist. He openly admits, for instance, ''that, in being social, each man has his end.'' Such ulterior motives would never occur to a fool, nor would a knave be so reckless as to admit to them to a potential victim like Pitch. Goodman's admission of the self-serving nature of social interaction suggests a wisdom beyond any con game gambit, and he concludes that Pitch must serve himself by making his ''end'' be ''a more genial philosophy.'' For Goodman, geniality is neither Christian pap nor a prelude to treachery; it is, as various Romantic humorists insist, a matter of social utility.

In his final words to Pitch, Goodman sizes up the false misanthrope's problems as though he has read Pitch's mind as clearly as Melville has read Pitch in chapter 23. The discussion turns to Diogenes. Giving up on converting Pitch from his charade of Timonism to geniality, the cosmopolitan proposes, for argument's sake, to view Diogenes as occupying a moral middle ground: He is a ''merry-Andrew, in the flower market'' but a skeptic all the same. In doing so, Goodman adheres to traditional cosmopolitan principles, for he recognizes the world's first ''cosmopolite'' as the kind of sociable cynic who, if not entirely admirable, is a step toward a more balanced sensibility. But Pitch sees all cynics—Timon, Diogenes, himself, and now (he presumes) Goodman—as one: ''a brace of misanthropes.'' With mock cordiality, he greets Goodman as a ''Diogenes masquerading as a cosmopolitan,'' a closet misanthrope, if you will. Pitch's splenetic vision is blind to Goodman's subtle distinctions. In response, Goodman regrets his attempt to offer Pitch an alternative to his false misanthropy. By ''conceding too much''—that is, by admitting a passing fondness for Diogenes' cynicism—he has been ''taken [by Pitch] to belong to a side which he but labors . . . to convert'' (138). With cosmopolitan versatility, he has modified his rhetoric to suit Pitch's needs, but only to find that Pitch has willfully misconstrued him. Pitch's misinterpretation is a minor league sarcasm and shallow victory. He feels he has bested a confidence man, but Goodman, striking to the heart of the matter, insists that Pitch has only conned himself: ''See how distrust has duped you.''

Here is the cosmopolitan's confirmation of Melville's diagnosis: Pitch is the victim of a jury-rigged misanthropy that he has constructed despite his good nature in the false hope that it will forestall the confidence games he inevitably blunders into anyway. Because Goodman's point in chapter 24 so clearly coincides with the analysis Melville has allowed us to glimpse in chapter 23, we come to see Goodman as Melville's moral agent. He knows what Melville knows, and thus within Melville's cagy rhetorical framework he earns our confidence.

This hint of Melville's hoaxing allows us to play along more fully with his characterization of Goodman. As a ''metaphysical scamp'' (i.e., confidence man *and* amiable humorist), Goodman does not abuse Pitch but cons him (as Coffin does Ishmael) into a more flexible sensibility, one that better prepares him for life than ''the solitude he [continues to hold] so sapient'' (138). As with Poe, Melville's rhetorical strategy tempts readers to build false conclusions out of false assumptions and false logic. If we take the ''sapient'' route in assuming that Goodman is a confidence man solely, then we give credence to Pitch's splenetic overreactions and validate his specious misanthropy. If, however, we take Goodman too sincerely, we risk accepting his benevolism uncritically. Thus readers find themselves torn between being duped by their faith or by their distrust, when quite naturally they would rather not be duped at all. If, however, we play along with Melville's hoaxing, we find in Goodman's indeterminacy the very model of survival for our own immersion in doubt.

Charlie Noble: The False Genialist

If "life is a pic-nic *en costume*," then "one must take a part, assume a character, stand ready in a sensible way to play the fool" (133). Pitch cannot comprehend this cosmopolitan advice; he is so afraid of being made a fool that he freezes his character into a caricature of "sapience." He forsakes sensibility to become a backwoods cynic and thereby becomes a fool all the same and all the more foolish for his professing to be wise. Goodman, however, fuses variant perspectives. As a "metaphysical scamp," he investigates the most foolish beliefs to extract from them redemptive values. Beneath the shallow optimism is an aggressive humanism designed to con us into a more reliable geniality. Like the chameleon Voltaire, Goodman dons a coat of many colors to address the many-colored defects of his fellow players. He is a *sensible* fool who intuits what others lack and mimicks the values they need. If Pitch is "surly," Goodman will be "boistrous." And if Charles Noble, Goodman's next interlocutor, is excessively genial, he will be "restrained."

Goodman's mimickery may be taken as mockery. That is, his self-conscious role-playing appears to be a performance designed to satirize. Thus, Goodman's good-humored rhetoric threatens to expose itself as the author's submerged caricature of Man the Fool. Accordingly, Melville's problem in maintaining Goodman's rhetorical credibility is to inculcate in readers an appreciation of the suppleness, not the rigidity, of Goodman's mind, to have readers experience the tense repose of his perpetual questioning that necessarily swings from one certainty to its opposite, to have them live the passion of his doubt. In thus playing upon the "marge" between humor and satire, Melville keeps us wondering if Goodman is there to console or to attack. Nowhere in Melville's fiction is this conflict in the comic debate rehearsed as in the Goodman's encounter with Noble.

As the episode unfolds, we quickly recognize a staging of the "con man conned" scenario. Noble's scheme is to bilk Goodman, and while his tactics shift to meet Goodman's dodges, his strategy remains the same: to impress upon Goodman that his own geniality is as sincere as the cosmopolitan's. But every step of the way Goodman's "velvet paw" reveals a hidden "fang" that pierces Noble's false notions of good humor. Noble's opening gambit is to gain Goodman's confidence by denigrating the misanthropic Pitch. The schoolyard logic is as follows: If Pitch has rejected Goodman, and if Noble rejects Pitch, then Goodman must accept Noble. This dichotomous thinking is doomed to fail, because Goodman sympathizes with Pitch's misguided dependence on sham misanthropy.

Although the cosmopolitan is not the easy "mark" Noble thinks he is, Goodman does all he can to appear to be the dupe Noble wants. Accordingly, he makes his benevolism border on the absurd. Goodman professes never to have heard of Indian hating, nor can he conceive of a reason that others might hate the Indian; he denies the possibility of the looting that followed Lisbon's famous earthquake; he believes the press to be objective; he cannot conceive of a virtuous man in debt. Critics generally read these astonishing quixotisms as Melville's burlesque of optimism. But, in fact, their most immediate function is to encourage Noble in his attempts to con Goodman by having Goodman make himself out to be a temptingly jejune booby. This act for Noble's sake is made all the more obvious by the fact that Melville has Goodman drop this mask as soon as it is of no rhetorical use to him. At the same time, and despite the shallowness of Goodman's professed benevolism, readers are drawn to Goodman's good humor, especially in light of the false wit Noble evinces in his responses to Goodman.

But Goodman's role is not only to beat Noble at his own game but to reveal through Socratic ironies the weaknesses of his views and to educate readers in need of a more complex vision of misanthropy and repose. Two con games operate at once: Goodman's staged undoing of Noble and Melville's undoing of the reader. This two-pronged offensive is most evident in the novel's much-debated section on Colonel Moredock and Indian hating.

Killing Indians

Like the tall tale and literary hoax, the Moredock story (chs. 27–28) is the staged performance of a liar duping a victim as well as the author's challenge to the reader to seize his knowledge and "catch me if you can." Complicating this structure are two problems: The intended victim (Goodman) turns out to be the better liar, and Melville has concealed himself so deeply within Goodman that more than the usual digging is required to find the hidden message at the center of his hoax. In this regard, we must return to the original source of the Moredock tale, Judge James Hall, whom Melville alludes to repeatedly in the text, as if to invite our investigation and comparisons.

In the first prong of Melville's hoax, Noble attempts unsuccessfully to draw an invidious connection between Pitch and Colonel Moredock. Noble begins by relating his own childhood encounter with Moredock; he then adopts Judge Hall's voice to give us the judge's philosophy of Indian-hating, to which is appended Moredock's life as exemplum. Having recounted instances of Indian treachery, Noble continues in Hall's voice to envision the white man's revenge in the form of the Indian-hater *par excellence,* a "Leatherstocking-Nemesis" committed to "a calm, cloistered scheme of strategical, implacable, and lonesome vengeance" (149–50). This occasions a bit of cagey Platonizing. The Indian-hater *par excellence* is an Ideal Form that we only assume exists. Since such a pure Indian-hater avoids all human contact, we have no direct biographical evidence of his existence. Since his Being cannot be confirmed, we must be satisfied with the study of "diluted" Indian-haters, those who like Colonel John Moredock actually return to normal society from time to time. Moredock, we learn, had lost his family to an Indian attack and has set out systematically to ambush the attackers methodically and without mercy. But his lust for revenge was not sated, and at times he would go into the woods and murder however many Indians he might find. He remained, according to Noble/Hall, a respected man of society: a misanthrope toward red men, a genialist among white. Thus Moredock's monomania is "diluted" with benevolence. Noble concludes by dissociating himself from Hall's unsavory "story, mind, or . . . thoughts" (155) and by identifying Pitch as a "comprehensive Colonel Moredock."

Despite his professed distaste for Hall and Moredock, Noble cannot conceal his actual affection. His tone belies his lie work. We recall that the day the young Noble met Moredock "is marked with a white stone" (141). Like any boy, he was drawn to outlaws, legends, and Cooperesque woodsmen, but presumably the adult Noble would have grown beyond this immature hero-worship. His description of the personal encounter, however, betrays a continued fascination. Traveling with his father, the young Noble had come upon an inn where Moredock was sleeping off a long night's slaughter. The boy cannot resist climbing the corn loft and taking a peek; here is what he sees:

> I saw what I took to be the wolf-skins, and on them a bundle of something like a drift of leaves; and at one end, what seemed a moss-ball; and over it, deer-antlers branched; and close by, a small squirrel sprang out from a maple-bowl of nuts, brushed the moss-ball with his tail, through a hole, and vanished, squeaking. That bit of woodland scene was all I saw. No Colonel Moredock there, unless that moss-ball was his curly head, seen in the back view. [141]

The language is adult, poetic, and mythic. As depicted, Moredock is not a human presence but, like the Indians he hates, a part of the woods. Indeed, he *is* the woods or, in Noble's boy-man vision, he partakes of the comprehensive spiritual ideal of Nature itself: wolf and squirrel, moss and nuts, leaves and antlers, the living and the dead. This initial apotheosis—it is our first view of Moredock—reveals Noble's affection (hence falsity) that may trap nature-worshiping readers into a respect for the charismatic Moredock.

As with Jim Doggett's heightened language, we must be careful not to let our instinctive benevolism discover a Nature Man who is not there. Young Noble only speculates that the moss-ball is Moredock's head. And it is our propensity for metaphor and transcendence, our passion for analogy, myth, and other puns, that predisposes us to create a human shape out of the indirections Noble provides. In point of fact, the moss is moss, and what might have happened is that an eager young boy has been tricked by an innkeeper to see if he can catch sight of a Dillinger upstairs. What is significant about Noble, of course, is that he prefers to believe that he *did* see Moredock. He sees because he wants to see, and the uncritical conveyance of that childhood desire only exposes his adult love for Moredock, even though the point of his narrative is to register his disdain. For the reader, the scene plays upon our Emersonian logic, which would place man at the heart of nature even when man is nowhere to be found. If we fall for the trap, we are no better than young Noble. But if we resist it, we are only set up for further ironies. And this leads us to the second prong in Melville's hoaxing.

No one, for instance, is likely to miss the irony of the self-contradictions unconsciously implied in Judge Hall's words on racism, which Noble borrows and in turn transmits, also unconsciously, to us. "It is terrible," Noble has the judge remark, "that one creature . . . should make it conscience to abhor an entire race. It is terrible; but is it surprising?" On the one hand, Noble's Hall deplores the white man's hatred, but on the other hand, with the pretense of a cool observer, he entertains, and thus validates, the *logic* of brutal revenge. Racism is wrong but clinically understandable. To demonstrate this logic, Hall allows that Indians have been "painted . . . in every evil light," and he proceeds to enumerate various Indian crimes. But in doing so, Hall methodically compares the Indian to *white* villains:

> now a horse-thief like those in Moyamensing; now an assassin like a New York rowdy; now a treaty-breaker like an Austrian; now a Palmer with poisoned arrows; now a judicial murderer and Jeffries, after a fierce farce of trial condemning his victim to bloody death. [146]

Melville has structured this crucial passage so that Hall seems utterly unaware that his analogies argue as much for the white man's ignominy as the Indian's; and in quoting Hall uncritically, Noble seems equally insensible of any ironic backfire. Readers cannot help but be drawn up short by the litany of criminal acts which argue that if the Indian is to be hated it is only because he shares the white man's capacity for theft, murder, and deceit. He is to be feared because he is like "us." In planting such obvious ironies, Melville is essentially testing his readers' ability to fashion a logic of their own separate from that of Noble and Hall.

Subtler ironies establish that Hall's discussion of Moredock effectively praises the very character it pretends to condemn. To make the point, we need to resurrect Melville's original sources. As Elizabeth Foster notes, Melville borrowed the basic structure and several passages directly from various texts, each written by James Hall. The principal source is *Sketches of History, Life and Manners in the West* (1835), which includes this sampling of the original Hall's unconscious acceptance of the murderous Indian hater. "The reader must not infer," he warns

> that Colonel Moredock was unsocial, ferocious, or by nature cruel. On the contrary, he was a man of warm feelings, and excellent disposition. At home he was like other men, conducting a large farm with industry and success, and gaining the good will of all his neighbours by his popular manners and benevolent deportment. He was cheerful, convivial, and hospitable; and no man in the territory was more generally known, or more universally respected.[2]

Adding a few more biographical details, Hall concludes without hint of irony that Moredock had been asked to run for the Illinois governorship "but refused to permit his name to be used."

There is a chilling failure of conscience in the original Hall's hurried insistence that we not condemn Moredock as "unsocial, ferocious, or by nature cruel." We are encouraged to see his Indian-hating as no detraction from this "man of feeling." Hall does not rationalize Moredock's practice by suggesting that it occurs *despite* his *otherwise* "benevolent deportment." Rather, by implying that Moredock is "by nature" good, he argues that Moredock's Indian-hating is only a minor blemish, a *jeu d'esprit,* or whim. In a sense, Moredock's geniality toward white men not only compensates for his bestiality toward Indians, it retroactively decriminalizes his acts. Hall's approach is equivalent to rationalizing away the Nazi past of a gentle neighbor or colleague, when the past should in fact argue for less gentility than we had previously assumed. In the original Judge Hall's view, Moredock is a good-natured man with one odd quirk.

The unexamined assumption beneath the original Hall's argument is that if the murder of an Indian does not invalidate Moredock's professed benevolence toward men, then Indians occupy a class of being below the white man; they are not human. It is no wonder that Hall unconsciously uses a vocabulary of love that betrays a secret affection. Moredock, he writes, never failed ''to embrace an opportunity to kill a savage.'' For the judge, the murder of a ''savage'' is an act of love, an ''embrace.'' Such is the inevitable failure of a doctrine of geniality spread to absurd extremes.

With Hall's original language before us, Melville's fictional transcription of that source is clearly an attack upon the good judge's racism. Drawing upon the passage quoted above, Melville has Noble render Hall almost word-for-word. ''It were to err to suppose,'' he begins, ''that this gentleman [Moredock] was naturally ferocious, or peculiarly possessed of [a tendency] to withdraw from social life.'' Noble also co-opts Hall's false geniality in his continued paraphrase of Hall: Moredock has ''a loving heart,'' ''humane feelings,'' and is ''very convivial'' and ''benevolent'' (*CM*, 154). But at this point Melville expands upon Hall to make explicit the inhumanity beneath Hall's false logic.

Where Hall merely records the fact of Moredock's refusal to run for governor, Melville ferrets out the reason:

> [Moredock] felt there would be an impropriety in the Governor of Illinois stealing out now and then, during a recess of the legislative bodies, for a few days' shooting at human beings, within the limits of his paternal chief-magistracy.   [*CM*, 155]

Melville's expansion clarifies the Judge's position. Rather than adopt Hall's term ''savage'' to refer to Indians, he has him elevate them to the status of ''human beings.'' But this happy improvement only belies Hall's false benevolence. What the original Hall hides, Melville's Hall acknowledges: that it is simply ''improper'' for a Governor to murder human beings (especially in the jurisdiction of one's own constabulary). It is a cool logic that parodies Hall's hidden absurdities. And Melville goes further with a final absurdity. Since Indian-hating forced Moredock to give up a promising political career, and since religion, too, has its sacrifices, then Indian-hating, Melville's Hall concludes, must be ''a devout sentiment'' (*CM*, 135). It is more of Charlie Noble's chop logic.

In the complex overlaying of voices (Melville reporting on Noble reporting on Hall), Melville's Poe-ish hoaxing invites us to adopt a mode of thinking that will lead us to an absurdity. Just as Noble hopes Goodman will ''fall'' for all this and acknowledge Pitch as a Moredock, so too does Melville try to make us fall for Hall. If we fail to detect Noble's admiration for the man he allegedly disdains, or fail to unpin the ironies Melville plants in Hall's mouth, then we are indeed victims of a rhetoric of deceit that would have us dismiss Pitch as a Moredockian racist despite the solid evidence of his worth. If, however, we detect those ironies that undermine Noble's and Hall's authority and reject their false geniality along with their false logic, we rise to Melville's challenge and ready ourselves to play along with the author's intellectual games in pursuit of a more effective form of geniality.

Of course, not all readers acknowledge the fundamental rhetorical conditions of the Moredock episode. Sharp analysts of the 1950s and 1960s argued strongly that since a distinct pattern of Devil imagery is applied to both Indians and con men, we must conclude that an Indian-hater is as much a con-man–hater. In such a reading, first proposed by William E. Sedgwick, then developed by John W. Shroeder, and then endorsed by Hershel Parker, Moredock becomes the novel's moral norm, for he alone stands as a resolute and undeterred destroyer of evil.[3] According to Parker's 1963 article "The Metaphysics of Indian-Hating," the irony in this "grotesquely satiric study" (MIH, 326) lies in that the novel's best Christian is a vengeful, monomaniacal murderer. Consolidating and affirming earlier readings, Parker also demonstrated Biblical precedence for the idea of "Christianity as a practice of Devil-hating" (327), thus lending credence to Melville's supposed inverted moral design.

But a reading that assigns normative value to Moredock is flawed, for in elevating a simple image pattern to the status of an allegorical structure we fail to account for the rhetoric of deceit which shapes that pattern.[4] Locating morality in Moredock is precisely the "self-contradicting" logic of racism that Noble's Judge Hall would have us entertain. It is a metaphysical man trap. Parker acknowledges in a 1971 revision of his article that his thesis does not account for certain structural problems, in particular that Moredock is part of a tale told by Noble. "No one would want to claim," Parker states in revision, "that Charlie is aware of the allegorical meaning of his story" (MIH, 330 n.1). But this corrective is not entirely to the point, for Noble is indeed an unconscious hypocrite fully capable of delivering a message— in Parker's reckoning, that message would be the Christian value of Moredock's hatred—without knowing what it means. As we have seen, Noble offers Moredock up as a reprehensible figure even though his childhood memories suggest a lingering affection for the man.

At issue is Noble's rhetorical ineptitude. Not only has he failed to perceive the corrosive ironies planted in Hall's narrative, ironies that clearly deny moral value to Moredock's monomaniacal hatred, but, more importantly, he has misdiagnosed Pitch as a Moredock and miscalculated Goodman's reaction to such a diagnosis. Because Goodman confirms Melville's more benevolent view of Pitch, we disavow Noble's and Hall's Moredock as a moral norm by which to judge Pitch. To insist upon the Indian-hater as a metaphysical hero is to make flesh and bones out of a straw man.

Melville, of course, tempts us to fall for Noble and Hall. His strategy is to make the reader experience both geniality and hatred fully. The Indian-hating chapters exhibit the same fascination with evil and wish-fulfillment of eradicating that evil as found in *Moby-Dick*. Moredock is a woodland Ahab, and as with any tragic figure, his *dramatic* centrality inevitably insists upon a notion of that character's *moral* centrality. What makes Moredock's candidacy for centrality logical though not acceptable is that the Indian-hater has, it seems, his genial side. Despite it all, that factor, which draws us to the heart of Melville's comic debate and the resolvent nature of cosmopolitanism, humanizes Moredock enough to make him a sociable isolato, more Ishmael than Ahab. That we might find Moredock appealing illuminates the rhetorical risk Melville was willing to take. By deepening our attachments to both sides of his debate, to misanthropy as well as to benevolence, he takes the chance of confusing readers for the sake of exposing them to the dilemmas of faith. He challenges us to reject a figure whom we are tempted to embrace but must finally deny.

And deny Moredock a moral centrality we must, for as with Noble and Hall his geniality is essentially a coverup for racism. His benevolence is as false as Pitch's misanthropy. To lionize Moredock exclusively is to freeze a perpetual polemic that must remain fluid if it is to be rendered psychologically realistic. The excitement of reading *The Confidence-Man* rests precisely on this intellectual engagement, for readers cannot seriously experience the passions of doubt unless they are made to reject an object they may secretly desire.

One of Melville's more insidious tactics in tempting us toward Moredock occurs when Hall directs our attention from the "Indian-hater *par excellence*" to Moredock's "diluted" variety, from the Ideal to the Actual. Although we have disqualified Hall as a reliable speaker, unreliable voices can lead us toward truths (as witness Plinlimmon in *Pierre* or Franklin in *Israel Potter*). Thus there are really two Judge Halls in this tale: the racist that Noble uncritically quotes and the historical biographer that Melville uses as a source. Departing from his original source, Melville has Hall discuss the problems of writing the biography of a pure isolato, one who never returns to society, for quite obviously (Melville observes with his characteristic fondness for metaphysical conundrums) one cannot truly know a person whom one can never meet. Direct knowledge must bow to legend, hearsay, and speculation. Putting words in Hall's mouth, Melville examines the biographer's dilemma:

> How evident that in strict speech there can be no biography of an Indian-hater *par excellence,* any more than one of a sword-fish, or other deep-sea denizen; or, which is still less imaginable, one of a dead man. The career of the Indian-hater *par excellence* has the impenetrability of the fate of a lost steamer. Doubtless, events, terrible ones, have happened, must have happened; but the powers that be in nature have taken order that they shall never become news.   [150]

Melville did not write a biography of a swordfish, but he wrote one of another "deep-sea denizen" and of the "dead man" Ahab who pursued it. That work was, for Ishmael, necessarily unfinished, and its exact meaning "shall never become news"; it can never be fully reported or known. Melville's notion of biography reflects upon his condition as a writer and of the impossibility of penetrating directly to the heart of human nature or universal Being.

Nevertheless, the biographer proceeds as best he can, speculating on the true nature of the ideal Indian-hater *par excellence* by observing intermediate forms. When, in *The Symposium,* Socrates asks Diotima how he might know the truth, his teacher responds that we know ideality only through emissaries or *daemons,* figures which like philosopher kings return blinded to the cave of our actual existence and speak cryptically of Reality. For Hall, Moredock is one such daemon, or rather a "diluted Indian-hater," one who has been into the wilderness, experienced its evil, and yet has returned to civilization with his sociability intact. Such "domestic adventurers," to use Judith Slater's apt term, mediate sunny society and dark woods.[5] They report to us "news" of unfathomed truths. The existence of the *daemon* Moredock is a positive boon for the biographer. "Luckily," Hall exclaims,

> "there is a species of diluted Indian-hater, one whose heart proves not so steely as his brain. Soft enticements of domestic life too often draw him from the ascetic trail; a monk who apostatizes to the world at times. Like a mariner, too, though much abroad, he may have a wife and family in some green harbor which he does not forget. It is with him as with the Papist converts in Senegal; fasting and mortification prove hard to bear." [*CM*, 150]

In this instance Melville associates the Indian-hater's return to society with the necessary condition of the writer. He is like Tommo who left a "wife and family" in the green Marquesas. He is an Ishmaelian "mariner" who ventures on deep seas but never forgets his "green harbor." His less steely heart, a weakness to the ideal pursuer of evil, is the artist's source of humor, which makes fiction possible. To do otherwise is to mortify one's art.

At this juncture, readers are bound to be confused. Previously, Melville's Hall was an unsettlingly unconscious racist. Now he is an admirable pragmatic Platonist and a self-portrait of Melville. Yet we cannot forget that the insights into biography are embedded within Charlie Noble's fallacious meanderings. Just how reliable is Hall's discussion of biography—a single text spoken with two voices? Interestingly, both voices harmonize on the single word "luckily." If read in the voice of the racist Hall, we are "lucky" to have such an emissary as Moredock to fulfill our secret wish to destroy. But in the contrapuntal voice of Melville speaking as metaphysician through Hall, we are "lucky" to have in Moredock a "daemon" through which lovers of wisdom can glimpse pure evil and somehow articulate and contain it. We are lucky, too, for the daemonic nature of language itself—lucky to have myth, metaphor, and words like "luckily," which allow a humorist to fuse the "steely" satiric reality of Moredock's hate within the domestic warmth of Hall's broader, although finally flawed, vision.

Goodman himself adopts Hall's mariner metaphor for the artist and thus lends deeper credence to the Melvillean self-portrait. For Hall, the diluted Indian-hater ships out into the wilderness but never forgets his "green harbor" home. Goodman similarly acknowledges: "I am at bottom almost in the condition of a sailor who, stepping ashore after a long voyage, ere night reels with loving welcomes, his head of less capacity than his heart" (158). "At bottom" Goodman possesses the tense repose of that picturesque moment in "The Enviable Isles" in which mind is situated "on the marge" between the sea's powerful hint of nihility and the land's alluringly insensate sleep. Through Melville's retroactive association of Goodman's "sailor" with Hall's "mariner," we entertain a validity in Moredock's half-wild, half-civil condition. If not the novel's moral center, Moredock appears in his "mariner" status to be an aesthetic template for the artist.

No certain reconciliation of Moredock as satirized racist and daemon artist is forthcoming, for neither Noble nor Hall is fully conscious of the double voice or aware that a reconciliation is needed. Hall allows racism and art to sleep side by side in his "green harbor" without any hint of conflict. Finally, it is Goodman's "sailor" metaphor that exposes the shallowness of Hall's geniality. His sailor-artist is a lover seeking the "reeling" passions of the night. Hall's mariner is a husband dozing before the fireplace, a "slumberer mere." Hall's geniality is too complacent to deal with the subtleties of mind and passion, to fuse the conflicting impulses of vengeance and love, destruction and creation, satire and humor. Thus his Moredock only *opens* the discussion of how to mediate misanthropy through a genial aesthetics of repose, better effected through the broad-minded love, the nighttime reeling, the liberal libertine vision of the cosmopolitan.

The Moredock episode only begins the Goodman-Noble encounter. It sustains the central problem of Pitch's false misanthropy while introducing Moredock's problematic geniality; it reveals Noble's tactical miscalculations and general ineptitude while preparing us for a tentative consideration of a synthesis in the genial misanthrope. And finally it provides a stage upon which Goodman can exercise his cosmopolitanism as both idealist and knave. The rest of the encounter, which climaxes with Goodman's table-turning on Noble, is an extended debate on the benefits and costs of humor.

False Wit, Good Humor

Goodman's Socratic mission is to educe from Noble a better way of thinking. He begins by playing the perfect fool, a benevolist who believes in newspapers and cannot conceive of hate. And yet he opens up for us, if not to the impercipient Noble, a deeper awareness. When asked, "What sort of sensation is misanthropy?" Goodman demurs: He cannot know because, like hydrophobia, it is a disease he never had or could survive to describe. But he launches into a paragraph of speculation that belies his ignorance:

> Can a misanthrope feel warm, I ask myself; take ease? be companionable with himself? Can a misanthrope smoke a cigar and muse? How fares he in solitude? Has the misanthrope such a thing as an appetite? Shall a peach refresh him? The effervescence of champagne, with what eye does he behold it? Is summer good to him? Of long winters how much can he sleep? What are his dreams? How feels he, and what does he, when suddenly awakened, alone, at dead of night, by fusilades of thunder?   [*CM*, 157–58]

Goodman may be America's first method actor. He asks the questions that will get him to the heart of a misanthrope. His questions act out the anxieties that clarify the misanthrope's rejection. In playing this part "to the life," Goodman fulfills his cosmopolitanism. But Noble, referred to repeatedly as "the stranger," misses the performance that proves Goodman's capacity to know hate: "Like you," he avers, "I can't understand the misanthrope." Noble fails to see that Goodman understands rather well, and from this point on he is Goodman's pawn.

Goodman tries to tease Noble out of his false geniality by testing the flexibility of his humor. It is his way of demonstrating the difference between good humor and false wit. Refusing, again with characteristic naïveté, to acknowledge the existence of vintners who would poison their wines, the cosmopolitan proposes a prototypical genial misanthrope who, "while convinced that on this continent most wines are shams, yet still drinks away at them." Sham wine is better than none despite the threat to good health, for "health without cheer [is] a bore" (162). To live genially, one must risk death.

Goodman extends this parable of the toper to a larger social context:

> "a man of a disposition ungovernably good-natured might still familiarly associate with men, though, at the same time, he believed the greater part of men false-hearted—accounting society so sweet a thing that even the spurious sort was better than none at all." [162]

Despite the threats that such a sham society might pose, "security without society [is] a bore; and society, even of the spurious sort, has its price, which I am willing to pay." The sham wine–sham society analogy encourages cosmopolitanism in that amiability can be preserved in the midst of "false-hearted men." Goodman will enjoy Noble's sham companionability but will not forget his motives. Just as Goodman's geniality humanizes his misanthropy, his misanthropic insight preserves his otherwise "ungovernably good-natured disposition." The cosmopolitan is a comic survivor, one made all the more valid by his cunning. He concludes: "And do you think I don't know" full well the threat of sham wine and sham society? He knows the risk of his cosmopolitanism.

While Melville infuses his narrative with the mode of thinking associated with genial misanthropy, Noble is oblivious to the indoctrination. He accepts Goodman's remark that his "spurious" man is just a fable, assuming that no fable can be "real." Readers who take to heart Melville's digression on fiction in chapter 33 will know that such a character is validated precisely *because* he is presented as a fable. Noble is satisfied with Goodman's misdirection that fables are joking words. As Goodman puts it, this business of sham wine and sham society is a "wicked thought, but conceived in humor" (164).

Noble has just enrolled in Melville's graduate seminar on amiable humor, conducted by a Bibundtucker professor named Goodman whose principal text is from Herr Teufelsdrockh. "Humor," Goodman intones,

> is, in fact, so blessed a thing, that even in the least virtuous product of the human mind, if there can be found but nine good jokes, some philosophers are clement enough to affirm that those nine good jokes should redeem all the wicked thoughts, though plenty as the populace of Sodom. At any rate, this same humor has something, there is no telling what, of beneficence in it, it is such a catholicon and charm—nearly all men agreeing in relishing it, though they may agree in little else—and in its way it undeniably does such a deal of familiar good in the world, that no wonder it is almost a proverb, that a man of humor, a man capable of a good loud laugh—seem how he may in other things—can hardly be a heartless scamp.[6]

As if on cue, Noble laughs good and loud at a passing beggar. Later he laughs at the anecdote of Phalaris, who reduces punning to sadism when he executes a prisoner on a horse-block in order to have a "horse-laugh." Noble fails miserably his first test of good humor.

He fails his midterm as well. Goodman will tell a joke, and Noble will assess its humor. "A mere wit" has suggested that only niggards and knaves join temperance unions, the former to save money by not drinking, the latter to make money by staying sober while others get drunk. Noble must determine whether the "sting" in this antitemperance witticism is "neutralized by the humor" or given "free play" by the "absence of humor." Is this jest a satire or gentle humor? Noble finds the sting too "free," and for his part he is right, for, given that he is trying to get Goodman drunk, he is the "knave" in Goodman's joke. A sworn drinker and antitemperance man, the bilious Noble is forced by his attempt to avoid the subject of his knavery into the odd position of protesting against an attack on temperance because it is as well an attack on himself. Noble must defend those temperance folk he would otherwise condemn. Whether the joke's sting is too deep or not, its function is to pull Noble out (to educe him) by undermining his pretenses. For Goodman's part, his little joke, though "wicked," is not conceived in wickedness. It is a "catholicon" that will heal Noble, a "charm" that will "redeem" him. But Noble is not redeemed; he fails to play along.

Noble fails his final orals in a discussion on Shakespeare's Polonius and Autolycus. The Mississippi operator reviles Polonius's advice to use one's friends and not love them. It is "false, fatal, and calumnious," Noble rails on: "I hate him" (*CM*, 170, 171). Goodman's blending of sensibilities has not rubbed off, for Noble's unrestrained attack leaves Goodman "unsettled"; he feels "immature" in the presence of Noble's "mature" mind. He confesses to being confused by Shakespeare. Noble is flattered; for once, the argument seems to go his way. But Goodman's apparent confusion is only his recognition of a depth in Shakespeare beyond Noble's reach. Shakespeare is "a queer man," Goodman allows:

> At times seeming irresponsible, he does not always seem reliable. There appears to be a certain—what shall I call it?—hidden sun, say, about him, at once enlightening and mystifying. Now, I should be afraid to say what I have sometimes thought that hidden sun might be. [171–72]

We cannot miss the echo here of Shakespeare's "flashings-forth" in Melville's review of Hawthorne's *Mosses*. But in this instance, Melville emphasizes the containment, not the exposure, of hidden suns, which are the mystifying and illuminating functions of art. Shakespeare may not seem "reliable" in offering characters like Polonius who bundle Chesterfieldian banalities with deeper wisdom. As with Judge Hall, we must be prepared to fuse opposing visions in order to recognize the character fully.

So, too, with Shakespeare's confidence man Autolycus. Goodman stresses that the validity of this rogue stems from his fictionality. Whereas Judge Hall seeks to know an unknowable misanthropical principle through biography, Shakespeare and Melville find truth through poetic creation. Similarly, Autolycus goes deeper than biography, because like Polonius he is designed to "puzzle" or "mystify." Thus, in his "paper-and-ink investiture [he] acts more effectively upon mankind than he would in a flesh-and-blood one." Autolycus's use of humor becomes crucial; it "oils his mischievousness . . . as a pirate schooner, with colors flying, is launched into the sea on greased ways" (172). This is neither Pitch's sentiment nor Noble's false wit, but an insidious good-natured humor that Goodman practices while preaching benevolence: insidious because it undermines the false assumptions of one-sided thinking; good-natured in that learning, not the exposure of defect, is its goal.

It is a cosmopolitan humor that Noble never really gets. Assuming that Autolycus's "grease" is reprehensible, Noble disapproves only to find Goodman championing him over Polonius, "for a moist rogue [Autolycus] may tickle the midriff, while a dry worldling [Polonius] may but wrinkle the spleen" (173).

Things have come round in circles, and Noble is dizzy. Goodman has begun by defending Polonius, but in comparing him to Autolycus, he has moved toward Noble's side. However, Goodman's conclusion that Autolycus is the better man neither embraces nor denies Noble's position. It is downhill from here on out. Sensing that he is being "had," Noble "excitedly" defames Polonius. His "earnestness" flares into anger, and when Goodman trots out Lear to affirm the "ripeness" of Polonius's old age, Noble slams the table in a sham fury that he hopes will be taken for sincerity, declaring it better to be "raw" than "rotten." Noble's last resort is to substitute volubility for reason, and he remains stuck fast to his false dichotomies of raw and rotten in the face of Goodman's delectable "ripe." Having worked his victim into a rage, Goodman urges Noble, just as he did Pitch, to be convivial, not censorious. Cosmopolitan to the last, he claims, "I will not prescribe my nature as the law to other natures. So don't abuse the sober man. Conviviality is one good thing, and sobriety is another good thing. So don't be one-sided" (175).

Goodman's antidote, the two-sided genial misanthrope, can sustain a good-natured love and a healthy hatred of man. He knows human iniquity but is fully committed to human society. Pitch, Moredock, Hall, Polonius, even Noble himself anticipate this figure, for each exhibits an experimental combination of geniality and misanthropy, but these fractional men only whet our taste for something whole, someone like Goodman, whose instinctual benevolence and misanthropy fuse in one cosmopolitan tide. In grounding his geniality upon a misanthropic awareness, Melville's new "monster" brings others in their ill-fated extremism toward his fused sensibility. He sets "the tickled world a'dancing."

Charlemont: The Genial Misanthrope

Goodman's request for a loan from Noble is the dramatic conclusion to his rhetoric of deceit. Noble's attempts to win Goodman's confidence involve one unpalatable misrepresentation of geniality after another. He began as an antimisanthrope hoping to defame Pitch. But in response to Goodman's unrelenting philanthropy, he shifted to a passionate pro-geniality. Yet this false genialist is a splenetic, censorious poser whose response to such "surly philanthropists" as Pitch is that he would "hang . . . the ungenial soul." No positive label can be pinned on Noble; he is an anti-antigenialist, a negation of a negative. As such he is easily caught in contradictions. Thus, when Noble defames Polonius for his claim that a "loan los[es] both itself and friend" (*CM*, 174), he erupts with no sense of irony at Goodman's request for fifty dollars. Suddenly, the discarded masks of both men's identities litter the stage. Goodman reveals his underlying knavery; Noble sheds his false geniality. Linked by a shock of recognition, one con man eyes another. But the flashing-forth is only a joke, Goodman says, and Noble readily allows that he has "humored" Goodman's act. He pretends he was only playing along.

In fleshing out the knavish dimension of Goodman's cosmopolitanism, the scene dramatizes the relationship of fiction and reality. Already Goodman has argued that "pen-and-ink" people like Autolycus and Polonius act "more effectively upon mankind" as comic characters than real individuals. True identity comes, as Melville confirms in chapter 33, through fiction, and in this case humor smoothes the way for "fictionalizing." Goodman fictionalizes himself into a comic sparring bent upon undoing the fictionality of Noble. He plays philanthropist to root out Noble's concealed misanthropist. His success lies in his play-acting versatility. He is a "magician," "necromancer," "metaphysical scamp," and "harlequin." To play a part, one must believe the part. Thus, the cosmopolitan confidence man is a comic liar who exercises faith in himself, his part, and us. Like Lorenzo Dow, he is also a "trickster for God," engaging us in self-conscious enactments of belief and disbelief. With Autolycus, humor "acts effectively"; that is, it effects belief. Thus, only the true humorist can succeed. The cosmopolitan is that true humorist. But as the novel's moral center, Goodman does not promote himself as hero. Even though his voice is finally the cosmopolitan One out of many voices on the *Fidèle,* it is only one of Many. Rather than holding center stage, he projects himself into a minor figure, too briefly onstage to be a character and yet compelling enough to claim a representative status. Like Autolycus, he appears in fable form: the story of Charlemont.

Charlemont, the "gentleman-madman," is a domestic manifestation of Goodman's prophetic humorist. As a young merchant, he blends a "captivating kindliness" with "gracefully devil-may-care and witty good-humor." But in his twenty-fifth year, he "turn[s] from affable to morose," cuts dead all friends, declares bankruptcy, and leaves home. No one can comprehend the "secret grief [that] had distempered him." Years later, he returns with a new fortune in hand and his old manner repossessed; he becomes "devoted henceforth to genial friendships." But, quizzed one night to explain the "enigma" of his sombre retreat, he feels a sense of melancholy returning. Since "art, and care, and time" can make "flowers . . . bloom over a grave," he will not attempt to mar that landscape and "dig all up again only to know the mystery" (184–85). "If ever, in days to come," he advises his friend,

> "you shall see ruin at hand, and, thinking you understand mankind, shall tremble for your friendships, and tremble for your pride; and, partly through love for the one and fear for the other, shall resolve to be beforehand with the world, and save it from a sin by prospectively taking that sin to yourself, then will you do as one I now dream of once did, and like him will you suffer; but how fortunate and how grateful should you be, if like him, and after all that had happened, you could be a little happy again." [185–86]

What is both realistic and compelling about Charlemont's fulfillment of the genial misanthrope type is his capacity to blend art and happenstance, personal biography and Christian myth.

While Charlemont has recreated himself into a genial misanthrope "by art and care," this process is controlled by "time," so that affability returns as providentially as moroseness "happened." Charlemont's genial misanthropy is not an act of will. He gained his cosmopolitanism through the whims of time and instinct. Moreover, it is not contrived to perform ethical con games; he is a cosmopolite by chance, and "lucky" to be so. By luck he has returned to the living, and by luck his encounter with the universe has not crippled him. Through benevolence he has taken on sin, but this Hawthornean project has not destroyed his sociality. Unlike his Protean counterpart Goodman, he will not set the tickled world a'dancing. His mission is simply to tend his garden (even as it decorates a grave), doing so with an outward aspect of joy despite an inward recognition of suffering.

If Goodman is the novel's comic God, an Old Testament scamp set out to vex man and test his faith, Charlemont is surely his New Testament Christ. The Christological allusions are clear: Charlemont's wilderness retreat from society, his taking on of sin, his resurrection. Like Christ, this "daemonic" cosmopolitan mediates for man both love and fear, benevolence and sin. We cannot, nor are we meant to, emulate Goodman; he is a comic scamp of revelation. But Charlemont is imitable, a "diluted" genial misanthrope whom we can know, for he reminds us of ourselves. He reminds us, too, of Melville.

Enriching the Christian allusions are personal associations, for Charlemont is a Melville family portrait. His French descent, merchant service, and youthful career reversal suggest any of a number of men in Melville's immediate family: his merchant father who spoke fluent French and died bankrupt; his Uncle Thomas, a cosmopolitan and emissary to France, who survived repeated bankruptcies; his brother Gansevoort, whose own diplomatic career came unglued just before his death at thirty-one; Herman himself, who at twenty-five in 1844 came home from sea, read profusely, and suddenly turned into a writer (both affable and morose). Charlemont also recalls the young Pierre (a version of Herman embroiled in the family rumors of his father's youthful indiscretions) who takes his father's sin "to himself" to save his mother, if not the world. Born to be gentlemen, these men failed—some went mad—and those who survived, Thomas and Herman, were indeed lucky to retain both humor and insight. John Wenke has argued, perhaps too cleverly yet incisively all the same, that Charlemont is an anagram of two names: "Charlie" Noble and "Timon" of Athens. Taken orthographically, this man of "self-possession" and tense repose is a commingling of one man's falsely practiced geniality and another man's foul misanthropy. The one letter in both names—Charlie and Timon—that is missing in the anagram, Wenke observes, is "i."[7] Quietly veiled within Charlemont, lowercase and invisible, but present because of exclusion, is Melville himself, the narrative first-person "I" so cagily hidden from view, indeed so severely contained, throughout this third-person novel.

But finally, like Goodman, Charlemont is a comic creation, "served" up as if a dream. He is, Noble reacts, "a very strange one . . . but is it true?" "Of course not," Goodman responds. He exists only "to amuse." "If it seem strange to you, that strangeness is the romance; it is what contrasts it with real life; it is the invention, in brief, the fiction as opposed to the fact" (*CM*, 187). This is all too much for Charlie, who, when asked if he might take on Charlemont's Christlike manner, quickly assents but quickly departs. Charlemont is a valid moral center for this novel without heroes; he is "real" precisely because he is fictional. He is normative because he is strange. He is serious because comic. If a moral center exists that sedulously upsets our notions of normative absolutes, it is to be found in the reader's relation to Melville's "other selves," in our participation in the unraveling drama of doubt surrounding the cosmopolite, and in our attempts to comprehend both this metaphysical scamp Frank Goodman and his self-projected gentleman-madman Charlemont, both genial misanthropes, both New World versions of a cosmopolitan ideal.

For all intents and purposes, Melville's professional writing career ended with *The Confidence-Man*. He had used humor throughout that career to express his deepest insights. It was a part of his picturesque sensibility, his cosmopolitan politics, and his aesthetics of repose. Fiction was a way to gain a sense of the Ideal, but as a pragmatic Platonist, Melville also felt the responsibility to give us a true taste of that ideality. He experimented continually to reach readers more fully. Although *Typee* was a success, it crumbled under the weight of its anxious encounter with both self and audience. Although *Moby-Dick* perfected the voice of genial desperation, its dramatism vies heavily with its amiable "first-personalism," suggesting the need for a more objective, voiceless voice. In the end, voice was everything and nothing to Melville. He found his Ishmael but immediately killed him off, sensing that only through the force of language itself, not personality, can writers and readers find "something beyond." And though *The Confidence-Man* leaves us unguided within a shifty fiction to taste that something, we sense in this problematic novel the loneliness of abstraction. Melville contained himself so fully that we can glimpse him only in formal digressions or as a "mariner" here and a Charlemont there, detached and indifferent, bit parts oddly removed from a drama that tests our ability to play along on the margin between allegory and life. His aesthetic self-effacement virtually complete, Melville achieves in *The Confidence-Man* his most precarious balance of self and nihility, and the brilliance of his fiction lies finally in its ability to make readers reenact that balance for themselves, to live the moment of Melville's tense repose.

Coda: Something Further

The recent emergence of the New Historicism encourages us to take stock of what any historicist approach can and ought to do. The fear is that historicists, traditional and new, will stereotype each other as mere source hunter and ideologist, respectively, and no fruitful synthesis of the two shall occur. To some extent, the two camps seem irreconcilable. On the one hand, traditional historicists in focusing their energies on verifiable biographical "facts" presume the validity of authorial intentionality. On the other hand, the new historicist presumes that social forces operate independently of the author to shape a text. One looks for brushstrokes as evidence of a conscious talent; the other, for larger structures that reflect the pressure of a culture beyond the conscious individual. One demands fact; the other, a relevant vision of America. The strength of traditionalism is that its grounding in fact (however speculative such a thing, in fact, must be) lends a certain reliability to its critical conclusions. The problem with much new historicist analysis is that, in rising above biography, authorial intent, and an obligation to historical cause and effect, it is too often simply unconvincing. But the power of the new historicism, this rhetorical limitation notwithstanding, is that it enacts the most vital function of criticism in its attempt to use the past to construct our present. This mission is valid and, I believe, imperative, for criticism is nothing unless it addresses the problem of who we are now. The problem for us is to find a comprehensive historicist approach that comprises the traditional and new, that is both factual and broad, biographical and cultural, relevant and convincing.

In *Melville and Repose,* I have used a kind of *pluralistic historicism* that is comprehensive largely to the extent to which it focuses on the *rhetorical conditions of creation* during the period of Melville's most active writing phase. By pluralistic and comprehensive, I mean that it gives access to the metaphysical grounding as well as political and sexual particulars of Melville's work; it treats the author as an independent consciousness and the reader as a historical force. My assumption is that the more we know about how Melville used the rhetorical models that prevailed in his time, the more we can come to understand the intersection of authors and audience in his creations as well as the motives within American Creativity. Such an understanding may be no more achievable than our understanding of a black hole, and yet how we create and why and for whom, these are the questions that take us to the most immediate sense of our metaphysical and political Self, both as Americans and as human beings. If these questions are finally unanswerable, they still remain the most compelling questions to ask. All that is needed is a critical vocabulary to articulate the questioning. For me, the discovery of humor at the heart of Melville's aesthetics of repose has led to one such critical vocabulary, but the ultimate problem of the kind of historicist approach I propose is to rise beyond local applications to a larger vision.

My exercise in pluralistic historicism is naturally limited in scope as far as a larger theory of American literature or America is concerned, for though Melville's brilliance continues to astound us, he remains only one creative mind. There are others seeking voices; others still seeking their own kind of voicelessness. And since the rhetorical conditions of creation vary remarkably from author to author, the more we inspect the creative conditions of each and every writer, the more we shall begin to see a larger pattern recapitulated in their varied works. Emerson and Thoreau hush or strengthen their ideas from journal to essay, just as Whitman's rhetorical strategies shift in successive versions of his poem. How does the creative act embody or deny transcendental modes of creativity? Can we find in the manuscript and editorial variants in Dickinson homologous acts buried in the textual matters in Charlotte Perkins Gilman's publications, and if so, what can these patterns tell us of the ways women writers confront male and female readers? We might compare, as well, the fascinating rhetorical dynamics of Joel Chandler Harris's nostalgic Uncle Remus (a white man poses as black) to Chestnutt's more powerful *Conjure Woman* (a black poses as white), or consider, too, the growth of a self through the various drafts and changing editions and audiences of Frederick Douglass's *Life* alongside Richard Wright's *Black Boy*. To be sure, these "assignments" have a familiar ring, but the challenge remains to discover in these diverse arenas suggestive continuities that link the philosophical, social, sexual, and racial determinants of the conditions of creativity in America. Perhaps, there is waiting for us a theory of American literary creativity and rhetoric; but that is another book. At present, I have been content to explore the conditions of one author, Herman Melville, whose many selves and many audiences seem world enough.

The case of Melville, however, is well suited to the pluralistic historicism that I employ. Here is a writer who struggled from one book to the next to adapt himself to one audience and fight another, to caress and hoax his readers, to mold them into the kind of reader who could best understand him and better understand themselves. Here is a writer who hoped to rein in and contain his linguistic and philosophical excesses, while at the same time he quarreled with heaven and with fiction. Here is one who intermixed comedy and tragedy, redefined the picturesque, moved on to something more dramatistic, and exploited the notion of cosmopolitanism, all in a series of prose fictions, but who eventually abandoned them for poetry. Ultimately the value in studying Melville—and perhaps the reason that Melville endures even as the canon does not—is not simply that his words expose the nation's recurrent problems but that his career by the very fact of its instability, rhetorical struggles, and experimentation stands as an allegory for our culture's search for voice and form. And to some extent the voiceless voice Melville searched for is the same condition America today is seeking as it works through and beyond the problem of exclusionary ethnicity versus inclusionary nationalism inherent in today's multicultural debate.

Melville came a long way in the business of making fictions. An anxious yarn-spinner of Polynesian exploits in *Typee,* he invented for himself, through his essaying, the symbolism of *Moby-Dick,* and dropped all that for the drama of *The Confidence-Man.* He came this far in fiction and quit. In the years after *The Confidence-Man,* he turned almost exclusively to poetry, but his *Battle-Pieces* found no readership to speak of, and subsequent volumes, *Clarel* included, were distributed in painfully small numbers. Why Melville made such a radical shift in genre from fiction to poetry has not been adequately addressed, nor is any answer forthcoming in this volume, except to say that the urge to contain selfhood that drove Melville deeper into the humor of fiction drove him deeper still into the structures of language itself. His poems were his final containment. Just as Melville perfected his moral picturesque and then abandoned it for more dramatic forms, and just as he sought to transform his reader from a partner to a participant in even deeper dramatistic engagements, so too did he finally "let go" of the comicalities of fiction for the personless realm of the poetic line. Typically, Melville insisted upon an experimental, elliptical, often tortured syntax that makes him an unacknowledged precursor of modern verse. Even though his intense poetry left little room for the rhythms of geniality, still, like the grass Israel Potter observes growing between paving stones, geniality resurfaced in Melville's last writings, along with such prose-and-poem pieces as "John Marr" and "Rip Van Winkle's Lilac." In like manner, *Billy Budd,* which grew from a poem into one of our age's most durable novellas, reverses Melville's shift to poetry as it attempts to retrieve in prose a detached voice that mediates tragedy and transcendence. But, as if emblematic of Melville's career and aesthetics, it was left an unpolished manuscript at his death. Always revising, Melville died an inveterate essayer. His search for voice was never complete, but the search itself was all that mattered; it was the warm sparking of his artful repose.

NOTES

Preface

1. Henry Clay Lukens [Erratic Enrique], "American Literary Comedians," *Harper's Magazine* 80 (April 1890): 793.

2. Philarète Chasles, "Voyages réel et fantastiques d'Hermann Melville," Paris *Revue des deux mondes*, 15 May 1849, pp. 541–70. Translation in Watson G. Branch, ed., *Melville: The Critical Heritage* (London and Boston: Routledge & Kegan Paul, 1974), p. 164.

3. Wylie Sypher, *Comedy* (Garden City, NY: Doubleday, 1956), p. 193.

4. James Cox, *Mark Twain: The Fate of Humor* (Princeton, NJ: Princeton University Press, 1966), p. 22.

1. A Great Intellect in Repose

1. Fitz-James O'Brien, "Our Authors and Authorship. Melville and Curtis," *Putnam's Monthly Magazine* 9 (April 1857): 384–93. Reprinted in Branch, *Melville: Critical Heritage*, p. 362.

2. Frederic Jameson, *The Political Unconscious: Narrative as Socially Symbolic Act* (New York: Cornell University Press, 1981).

3. Ralph Waldo Emerson, "The Poet," *Selections from Emerson*, ed. Stephen Whicher (Boston: Houghton Mifflin, 1957), p. 227.

4. Edgar Allan Poe, "The Philosophy of Composition," *Selected Writings of Edgar Allan Poe*, ed. Edward H. Davidson (Boston: Houghton Mifflin, 1956), p. 453.

5. Robert Milder, "Knowing Melville," *Emerson Society Quarterly* (ESQ) 24 (2nd Q 1978): 96–117. Merton M. Sealts, Jr., *Pursuing Melville, 1940–1980: Chapters and Essays* (Madison: University of Wisconsin Press, 1982), p. 342.

6. Most of Melville's revivalists generally acknowledge that the author's major creative phase came to a screeching halt in mid-career. Carl Van Doren, "Fiction II: Contemporaries of Cooper," in W. P. Trent *et al.*, eds., *The Cambridge History of American Literature* (New York: Putnam, 1917–21), pp. 307–25, 536–38. Raymond M. Weaver, *Herman Melville* (New York: Doran, 1921). John Freeman, *Herman Melville* (London and New York: Macmillan, 1926). Lewis Mumford, *Herman Melville* (New York: Harcourt Brace, 1929). Unfortunately, subsequent inquiry has not fully outgrown the habit of thinking of the early works as a building up to *Moby-Dick* and the later works as a deterioration of talent. Brooks, for instance, called *The Confidence-Man* an "abortion." See Van Wyck Brooks, "Herman Melville," New York *Herald Tribune Books*, 16 May 1926, pp. 1–2. F. O. Matthiessen, *American Renaissance: Art and Expression in the Age of Emerson and Whitman* (New York: Oxford University Press, 1940), and William Ellery Sedgwick, *Herman Melville: The Tragedy of Mind* (Cambridge, MA: Harvard University Press, 1944), devote little space to the fictions after *Moby-Dick*. Charvat also considers *Pierre* the beginning of the end for Melville's

creative life. See William Charvat, "Melville's Income," in Matthew Bruccoli, ed., *The Profession of Authorship in America, 1800–1870* (Columbus: Ohio State University Press, 1968), p. 255. Berthoff expresses the general view succinctly: By 1852, "the rush of [Melville's] mind's unfolding appears to be at an end." See Warner Berthoff, *The Example of Melville* (New York: Norton, 1962), p. 55.

7. Walter Blair, "A Man's Voice, Speaking,': A Continuum in American Humor," in *Veins of Humor,* Harvard English Studies 3 (Cambridge, MA: Harvard University Press, 1972), pp. 185–204.

8. George Meredith, "An Essay on Comedy," in *Comedy,* introd. Wylie Sypher (Garden City, NY: Doubleday, 1956), p. 47.

9. Joseph Addison, *The Spectator,* nos. 61 and 62 [True and False Wit], in *Selections,* ed. Robert J. Allen (New York: Holt, Rinehart, 1957). Addison begins with Locke's idea of wit as the resemblance of ideas and adds to it the notion of surprise. Addison also discusses "mixt Wit," which balances the strength in both true and false wit, i.e. "the Resemblance of Ideas, and . . . the Resemblance of Words" (p. 106). In a sense, the push throughout the period for an aesthetic mixture or mingling of these modes shapes much of the development of British humor and is an integral dialectic in what I call here the "comic debate" in America. For a full discussion of the development of wit and amiable humor, see Stuart M. Tave, *The Amiable Humorist: A Study in the Comic Theory and Criticism of the 18th and Early 19th Centuries* (Chicago: University of Chicago Press, 1960). For the discussion of Addison, in particular, see pp. 58–63. The present study owes a great deal to Tave's work, and chapter 2, in particular, is an attempt to apply notions of amiability to the American scene.

10. Meredith, "Essay on Comedy," p. 42.

11. Austin traces the idea of mixed modes of humor in his discussion of the development of French views on America's comic spirit. In particular he examines Robert Escarpit's 1963 thesis that humor consists of a dialectic between intellectual and emotional (affective) movements, the recognition of the absurd and yet the creation of faith between humorist and audience. See James C. Austin, *American Humor in France: Two Centuries of French Criticism of the Comic Spirit in American Literature* (Ames: Iowa State University Press, 1978), p. 33.

12. Paul de Man, "The Intentional Structure of the Romantic Image," in *The Rhetoric of Romanticism* (New York: Columbia University Press, 1984), p. 7.

13. This "camp" includes Sedgwick's *Tragedy of Mind;* Harry Levin, *The Power of Blackness* (New York: Knopf, 1958); and Richard Boyd Hauck, *A Cheerful Nihilism: Confidence and "The Absurd" in American Humorous Fiction* (Bloomington: Indiana University Press, 1971). Here we must also include Marjorie Dew, "Black-Hearted Melville: Geniality Reconsidered," in Robert J. DeMott and Sanford E. Marovitz, eds., *Artful Thunder* (Kent, OH: Kent State University Press, 1975), pp. 177–94.

14. The image is from Melville's "Hawthorne and his *Mosses,*" which I treat more fully later on. Dryden's point is that ontology dictates form, and that after *Moby-Dick,* Melville's critical shift in the understanding of Being led him to abandon "truth-seeking" forms for more verbose fictions, which destroy themselves, as all, according to Dryden, "wise fictions" should. Edgar Dryden, *Melville's Thematics of Form: The Great Art of Telling the Truth* (Baltimore: Johns Hopkins University Press, 1968), pp. 6, 151, 124.

15. Nina Baym "Melville's Quarrel with Fiction," *Publication of the Modern Language Association* (PMLA) 94:919.

16. Neither Dryden nor Baym is strictly speaking a deconstructionist. I include them here only to the extent that they anticipate de Man's point, and to this extent we might call Dryden and Baym pre-poststructuralist.

17. Warwick Wadlington, *The Confidence Game in American Literature* (Princeton, NJ: Princeton University Press, 1975), p. 73. The camp that argues for Melville's more positive sense of language and fiction (of which Wadlington is a member) may be said to have its roots in Walter E. Bezanson's placement of Ishmael at the center of *Moby-Dick* in *"Moby-Dick:* Work of Art." See also Paul Brodtkorb, Jr., *Ishmael's White World: A Phenomenological Reading of Moby-Dick* (New Haven: Yale University Press, 1965), and Richard Brodhead, *"Mardi:* Creating the Creative," in Faith Pullin, ed., *New Perspectives on Melville,* (Kent, OH: Kent State University Press, 1978), pp. 229–50.

18. Anne K. Mellor, *English Romantic Irony* (Cambridge, MA: Harvard University Press, 1980), p. 5.

19. John Seelye devotes part of his first chapter to Melville's connection to Schlegel's view of irony in *Melville: The Ironic Diagram* (Evanston, IL: Northwestern University Press, 1970).

20. Samuel Taylor Coleridge, *Biographia Literaria,* p. 433 (my italics).

21. Thomas Carlyle, *Sartor Resartus: The Life and Opinions of Herr Teufelsdrockh* (Indianapolis and New York: Odyssey Press, 1937), p. 32.

22. Tave, *Amiable Humorist,* pp. 238–40. Tave ranks Richter beside such principal amiable humorists as Lamb and Hazlitt.

23. According to Henry A. Pochmann, *German Culture in America: Philosophical and Literary Influences, 1600–1900* (Madison: University of Wisconsin Press, 1957), Jean Paul Richter had "an amazingly strong hold on American interest" in the 1830s. Margaret Fuller, for instance, taught *The Titan* at Alcott's school (pp. 330 and 332). See Tave, *Amiable Humorist,* p. 290, n. 48, for Richter's European popularity.

24. Thomas Carlyle, *Edinburgh Review,* 1827, p. 14.

25. Probably the most comprehensive survey of Melville's aesthetics is Shirley Dettlaff's chapter in John Bryant, ed., *A Companion to Melville Studies* (Westport, CT: Greenwood Press, 1986), pp. 625–65.

26. William Cullen Bryant, *Representative Selections,* ed. Tremaine McDowell (New York: American Book Co., 1935), p. 4, l. 33.

27. Edgar Allan Poe, *Collected Works of Poe,* ed. Thomas Ollive Mabbott (Cambridge, MA: Harvard University Press, 1969), p. 322.

28. Henry Wadsworth Longfellow, *Longfellow's Poems* (New York: Dutton, 1970), p. 5.

29. Ralph Waldo Emerson, *Emerson in His Journals,* ed. Joel Porte (Cambridge, MA: Harvard University Press, 1982), p. 288.

30. *Letters,* p. 79. An excellent discussion of Melville's probable reading and relationship to Emerson can be found in Merton M. Sealts, Jr., "Melville and Emerson's Rainbow," *ESQ* 26 (2nd Q, 1980): 53–78; rpt. in Sealts, *Pursuing Melville,* pp. 250–77.

31. "Statues in Rome," in *Piazza Tales,* p. 408. Hereafter cited as "Lectures."

32. Gotthold Lessing, *Laocoön: An Essay on the Limits of Painting and Poetry,* trans. Edward Allen McCormick (Indianapolis: Bobbs-Merrill, 1962), p. 17.

33. Matthiessen's notion of symbolism, while not owing any particular debt to Lessing, operates on the similar idea that symbol provided Hawthorne and Melville an avenue for the heightening of reality. Matthiessen, *American Renaissance,* p. 269. Nor does Matthiessen attempt to show the link in Melville's thought to notions of Greek restraint. Although he notes in passing that Melville had marked in his copy of the *French and Italian Notebooks* Hawthorne's admission that "all this Greek beauty has done something towards refining me," Matthiessen seems more intent upon the gothicism in both writers. It could be argued that, since the critic did not have available to him the reconstruction of Melville's lecture on Roman Statuary (first published in 1957) which reveals the link to Laocoön, he was simply not privy to this significant aspect of Melville's aesthetics. And yet, like the early

Melville revivalists, he was inclined to portray the author as more stormy than calm, more the Goth than the Hellene. This presumption infects his interpretation of Melville's persistent imagery of sea-calms to the point of misreading. Says Matthiessen: "As Melville construes it, calm is but the fragile envelope of storm; it is mere delusive appearance, like the treacherous repose of Moby-Dick himself, for the truth is violent and tempestuous" (p. 289). Citing the famous passage from "The Grand Armada," Matthiessen allows that the author "varies this interpretation." But, in fact, Melville fairly consistently acknowledged, as I argue throughout this chapter, the deeper power of calm over storm.

34. Melville marked this passage in his copy of Hawthorne before writing his famous review. See Nathaniel Hawthorne, *Mosses from an Old Manse* (New York: Wiley, 1846), p. 25.

35. The analysis of Melville's aesthetics as it relates to movements in the fine arts has focused largely upon the author's use of Burke's sublime and, in addition, Melville's rejection of the picturesque as a comparatively weak or even dishonest alternative. Probably the most ambitious study to date is by Richard S. Moore, *That Cunning Alphabet: Melville's Aesthetics of Nature* (Amsterdam: Rodopi, 1982), who argues, as did Poenicke, Breinig, and Fisher before him, that Melville used the sublime to remind Americans of the essentially delusive nature of a picturesque vision which had become in the 1850s a "vital element of the nation's self-image." (p. 53). See Klaus Poenicke, "A View from the Piazza: Herman Melville and the Legacy of the European Sublime," *Comparative Literature Studies* 4 (1967): 267–81, who entertains the possibility of Melville's attraction to the picturesque only to suggest its final inadequacy to explore "associational and thematic implications" (pp. 272–73). See also Helmbrecht Breinig, "The Destruction of Fairyland: Melville's 'Piazza' in the Tradition of the American Imagination," *English Literary History* 35 (1968): 254–83, and Marvin Fisher, *Going Under: Melville's Short Fiction and the American 1850s* (Baton Rouge: Louisiana State University Press, 1977), pp. 13–28. Neither of these studies, however, shows awareness of Melville's explicit writings on his preference for the Picturesque in the Burgundy Club Sketches and "Rip Van Winkle's Lilac," nor can an aesthetics of the sublime fully account for Melville's comic sensibility, or Coleridgean "inverse sublimity."

36. The earliest of the more comprehensive analyses of the picturesque in America is Ringe's study of the mode's philosophical groundings in the Scottish common sense tradition and its techniques and thematic potentials: Donald A. Ringe, *The Pictorial Mode: Space and Time in the Art of Bryant, Irving and Cooper* (Lexington: University of Kentucky Press, 1971). Blake Nevius, in *Cooper's Landscapes: An Essay on the Picturesque Vision* (Berkeley: University of California Press, 1976), applies the ideas of E. H. Gombrich to argue for a picturesque way of seeing. An excellent and promising extension of these two studies is Dennis Berthold, "Charles Brockden Brown, *Edgar Huntly,* and the Origins of the American Picturesque," *William and Mary Quarterly* 41 (June 1984): 62–84. Berthold writes that the picturesque "mode of seeing provided an organized, cool aesthetic that restrained exaggerated emotion and framed one's view of rude nature with the artistic perspective of the landscape painter" (p. 69).

37. Nathaniel Hawthorne, *Tales and Sketches,* ed. Roy Harvey Pearce (New York: Library of America, 1982), pp. 714, 718, my emphasis. Two useful studies of Hawthorne's picturesque are by Leo B. Levy, "Picturesque Style in *The House of the Seven Gables,*" *New England Quarterly* 39 (June 1966): 147–60, and *idem,* "The Landscape Modes of *The Scarlet Letter,*" *Nineteenth-Century Fiction* 23 (1969): 377–92. Levy does not allude to the phrase "moral picturesque" as found in "The Old Apple Dealer," but in both studies he explores the "moral and aesthetic" dimensions of the visual mode.

38. Darrel Abel has, in his collection of essays *The Moral Picturesque: Studies in Hawthorne's Fiction* (West Lafayette, IN: Purdue University Press, 1988), p. 2, used the term

"moral picturesque" to describe Hawthorne's "attempt to express meanings through figures rather than in explicit statement." He does not, however, attempt to locate the concept in fine arts traditions or explore the dynamic nature of its aesthetics.

39. Still an excellent guide to the development of the picturesque in its British context is Walter J. Hipple, Jr., *The Beautiful, the Sublime, and the Picturesque in Eighteenth-Century British Aesthetic Theory* (Carbondale: Southern Illinois University Press, 1957).

40. As quoted in Christopher Hussey, *The Picturesque: Studies in a Point of View* (New York: Putnam, 1927), p. 13. Burke's physiological metaphor of a suspension of nerves coincides with Melville's poetic placement of the self "on the marge," suspended between full tension (of the sea) and utter relaxation (inland), which we shall examine more fully later on. Here, too, are the curiosity (a combination of wonder and doubt) and irregularity (improvisation) that typify Melville's compositional processes.

41. Taking the associationist approach to the picturesque, certain scholars have begun recently to show how Melville adapted his prose to specific, and fairly diverse, modes of painting, in particular the Dutch Genre School and J. M. W. Turner. See Dennis Berthold, "Melville and Dutch Painting," *Melville Society Extracts*, no. 69, February 1987, p. 4; and Robert K. Wallace, "New Evidence for Melville's Use of Turner in *Moby-Dick*," *Melville Society Extracts*, no. 67, September 1986, pp. 4–9. Oddly enough, there is as yet no study of Melville's attraction to the American artist Elihu Vedder, to whom Melville dedicated *Timoleon*.

42. The utility of Martin Price's formulation is that it allows us to see the picturesque as a dynamic middle ground between the aesthetic domains of sublime and beautiful. The error, as I see it, in most critiques that denigrate the picturesque in America is the failure to see this inherent dynamism and to recognize that the picturesque could at the same time tame the sublime and enliven or deepen the merely beautiful. Richard Moore's view that Melville "deride[s] the passive state of aesthetic repose connected with the picturesque"(53) therefore misses Melville's attempts to grasp the full potential of Price's "picturesque moment," both the insight and the repose. Some sense of the dual effect of the picturesque can be seen in the opposite conclusions derived by two critics, both favorably disposed toward the picturesque. Nevius's point, for instance, is that the picturesque allowed Cooper to move from a fairly uninspired use of landscape toward a more Romantic vision (104). Berthold argues for the restraining influences of the picturesque which provided Brockden Brown and others "a congenial, respectable, eminently civilized standpoint" (69). My purpose here is to expand our notions of the picturesque so that its capacity for containing both the wild and the genial can be better appreciated.

43. This "marginal" point of view has its most memorable application in his image of the two-sided tortoise. As the jokey narrator of "The Encantadas" puts it, one must keep the bright side up, "but be honest, and don't deny the black" (*Piazza Tales*, 130). William Bysshe Stein in "Melville's Comedy of Faith," *ELH 27* (December 1960): 315–33, attempts an ironic reading of this famous passage by observing that when a tortoise is turned bright side up, it is on its back and therefore helpless (p. 323). Melville, however, does not press or even allude to this natural fact; hence, the irony, if it exists, does not seem intended, nor is it strong enough to invert a straight reading of his message. (One update in all this is that Walter Bezanson, a mariner in Melville's seas, reports first hand that the Galapagos tortoise has no bright side at all.) Both images of marge and tortoise imply that our bright vision, no matter how rooted it is in our awareness of nihility, must have ascendency over the dark. At the end, Ishmael is not an enthusiast plunging into the "closing vortex" of the sinking *Pequod* but an observer gently circling "on the margin" (*MD*, 573) of the maelstrom. Carolyn Porter explores Ishmael's liminality or marginal character in her excellent dialogic analysis "Call Me Ishmael, or How to Make Double-Talk Speak," *New Essays on Moby-*

Dick, ed. Richard H. Brodhead (New York: Cambridge University Press, 1986), pp. 73–108. Porter does not discuss "The Enviable Isles" or attempt to place Ishmael's ability to recognize the fragility of "boundaries" in the picturesque or comic traditions.

44. "Sendak on Melville: An Interview," by Richard Kopley, *Melville Society Extracts,* no. 87, November 1991, p. 6.

45. Lawrance Thompson, in *Melville's Quarrel with God* (Princeton, NJ: Princeton University Press, 1952), tends to overstate the strictness of Melville's Calvinistic upbringing in order to dramatize more fully the author's reaction to Puritanism. In fact, Melville grew up with his Unitarian father as well as his Dutch Reformed mother. T. Walter Herbert, in *Moby-Dick and Calvinism: A World Dismantled* (New Brunswick, NJ: Rutgers University Press, 1977), provides a more measured assessment of the tensions between liberal and conservative elements in Melville's religious upbringing.

46. Gansevoort-Lansing Collection, New York Public Library (my italics).

47. Maria Gansevoort Melville's letters, as yet unpublished, may be found in the recently discovered cache of Augusta Melville's papers now located at the New York Public Library. Neal Tolchin in his treatment of *Melville and Mourning* (New Haven: Yale University Press, 1989), was the first to incorporate the Augusta Letters in a major critical study.

48. In speaking of the victims of the confidence man, James E. Miller, Jr., strikes at the central problem of nearly all of Melville's more interesting characters: They "are ultimately victims of their own weaknesses and evil impulses. They suffer some imbalance of head and heart that makes them vulnerable." James E. Miller, Jr., *A Reader's Guide to Herman Melville* (New York: Farrar, Straus & Cudahy, 1962), p. 181. Miller's readings in his *Guide* remain fresh and useful. My point, in extension of his view, that we are victims of instinct presumes that "head and heart" are the faculties not of will but of instinct; hence they are not *per se* "evil impulses" but rather impulses pure and simple.

49. My argument that Melville attacks geniality in order to strengthen it varies from the general view, voiced by Marjorie Dew, that Melville "lacerates his persistently genial men." See "Black-hearted: 'Geniality' Reconsidered," in *Artful Thunder,* p. 177. Dew's essay is in response to Merton M. Sealts, Jr., "Melville's 'Geniality,'" in Max F. Shulz, ed., *Essays in American and English Literature Presented to Bruce R. McElderry* (Athens: University of Georgia Press, 1967), pp. 3–26, reprinted in *Pursuing Melville,* pp. 155–70. Sealts demonstrates through examples throughout the canon that geniality is a "persistent strain of sensibility" (Sealts, 156). I also differ with those who take *The Confidence-Man* to be Melville's principal satire or burlesque on the "philosophy of geniality." See Elizabeth Foster, ed., *The Confidence-Man: His Masquerade,* by Herman Melville (New York: Hendricks House, 1954), p. xiv, and Joseph Flibbert, *Melville and the Art of Burlesque* (Amsterdam: Rodopi, 1974), p. 149.

50. Richard H. Brodhead, *Hawthorne, Melville, and the Novel* (Chicago: University of Chicago Press, 1976), p. 165.

51. For Lawrance Thompson, Melville's concealment of his "quarrel with God" from readers was a success, but for Edgar Dryden such concealment became aesthetically self-defeating.

52. Edward FitzGerald, *Polonius: A Collection of Wise Saws and Modern Instances* (London: Pickering, 1852), p. xv, Sealts, no. 218. See also *Marginalia.*

53. Brodhead's point is that Melville differed from Hawthorne as a novelist in that "the natural bent of his imagination is not toward submerging his own identity and evoking images of the experience of others." Brodhead, *Hawthorne, Melville, and Novel,* p. 122. In this regard Hawthorne more fully anticipates James's notion of self-distancing and dramatization. While this may be true of Melville's natural tendency, especially in the novels Brodhead treats (*Moby-Dick* and *Pierre*), my point is that in the later fiction Melville clearly develops

along more Jamesian lines by submerging himself in third-person narratives and letting characters interact naturally in their dramatic context. This is particularly true of "Benito Cereno" and *The Confidence-Man*.

54. "Nor," as Melville notes, "need you fix upon that blackness in him, if it suit you not" (*"Mosses,"* 245). I am taking Melville at his word here, not to insist upon a shallow reading of the text but rather to stress its deeper complexity. In my view, we have "fixed" so much upon Melville's discovery of blackness that we fail to see the dynamism of his more comprehensive image of Hawthorne's dualism, his mixture of bright humor and dark insight.

55. I insert the word "else" here to clarify the meaning of "or." Melville's "or" does not mean that what follows is an alternate phrasing for what comes before. Rather, the "or" along with "only" suggests the negative consequences of not combining intellect with good humor and love.

56. "Tintern Abbey," l. 97.

57. Melville may have drawn his sense of the picturesque from Hazlitt, who in a passage from *The Round Table* marked by Melville notes that art makes "sunshine in a shady place." See *The Round Table: A Collection of Essays on Literature, Men, and Manners* (Edinburgh: Constable, 1817), II: 256 (Sealts, no. 265). Melville's dawn metaphor resembles an image from Hazlitt's discussion of the periodical essayists (Addison, *et al.*) in *Lectures on the English Comic Writers:* "How airy these abstractions of the poet's pen stream over the *dawn of our acquaintance with human life!* how they glance their fairest colours on the prospect before us! how pure they remain in it to the last, like the rainbow in the evening cloud." *Complete Works of William Hazlitt,* ed. P. P. Howe (London: J. M. Dent, 1930–34), 6: 98. It is tempting to draw a direct link, but Melville did not purchase his volume of the *Lectures* (Sealts, no. 263b) until 1862. Of course, Melville read Hazlitt throughout his life, from the first time he borrowed *Table-Talk* in 1848 to 1890, when he borrowed *Political Essays,* and he may have read the *Lectures* before purchasing them. In any event, Hazlitt's passage, while its dawn is enticing, wanes in a Wordsworthian mode with "the rainbow in the evening cloud," an image that lacks the tension in Hawthorne and Melville's picturesque humor.

58. Nathaniel Hawthorne, *American Notebooks,* pp. 147 and 244. Both passages are also quoted in Robert Dusenberry, "Hawthorne's Merry Company: The Anatomy of Laughter in the Tales and Short Stories," *PMLA* 82 (1967): 285.

59. Nathaniel Hawthorne, *The House of the Seven Gables, A Romance* (Boston: Ticknor, Reed & Fields, 1851), p. 178. Melville marked this passage (*Marginalia,* 286) in his copy of the novel (Sealts, no. 246), perhaps because it echoed Babbalanja's "deep thought" of laughter.

60. E. P. Whipple, "The Literature of Mirth," in *The Boston Book* (Boston: Ticknor, Reed & Fields, 1850), p. 37.

61. [William Gilmore Simms], "Writings of Cornelius Mathews," *Southern Quarterly Review* 6 (October 1844): 325.

62. Richard Haywarde [Frederick S. Cozzens], "On Wit and Humor," *The Knickerbocker* 36 (December 1850): 496.

2. America's Repose

1. Thomas Hobbes, *Leviathan: Or the Matter, Forme and Power of a Commonwealth Ecclesiasticall and Civil,* ed. Michael Oakeshott (New York: Collier Books, 1962), I, vi, p. 52.

2. Anthony Ashley, Lord Shaftesbury, *Characteristics of Men, Manners, Opinions, Times* (New York: Bobbs-Merrill, 1964), p. 74.

3. One might argue that the convoluted ironies and burlesquing in Melville's later fiction fulfills the Shaftesburyan prediction that authors living under the pall of the demands of the marketplace or of political oppression and censorship will resort to forms of parabolic humor that by the very nature of their necessary indirection confuse more than they entertain. Of course, Melville was aware of this phenomenon, for in his *"Mosses"* review he wonders how Shakespeare might have fared had he lived in freer times; the Declaration of Independence, he says, makes a difference. But if Melville was living under any form of oppression, it was likely to be as much familial as political. Married to the daughter of Massachusetts Chief Justice Lemuel Shaw, upholder of the repugnant Fugitive Slave Law, the author may have felt obliged to debase his forthright political attacks into obscure ironies, especially in his portrait of the man with gold sleeve-buttons in *The Confidence-Man.* See Jonathan Cook, "Melville's Man in Gold Sleeve Buttons: Chief Justice Lemuel Shaw," *ESQ* 34 (4th Q 1988): 257–81.

4. Ronald S. Crane, "Suggestions Toward a Genealogy of the 'Man of Feeling,' " in Wayne C. Booth, ed, *The Idea of the Humanities,* 2 vols. (Chicago: University of Chicago Press, 1967), I:188–213.

5. William Empson, *Some Versions of Pastoral* (London: Chatto & Windus, 1935), and Leo Marx, *The Machine in the Garden: Technology and the Pastoral Ideal in America* (New York: Oxford University Press, 1964).

6. I am borrowing John K. Sheriff's terms as found in *The Good-Natured Man: The Evolution of a Moral Ideal, 1660–1800* (University, AL: University of Alabama Press, 1982).

7. Roger B. Henkle, *Comedy and Culture: England 1820–1900* (Princeton, NJ: Princeton University Press, 1980), p. 26.

8. Sheriff, *Good-Natured Man,* p. 34.

9. William Hazlitt, *Lectures on the Comic Writers,* in P. P. Howe, ed., *The Complete Works of William Hazlitt* (London: Dent, 1910), 6: 92. Hereafter cited as *CW.*

10. William Hazlitt, *The Spirit of the Age: or Contemporary Portraits* (London: Oxford University Press, 1954, 1970), pp. 294, 296.

11. Henkle stresses the tendency of most British comic novels in the first half of the century to assuage anxieties over social change through the valorization of "more traditional relationships—those of country life, . . . home, and so on. Thus, whenever the urge to rebel . . . grew potentially antisocial, it was resolved in favor of middle-class stability." Henkle, *Comedy and Culture,* p. 57.

12. Hazlitt, *CW,* 4: 101. Melville's copy is registered as Sealts, no. 265.

13. Ralph Waldo Emerson, *Emerson in His Journals,* ed. Joel Porte (Cambridge, MA: Harvard University Press, 1982), pp. 196, 387.

14. *Ibid.,* p. 363; Walter Blair and Hamlin Hill, *American Humor: From Poor Richard to Doonesbury* (New York: Oxford, 1978), p. 175.

15. Ralph Waldo Emerson, "Self Reliance," in *Selections from Ralph Waldo Emerson,* ed. Stephen E. Whicher (Boston: Houghton Mifflin, 1957), p. 150.

16. Ralph Waldo Emerson, "The Comic," in *ibid.,* p. 204. Hereafter cited as "Comic."

17. Blair and Hill, *American Humor,* p. 176.

18. Edwin P. Whipple, "The Literature of Mirth," in *The Boston Book* (Boston: Ticknor, Reed & Fields, 1850), p. 38.

19. [C. A. Munger], "A Chapter on Laughing," *The Knickerbocker* 44: 164, 163.

20. Charles A. Munger, "A Second Chapter on Laughter," *The Knickerbocker* 44: 600.

21. Donald Yannella and Kathleen Malone Yannella, "Evert A. Duyckinck's 'Diary': May 29–November 8, 1847," in Joel Myerson, ed., *Studies in American Renaissance 1978* (Boston: Twayne, 1978), p. 242.

22. Evert A. Duyckinck, Review of Mathews's *Motley Book, New York Review* 7 (October 1840): 433. Hereafter cited as ED.

23. Clifford in Hawthorne's *The House of the Seven Gables* provides an excellent example of the failure to maintain comic distance. Standing in his arched window and contemplating a suicidal plunge into a political procession below him, he is shocked by the presence of an organ grinder's monkey. "Destitute of the fiercer, deeper and more tragic power of laughter," he is reduced to mawkish tears over the ugliness of the animal. Without humor, Clifford is forever a victim of sentimentality. He would either remove himself entirely from social intercourse or plunge to his death into the midst of it. He cannot sustain the picturesque perspective on the margins of humanity that Duyckinck's poet-humorist maintains.

24. ED, 433. In his brief discussion of Young America's humor, Stafford stresses Duyckinck's notion of the humorist as poet. See John Stafford, *The Literary Criticism of "Young America": A Study in the Relationship of Politics and Literature, 1837–1850* (Berkeley: University of California Press, 1952), pp. 74–75.

25. Perry Miller, *The Raven and the Whale: The War of Words and Wits in the Era of Poe and Melville* (New York: Harcourt Brace & World, 1956), p. 138.

26. [William Gilmore Simms], "Writings of Cornelius Mathews," *Southern and Western* 6 (October 1844): 335, 339. Hereafter cited as Simms.

27. William A. Jones, "American Humor," *Democratic Review* 17 (September 1845): 215. Hereafter cited as AH.

28. Edgar Allan Poe, Notice of *Democratic Review, Broadway Journal* 2 (20 September 1845): 169. Some hint of the volatility of this episode in America's comic debate can be found in the fact that five years later, in a piece published shortly after his death, Poe revised his notion of Jones a bit, noting that the quondam "quack" was America's "most analytic, if not altogether our best critic." See *Edgar Allan Poe: Essays and Reviews,* Library of America, ed. G. R. Thompson (New York: Literary Classics of the United States, 1984), p. 1039

29. See Stafford, *"Young America,"* and Miller, *Raven and Whale.* I stress the *if,* for there is no mention of the affair in Blair and Hill's study at all.

30. AH, 215. Jones refers to Shaftesbury's remark, "'Tis the persecuting spirit [that] has raised the bantering one; and want of liberty may account for want of a true politeness, and for the corruption or wrong use of pleasantry and humour. . . . The greater the weight is, the bitterer will be the satire. The higher the slavery, the more exquisite the buffoonery." See William A. Jones, "Freedom of Wit and Humour," *Characters and Criticisms,* 2 vols. (New York: Westervelt, 1857), I: 49.

31. William A. Jones, "Literary Egotism," in *Characters and Criticisms,* I: 223. Hereafter cited as LE.

32. William A. Jones, "The Familiar Philosophy," in *Characters and Criticisms,* I: 247. Hereafter cited as FP.

33. William A. Jones, "Satire and Sentiment," in *Characters and Criticisms,* I: 88. Hereafter cited as SS.

3. The Example of Irving

1. See Leon Howard, *Herman Melville: A Biography* (Berkeley: University of California Press, 1967), pp. 98, 104–55.

2. For a lively rendition of "the war of words and wits" waged between Young America and the Knickerbockers, see Miller, *Raven and Whale.*

3. Evert A. Duyckinck, *Irvingiana: A Memorial of Washington Irving* (New York: Charles B. Richardson, 1860), p. xx.

4. William Hedges, *Washington Irving: An American Study, 1802–1832* (Baltimore: Johns Hopkins University Press, 1965), devotes a final chapter to Irving's influence on such major writers as Poe, Hawthorne, Melville, and Thoreau. Roth speaks of the Irvingesque nature of *Typee*. Martin A. Roth, *Comedy and America: The Lost World of Washington Irving* (Port Washington, NY: Kennikat Press, 1976), p. 180. Dillingham argues that Melville's tales reveal the development of a character that is "submerged beneath layers of inoffensive wit, congenial reminiscing, and Irvingesque worldly maturity." William B. Dillingham, *Melville's Short Fiction: 1853–1856* (Athens, University of Georgia Press, 1977), p. 11. R. Bruce Bickley, Jr., in *The Method of Melville's Short Fiction* (Durham, NC: Duke University Press, 1975), provides more specific links between Melville and Irving (see pp. 26–44), as does Jane Mushabac, *Melville's Humor: A Critical Study* (Hamden, CT: Archon Books, 1981).

5. William Hazlitt, *Spirit of the Age*, pp. 299–300, and *idem.*, *Conversations of James Northcote*, in Hazlitt 11:239.

6. Hazlitt, *Spirit of the Age*, p. 300.

7. Hedges, *Irving*, p. 129.

8. Irving was also working out personal anxieties—failures in love and finance, the inability to settle at home—in his seemingly cheery writings. See Jeffrey Rubin-Dorsky, *Adrift in the Old World: The Psychological Pilgrimage of Washington Irving* (Chicago: University of Chicago Press, 1988).

9. The letters suggest the latter. Writing to Mary Fairlie in 1807, Irving complained of the graft in Democratic politics: "Truly this serving of one's country is a nauseous piece of business." See Stanley T. Williams, *The Life of Washington Irving* (New York: Oxford Press, 1935), p. 96. According to Roth, politics of this sort was a matter of "revulsion" for the author. See Roth, *Comedy and America*, p. 78.

10. Williams, II: 269. It might be argued that Irving disregarded *Salmagundi* because it was a collaborative effort, and scholars as early as Duyckinck and as recent as Bruce Granger in the now standard edition of the text have mulled over just how much Irving contributed. But all, especially Stanley Williams, seem to agree that Irving made substantial contributions (26 out of 59, according to Granger, pp. 327–29) and that he edited Paulding and his brother as well. In short, Irving had every good reason to include the early work. His honesty on this score finally outweighed his reluctance. Excluding his next work would have been unthinkable, and yet he felt the need to defend its tone. In his "Apology" to the 1848 edition of *The History of New York,* he disavowed any satiric intentions, claiming only to be humorous. Hedges, *Irving*, p. 80.

11. According to Hedges, Dana found "gentle good-naturedness and touching pathos mixed with humor" in *Salmagundi* and no hint of satire. Clearly, he was reading the early work in light of *The Sketch Book* (56–57).

12. Williams, I: 79.

13. Roth, *Comedy and America*, p. 80.

14. Hedges, *Irving*, p. 45, reminds us that, rather than imitating, Irving and his co-authors James Kirke Paulding and brother William Irving were parodying British, and also American, periodicals of the day.

15. *Ibid.*, p. 6; Roth, *Comedy and America*, pp. 32, 38–39; Hedges, *Irving*, p. 7.

16. Hedges argues that the burlesque pervades much of Irving's work, and from a modernist's perspective he finds a valorizing connection between Irving and modern absurdism. *Salmagundi*, for instance, "pushes the tendency of self-mockery to the point of explicitly defying its readers to make sense of the contents." Hedges, *Irving*, p. 45. Roth extends the

argument, using the burlesque as a measuring stick of excellence against which Irving at times succeeds or fails. My sense is that Irving eventually grew beyond the constraints of burlesque toward a more amiable accommodation of whim and politics.

17. Washington Irving, *Salmagundi; or The Whim-whams and Opinions of Launcelot Langstaff, Esq. & Others,* ed. Bruce I. Granger and Martha Hartzog (Boston: Twayne, 1977), p. 239. Hereafter cited as *Sal.*

18. It would be another two decades before Frederic Church would supply an Andean alternative to the sublime Alps with his monumental paintings of the Andes.

19. Washington Irving, "Rip Van Winkle," in *The Sketch Book of Geoffrey Crayon, Gent.,* ed. Haskell Springer (Boston: Twayne, 1978), pp. 38–39. Hereafter cited as *Rip.*

20. Philip Young, "Fallen from Time: Rip Van Winkle," in *A Century of Commentary on the Works of Washington Irving, 1860–1974,* ed. Andrew B. Myers (Tarrytown, NY: Sleepy Hollow Restorations, 1974); Donald E. Pease, *Visionary Compacts: American Renaissance Writings in Cultural Context* (Madison: University of Wisconsin Press, 1987), pp. 14–15; Rubin-Dorsky, pp. 111–15.

21. Washington Irving, *Oliver Goldsmith: A Biography* (New York: Putnam's, 1864), p. 211. My italics. Hereafter cited as *OG.*

4. Playing Along: America and the Rhetoric of Deceit

1. Michel de Montaigne, "On Liars," in *Essays,* trans. J. M. Cohen (New York: Penquin, 1958), p. 31.

2. *Ibid.,* pp. 30–31.

3. "Mendacem memorem esse oportet," *De Institutione Oratoria* IV, no. 2:91.

4. Michel de Montaigne, "On Democritus and Heraclitus," p. 133.

5. As quoted in Sissela Bok, *Lying: Moral Choice in Public and Private Life* (New York: Pantheon, 1978), p. 262.

6. Jean Starobinski, "Montaigne on Illusion: The Denunciation of Untruth," *Daedalus* 108, no. 3 (Summer 1979): 93.

7. *Ibid.,* p. 95.

8. Quoted in Bok, *Lying,* p. 262.

9. As Starobinski observes, "The supreme illusion [for both Montaigne and Bacon] was to believe that one had escaped illusion." "Montaigne on Illusion," p. 100.

10. Evidence of this may be found in the Restoration debate over the acceptability of Dorimant's dissembling in Etherege's *The Man of Mode.* See James Thompson, "Lying and Dissembling in the Restoration," *Restoration* 6 (1982): 15–17.

11. Gary Lindberg, *The Confidence Man in American Literature* (New York: Oxford Press, 1982), p. 3.

12. Quoted in Bok, *Lying,* p. 262.

13. Philip Dormer Stanhope, Lord Chesterfield, *Lord Chesterfield's Letters to His Son,* intro. R. K. Root (London: Dent, 1929), p. 148.

14. [T. Dobson], *Lord Chesterfield's Advice to his Son, on Men and Manners; or, a New System of Education* (Philadelphia: T. Dobson, 1789), p. 104.

15. Chesterfield, *Letters,* p. 149.

16. Rev. John Trusler, ed. *Principles of Politeness and of Knowing the World, By the Late Lord Chesterfield. With Additions by the Rev. John Trusler* (Carlisle, PA: Alexander & Philips, 1809), p. 3.

17. "A Member of the Philadelphia Bar," *The American Chesterfield, or Way to Wealth, Honour and Distinction* (Philadelphia: John Grigg, 1827).

18. *Ibid.,* p. 14.

19. Neil Harris, *Humbug: The Art of P.T. Barnum* (Chicago: University of Chicago Press, 1973), p. 23. Hereafter cited as Harris.

20. "Humbugiana," *Titan* 13 (1854): 233.

21. Melville, casting his confidence man in an apocalyptic frame, makes a similar but less acrimonious claim for his genial misanthrope as a "new monster" for a new age.

22. R. L., "An Essay on Humbug. By a Manchester Man," *Fraser's Magazine* 7 (July 1855): 30, 31.

23. "Lectures on the Comic Writers," in William Hazlitt, *Complete Works* 6: 11.

24. Laman Blanchard, "Every-Day Lying," *Colburn's New Monthly Magazine*, 1842, p. 264.

25. "Prospectus of an Intended Course of Lectures on the Philosophy of Humbug. By Professor Wolfgang von Bibundtucker," *Bentley's Magazine*, 1839, p. 601.

26. Mu [George Henry Lewes], "On the Physiology of Lying," *Colburn's New Monthly Magazine*, 1842, p. 55. See also Lewes's essay on Humbug, "Proposal for a Dictionary of a not 'Unknown Tongue," *Colburn's New Monthly Magazine*, 1842–43, pp. 190–99. Like Bibundtucker, he finds that education as it is presently designed "to prevent the possibility of straightforward progression" is our most pernicious humbug (p. 197).

27. [D. McCauley], "Humbugiana," *Debow's Commercial Review*, 1846, p. 444.

28. Johannes Dietrich Bergmann, "The Original Confidence Man," *American Quarterly* 21 (Fall 1969): 561.

29. Lindberg distinguishes between the trickster and the confidence man. The former is a culturally marginal figure; the latter, "culturally representative." See Gary Lindberg, *The Confidence Man in American Literature* (New York: Oxford University Press, 1982), p. 8. But in American society, where marginal subcultures are continually engaged in the complex (and perhaps paradoxical) process of self-legitimization and assimilation, this distinction is not so important a focus as is the means by which a formerly "marginal" figure becomes "representative." Stately Uncle Sam was once a thieving Yankee Peddler; today's rappers may soon become streetcorner bards.

30. Quoted in Bergmann, "Original Confidence Man," pp. 561–62.

31. Quoted in *Ibid.*, p. 566; see also Paul Smith, "*The Confidence-Man* and the Literary World of New York," *Nineteenth-Century Fiction* 16 (March 1962): 329–37.

32. Swapping anecdotal tall tales remains a fairly common phenomenon. Literary tall tales are relatively scarce, although some of our best modern writers—John Barth, Thomas Berger, Joseph Heller, Bernard Malamud, Thomas Pynchon, Philip Roth—have used "tall" fiction techniques for their own individual aesthetic ends. The genre did not die with the frontier.

33. Richard Dorson, "Comic Indian Anecdotes," *Southern Folklore Quarterly* 10 (June 1946): 114. Dorson contends that early American Indians were "ingenious fabricators" intent upon deluding America's first visitors.

34. William Wood, *New England's Prospect*, ed. Alden T. Vaughan (Amherst: University of Massachusetts Press, 1977), p. 85.

35. Blair and Hill, *American Humor*, p. 130.

36. Wood, *New England's Prospect*, p. 29.

37. See Montaigne, "On Liars," p. 27. "If falsehood, like truth, had but one face, we should know better where we are, for we should then take for certain the opposite of what the liar tells us. But the reverse of the truth has a hundred thousand shapes and a boundless field."

38. Carolyn Brown's recently published dissertation combines anthropological and rhetorical approaches to derive a satisfyingly similar conclusion. For her, the tall tale is "a dalliance at that hazy border between the credible and incredible" that effectively reinforces

a group identity. See Carolyn S. Brown, *The Tall Tale in American Folklore and Literature* (Knoxville: University of Tennessee Press, 1987), pp. 38, 36.

39. Kenneth Lynn, *Mark Twain and Southwestern Humor* (Boston: Little, Brown, 1959), p. 28.

40. Joseph G. Baldwin, "Flush Times in Alabama and Mississippi" (1853) in Blair, *Native American Humor*, p. 357.

41. Mody C. Boatwright, "The Art of Tall Lying," *Southwest Review* (Fall 1949): 358.

42. Lynn, *Mark Twain*, p. 18.

43. Neil Schmitz, "Tall Tale, Tall Talk: Pursuing the Lie in Jacksonian Literature," *American Literature* 48 (January 1977): 471, 474.

44. William Lenz, *Flush Times and Fast Talk: The Confidence Man as Literary Convention* (Columbia: University of Missouri Press, 1985).

5. E. A. Poe and T. B. Thorpe: Two Models of Deceit

1. Paul Brodtkorb, Jr., *"The Confidence-Man:* The Con Man as Hero," *Studies in the Novel* 1 (Winter 1969): 421.

2. See "The Duc de L'Omlette" and "Bon-Bon" in Thomas Ollive Mabbott, ed., *The Collected Works of Edgar Allan Poe: Tales and Sketches (1831–1842)* (Cambridge, MA: Harvard University Press, 1978), pp. 34, 105. Hereafter cited as *Tales and Sketches*. This patterned joke also appears in a letter to Beverley Tucker (1 December 1835), in which Poe walks a thin line in sorting out the proper use of humor. On the one hand, he admires one critic's comic attacks as "annihilating"; on the other, he thinks that very critic should be "horsewhipped" for his "indecency." Clearly, he saw humor as a weapon, but one that it is wrong to use. See *The Letters of Edgar Allan Poe*, ed. John Ward Ostrom (New York: Gordian Press, 1966), p. 77. Hereafter cited as Poe's *Letters*.

3. Responding to Evert Duyckinck's rejection of "Von Kempelen's Discovery," Poe wrote, "It is a kind of 'exercise,' or experiment, in the plausible or verisimilar style. Of course, there is *not one word* of truth in it from beginning to end" (Poe's *Letters*, II: 443).

4. Taylor classifies "Loss of Breath" along with the equally odd "Berenice" as another satire of the lurid Blackwood Magazine tale. See Walter Fuller Taylor, "Israfel in Motley: A Study of Poe's Humor," *Sewanee Review* 42: 336–37.

5. Poe's first proposal for a collection of short pieces, which became *Tales of the Grotesque and Arabesque*, was to be a gathering of parodies of contemporary writers and styles entitled "Tales of the Folio Club." Alexander Hammond, "A Reconstruction of Poe's 1833 *Tales of the Folio Club:* Preliminary Notes," *Poe Studies* 5 (December 1972): 25–32. Hammond's work significantly expands upon T. O. Mabbott, "On Poe's Tales of the Folio Club," *Sewanee Review* 36 (1928): 171–76.

6. G. R. Thompson, *Poe's Fiction: Romantic Irony in the Gothic Tales* (Madison: University of Wisconsin Press, 1973), pp. 34, 164.

7. Critics generally read Poe's hoaxing as constructive rather than deconstructive, in that its satire brings readers to a fresh vision. Mooney is a case in point: "Behind all of Poe's doors lurks the ghost of the hoaxer, secretly working toward the construction of fantastic ironies with which to plague the literalist." Stephen L. Mooney, "Poe's Gothic Wasteland," *Sewanee Review* 70 (1962): 281. While this may be true in certain instances, I tend to see Poe's hoaxing as more pathological in its teasing of readers about conflicts that obsessed him. In "Rue Morgue," for instance, the hoax is so artfully submerged that the reader has little chance of uncovering it all; it is Poe's private joke, and attack, rather than a shared experience. Daniel Hoffman coined the term "hoaxiepoe," in *Poe Poe Poe Poe Poe Poe Poe* (Garden City, NY: Doubleday & Co., 1973), p. 153. Dennis W. Eddings has also

assembled a useful collection of essays entitled *The Naiad Voice: Essays on Poe's Satiric Hoaxing* (Port Washington, NY: Associated Faculty Press, 1983).

8. In *Edgar Allan Poe: Essays and Reviews,* ed. G. R. Thompson (New York: Library of America, 1984), pp. 778–96.

9. Robert Regan, "Hawthorne's 'Plagiary'; Poe's Duplicity," *Nineteenth-Century Fiction* 25 (December 1970): 282.

10. Edgar Allan Poe, "The Murders in the Rue Morgue," in *Tales and Sketches,* p. 526. Hereafter cited as RM.

11. Edgar Allan Poe, "The Philosophy of Composition," in *Selected Writings of Edgar Allan Poe,* ed. Edward H. Davidson (Boston: Houghton-Mifflin, 1956), p. 454. Hereafter cited as PC.

12. For a thorough assessment of Poe's hoaxing in "Rue Morgue," see Burton R. Pollin, "Poe's 'Murders in the Rue Morgue': The Ingenious Web Unravelled," in *Insights and Outlooks: Essays on Great Writers* (New York: Gordian Press, 1986), pp. 101–29.

13. David Ketterer, *The Rationale of Deception in Poe* (Baton Rouge: Louisiana State University Press, 1979), pp. i, xiii.

14. Dennis W. Eddings, "A Suggestion for the Unity of Poe's Fiction," in *The Naiad Voice,* pp. 161–62.

15. Poe's *Letters,* pp. 22–23.

16. Elsewhere, in discussing the styles of Margaret Fuller, Emerson, and Carlyle, Poe defined "affectation" as "an assumption of airs or *tricks* which have no basis in reason or common sense." See "About Critics and Criticism," in *Poe: Essays and Reviews* (New York: Library of America, 1984), p. 1040.

17. Basler first established the unreliability of the obsessed narrator and substantiated the claim that the narrator murdered Rowena. Roy Basler, "The Interpretation of 'Ligeia,' " *College English* 5 (April 1944): 363–72. Ten years later Griffith determined that the struggle of wills between the dark, Germanic Ligeia and the fair-haired English Rowena constitute a satire on British transcendentalism. Clark Griffith, "Poe's 'Ligeia' and the English Romantics," *Toronto Quarterly* 24 (1954): 3–16, 19–25. And in the 1960s Stovall argued that Ligeia is, in fact, the narrator's fantasy creation. Floyd Stovall, "The Conscious Art of Edgar Allan Poe," *College English* 24 (March 1963): 417–21. Countering them, however, are such critics as James Schroeter and John Lauber, who call for a "literal" reading of the text as Poe's attempt to achieve a unified Gothic effect. That is, his supernaturalism is to be taken, with appropriate suspensions of disbelief, at face value. A key argument offered by the literalists is that Poe altered his text at Philip Cooke's suggestion to increase verisimilitude. James Schroeter, "A Misreading of Poe's 'Ligeia,' " *PMLA* 75 (September 1961): 397–406, and John Lauber, " 'Ligeia' and Its Critics: A Plea for Literalism," *Studies in Short Fiction* 4 (1966): 28–32. But G. R. Thompson's closer inspection of the timing of Poe's revisions reveals that Poe ignored Cooke's advice, that he made Ligeia's supposed possession of Rowena more abrupt rather than more gradual; hence his revisions created a less believable (thus more hoaxy) fiction. Thompson, *Poe's Fiction,* p. 87.

18. Edgar Allan Poe, "Ligeia," in *Tales and Sketches (1831–1842),* p. 330. Hereafter cited as L.

19. Thompson's own reading uncovers numerous ironic twists, all of which corroborate the notion that the "real subject" of "Ligeia" is that "delusive madness of the narrator," which amounts to a burlesque or "insinuated mockery of transcendentalism." Thompson, *Poe's Fiction,* pp. 82, 87.

20. "Exordium to Critical Notices," in *Poe: Essays and Reviews,* p. 1031.

21. Ralph Waldo Emerson, "The Poet," in *Selections from Ralph Waldo Emerson,* p. 225.

22. Edgar Allan Poe, "About Critics and Criticism," in *Poe: Essays and Reviews* (New York: Library of America, 1984), p. 1040, Poe's italics.

23. Thomas Bangs Thorpe, "The Big Bear of Arkansas," in Walter Blair, *Native American Humor* (San Francisco: Chandler Press, 1960), pp. 345, 347. Hereafter cited as Big Bear.

24. Blair and Hill, p. 212. This discussion is an expansion of Blair's earlier essay, "The Technique of The Big Bear of Arkansas," *Southwest Review* 28 (1943): 426–35.

25. *Ibid.*, p. 211.

6. The Genial Misanthrope: Melville and the Cosmopolitan Ideal

1. Hector St. John de Crèvecoeur, *Letters from an American Farmer* (London: J. M. Dent, 1951), p. 43–44. Hereafter cited as *LAF*.

2. Thomas R. Preston, *Not in Timon's Manner: Feeling, Misanthropy, and Satire in Eighteenth-Century England* (University: University of Alabama Press, 1975), p. 107.

3. Thomas J. Schlereth, *The Cosmopolitan Ideal in Enlightenment Thought: Its Form and Function in the Ideas of Franklin, Hume, and Voltaire, 1694–1790* (Notre Dame, IN: University of Notre Dame Press, 1977), pp. 14, 18. Hereafter cited as Schlereth.

4. Immanuel Kant, "Idea for a Universal History with Cosmopolitan Intent," in *The Philosophy of Kant*, ed. Carl J. Friedrich (New York: Modern Library, 1949), p. 120.

5. Johann Wolfgang von Goethe, "Theory of World Literature" (1828), in *Goethe's Literary Essays,* arr. J. E. Springarn (New York: Ungar, 1921), pp. 92, 96.

6. Johann Wolfgang von Goethe, *Conversations of Goethe with Eckermann* (London: J. M. Dent, 1930), pp. 165, 361.

7. "On Sterne" (1827), in *Goethe's Literary Essays*, p. 222.

8. Samuel Johnson, *The History of Rasselas, Prince of Abyssinia,* ed. Gwin J. Kolb (Northbrook, Ill.: AHM Publishing, 1962), pp. 75–76.

9. Quoted in Washington Irving, *Oliver Goldsmith: A Biography* (New York: Putnam's, 1864), p. 53.

10. Alan D. McKillop, "Local Attachment and Cosmopolitanism: The Eighteenth-Century Pattern," in Frederick W. Hilles and Harold Bloom, eds., *From Sensibility to Romanticism: Essays Presented to Frederick A. Pottle* (New York: Oxford University Press, 1965), pp. 191–218.

11. Oliver Goldsmith, *The Citizen of the World, in The Vicar of Wakefield and Other Writings*, ed. Frederick W. Hilles (New York: Modern Library, 1955), p. 126. Hereafter cited as *CW*.

12. Henry A. Pochmann, *German Culture in America: Philosophical and Literary Influences, 1600–1900* (Madison: University of Wisconsin Press, 1957), p. 330.

13. *The Stranger: A Play in Five Acts,* by Augustus Frederick Ferdinand von Kotzebue, trans. Benjamin Thompson and emended by Richard Brinsley Sheridan and John P. Kemble, in Epes Sargent, ed., *Modern Standard Drama* 9 (New York: William Taylor, 1846): iii. Hereafter cited as *Stranger*. The first edition to be published on American soil seems to be *The Stranger; or, Misanthropy and Repentance,* trans. George Papendick (Salem, MA: Barnard B. Macanulty, 1799).

14. Although no direct evidence indicates that Melville saw Kotzebue's play, he surely knew of it. He might have seen a Western production of it in Galena, Illinois, when he visited his uncle in 1840, or a New York production in 1846 at the Park Theater. See Stanton Garner, "The Picaresque Career of Thomas Melvill, Junior: Part II," *Melville Society Extracts,* no. 62 (May 1985), p. 7. Melville certainly knew of John Kemble, who played the role of Charles, according to Hazlitt, "as if his whole life had been a suppressed sigh!"

(Hazlitt, *Collected Works* 5:376). John was the brother of Fanny Kemble Butler, Melville's Berkshire neighbor, whose stormy divorce may have inspired Melville's Goneril in *The Confidence-Man*. See "Melville's Goneril and Fanny Kemble," *New England Quarterly* 18 (1945): 489–500. Foster virulently disputes that satiric reading. Elizabeth Foster, ed. *The Confidence Man* by Herman Melville (New York: Hendricks House, 1954), 311–14. Reflecting upon *The Stranger* and the Kembles, Melville may have sensed the ironies of domestic disintegration incumbent upon the brother's role and the sister's unhappy marriage. Whatever the associations to Kemble (*fils* or *fille*), one cannot ignore the portrait temptingly entitled "The Stranger" toward the end of *Pierre,* or the use of the term "stranger" in the tales, which becomes an idiomatic pattern in *The Confidence-Man,* or the possibility that Frank Goodman's and Charlie Noble's verbal duel over benevolence and misanthropy parallels the similar debate conducted in Act One of *The Stranger* by the servant Francis, who is a good man, and Charles, a noble.

15. Thomas Carlyle, "Jean Paul Friederick Richter" (1827), in *Critical and Miscellaneous Essays,* 5 vols. (London: Chapman & Hall, n.d.), I: 13–14.

16. Review of *Walt und Vult, Literary World,* no. 17, 29 May 1847, p. 387.

17. Hans-Joachim Lang and Benjamin Lease, "Melville's Cosmopolitan: Bayard Taylor in *The Confidence-Man,*" *Amerikastudien* 2 (1977): 286–89. N. P. Willis, *Inklings of Adventure,* 3 vols. (London: Saunders & Otley, 1836). The epigram is from Colley Cibber's "Love Makes a Man."

18. James Lawson, *Tales and Sketches, by a Cosmopolite* (New York: Elias, 1830). Born in 1799 to a Scots merchant family, Lawson earned his sobriquet by advancing the cause of American literature abroad. Duyckinck credited his selection of American writers in John Mennon's *Literary Coronal* (1821) for introducing the best of American literature to the British. According to Poe, he was "generally respected and beloved." See "Literati of New York City," in *Poe: Essays and Reviews,* p. 1180.

19. Evert Duyckinck, "Cornelius Mathews's Writings," *New York Review* 7 (October 1840): 430.

20. "Monologues Among the Mountains, By a Cosmopolite," *Graham's* 26 (January 1845): 170. Poole's provides no attribution, but a likely suspect is James Lawson.

21. "Monologues Among the Mountains—No. II, By a Cosmopolite," *Graham's* 27 (April 1845): 1. My italics.

22. "*Mosses,*" pp. 244, 249, 245.

23. John Rathbun, *American Literary Criticism, 1800–1860* (Boston: Twayne, 1979), pp. 20, 42.

24. Quoted in Odell Shepherd, "The New England Triumvirate," in Robert E. Spiller *et al.,* eds., *Literary History of the United States,* rev. 3d ed. (London: Macmillan, 1963), p. 601.

25. Ralph Waldo Emerson, *Representative Men: Seven Lectures* (Boston: Phillips, Sampson, 1850), pp. 224, 279. Hereafter cited as *RM.*

26. Herman Melville, *Israel Potter: His Fifty Years of Exile* (Evanston and Chicago: Northwestern University Press and the Newberry Library, 1982), 48.

27. Poe objected to the worldliness of the cosmopolitan ideal: "An infinity of error makes its way into our Philosophy, through Man's habit of considering himself a citizen of the world solely." See *Marginalia,* in *The Complete Works of Edgar Allan Poe,* vol. 16, ed. James A. Harrison (rpt. New York: AMS Press, 1965), p. 167. Our goal must be to leap into the world of Reason. Preferring to be "a denizen of the universe," Poe insisted upon a return to the true transcendental spirit of the ideal.

28. Citizen of the World [James Boardman], *America and the Americans* (n.p., 1833). Dedicated to the memory of Lafayette, this defense of America emphasizes the nation's

advancement in "all the useful arts" (p. vi). As an international merchant, philanthropist, and pragmatist, Boardman typifies the mercantile degeneration of the cosmopolitan ideal that is best exemplified by the international trickster Vincent Nolte, discussed below.

29. Voltaire, Letter of 23 April 1754, quoted in Schlereth, *Cosmopolitan Ideal,* p. 12.

30. [Anonymous], "Prospectus of an Intended Course of Lectures on the Philosophy of Humbug," *Bentley's Magazine,* 1839, p. 599. Like Poe, he calls himself "a denizen of the universe."

31. Vincent Nolte, *Fifty Years in Both Hemispheres; or, Reminiscences of the Life of a Former Merchant* (New York: J. S. Redfield, 1854), p. xxii. Hereafter cited as Nolte.

32. [Donald MacLeod], "The History of a Cosmopolite," *Putnam's Monthly,* September 1854, pp. 325–30. Hereafter cited as HC.

33. For a fuller discussion of this source, see John Bryant, " 'Nowhere a Stranger': Melville and Cosmopolitanism," *Nineteenth-Century Fiction* 39 (December 1984): 275–91.

34. Constance Rourke, *American Humor: A Study of the National Character* (New York: Harcourt Brace, 1931), pp. 50–52.

35. Review of *The Life and Adventures of John James Audubon, the Naturalist,* ed. Robert Buchanan, *Edinburgh Review* 133 (July 1870): 140.

36. John James Audubon, *Audubon and His Journals,* 2 vols., ed. Maria R. Audubon (New York: Scribners, 1897; rpt. New York: Dover, 1960), II: 220–21. Audubon writes: "I met at the crossings of the Juniata River a gentleman from New Orleans, whose name is Vincent Nolte. . . . From that day [in 1811] Vincent Nolte has been a friend to me." Apparently Nolte gave Audubon several letters of introduction, which advanced his cause in Europe. Later the relationship cooled, for Audubon calls Nolte his "old but too rich acquaintance." See *Audubon's America: The Narratives and Experience of John James Audubon,* ed. Donald C. Peattie (Boston: Houghton Mifflin, 1940), p. 176.

37. Donald MacLeod, *Pynnshurst: His Wanderings and Ways of Thinking* (New York: Scribner's, 1852), pp. 412 and 297.

38. *Hunt's Merchants' Magazine,* 1854, p. 414.

39. *Littell's Living Age,* 1854, p. 3.

40. Introduction to *History of Cosmopolite: or the Writings of Rev. Lorenzo Dow,* 8th ed. (1848; rpt. Cincinnati: Applegate, 1851), p. vi. Hereafter cited as Dow. The title page of this edition boasts "30,000 copies" in print. Dow's memoirs and other writings were published under various titles and at various times up through the Civil War. They first appeared as *History of Cosmopolite* in at least five editions in 1814. Multiple editions under that title were published in each of the years 1848–51, 1854–60, and 1864. As noted, the title of MacLeod's review of Nolte's memoirs was clearly intended to echo Dow's title. Other Dow titles include *The Yankee Spy: or Cosmopolite's Interesting Analects of Common Sense* (1814); *Perambulations of Cosmopolite* (1842, 1855); and *Life, Travels, Labors, and Writings of Lorenzo Dow* (1859).

41. For a fuller discussion of the benevolent nonsectarians, see John Bryant, "Citizens of a World to Come: Melville and the Millennial Cosmopolite," *American Literature* 59 (March 1987): 20–36.

42. Dorothy Ripley, *The Bank of Faith and Works United* (Philadelphia: J. H. Cunningham, 1819), title page.

43. James F. Findlay, *Dwight L. Moody* (Chicago: University of Chicago Press, 1969), p. 148. See also Richard Carwardine, *Transatlantic Revivalism: Popular Evangelism in Britain and America, 1790–1865* (Westport, CT: Greenwood Press, 1978), p. 104.

44. Charles Coteman Setters, *Lorenzo Dow: The Bearer of the Word* (New York: Minton, Balch, 1928), p. 256. Hereafter cited as Setters. Jackson received Dow in Washington in 1832 and met him again that year in Dow's Vermont home.

45. S. G. Goodrich, *Recollections of a Lifetime, or Men and Things I Have Seen* (New York: Miller, Orton, 1857), p. 210. Hereafter cited as Goodrich.

46. Lewis Gaylord Clark, "Editor's Drawer," *Harper's* 10 (December 1854): 136.

47. The attractive, militant, and intolerant Peter Cartwright, for instance, resembles in build and manner the militant Methodist of Chapter 3. Russel B. Nye speaks of Cartwright's "manhandling" in *The Cultural Life of the New Nation: 1776–1830* (New York: Harper & Row, 1960), pp. 220, 231. Joseph Thomas, known as "the white pilgrim," might well be Melville's cream-colored mute, who similarly characterized himself as "a Lamb sent among wolves" to preach a cosmopolitan line: "the union and oneness of all God's people." *The Life of the Pilgrim Joseph Thomas* (Winchester, VA: J. Foster, 1817), pp. 36, 64. Dow's "City of Peace," like innumerable other Western utopias, both projected and realized, resembles Truman's planned community, aptly named New Jerusalem (*CM*, 50).

48. Bryant, "Citizens of a World to Come," pp. 34–36.

49. Setters, pp. 59, 69, and p. 45.

50. John Dowling, Introduction to *The Dealings of God, Man, and the Devil*, by Lorenzo Dow (Cincinnati: Applegate, 1858), pp. iii, iv. Hereafter cited as Dowling.

51. John W. Francis, *New York During the Last Half Century* (New York: John F. Trow, 1857), p. 95. Goodman is also referred to as "quite an original" (*CM*, p. 238). Francis was, according to Perry Miller, the Rabelaisian "patriarch" of Clark's Knickerbocker "Sanctum" and "conspicuous guest" at the wedding of Herman's young brother, Allan. *The Raven and the Whale: The War of Words and Wits in the Era of Poe and Melville* (New York: Harcourt Brace, 1956), pp. 16–17.

52. Dow, pp. 18, 94. See also pp. 203, 208, 239, and 322.

53. Bryant, "Citizens of a World to Come," p. 34.

54. Dow Jr. [Elbridge G. Paige], *Short Patent Sermons,* rev. and corrected (New York: Lawrence Labree, 1841), p. [i]. Paige also published a two-volume set of sermons with a humorously illustrated title page (New York: L. Long, 1850).

55. "A Short Patent Sermon," *Yankee Doodle,* 2, no. 40 (10 July, 1847): 131. See *Piazza Tales,* 443–44, 786–87.

7. The Anxieties of Humor

1. See in particular the chapter "Truth and Fiction in '*Typee*,' " in Charles Roberts Anderson, *Melville in the South Seas* (New York: Columbia University Press, 1939), pp. 179–195. More factual material can be found in the writings of Wilson Heflin and Robert Forsythe. For an overview of Melville's travels, see Thomas Farel Heffernan, "Melville the Traveler," in John Bryant, ed., *A Companion to Melville Studies* (Westport, CT: Greenwood Press, 1986), pp. 35–61. For a sociological reading of Melville's transformation of experience into text, see T. Walter Herbert, Jr., *Marquesan Encounters: Melville and the Meaning of Civilization* (Cambridge, MA: Harvard University Press, 1980).

2. Leon Howard's "Historical Note" to the NN edition of *Typee* (pp. 277–302) is still a useful resource for the background on Melville's first novel, despite twenty years of new findings. A helpful guide for updates is Bette S. Weidman's chapter "*Typee* and *Omoo*: A Diverging Pair" in Bryant, *Companion,* pp. 85–121.

3. Weidman, "*Typee* and *Omoo*," p. 98. Milton R. Stern collects the major reviews of *Typee* in *Critical Essays on Herman Melville's Typee* (Boston: G. K. Hall, 1982).

4. Charles Fenno Hoffman "commended" Melville's critique of the missionaries to the readers of the New York *Critic and Times* (30 March, 1846) for frank and open discussion. See Watson G. Branch, ed., *Melville: The Critical Heritage* (London: Routledge & Kegan

Paul, 1974), p. 70. The Transcendentalist John Sullivan Dwight provided the most spirited and politically advanced defense of Melville's attacks in the Brook Farm *Harbinger,* 4 April 1846, pp. 263–66. The review is reprinted in Stern, *Critical Essays,* pp. 24–27.

5. William Oland Bourne, "Typee: The Traducer of Missions," *Christian Parlor Magazine* 3 (July 1846): 74–83, reprinted in Stern, *Critical Essays,* p. 40.

6. Weidman, *"Typee* and *Omoo,"* p. 96.

7. Seelye argues that Melville's attempt to adopt an "Irvingesque style," or "ironic mask . . . whose jolliness is mockery," fails because it cannot accommodate the author's formal two-step of trying to be a Polynesian expert and yet "unsuspecting dupe of cannibal tricks." See John Seelye, *Melville: The Ironic Diagram* (Evanston: Northwestern University Press, 1970), p. 23. Rather than stress Melville's fatal adherence to Irving, I argue for his conscious stretching beyond the model.

8. Milton R. Stern, *The Fine Hammered Steel of Herman Melville* (Urbana: University of Illinois Press, 1957), p. 49.

9. See Janet Giltrow, "Speaking Out: Travel and Structure in Herman Melville's Early Narratives," *American Literature* 52 (March 1980): 18–32; Mitchell Breitwieser, "False Sympathy in Melville's *Typee," American Quarterly* 34 (Fall 1982): 396–417; John Samson, "Perception and Preconception in Polynesia," in *White Lies: Melville's Narratives of Facts* (Ithaca, NY: Cornell University Press, 1989), pp. 22–56; and Bryan C. Short, " 'The Author at the Time': Tommo and Melville's Self-Discovery in *Typee,"* in James Duban, ed., *Melville and His Narrators,* a special issue of *Texas Studies in Literature and Language* 31 (Fall 1989): 386–405.

10. This irony is not entirely a literary construction. Melville would have been aware of an equivalent irony regarding the fate of the crew of the *Essex,* the whaling ship that was struck and sunk by a whale in 1820. These unfortunates in their lifeboats avoided touching the nearby Marquesan islands because they feared native cannibalism and were eventually forced to kill and eat one another before their rescue. In fact, as Anderson notes (*Melville in South Seas,* pp. 106–7), island cannibalism was virtually nonexistent and possibly a sailor or native ruse, making the sailor's experience all the more grim: Fearing the worst from the "alien other," they committed upon themselves the very crime they would expect only of a "savage." Inverting this irony, Melville has Tommo risk native cannibalism to avoid that of his fellow mates. See also Thomas Farel Heffernan, *Stove by A Whale: Owen Chase and the Essex* (Middletown, CT: Wesleyan University Press, 1981), p. 78.

11. Edward H. Rosenberry, *Melville and the Comic Spirit* (Cambridge, MA: Harvard University Press, 1955), p. 5.

12. Breitwieser precedes me in this source attribution. See Mitchell Breitwieser, "False Sympathy in Melville's *Typee," American Quarterly* 34 (Fall 1982): 400–401.

13. Generalizing upon the *Typee* expurgations, Bryan C. Short justifies the cuts, contending that the excised "segments draw attention away from Tommo's half-innocence and the essential contradictions in his situation." Short, "Author at the Time," p. 392. My point here and in succeeding chapters is that what Short calls Melville's "aggressive wit" often induced editors to cut, but that those cuts at times damaged rhetorical gambits designed to balance out the aggressions, and that when Melville encased his sharp wit in a more genial frame he was *not* censored, even though the artfully contained message is more subversive than those actually expurgated.

14. Michel de Montaigne, "On Cannibals," in *Essays,* p. 110. In noting Melville's borrowing from both Shakespeare and Montaigne, Scorza places this passage in the context of Rousseau. See Thomas J. Scorza, "Tragedy in the State of Nature: Melville's *Typee,"* *Interpretation* 8 (January 1979): 103–20; reprint in Stern, *Critical Essays,* pp. 233–37.

8. *Typee* in Manuscript

1. Only a handful of scholar-critics has commented on the *Typee* fragment thus far. Aside from my own contributions reprinted later on in this chapter, there are Susan Davis, "More for the NYPL's Long Vaticans," *Melville Society Extracts,* no. 57, February 1984, pp. 5–7; Bette S. Weidman, "*Typee* and *Omoo:* A Divergent Pair," in John Bryant, ed., *A Companion to Melville Studies* (Westport, CT: Greenwood Press, 1986), pp. 93–95; David Ketterer, "Censorship and Symbolism in *Typee* Revisited: The New Manuscript Evidence," *Melville Society Extracts,* no. 69, February 1987, pp. 6–8; and Bryan C. Short, "The Author at the Time: Tommo and Melville's Self-Discovery in *Typee,*" *Texas Studies in Literature and Language* 31 (Fall 1989): 386–405.

2. MS leaf 2. As yet no transcription of the manuscript has been published, and the leaf references I offer may vary with those designated by future scholars. Brackets indicate Melville's canceled words, which are followed by the word or words Melville substituted for the cancellation. The manuscript fragment is at present housed in the New York Public Library's Gansevoort-Lansing collection, Box 310.

3. It is anyone's guess who edited any particular passage in *Typee.* Before it went to press, Melville's brother Gansevoort made changes, as did Murray's house editor, Henry Milton. But the cancellations and revisions in manuscript are in Melville's hand.

4. Compare Melville with the following notice in the *Minnesota Pioneer* description of the Reverend Gideon H. Pond's periodical *The Dakota Friend,* which offered articles written in an English transcription of Lakotan. The transcription is done "imperfectly, but as well, probably, as our alphabet can be made to represent the hissing, sputtering, hawking, grunting, clucking, gutturals and *unutterals* of the Dakota language, composed as it is, of words which fall upon the tympanum less like soft flakes than like a mingled tempest of tomahawks, hedgehogs and wild cats." Reprinted in *Nantucket Inquirer,* 13 January 1851, p. 2. Melville could not have read this before writing *Typee,* nor could the editors of the *Minnesota Pioneer* have known Melville's manuscript lampooning of the Polynesian language. The similarities in comic structure and wording are remarkable. Perhaps both writers were drawing upon a common mode in the popular culture of describing native and primitive language. If so, Melville may have canceled his version because he realized that he was doing unto the Polynesians what other English speakers had typically done unto the American Indian. As with Melville's treatment of "Little Henry," to be discussed later, the author seems to have discovered his liberal ideology only after trying out and purging himself of the cultural stereotypes of his own native culture.

5. See John Bryant, "Melville's L-Word: First Intentions and Final Readings in *Typee,*" *New England Quarterly* 63 (March 1990): 120–31.

6. Mrs. [Mary Martha] Sherwood, *Little Henry and His Bearer* (1814), tract no. 107 in *The Publications of the American Tract Society* (New York: American Tract Society, n.d.), 4: 165–96. Hereafter cited as Sherwood.

7. *Dictionary of National Biography* 18: 103. See also Sophia Kelly, *The Life of Mrs Sherwood, Chiefly Autobiographical* (London: Darton & Co., 1857).

9. Tommo's Rhetoric of Deceit

1. Sedgwick calls *Typee* a recollection not in tranquility, but "amidst the stress of a consciousness which has expanded far beyond the simplicities of sensual instinctive being." (See William Ellery Sedgwick, *Herman Melville: The Tragedy of Mind* (Cambridge, MA: Harvard University Press, 1944), p. 28. But Dryden argues that Melville's reconstruction

of Typee is a "creative remembering" that allows him to maintain "sanity and discover truth by the creation of a rational lie, a fiction." Edgar Dryden, *Melville's Thematics of Form: The Great Art of Telling the Truth* (Baltimore: Johns Hopkins Press, 1968), pp. 35, 37. By placing Melville in this Wordsworthian frame, we tend to lose sight of the fact that Melville was creating "rational lies," not solely as necessary ontological extensions of self but also as strategies for conning readers into his political and sexual visions.

2. Anderson's chapter on "The French at Nukahiva" provides a careful description of the colonial political tensions in the Marquesas during Melville's visit. Anderson remarks that Melville, despite his experience on the island, "seems to have remained strangely ignorant" of the French attempts to unite the warring tribes.

3. Breitwieser's point is that Tommo's "ignorance" is not entirely genuine. He is alive to Polynesian political injustices as they serve to negate Western practices and culture, but he fails to comprehend Typee as a coherent culture in and of itself. See Mitchell Breitwieser, "False Sympathy in Melville's *Typee*," *American Quarterly* 34 (Fall 1982): 403.

4. Nearly all readers of *Typee* acknowledge some form of this duality. Along with Breitwieser, see Milton R. Stern, *The Fine Hammered Steel of Herman Melville* (Urbana: University of Illinois Press, 1968), p. 35; Thomas P. Joswick, "*Typee:* The Quest for Origin," *Criticism* 17 (Fall 1975): 353; John Wenke, "Melville's *Typee:* A Tale of Two Worlds," in Stern, *Critical Essays,* p. 252; and Herbert, *Marquesan Encounters,* pp. 149–91.

5. Anderson discourages us from adopting various misperceptions Melville had about the tattoo, in particular the view that Marquesan tattooing was specifically religious in nature (pp. 149–56). Handy speculates that Marquesan tattooing was primarily a sign of family, class, and power. See Willowdean Chatterson Handy, *Tattooing in the Marquesas,* Bernice P. Bishop Museum *Bulletin* 1 (Honolulu: Bernice P. Bishop Museum, 1922).

6. Richard Ruland, "Melville and the Fortunate Fall: Typee as Eden," in Stern, *Critical Essays,* p. 189.

7. Robert Brain, *The Decorated Body* (New York: Harper, 1979), p. 59. We see this demonstrated when Queequeg signs his "name" by copying onto paper "an exact counterpart of a queer round figure which was tattooed upon his arm" (*MD,* 89), although printers to this day insist upon rendering Queequeg's "mark" as a cross.

8. At least, this is Tommo's logic, which is all that concerns us in the fiction. However, Anderson notes that the "most common cause [of tribal warfare on Nukuhiva] was the seizure of victims for the purpose of religious sacrifice, upon the death of a priest or chief." Anderson, *Melville in South Seas,* p. 138.

9. Joswick also reads the leg wound as a "mediat[ion of] the antithesis" of two cultures. Thomas Joswick, "*Typee:* The Quest for Origin," 352–53.

10. See Gerard M. Sweeney, "Melville's Smoky Humor: Fire-Lighting in *Typee,*" *Arizona Quarterly* 34 (1978): 371–76, and David Ketterer, "Censorship and Symbolism in *Typee* Revisited: The New Manuscript evidence," *Melville Society Extracts* no. 69 (1987), p. 6.

11. My italics. These canceled lines appear in correspondence to p. 109, lines 17–19.

12. Sweeney's idea that Melville's reference to the College of Vestals is an argument for the establishment of "an easily accessible whorehouse" ("Smoky Humor," p. 375) is untenable both for the fact that Vestals were sworn to virginity on pain of death and that given Polynesian economic and sexual practices, prostitution seems unlikely. Bryan C. Short's investigation of the manuscript (which was not available to Sweeney at the time of his 1978 article) corroborates my interpretation.

13. Anderson provides the earliest and best overview of Melville's use and sometimes abuse of sources. Drawing upon the work of Clifford Geertz, T. Walter Herbert's *Marquesan*

Encounters: Melville and the Meaning of Civilization (Cambridge, MA: Harvard University Press, 1980) is not so much a source study as a fascinating analysis of how Americans responded to the cultural threat of Polynesia.

14. Calling Tommo "the Increase Mather of Polynesia," Mitchell Breitwieser rightly acknowledges the strain between jocularity and parodic satire in this comic passage. Breitwieser, "False Sympathy," p. 403.

15. For other expurgations, presumably made with the Shaw family in mind, see Michael Paul Rogin, *Subversive Genealogy: The Politics and Art of Herman Melville* (New York: Knopf, 1983), p. 45.

16. Most critics acknowledge Marnoo's moral status above Tommo. For Stern, he possesses the "border-crossing eclecticism" that Tommo lacks. *Fine Hammered Steel,* pp. 49, 60. Witherington praises the fact that he is a thoroughly "non-compartmentalized" individual. Paul Witherington, "The Art of Melville's *Typee,*" *Arizona Quarterly* 26 (1970): 146. And in Joswick's mythopoeic view, Marnoo's tattoo is a " 'sacramental' fiction" which outstrips Tommo's leg wound as an emblem of a mediation of two cultures (Thomas Joswick, "*Typee:* The Quest for Origin," 353–54).

17. Interestingly enough, Hawthorne sensed in his review of *Typee* that Melville had made a significant step in achieving the modulations of a cosmopolitan voice: "He has that freedom of view—it would be too harsh to call it 'laxity of principle'—which renders him tolerant of codes or morals that may be little in accordance with our own; a spirit proper enough to a young and adventurous sailor, and which makes his book the more wholesome to our staid landsmen. The narrative is skillfully managed." *Salem Advertiser,* 25 March 1846; reprinted in Stern, *Critical Essays,* p. 34. Although Hawthorne does not denominate as specifically cosmopolitan Melville's ability to maintain tolerance without a "laxity of principle," Hawthorne's wording is reminiscent of language typically associated with the cosmopolite sensibility. Herbert's view of Tommo as a "gentleman-beachcomber" is also cosmopolitan (pp. 151–57).

10. Ishmael: Sounding the Repose of If

1. For a fuller discussion of Melville's use of Mary Shelley's *Frankenstein* and Thorpe's "Big Bear of Arkansas," see my forthcoming "Essaying the Romance: The Comic in *Moby-Dick,*" in Jeffrey Rubin-Dorsky and Donald Pease, eds., *The Other Romance* (Chicago: University of Chicago Press, in press).

2. The notion of "essaying" one's being derives primarily from Montaigne. Dryden argues that Melville departs from Montaigne in that Montaigne examines the "passage," not the "being," of the world, whereas Melville focuses only on the nature of being. Edgar A. Dryden, *Melville's Thematics of Form: The Great Art of Telling the Truth* (Baltimore: Johns Hopkins Press, 1968), pp. 33–37. Feidelson, however, indicates a deeper affinity between the two writers when he writes that Melville sought to bridge the gap between object and idea "by treating the moment of passage as an end in itself, not a means." Charles Feidelson, *Symbolism and American Literature* (Chicago: University of Chicago Press, 1953), p. 168. Nevertheless, Feidelson concludes that Melville failed in this Montaignean symbolistic enterprise. I argue that Melville's use of symbolism is itself a trying out of experience into pure knowledge, and that while the process cannot be fully successful, it is nevertheless carefully contained in *Moby-Dick* within Melville's picturesque aesthetic.

3. Melville's sense of the other is best treated in Paul Brodtkorb, Jr., *Ishmael's White World: A Phenomenological Reading of Moby Dick* (New Haven: Yale University Press, 1965), esp. pp. 58–88.

4. Feidelson, *Symbolism,* p. 173, locates the doctrine of symbolism in the Mardian notion of "creating the creative," discussed earlier in this book.

5. Taverns often served double duty in Early America as places of worship. Duban considers this episode a sign of Ishmael's latent ambivalence toward abolitionism. James Duban, *Melville's Major Fiction: Politics, Theology, and Imagination* (Dekalb: Northern Illinois University Press, 1983), p. 123.

6. Probably the fullest literary treatment of Melville's homoeroticism is Leslie Fiedler, *Love and Death in the American Novel* (New York: Criterion Books, 1960). Miller provides fairly weak literary interpretations to substantiate his psychological claim that, in searching for a substitute father figure, Melville fixated, with repressed homosexual desire, upon Hawthorne. See Edwin H. Miller, *Melville* (New York: Braziller, 1975). More recently, Robert K. Martin has reoriented thinking on the matter to stress the creative and healthy rather than infantile and pathological aspects of Melville's homosexual tendencies.

7. Miller, *Melville,* p. 200, considers the scene to be one of Ishmael's ''sterile fantasies.'' I argue that Ishmael's autoeroticism is palpable evidence of his creativity.

8. See David R. Eastwood's as yet unpublished study ''Melville, Madness, and Medical Fallacies.''

9. Fiedler hints at this connection, and others have filled in details. See E. Hale Chatfield, ''Levels of Meaning in Melville's 'I and My Chimney,' '' *American Imago* 19 (Spring 1962):163–69, and Darwin T. Turner, ''Smoke from Melville's Chimney,'' *College Language Association Journal* 7 (December 1963):107–13. Merton M. Sealts, Jr., whose 1941 essay ''Melville's 'I and My Chimney''' was the first critical analysis of that tale, has also written a detailed discussion of the tale's critical history. Both are reprinted in *Pursuing Melville, 1940–1980* (Madison: University of Wisconsin Press, 1982). pp. 11–22, 171–92.

10. The scene is an all-male enactment of the far less graphic shipboard scenes of heterosexual ''gratification'' only vaguely alluded to in *Typee,* scenes Melville was forced to cut. British editors of *Moby-Dick,* however, did not expurgate sexual references in ''Midnight, Forecastle,'' only certain barely irreverent allusions to resurrection and Christ. What Melville was likely to have learned from editors and reviewers was that he could dramatize his sexuality symbolically—as in Kory-Kory's fire lighting and Fayaway's canoe scenes or here in ''Midnight, Forecastle''—but not speak of it directly. Thus, through symbolism Melville could in *Moby-Dick* avoid the censors, and the result was that while reviewers acknowledged its raciness (*Graham's*) and even its ''hermaphrodite craft'' (*Boston Daily Evening Traveller*), they allowed its sensuality to pass as ''a story of peculiar interest'' (*Spirit of the Times*). Although one or two condemned the book for its ''flings at religion, and even . . . vulgar immoralities'' (*Methodist Quarterly Review*), most recognized Melville's ability to contain the sexual within acceptable linguistic patterns of sensuality and would have agreed with the *National Intelligencer* (Washington, DC) that ''Mr. Melville has the strange power to reach the sinuosities of thought, sweet or wild.'' For review citations see Hershel Parker and Harrison Hayford, *Moby-Dick as Doubloon: Essays and Extracts (1851–1970)* (New York: Norton, 1970), pp. 89, 32, 64, 82–83, 68.

11. Critics remain skeptical of Mapple's relevance. For James E. Miller, Jr., Mapple's wisdom is something Ishmael (through Queequeg) is in the ''process of unlearning.'' See James E. Miller, Jr., *A Reader's Guide to Herman Melville* (New York: Noonday Press, 1962), p. 89. Taking Mapple as a parody of American preachers, Paul Brodtkorb, Jr., argues that the ''sacramentalism [of Mapple's sermon] is neutralized by its style'' and concludes that Mapple's ''total religious commitment'' in the sermon ''has little relevance *to* Ishmael (though . . . a great deal to Ahab). Ishmael cannot appropriate the sermon in Father Mapple's terms, he can only reproduce it.'' Brodtkorb, *Ishmael's White World,* pp. 57, 58; his italics. Brodtkorb is correct that Mapple's model of religiosity is aimed at Ahab, but he underestimates its relevance to Ishmael as an ironic model of the artist. The problem is that Mapple's sermon undermines Melville's own declaration of artistic containment.

12. Howard P. Vincent, *The Trying-Out of Moby-Dick* (Kent, Ohio: Kent State University Press, 1980), pp. 93–102.

13. Melville borrowed this idea directly from Beale, although it was Melville, not Beale, who set it in a cosmopolitan frame. See *ibid.*, pp. 96–97.

14. *Ibid.*, p. 99.

15. Franklin's distinction between myth as a narratorial enactment of psychological constants rather than an exaggerated narrative of forgotten historical event is useful here. H. Bruce Franklin, *The Wake of the Gods: Melville's Mythology* (Stanford, CA: Stanford University Press, 1963), pp. 56–58.

16. I am indebted to Emma Bryant for her discussions on her eighth grade science labs, which reminded me of this venerable truth that I so imperfectly learned some years ago.

17. The Blue Whale is considerably larger than the Sperm, but Ishmael whimsically omits it as "obsolete." Lauriat Lane, Jr., "Melville and the Blue Whale," *Melville Society Extracts*, no. 87 (November 1991):7–8.

18. Feidelson, *Symbolism*, argues that Ishmael's project of fusing rational (or empiricist) and symbolic modes ultimately fails, for each method finally "damns" the other (p. 175). To some degree this is true, especially if we emphasize the logical or philosophical incompatibility of the scientific and poetic modes, as Feidelson seems to be doing. My point, however, is that while Melville recognizes in "The Whiteness of the Whale" that pushing his symbolic method to its logical extremes will lead to disaster, he nevertheless has Ishmael contain his symbolism within the artful boundaries of a picturesque aesthetic wherein (like an atomic pile) destructive antipathies can be controlled without an annihilating explosion. This, it would seem, is Ishmael's final revelation in "The Try-Works" (ch. 96). Once again, it is Ishmael's attempt as an artist to forestall the deconstruction of his language that creates the tension in his reposeful rhetoric.

19. Feidelson, *Symbolism*, ties Melville's circular symbology in *Typee* to Emerson in "Circles" (p. 165). Brodtkorb, however, finds a certain metaphysical sterility in Melville's images of circular motion, preferring the depth implicit in vertical movement. Brodtkorb, *Ishmael's White World*, pp. 34–41. But it is important to recall Melville's explicit endorsement of circles in *Pierre* (p. 283): "Most grand productions of the best human intellects ever are built round a circle." (Evanston and Chicago: Northwestern University Press and the Newberry Library, 1971). Circle imagery has also been a subject treated in various unpublished dissertations, notably those by Robert G. Waite, John S. Tumlin, Jr., and Marilyn J. Atlas. See *Melville Dissertations, 1924–1980* (Westport, CT: Greenwood Press, 1983), nos. 336, 369, and 490.

20. Leo Marx's analysis of *Moby-Dick* in *The Machine in the Garden* focuses primarily upon "The Try-Works" as the fiery industrial image in contrast to Melville's sea-pastoral vision. For an analysis of the analysis, see John Bryant, "A Usable Pastoralism: Leo Marx's Method in *The Machine in the Garden*," *American Studies* 16 (Spring 1975):63–72.

21. In *Empire for Liberty*, pp. 3–41, Dimock argues that sovereignty and freedom are opposing concepts tightly bound together in a process of social and aesthetic self-definition.

22. Whether these and countless other "unnecessary duplicates" noted by Hayford can be taken as evidence of various phases in the genesis of *Moby-Dick* remains speculative, but their rhetorical effect is to lend a structural inevitability to the metaphysical and aesthetic necessity of circular essaying. See Harrison Hayford, "Unnecessary Duplicates: A Key to the Writing of *Moby-Dick*," in Faith Pullin, ed., *New Perspectives on Melville* (Kent, OH, and Edinburgh: Kent State University Press and Edinburgh University Press, 1978), pp. 128–61, and his contributions in the "Discussions of Adopted Readings" in the Northwestern-Newberry edition of *Moby-Dick*, pp. 809–906.

23. Herman Melville, *Moby-Dick; or, The Whale,* ed. Luther S. Mansfield and Howard P. Vincent (New York: Hendricks House, 1952), p. 818.

24. Dillingham argues in his study of gnosticism, alchemy, and Melville that gold "stands for the precious and the permanent which [Ahab] yearns for" and yet "is never to find." See William B. Dillingham, *Melville's Later Novels* (Athens: University of Georgia Press, 1986). p. 86.

11. Ahab: Personifying the Impersonal

1. In *Hawthorne, Melville, and the Novel* (Chicago: University of Chicago Press, 1976), p. 156, Richard H. Brodhead argues that "what most distinguishes Ahab from Ishmael is not his habit of symbolic perception but his inability to understand the meanings he sees as products of his own imagination." In separating from this view, I try to show that Ahab's problem does, in fact, lie with his "habit" of symbolizing, which is more allegorical than symbolist, and that his theatrical and allegorizing skills delude not only the crew but himself.

2. Dimock makes a similar argument regarding the logic of Melville's naming patterns in *Mardi,* that is, that the author's arbitrary names signify his attempts to gain dominion over the novel's plot and readers. But in *Moby-Dick,* Melville has come to see himself as a victim of readers, and Ahab (like the American Indian) becomes a personification representing a broad form of social and literary "negative individualism." Dimock does not examine Ahab's own personifications in "The Candles" as an enactment of his notions of sovereignty. See Dimock, *Empire for Liberty,* pp. 110, 136.

3. Brodtkorb, *Ishmael's White World,* p. 82.

4. H. Bruce Franklin offers one of the most forthright interpretations of Melville's aesthetic use of Ahab's impotence when he demonstrates its relation to the Osiris and Typhon myth in his study of Melville's comparative mythologizing. See Franklin, *Wake of the Gods,* p. 73.

5. Brodtkorb contends that Melville is doing this already through Ishmael's language, which "seeks to create . . . a literary world of which the reader must become a part before its final reality comes into being." *Ishmael's White World,* p. 148. I argue, however, that while Melville was attempting to achieve this rhetorical effect, he did not fully create it until he eliminated his Ishmaelian voice, for finally in *Moby-Dick,* our awareness of the wise, first-person Ishmael actually undercuts our sense of an independently derived experience of ontological doubt. With *Moby-Dick,* Melville was working with a safety net, but in *The Confidence-Man,* all nets are removed.

6. Arac skillfully argues that Ahab's disregard for the distinction between agent and principal also parallels a similar disregard in industrial law sanctioned by Melville's father-in-law, Lemuel Shaw. See Jonathan Arac, " 'A Romantic Book': *Moby-Dick* and Novel Agency," *Boundary 2,* no. 17 (Summer 1990): 40–59.

7. Bezanson writes: "Yet the tragedy of Ahab is not his great gift for symbolic perception, but his abandonment of it. Ahab increasingly reduces all pluralities to the singular." Walter Bezanson, "*Moby-Dick:* Work of Art," in Tyrus Hillway and Luther S. Mansfield, eds., *Moby-Dick: Centennial Essays* (Dallas: Southern Methodist University Press, 1953), pp. 47–48.

8. Franklin, *Wake of the Gods,* p. 98, also argues that in playing the role of a savior god (Prometheus) for man, Ahab commits the "most complete ungodliness." See also Leo Marx, *Machine in the Garden.*

9. Brodtkorb concludes: "*Moby-Dick* tries to persuade us to become these moods in order to discover their meanings within ourselves; it does so by submerging the initially amusing

character Ishmael into the ambiguous voice of the narrator, whose feelings in relation to his strange world provide analogues for ours." *Ishmael's White World,* p. 148. Building upon this phenomenological view, I argue that Ishmael's projections allow for a certain but not total, degree of aesthetic self-effacement.

10. Of course, the desire to find or place upon *Moby-Dick* a particular political or social referent has been a major impetus in the modern resurgence of Melville from Matthiessen and Perry Miller to more recent historicists and "New" historicists. Charles H. Foster, in "Something in Emblems: A Reinterpretation of *Moby-Dick,*" *New England Quarterly* 34 (March 1961):3–35, and Alan Heimert, in *"Moby-Dick* and American Political Symbolism," *American Quarterly* 15 (Winter 1963):498–534, attempt to identify characters and images with historical individuals and events concerning the Compromise of 1850. More recently, Michael Paul Rogin, in *Subversive Genealogy: The Politics and Art of Herman Melville* (New York: Knopf, 1983), and James Duban, in *Melville's Major Fiction: Politics, Theology, and Imagination* (DeKalb: University of Northern Illinois Press, 1983), have extended that approach to include the additional dimensions of family and religion. Intelligent and challenging analyses of Melville and agency can be found in the works of Jonathan Arac, Wai-chee Dimock, Donald Pease, and Brook Thomas. But though Melville requires a historicist approach, few historicists, traditional or new, have been able to resist making political allegory out of Melville's texts. And yet finding a satisfying balance of aesthetic and sociological methods is imperative, if only for the fact that Melville seemed intent in his writing upon lessening allegory and minimizing specific satiric attacks. To know Melville's private world of ideas and to use him effectively in our own modern world of ideas, we need an approach that can illuminate the growth of his political ideology in the context of his creativity.

11. Foster contends that Ahab's rejection of Pip represents Judge Lemuel Shaw's verdict against the fugitive slave Thomas Sims in 1850. See Charles H. Foster, "Something in Emblems: A Reinterpretation of *Moby-Dick,*" reprinted in *Moby-Dick as Doubloon,* pp. 281–82.

12. Melville's Comedy of Doubt

1. Hershel Parker and Harrison Hayford, eds., *Moby-Dick as Doubloon* (New York: W.W. Norton, 1970), p. 89, my emphasis. Hereafter cited as *D.*

2. *John Bull* said the entire novel had "charm" (*D,* 9), and the *National Intelligencer* related Melville's stylistic "charm" to his humor (*D,* 68). The *Courier* called the style "witching" (*D,* 32), and *Graham's* reiterated these notions, emphasizing the "raciness" of the prose (*D,* 89).

3. Critics tend to read "The Piazza" as an ironic critique of faith—William Bysshe Stein, "Melville's Comedy of Faith," *ELH* 27 (December 1960): 315–33—of the sublime—Klaus Poenicke, "A View from the Piazza: Herman Melville and the Legacy of the European Sublime," *Comparative Literature Studies* 4 (1967):267–81—and of the picturesque—Marvin Fisher, *Going Under: Melville's Short Fiction and the American 1850s* (Baton Rouge: Louisiana State University Press, 1977), pp. 13–28, and Richard S. Moore, *That Cunning Alphabet: Melville's Aesthetics of Nature* (Amsterdam: Rodopi, 1982), pp. 3–53. But if, as Poenicke (p. 271) aptly observes, the tale is "an inquiry into what such an experience [as the sublime] may do to human beings," we must begin with the notion that Melville's "inquiry" is just that, an inquiry, and that the inquirer remains open to various new possibilities. Hence the speaker's disillusionment with the sublime is only one phase of investigation, a prelude to a more resolvent picturesque sensibility, which is itself a prelude to a new dramatism. The fact that Melville returned to the picturesque, after *The Confidence-Man,* in his later poems is enough to tell us that Melville does not in his thinking reject

former intellectual or aesthetic stances but rather expands his ever growing ideology to incorporate old (the sublime and the picturesque) and new (the dramatistic).

4. Watson G. Branch, *Melville: The Critical Heritage* (London: Routledge & Kegan Paul, 1974), pp. 380, 385.

5. John Bryant, *"The Confidence-Man:* Melville's Problem Novel" in *Companion,* pp. 315–50, provides a lengthy analysis of different critical approaches. For a recent update, see Michael S. Kearns, "How to Read *The Confidence-*Man," *ESQ* 36:209–37.

6. These positions are argued, respectively, by Hershel Parker, "The Metaphysics of Indian-hating," *Nineteenth-Century Fiction* 18 (September 1963): 165–73; Christopher W. Sten, "The Dialogue of Crisis in *The Confidence-Man:* Melville's 'New Novel,' " *Studies in the Novel* 6 (Summer 1974): 165–85; Lawrence Buell, "The Last Word on *The Confidence-Man?" Illinois Quarterly* 35 (November 1972): 15–29; John Seelye, *Melville: The Ironic Diagram* (Evanston, Il: Northwestern University Press, 1970); Elizabeth S. Foster, "Introduction," *The Confidence-Man: His Masquerade* (New York: Hendricks House, 1954); Michael Davitt Bell, *The Development of American Romance: The Sacrifice of Relation* (Chicago: University of Chicago Press, 1980); and Daniel Hoffman, *Form and Fable in American Fiction* (New York: Oxford University Press, 1961), p. 311.

7. Most recently Trimpi, taking the novel to be purely satiric, has attempted with some success to correlate Melville's characters with contemporaries in the political milieu of the 1850s. See Helen P. Trimpi, *Melville's Confidence Men and American Politics in the 1850s* (Hamden, CT: Archon Books, 1987).

8. Edwin Honig, *Dark Conceit: The Making of Allegory* (New York: Oxford University Press, 1966), and Stephen A. Barney, *Allegories of History, Allegories of Love* (Hamden, CT: Shoestring Press, 1979).

9. Foster, "Introduction," pp. xci, xviii, xlvi.

10. Hershel Parker, "The Metaphysics of Indian-hating," rev. in Hershel Parker, ed., *The Confidence-Man: His Masquerade* (New York: Norton, 1971), pp. 324, 322. All references are to this revised version.

11. Honig, *Dark Conceit,* p. 84, and Barney, *Allegories,* p. 158.

12. Sheldon Sacks elaborates this distinction between the mimetic and didactic in his discussion of satire, apologue, and represented actions in *Fiction and the Shape of Belief: A Study of Henry Fielding with Glances at Swift, Johnson, and Richardson* (Berkeley: University of California Press, 1964), pp. 1–69. See also R. S. Crane, *The Languages of Criticism and the Structure of Poetry* (Toronto: University of Toronto Press, 1953), pp. 122–23, and Bainard Cowan, *Exiled Waters: Moby-Dick and the Crisis of Allegory* (Baton Rouge: Louisiana State University Press, 1981), p. 30. Dimock alludes to this pattern in allegory in *Empire for Liberty.*

13. Buell, "Last Word," p. 20. John G. Cawelti argues a similar position in "Some Notes on the Structure of *The Confidence-Man,*" *American Literature* 29 (November 1957):278–88. Those finding clear, normative values amid such ambiguities include Walter Dubler, "Theme and Structure in Melville's *The Confidence-Man,*" *American Literature* 33 (November 1961): 307–19, and Merlin Bowen, "Tactics of Indirection in Melville's *The Confidence-Man,*" *Studies in the Novel* 1 (Winter 1969):401–20.

14. Wayne Booth, *The Rhetoric of Fiction* (Chicago: University of Chicago Press, 1961), p. 293.

15. Rosenberry writes that *The Confidence-Man* is "a philosophical leg-pull, not a drama in any sense" but rather a "satiric barrage." See Edward Rosenberry, *Melville and the Comic Spirit* (Cambridge, MA: Harvard University Press, 1955), pp. 142, 168. Daniel Hoffman calls the novel simply "nondramatizable." Hoffman, *Form and Fable,* p. 310.

16. Wolfgang Iser, *The Act of Reading: A Theory of Aesthetic Response* (Baltimore: Johns Hopkins University Press, 1978), p. 54.

17. Lewis was one of the first to imply that Melville's reader is a victim when he argues that the narrator is a confidence man. See R. W. B. Lewis, "Afterword," *The Confidence-Man: His Masquerade* (New York: Signet, 1964). Edgar Dryden offers a similar position in *Melville's Thematics of Form* (Baltimore: Johns Hopkins University Press, 1968). A fuller elaboration of the idea of Melville's reader as victim can be found in Dimock, *Empire for Liberty*.

18. Angus Fletcher, *Allegory: The Theory of a Symbolic Mode* (Ithaca, NY: Cornell University Press, 1964), pp. 278, 343, and p. 322.

19. Booth, *Rhetoric of Fiction*, p. 378.

20. Edward Rosenberry, "Melville's Ship of Fools," *PMLA* 75 (December 1960): 604–8.

21. Fletcher, *Allegory,* pp. 68, 151. Warwick Wadlington also likens the confidence man to Socrates in *The Confidence Game in American Literature* (Princeton, NJ: Princeton University Press, 1975), p. 19.

22. *Ibid.*, pp. 172, 190, 195.

23. Black Guinea's list may be explained away as being incomplete due to authorial oversights. See Watson G. Branch, "The Genesis, Composition, and Structure of *The Confidence-Man*," *Nineteenth-Century Fiction* 28 (March 1973): 432. But if Melville intended a "consistent allegory" keyed to a single list established early in the narrative, the failure to see his list through would be a remarkable oversight, tantamount to forgetting the names of his principal characters at mid-novel. If Melville did make such a blunder, why did he not alter his list, in retrospect, to fit the characters that did finally emerge in his fiction, the way a freshman might alter his or her thesis sentence to fit the essay as it has finally evolved? My suggestion is that the accuracy of the list mattered little to Melville because he was not writing allegory. Rather than an oversight on Melville's part, the faulty list is just as likely to be Melville's printer's error, which went undetected by the author, who, according to the NN editors, did not supervise proofs (*CM*, 313). Whatever caused the disparity between list and characters, the effect, as I argue here, is to enhance our sense of allegorical breakdown, which increases in the novel's second half.

24. See *The Confidence-Man: His Masquerade,* ed. H. Bruce Franklin (New York: Bobbs Merrill, 1967), p. 164. See also Buell, "Last Word," pp. 15–29, Philip Drew, "Appearance and Reality in Melville's *The Confidence-Man*," *ELH* 31 (December 1964): 442, and, in particular, Elizabeth Keyser, " 'Quite an Original': The Cosmopolitan in *The Confidence-Man*," *Texas Studies in Literature and Language* 15 (Summer 1973): 279. Most recently, Quirk has found Goodman to be the culmination of the "evolving significances" of the confidence man figure in Melville's imagination; see Tom Quirk, *Melville's Confidence Man: From Knave to Knight* (Columbia: University of Missouri Press, 1982), pp. 11, 17.

25. Ringman, for instance, moves from amiable to serious with the troubled merchant Roberts (*CM*, 21) and returns to heightened sociability with the shallow collegian (25). The same pattern occurs with the man in gray (38 and 43) and Truman (64).

26. Black Guinea sets Roberts up for Ringman and the Episcopalian for the man in gray (19). Ringman sets up Roberts and the collegian for Truman (22) who in turn sets the miser up for the herb doctor (74).

27. Ringman vouches for Black Guinea to Roberts (*CM*, 19); Truman assures the collegian of the man in gray's and Ringman's good nature; the man in gray (we learn from Roberts) has confirmed Ringman (59); and the PIO man tells Pitch that the herb doctor looks "like a very mild Christian sort of person" (115). The man in gray confirms Black Guinea to the

Episcopalian (29); the herb doctor confirms the man in gray to the passengers (90), Black Guinea to the solder of fortune (99), and Truman to the miser (102).

28. The early confidence men are invariably associated with the ship's forward section, where the mute sleeps, Black Guinea performs, and Ringman first appears. Ringman, Truman, and the PIO man are associated with the gangplank, and along with the mute are said to come from the East.

29. Similar openings occur in chapters 4, 5, 6, 9, 21, and 22.

30. Parenthetical notations after each character indicate the number of times that character is referred to as "the stranger" or "the other," respectively: Mute (8, 0), Ringman (9, 1), Man in Gray (4, 1), Truman (6, 6), Herb Doctor (1, 3), PIO Man (1, 8), Cosmopolitan (5, 9), Noble (14, 15), Winsome (17, 3), and Egbert (1, 0).

31. *The Republic of Plato,* trans. Taylor and Sydenham (London: Methuen, n.d.), p. 159. The language here is from a reprint of the 1804 Taylor–Sydenham translation that Melville read; see Merton M. Sealts, Jr., *Melville's Reading* (Columbia: University of South Carolina Press, 1988), p. 40.

13. Comic Debates: The Uses of Cosmopolite

1. T. B. Thorpe, "The Big Bear of Arkansas," in Walter Blair, ed., *Native American Humor* (San Francisco: Chandler Publishing, 1960), p. 337.

2. I am using the text included in *The Confidence-Man: His Masquerade,* ed. Hershel Parker (New York: Norton, 1971), p. 254.

3. William Ellery Sedgwick, *Herman Melville: The Tragedy of Mind* (Cambridge, MA: Harvard University Press, 1944), p. 187–93; John W. Shroeder, "Sources and Symbols for Melville's *The Confidence-Man,*" *PMLA* 66 (June 1951): 363–80; and Hershel Parker, "The Metaphysics of Indian-hating," *Nineteenth-Century Fiction* 18 (September 1963): 165–73. Parker reprinted a revised version of his essay in his Norton Critical Edition of *The Confidence-Man* (pp. 323–31). All references here to Parker's essay are from the Norton edition and are hereafter cited in the text as MIH. Significant rebuttals to the notion that Moredock is the novel's moral center have been registered in Roy Harvey Pearce, "Melville's Indian-Hater: A Note on a Meaning of *The Confidence-Man,*" *PMLA* 67 (December 1952): 942–48; Elizabeth S. Foster, "Introduction," *The Confidence-Man: His Masquerade* (New York: Hendricks House, 1954); Edwin S. Fussell, *Frontier: American Literature and the American West* (Princeton, NJ: Princeton University Press, 1965); Joyce Sparer Adler, *War in Melville's Imagination* (New York: New York University Press, 1981); and William Ramsey, "The Moot Points of Melville's Indian-Hating," *American Literature* 52 (May 1980): 224–35.

4. In fact, Mary K. Madison's survey of *Confidence-Man* criticism indicates that Parker's position is a minority view. See "Hypothetical Friends: The Critics and *The Confidence-Man,*" *Melville Society Extracts,* no. 46, May 1981, pp. 10–14.

5. Judith Slater, "The Domestic Adventurer in Melville's Tales," *American Literature* 37 (November 1965): 267–79.

6. *CM,* 163. The concluding proverb belongs to that hearty scamp in Carlyle's *Sartor Resartus* who concludes that he "who cannot laugh is not only fit for treasons, stratagems, and spoils; but his whole life is already a treason and a stratagem" (34). It belongs as well to that "clement" philosopher Shakespeare, who first applied the idea to music. *Merchant of Venice,* V, i, 85.

7. John Wenke, "No 'i' in Charlemont: A Cryptogrammic Name in *The Confidence-Man,*" *Essays in Literature* (Macomb, Ill.) 9 (Fall 1982): 269–78.

Index

"Ligeia" (Poe), 88, 89, 95–100, 107,
282nn.17, 18; mimetic transcendence in, 99;
narrator as transcendentalist, 96–97, 99; and
repose, 98; and "Rue Morgue," 96
Lindberg, Gary, 280n.29
"Line, The" (*Moby-Dick*), 200
"Literary Egotism" (Jones), 48–50
Literary World, 52, 82, 116, 120. *See also*
Young America
Little Henry and His Bearer (Sherwood), 157–
60
Locke, John, 196, 270n.9
Lombardo (*Mardi*), 14–15, 217, 218
Longfellow, Henry Wadsworth, 10, 11, 14
Longstreet, Augustus B., 90; and Poe, 46, 87
"Loss of Breath, A" (Poe), 89
Lost generation, 117
Lowell, James Russell, 95
Lukens, Henry Clay ("Erratic Enrique"), vii
Lying: aesthetics of 85–86; Americans and, 78–
79, 80–82; amiable humorists and, 78–80; and
belief, 82, 107; in "Big Bear," 101; and
creativity, 85; culture of, 85; as education,
80–81; epistemology, 85; forms of, 82–87; on
frontier, 76; history of, 72–82; humanists and,
72–75; and imagination, 80; and memory, 72–
73; and picturesque, 80; and poetry, 85–86;
simulation and dissimulation, 72, 75, 76, 78,
83; as sin, 72, 75; sociology of, 85;
utilitarians and, 75–78. *See also* Playing
along; Reliability; Rhetoric of deceit; Tall
tale; Tall talk
Lynn, Kenneth, 86

Macbeth (Shakespeare), 221
MacHeath (*Beggar's Opera*), 168
Machiavelli, Nicolo, 213
Mackenzie, Henry, 37, 50
MacLeod, Donald, 120–22
Macy, Obed, 193
Man in black, 55, 183, 212, 245. *See also*
Drybone; *The Stranger*; Toby
Manifest Destiny, 194. *See also* Politics
Mansfield, Luther S., 205
Manuscript, 146, 167–69, 173, 288nn.1,2. *See
also Typee*
Mapple (*Moby-Dick*), 193, 291n.11
Mardi, 7, 9, 14, 52, 70, 217, 293n.2. *See also
specific characters*
Margin (the marge), image of the, 18, 185, 186,
190, 201, 204, 217, 228, 250, 257, 264,
273n.43. *See also* Symbolism
Marketplace, 241; literary, 5, 23, 40
Marnoo (*Typee*), 162, 163, 164, 171; as artist,

183–84; as cosmopolitan, 179, 184; and
Tommo, 183–84. *See also* Queequeg
Martin, Robert K., 291n.6
Marx, Groucho, 57, 89
Marx, Leo, 36
"Mast-Head, The" (*Moby-Dick*), 193–94, 196,
225
Masturbation: in *Moby-Dick*, 189–91, in *Typee*,
167, 168. *See also* Fire; Sexuality
Mathews, Cornelius, 28, 43, 45–47, 49
Matthiessen, F. O., 271n.33
Mehevi (*Typee*), 141, 164
Mellor, Anne K., 7
Melvill, Allan (father), 263
Melvill, Thomas (uncle), 263
Melville Revivalists, 269n.6, 272n.33
Melville's L-Word, 155–57, 160. *See also*
Manuscript; *Typee*
Melville, Augusta (sister), 20
Melville, Elizabeth Shaw (wife), 182. *See also*
Shaw, Lemuel
Melville, Gansevoort (brother), 263
Melville, Herman: and bachelor whim, 57; as
biographer, 256–57; in *The Confidence-Man*,
257; as cosmopolitan, 258; creative process,
146–60; critical camps, 270n.13, 271n.17; as
customs inspector, vii; deep thought of
laughter, 70–72; and Dow, 127; and
Duyckinck, 11, 44, 52–53; and Emerson, 11;
as essayer, ix, 267; in Europe, 12; as
experimenter, 28; and fine arts, 272n.35; and
Hawthorne's humor, 23–27; and Hazlitt,
275n.57; and Irving, 52–69; as literary
comedian, vii; as melancholiac, vii; and
missionaries, 157–60; and John Murray, 132;
and pluralistic historicism, viii, 266; as poet,
266–67; as pragmatic platonist, 40, 210, 213,
243, 246; and reader, 27–28; at sea, 132; and
sexuality, 189; and Shakespeare, 11, 142,
217, 220–21, 229, 260–61; and the Shaws,
182; silencing Ishmael, 230–31; and Sunday
school, 159; and voice, 70, 230–31, 266; and
world literature, 116. *See also specific titles
by author*
Melville, Maria Gansevoort (mother), 20–21,
274n.45
Melville, Thomas (brother), 13–14
Memory, 72–73. *See also* Lying; Montaigne
Meredith, George, 5, 6; and irony, 7
Michael Angelo, 19
"Midnight, Forecastle" (*Moby-Dick*), 192, 197,
206, 217, 222, 223, 225, 227, 291n.10
Milder, Robert, 4
Miles Gloriosus (Plautus), 83